NAPOLEON AND WATERLOO

NAPOLEONIC LIBRARY

NAPOLEON AND WATERLOO

The Emperor's Campaign
With The Armée Du Nord
1815

by A.F. Becke

Greenhill Books, London
Stackpole Books, Pennsylvania

This edition of *Napoleon and Waterloo* first published 1995
on the 180th Anniversary of the Battle of Waterloo
by Greenhill Books, Lionel Leventhal Limited, Park House
1 Russell Gardens, London NW11 9NN
and
Stackpole Books
5067 Ritter Road, Mechanicsburg, PA 17055, USA

British Library Cataloguing in Publication Data available

ISBN 1-85367-206-8

Library of Congress Cataloging-in-Publication Data available

Publishing History
Napoleon and Waterloo was first published in 1936 (Kegan
Paul, Trench, Trubner & Co. Ltd.) and is reproduced now
exactly as this original edition, complete and unabridged.
The 1936 edition was revised and rewritten from the author's
Napoleon and Waterloo, published in two volumes in 1914.

Printed and bound in Great Britain
by Biddles Limited, Guildford and King's Lynn

DÉDIÉ
À LA MÉMOIRE
DE S. M. L'EMPEREUR
NAPOLÉON
L'EMPEREUR DES BATAILLES

" Plutôt maintenant que demain, plutôt demain qu'après."

JEANNE D'ARC.

" Activité, Activité, Vitesse ! Je me recommande à vous."

NAPOLÉON.

TABLE OF CONTENTS

TABLE OF CONTENTS

Footnote.—Except in Appendix I, *von* is omitted all through
this study.

LIST OF MAPS AND SKETCHES

SKETCHES

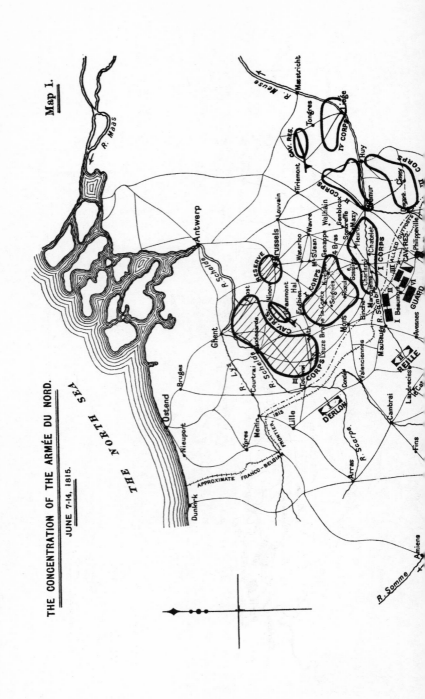

THE CONCENTRATION OF THE ARMÉE DU NORD.

JUNE 7-14, 1815.

Map I.

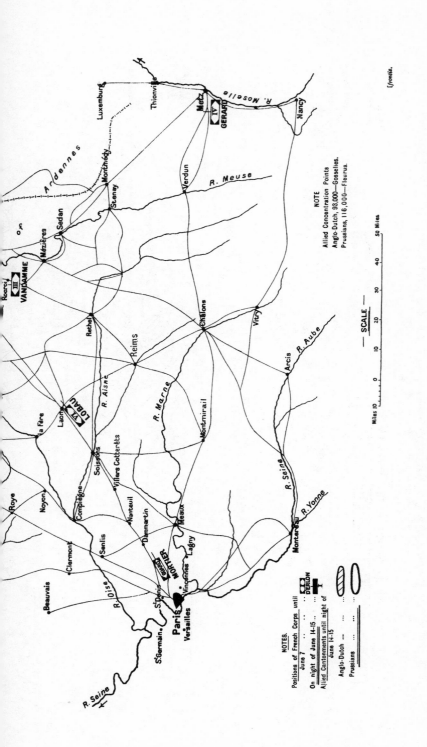

NOTES.

Positions of French Corps until
  June 7 ... ...
On night of June 14-15 ... ...
Allied Cantonments until night of
  June 14-15

Anglo-Dutch ... ...
Prussians ... ...

NOTE

Allied Concentration Points
Anglo-Dutch, 93,000—Gosselies.
Prussians, 116,000—Fleurus.

SCALE

Miles 10   0   10   20   30   40   50 Miles

[*frontis.*]

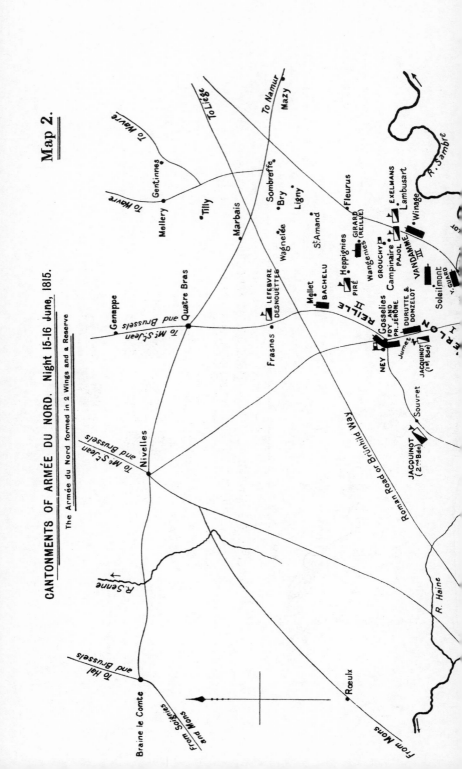

CANTONMENTS OF ARMÉE DU NORD. Night 15-16 June, 1815.

Map 2.

The Armée du Nord formed in 2 Wings and a Reserve

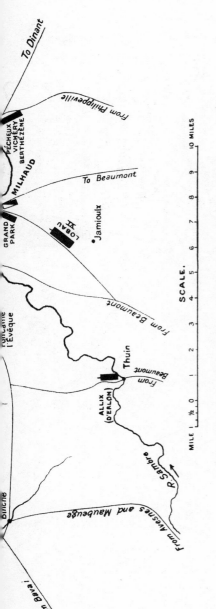

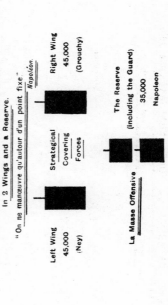

NAPOLEON'S FORMATION FOR THE ADVANCE OF THE ARMÉE DU NORD
FOR THE INVASION OF BELGIUM, JUNE 1815.

In 2 Wings and a Reserve.

"On ne manœuvre qu'autour d'un point fixe".
Napoléon.

SCALE.

MILE 1   ½   0   1   2   3   4   5   6   7   8   9   10 MILES

Left Wing
45,000
(Ney)

Strategical
Covering
Forces

Right Wing
45,000
(Grouchy)

La Masse Offensive

The Reserve
(Including the Guard)
35,000
Napoleon

[face p. 53

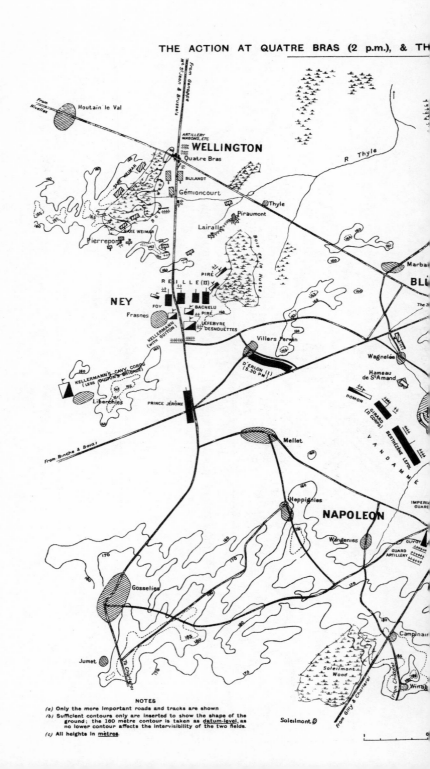

NOTES

(a) Only the more important roads and tracks are shown

(b) Sufficient contours only are inserted to show the shape of the ground; the 160 metre contour is taken as datum-level, as no lower contour affects the intervisibility of the two fields.

(c) All heights in métres.

Mellery

Gentinnes

St.Géry

To Liège

Gembloux

Tilly

160

160

160

160

165

160

160

165

160

ROMAN ROAD OF BRUNHILDA WAY

160

160

170

170

170

170

170

170

160

160

PIRCH I (II)

JÜRGASS

160

160

BRAUSE   LANGEN

RÖDER

Ligny

HENCKEL

ZIET

Sombreffe

LUCK

BORCKE

STEINMETZ

VICHERY PÉCHEUX

GÉRARD (IV)

HULOT

Tongrinnelle

Tongrinne

KEMPFEN

Point du Jour

T   H   I   E   L   M   A   N   N

170

170

170

170

160

HOBE

Mazy

To Namur

BIGOW

EXELMANS

GROUCHY

PAJOL

Boignée

Balâtre

R. Ligny

160

160

164

160

160

LOBAU (VI)
(AFTER 7 P.M.)

LYAUD

170

170

170

180

180

170

170

R. Orneau

R. Sambre

R. Sambre

usart

180

Map 4.

THE BATTLE OF WATERLOO

11.30 a.m., 18th JUNE, 1815.

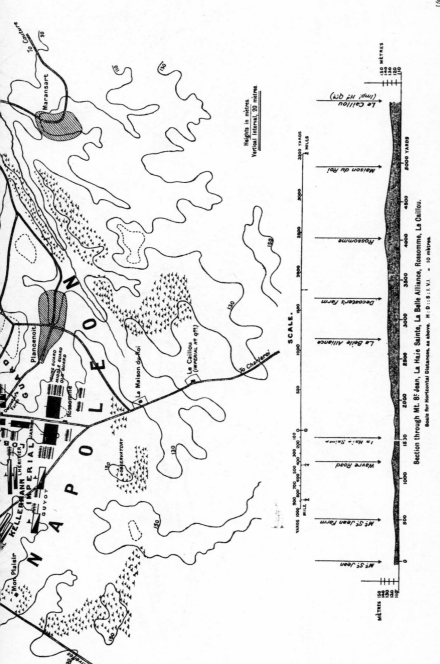

Heights in metres.
Vertical Interval, 20 metres.

SCALE.

Section through Mt. St Jean, La Haie Sainte, La Belle Alliance, Rossomme, Le Caillou.

Scale for Horizontal Distances, as above. H : D :: 5 : 1. V.I. = 10 metres.

[face p. 165

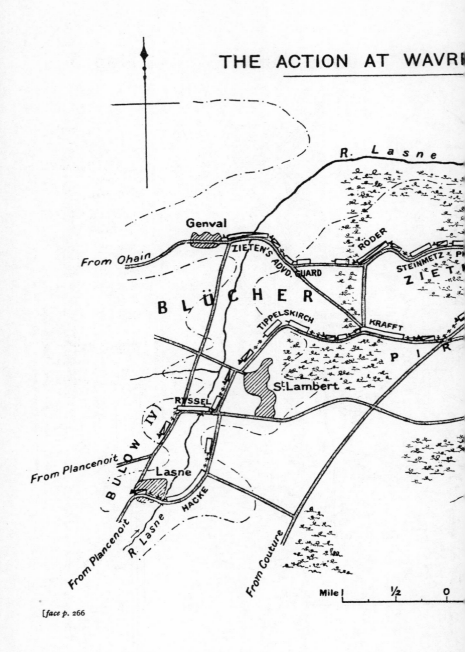

4 P.M., 18 JUNE, 1815.   Map 5.

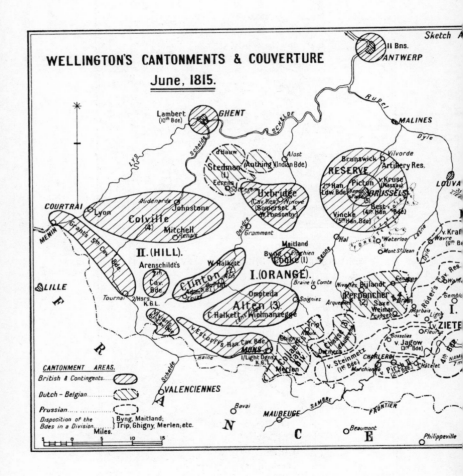

Sketch A

WELLINGTON'S CANTONMENTS & COUVERTURE
June, 1815.

II Bns.
ANTWERP

MALINES

Lambert (10th Bde)   GHENT

Schelde   Rupel   Dyle

d'Hauw   Alost   Vilvorde   LOUVA

Stedman (1)   (Anthing's Indian Bde)   Brunswick   Artillery Res.

Eerens   RESERVE   v. Kruse (Nassau)

Stevenen   Uxbridge   2nd Han   Picton   BRUSSELS   Best (4th Han Bde)

(Cav. Res.   Edw. Bde   (Kempt)   (5)

COURTRAI   Audenarde   Johnstone   (Somerset &   Vincke   v. Kraf

Lyon   Colville   M. Ponsonby)   (5th Han Bde)   (6th Bd)

Grant's 5th Cav. Bde   (4)   Mitchell   Dendre   Maitland   Hal   Waterloo   v. Wavre

MENIN   Mehan   Grammont   Byng   Enghien   Mont St. Jean   Lasne   Res.

II. (HILL).   Arenschildt's   W. Halkett   Cooke (1)   FOREST   v. Wal...

LILLE   7th   Clinton   I. (ORANGE)   Braine le Comte   Nivelles   Bijlandt   Gemble

Cav. Bde   (2)   Nivelles   Perponcher   I.

Tournai   2/Hsrs.   Adam   K.G.L.   Ompteda   Soignies   Arquen...   (2)   Rogier's   I.

K.G.L.   Keuz   Alten (3)   Saxe   Bro...

F   C. Halkett & Wielmansegge   Weimar   v. ZIETE

R   Westarp's Han Cav. Bde   Tripl   Grange   Fleurus

MONS   Ghigny   Chasse (3)   Gosselies   v. Jagow   4th Bd   NAM

Navarre   I/Light Dgns.   Dutmers   (3rd Bde)   7 m

Schelde   K.G.L.   v. Steinmetz   Marchienne   PI   (1st Bde)   Châtelet

Haine   Merlen   (1st Bde)

VALENCIENNES   FRONTIER

CANTONMENT AREAS.
British & Contingents....
Dutch – Belgian..........
Prussian.................
Disposition of the   } Byng, Maitland;
Bdes in a Division   } Trip, Ghigny, Merlen; etc.

Miles.   0   5   10   15

Bavai   MAUBEUGE   SAMBRE

N   C   Beaumont   E   Philippeville

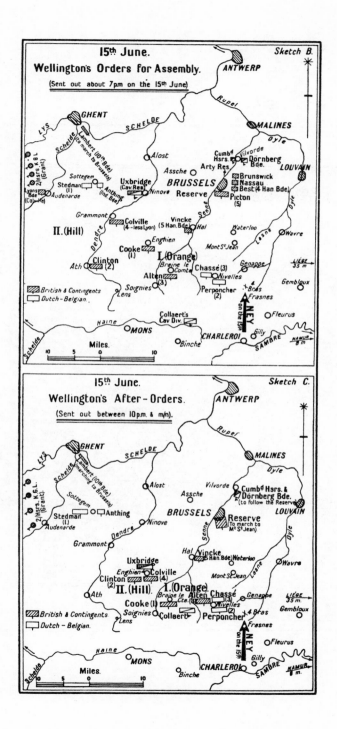

16th June.

Concentration of the Anglo-Dutch Army.
The Move to Quatre Bras.

Sketch D.

ANTWERP

GHENT

Schelde

Rupel

MALINES

Lys

Schelde

Dyle

Vilvorde

(Reached Waterloo at 10 a.m. on 18th June)

Lambert (10th Inf. Bde.)

Alost

Assche

LOUVAIN

Sottegem

Anthing

Stedman (I.)

BRUSSELS

Ninove

Reserve. (Marched about 5 a.m. from Brussels)

Audenarde

Dendre

Colville

Uxbridge

Senne

Hal

Vincke

10·30

Waterloo

Dyle

Wavre

Grammont

Noon

10·30

Enghien

Reserve (Picton leading)

Noon

Mt. St Jean

Walhain

REFERENCE.
Reserve.
Cooke.
Clinton.
Alten.
Colville.
Uxbridge.
Chassé.

Clinton. Grant, Vivian Arenschildt

Braine le Comte

Noon

Nivelles

1 p.m.

Genappe

Gembloux 2 p.m.

Ath

Noon

8·30

6·30

3 p.m.

Perponcher (2) 2 p.m.

Lens

Saignies

Merlen 3 p.m.

4 Bras

NOTE:—
Times of arrival at Quatre Bras are shown.

Estorff

Collaert (less Merlen)

Merlen

Frasnes

Fleurus

Haine

MONS

NEY'S Attack on the 16th

Gilly

Schelde

Binche

CHARLEROI

SAMBRE

Miles.
10 5 0 10

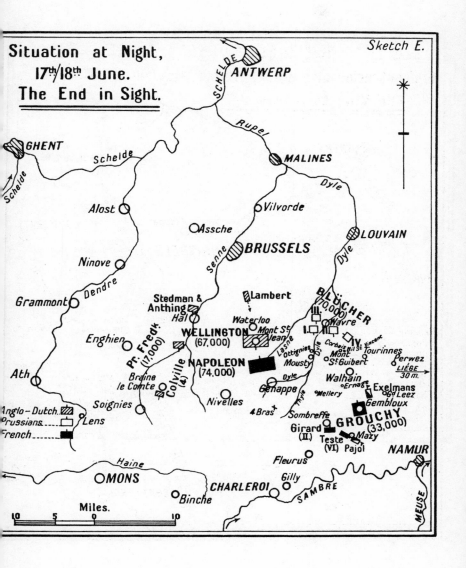

Situation at Night,
17th/18th June.
The End in Sight.

Sketch E.

ANTWERP

Schelde

Rupel

GHENT

MALINES

Schelde

Dyle

Schelde

Alost

Vilvorde

LOUVAIN

Assche

Ninove

Senne

BRUSSELS

Dyle

Grammont

Dendre

Stedman & Anthing

Lambert

BLÜCHER (70,000)

Enghien

Pr. Fredk. (17,000)

Hal

Waterloo

Wavre

WELLINGTON (67,000)

Mont St. Jean

Lasne

Corbais

St. Vincent

Braine le Comte

Colville (4.)

NAPOLEON (74,000)

Ottignies

Mont St. Guibert

Tourinnes

Ath

Mousty

Dyle

Walhain

Perwez

LIÈGE 30 m.

Nivelles

Genappe

Dyle

Mellery

Ernage

Exelmans

Leez

Gembloux

Soignies

4 Bras

Sombreffe

Anglo-Dutch

Prussians

Lens

Girard (II.)

GROUCHY (33,000)

French

Teste (VI.)

Mazy

Pajol

NAMUR

Haine

Fleurus

MEUSE

MONS

Gilly

CHARLEROI

SAMBRE

Binche

Miles.

10   5   0   10

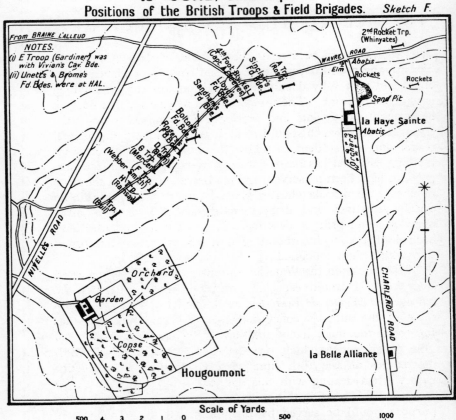

18ᵀᴴ JUNE, about 7 p.m.
Positions of the British Troops & Field Brigades.   *Sketch F.*

The guns of Mercer's Troop
at the close of the Battle.

PREFACE TO THE REVISED EDITION

THIS can claim to be a new study of the Waterloo Campaign. Twenty-one eventful years have passed since I published a detailed and very fully documented work on this subject ; which is now out of print. The time seems to be ripe for this book to be brought up to date and presented in a single volume, the arrangement of which should make it easier for both the general reader and the student to follow the campaign in its entirety. Nothing essential has been sacrificed by compression ; the proportions have been preserved, and the human element in the story remains. Six new sketches are given, in order to show graphically certain situations and dispositions which previously required many pages of print to describe. Nearly all the footnotes have been eliminated, by incorporating in the text the essential information which they contained.

Of the books on the Waterloo Campaign which have appeared since 1914, I would especially mention M. E. Lenient's *La solution des énigmes de Waterloo*. Although I cannot agree with some of the author's conclusions, yet I consider that he has suggested the most likely solution of the baffling mystery of ' the pencil note ', which was the cause of D'Erlon's fruitless manœuvres on the 16th June. I have adopted M. Lenient's theory when dealing with this episode.

When I was revising this study, it seemed to me that no useful purpose would be served by imagining that the opponents in the Waterloo Campaign were provided with all the most modern weapons and equipment, and then attempt to criticize or reconstruct the manœuvres and engagements on this assumption. In such circumstances the Campaign, as we know it, could not have been fought. That, however, is far from saying that it is too antiquated and out of date to be of any interest for present-day study. The interest of past campaigns lies in the study of human nature, which changes far more slowly than armaments ;

and the Waterloo Campaign provides an absorbing study of commanders of all ranks faced with unexpected situations, and the reaction of their minds to the varying strains which they underwent during the operations. For an inquiry of this description, few campaigns will ever be out of date.

In this book I have concentrated on following the working of Napoleon's plan, the employment of their detachments by Marshals Ney and Grouchy, and the fortunes of the *Armée du Nord*. In addition, the handling of the Allied Armies is given in sufficient detail to allow the reader to comprehend the manœuvres of the Emperor and of his two lieutenants.

It is thirty years since I first began to analyse the Waterloo Campaign seriously ; nevertheless I am still convinced that it is impossible to appreciate Napoleon's movements in Belgium, unless one clearly understands Napoleon's plan of organizing the *Armée du Nord* in ' two Wings and a Reserve ', which he outlined in his letter of the 16th June to Marshal Ney. This simple but masterly arrangement must be grasped before anyone can venture to criticize the Emperor's operations in Belgium.

As far as possible in this study, events are judged as they presented themselves at the time. Several critics, knowing the overwhelming disaster which overtook the mighty Emperor and his devoted Army on the fatal field of *la Belle Alliance*, have evolved many, and often quite fictitious, reasons for that failure. The correct method, however, of writing history is that of Michelet : ' Acts must be judged as they present themselves, day by day and hour by hour. Criticism, forgetful and harsh, too often condemns beginnings which are laudable, having in view the end which it knows, and which it has in sight at the outset. We do not choose to know this end. Whatever this man may do tomorrow, we note for his advantage the good work which he does to-day. The end will come soon enough.'

Further, in studying Napoleon, one is always made only too acutely conscious that genius, such as he possessed, requires genius to measure it. One has constantly to remind oneself that things must have looked very different to the Emperor on his dizzy height, from what they now appear to an ordinary mortal below. Probably many of Napoleon's accusers would have been far giddier than he.

Keeping this in mind, I have dedicated this study of Napoleon's

Campaign with the *Armée du Nord* in 1815, to the memory of the most famous of all Artillerymen. I am convinced that the deathless honour which is his in France is only the shadow of the Splendour of his world-wide fame.

PUTNEY, 1936.   A. F. B.

NAPOLEON AND WATERLOO

CHAPTER I

NAPOLEON'S RETURN FROM ELBA AND THE OPENING EVENTS OF THE HUNDRED DAYS

NOTE.—*The Napoleonic Strategy*

(Map 1 ; Sketch A)

It is impossible to bear the torch of truth through the throng without singeing somebody's beard.

LICHTENBERG.

NAPOLEON'S campaign in Belgium with the *Armée du Nord* lacked the dazzling brilliance of the First Consul's operations in 1800, had not the grand resistless sweep of the manœuvre of Ulm, did not end in a glorious crowning triumph like Austerlitz ; yet, despite the final disaster, it has an interest entirely its own, exhibiting, as it does, Napoleon's system of advancing in mass.

No useful purpose can be served by comparing what happened in 1815 with what occurred in 1914–18. In an interminable mutual siege, like the Great War, in which the opposing sides were nearly equal in numbers, the blunders committed by one side were often cancelled by mistakes which the opponents made in their turn. On the other hand, in a war of manœuvre, like 1815, which was bound to be of short duration, and with one side heavily outnumbered by its opponents, there was no time or opportunity for the weaker to recover from any errors which might be made.

In 1815, the Emperor, his lieutenants, and his troops had to surpass themselves, if victory was once more to crown the Eagle Standards of France.

' With the violets in the spring ' the Emperor returned. Whilst he was at Elba Napoleon had kept in touch with public feeling, and early in 1815 he deemed that the time had arrived when he could reseat himself on the Imperial Throne. So on the *27th February* Napoleon, with a small, devoted band of followers (1,000 strong with four cannon) and accompanied by Bertrand, Drouot, and Cambronne, set sail for the southern shores of France. On the *1st March* these adventurers landed in the Gulf of Juan, near Cannes. Masséna at Marseille was at once warned by semaphore, but the news only reached Paris on the 5th and London on the 9th.

Napoleon's small escort sufficed to act as a bodyguard to safeguard him from arrest by the local *gendarmerie* and protect him from the too officious zeal of some unsympathetic or over-zealous battalion leader, for any more serious operation it was useless. For his advance on Paris Napoleon purposely avoided the easy route through Marseille, where Masséna would have been encountered, and took the more difficult road over the French Alps past Grenoble and Lyon. By adopting this route he expected to take his enemies by surprise, and make it extremely difficult for them to intercept him before he gained Grenoble. Advancing with amazing rapidity, even over the difficult country which he encountered in his first marches, the speed of his advance took his opponents' breath away and they failed to combine and oppose his progress.

The critical moment in the adventure was on the *7th March*, when Napoleon's advanced guard struck into the Royalist troops at Lafrey, a small village 15 miles from Grenoble. Napoleon, however, rose to the occasion and dominated the whole scene, and his personal conquest of the 5th Regiment of the Line showed the hold which he still retained over his old soldiers. The men's muskets were levelled to fire, but Napoleon, alone and on foot, advanced to within pistol range and addressed the soldiers in ringing words : ' Soldiers of the Fifth of the Line, do you remember me ? ' There was a volley of assent ; and the clear, strong voice continued : ' If there is in your ranks a single soldier who would kill his Emperor, let him fire. Here am I ! ' Napoleon's calmness, confidence, and magnificent audacity triumphed and overcame all ideas of resistance at this moment of pressing danger. The test was too severe for the troops. Instead of being greeted by a volley of lead, Napoleon was welcomed by a ringing cry of homage, ' *Vive l'Empereur* ! ' Ranks were broken, white cockades torn off and trampled underfoot, shakos raised on bayonets ; and the soldiers, precipitating themselves on their Emperor surrounded him, and in their idolatry sought to touch even the skirts of his overcoat. Acclaimed by his soldiers Napoleon had become a power to reckon with. At one bound he passed from the rôle of adventurer and stood on the very steps of the Throne itself.

As in his progress to Paris on his return from his Egyptian expedition in 1799, all along his way to the capital there was the same wild and unrestrained outburst of enthusiasm and excitement directly the well-known figure of the Emperor was sighted. He charmed all with whom he came in contact by his unfailing tact and faultless demeanour, and his march to Paris became a triumph.

On the 14*th March*, near Auxerre, Napoleon encountered Marshal Ney. The Marshal had told Louis XVIII that he would bring Napoleon back to Paris ' in an iron cage '. But Ney soon found the temptation to join his former master was too strong to be resisted, and with his whole force he went over to the other side and joined his Emperor without firing a shot. Even so the Marshal did not make his final surrender until he had abundant proofs of the feeling pervading the Army. As he said : ' How could I hope to stay the incoming ocean merely with my own hands ? '

Ever onward from steeple to steeple the Eagle continued his irresistible flight ; and on the 20*th March*, the very day which he had foretold, Napoleon reached Paris to find that the Bourbons had fled. The Emperor realized that the time for preparation was short, and on the very evening of his return he started to reorganize the machinery of the Empire. The Cabinet, as announced, contained two distinct surprises. Marshal Davout was appointed Minister of War, though so fitted for high and independent command with the Grand Army in the field ; and Fouché figured once more as the Minister of Police.

Napoleon, during his brief reign at Elba, had undoubtedly heard of the dissensions in the Allied Congress at Vienna and probably reckoned that his return would further widen the existing breaches between the Allies. In this he was doomed to be disappointed. The Allies, appreciating the danger which threatened them after Napoleon had regained the throne of France, determined to sink their differences and work together until their common enemy had been utterly crushed.

It was on the 13*th March* that the Allied Congress in Vienna settled Napoleon's fate by issuing a solemn and somewhat turgid declaration that Napoleon Bonaparte, the enemy and disturber of the peace of the world, was forthwith to be handed over to the vengeance of Europe. The four Great Powers—Russia, Prussia, Austria, and Great Britain—each pledged themselves to put 150,000 men in the field, and keep them under arms until Bonaparte should have been rendered absolutely incapable of stirring up further trouble.

By diplomacy the Emperor attempted to gain the time requisite to set his military house in order, and he despatched accredited representatives to Austria and to Great Britain. Could these two Powers be persuaded to stand aside, even for a time, then Prussia could be overrun. Russia could be dealt with, once Prussia was struck down. It was not to be. Neither ' Papa François ' nor the Prince Regent would listen to Napoleon's pacific protestation. Thus war was made by the pen ; it was left to the sword to bring peace.

Faced with inevitable war the task which confronted Napoleon was an Herculean one. The Army, which he had taken over from Louis XVIII, numbered at most 100,000 men, and it was quite insufficient for the defence of France against the masses of the Seventh Coalition. Nor was the Army in an efficient condition to take the field : the clothing was in a bad state, the cavalry was deficient, the artillery lacked horses, harness, and ammunition, the infantry, as well as the cavalry, were below strength, no reserve of muskets or bayonets was in existence, and cartridges were not available in sufficient numbers for a serious campaign.

On the 13th May the Emperor wrote to Marshal Davout and demanded a detailed report of the breadth of the Condé canals, of the Schelde near Mons, and the Sambre near Charleroi, and the same of the Bruges canal, Brussels canal, and the Meuse near Maestricht. Napoleon also asked for the number of pontoons which would be necessary to bridge each river or canal, and the number of pontoon or field-service wagons available in

Paris; and the date on which they could be massed between Avesnes and Laon. The Emperor, with his thoughts already concentrated on Belgium, was collecting information about the natural obstacles which an advance would have to encounter. But he did not rest content with collecting information. He ordered third, fourth, and fifth battalions to be raised for the various regiments and the old well-known numbers, associated with many a triumph, were given back. All men on furlough were recalled, and 200 battalions of the National Guard were raised, marched off to the fortresses assigned to them, and clothed, armed, and completed after arrival. The fortresses and the coast defences were overhauled and put in order. Twenty veteran battalions were formed to stiffen the National Guard levies, serve as training battalions for them, and encourage the inhabitants. In the short available time, everything that energy and determination could do, was done and was done well.

On reviewing the situation the Emperor decided that although, broadly speaking, he was on the defensive, yet he was free to choose the nature of his operations. At the beginning of April he could have taken the offensive with all the available strength he could collect, and, marching at once into Belgium, have achieved some measure of success. But this course had several grave disadvantages : the Allies would have moved up Armies which would have speedily crushed the force which France could place in the field at this period, and the Emperor, fully engaged in operations in the field, could not have devoted the necessary time and energy to consolidating his power, reorganizing his Army, and rallying his people. By opening an immediate offensive Napoleon would have put himself in the wrong with the French Nation, who believed it was still possible to preserve peace. Such measures, too, would falsify any pacific protestations which the Emperor might wish to address to the Allies. So he held his hand.

On the 1st June the Emperor had a spectacular display called, as in former times (1790), the ' Champ de Mai '. The meeting was inaugurated with a civil ceremony, in which Napoleon, clad in gorgeous silken raiment, was almost unrecognizable. Fortunately the day concluded with the presentation of Eagles to the various regiments by the Emperor himself, now dressed in uniform. He stirred his men to the depths of their feelings by recalling former glories in which they had shared. To the Guard, who advanced last of all, he addressed these impressive words : ' You, Soldiers of the Imperial Guard, you swear to surpass your previous exploits in this campaign which is about to open ; and you will die rather than permit the foreigner to dictate his terms to your country.' The civil part of the function was a failure, but the second phase provided an imposing pageant.

To return to the general situation. The Emperor stood alone to meet the oncoming tide of invasion. He did not possess any ally, whose skilfully led army might be utilized to contain a large force of the Coalition in some secondary and unimportant theatre of operations. His situation was aggravated by the fact that the whole of France's long land boundary did not march for a single mile with any neutral power. Danger, too, was near at hand. The Anglo-Dutch and Prussian Armies were concentrating in Belgium and menaced France from this quarter.

When Napoleon returned from Elba he possessed one supporter on whose service he could reckon—his brother-in-law, Joachim Murat, King of Naples. Before he left Elba Napoleon warned Murat to prepare the Neapolitan Army, so as to be ready for any eventuality. But Murat was on no account to take the initiative and open hostilities, he was to play a waiting game. If the Austrian forces did press on, Murat was advised to draw back and avoid a decisive engagement as long as possible.

Murat's own position at this time was by no means secure, and his unreliable Army had little fighting value and was unlikely to stand the strain of a serious action. If it was defeated it would certainly dissolve. So long as Murat remained at the head of an undefeated Army the Emperor need not detach French troops to secure France's south-eastern boundary ; and, well handled, Murat's Army might have been of incalculable assistance. Unfortunately Murat was not an Ally on whom the Emperor could depend, as although ' in battle perhaps the bravest man in the world, yet, left to himself, Murat was without judgment '.

Murat considered that prompt action on his part would tend to secure his crown ; and, hearing that Napoleon had landed in France, he declared war on the Allies (15*th March*) before Napoleon was in any position to assist him. As soon as his Army was ready to take the field, Murat pushed forward a strong detachment (about 10,000–12,000 men) to Rome, whilst he himself marched at the head of the main Army (some 30,000 strong) along the Adriatic coast road. Had the King halted at Ancona the Austrians could not have advanced along the Po valley with this formidable collection of men on their left flank. But this was not Murat's method ; and he decided to take the initiative and destroy the Austrians, before they could concentrate sufficient forces to deal with him.

At first Murat achieved a slight success. He advanced against Bologna, pushed the Austrians out of the city and half-way to Mantua. Then he halted, instead of massing his whole force and attacking boldly. He had shot his bolt, and shortly afterwards he decided to fall back. This retreat upset the *moral* of his Army.

On the *2nd May*, however, Murat turned at Tolentino and attacked Bianchi. The opposing forces were : Austrians, about 11,000 (including 1,000 horse) and 28 guns ; Neapolitans, 28,000 (including 3,500 horse) and 35 guns. The fighting proceeded with fluctuating results until darkness fell, and Murat determined to attack again next morning. In this attack, Murat at first gained a temporary success and drove back the Austrian advanced troops ; but the final Neapolitan attack was checked. Bianchi then launched two squadrons and a regiment of infantry in a vigorous counter-attack, and the Neapolitans were overthrown and withdrew in considerable disorder followed by Bianchi. Under the pressure of pursuit the Neapolitan Army broke up and fled in small bodies to the eastward, leaving its *impedimenta* in the power of the Whitecoats. In these operations the Neapolitans lost about 4,000 men, though the Austrian casualty list did not exceed 800. Later, in the retreat, the demoralized Neapolitans deserted in thousands.

The result of Murat's premature campaign was most inopportune. The greater proportion of the Austrian forces in this subsidiary theatre were released at once for a closer and more direct attack on France, and Frimont began to concentrate in Lombardy. Murat fled to reunite his fortunes with Napoleon, but in this hope he was disappointed. Napoleon, furious at the light-hearted manner in which the King had opened and conducted his campaign, could not forgive its miserable failure. He refused to see Murat and would not consent to give him a command in the *Armée du Nord*. It was an unfortunate decision since it wronged France. 'At Waterloo Murat might have given us the victory. It required but little to break three or four English squares ; and Murat was the best cavalry officer in the world.'

Henceforward the Emperor stood alone. Not only was he without an ally he could not even reckon on any state remaining neutral, and the odds which he had to face were tremendous. The Emperor, however, made the most of the short breathing space which was accorded to him. He established his Government and raised fresh armies from the war-weary, but far from sterile soil of France. Unhappily for him the internal affairs of France were complicated by a revolt in the disturbed district of La Vendée, and this insurrection was still smouldering.

Before the middle of June the Emperor had organized his Armies as follows :

The *Armée du Nord* [1] (to operate in Belgium) :

The Guard (20,000), Cavalry Reserve (13,500), and the I (20,000), II (25,000), III (17,000), IV (15,500), and VI (10,500) Corps, with 370 guns ;

On the Upper Rhine (covering Alsace) : Generals Rapp (V Corps) and Lecourbe (23,000) ;

Covering the Italian frontier : Marshals Suchet and Brune (15,500) ;

Masking the Pyrenean defiles against Spain : Generals Clausel and Decaen (8,000) ; and

Quelling the Vendean insurrection : General Lamarque (10,000).

Map 1.—The actual distribution of the various Corps facilitated a concentration on the Franco-Belgian or on the Rhine frontier. In either case the VI Corps, Cavalry Reserve, and Guard could be pushed up to the concentration point.

The Armies of the Seventh Coalition, however, were in distinctly better case than the French. They had the *moral* of their conquest in 1814 to strengthen them ; and the Allied Armies, which had made the campaign in France, had not yet been disbanded. During May the Allies decided to close in on the French frontiers with five main Armies :

Map 1.—1. *Anglo-Dutch Army*, about 110,000 strong, was

[1] For detailed Order of Battle of the *Armée du Nord* see Appendix I—A.

cantoned in Belgium to the west of the Brussels–Charleroi road. It was under the command of Field-Marshal the Duke of Wellington (who had reached Brussels from Vienna on the 5th April) ; and it was to cross the Franco-Belgian boundary to the south-west of Mons.

2. *Prussian Army*, about 117,000 strong, was cantoned in Belgium between the Charleroi–Brussels road and Liége (under Field-Marshal Prince Blücher von Wahlstatt) ; it was to cross the Franco-Belgian frontier to the south-west of Namur.

3. *Russian Army*, 150,000 (under Barclay de Tolly), was to cross the Middle Rhine and advance in the second line, acting as Reserve Army. It was still far distant from the French frontier.

4. *Austrian Army*, 210,000 (under Prince Schwartzenberg), was to cross the Upper Rhine and advance in conjunction with Wellington's and Blücher's forces. In June this Army also was out of striking distance of the French frontier.

5. *Austrian Army of Italy*, 75,000 (under Frimont), was to debouch across the Alps with Lyon as its objective.

Both flanks rested on the sea and were secured by the fleets of Great Britain.

Their numerous wars against Napoleon had taught the Allies something. Of all the commanders, none realized more clearly than Blücher that only in unity was safety to be found when operating as part of an Allied Army. Consequently in the campaign in Belgium, opposed to the resolute old Prussian Field-Marshal and his loyal ally, Wellington, Napoleon found jealousy, intrigue, and incapacity playing a far smaller part than he expected.

To sum up the situation. On the one side France was standing alone, without the aid of any external allies, and she was unable to place in the field more than 200,000 men to safeguard herself from violation. On the other side were gathering the armed hosts of Europe—Austria, Prussia, Russia, and Great Britain— the Seventh Coalition. The Generalissimo directed 1,000,000 men, and behind this host were adequate reserves. The alliance was welded together by the gold of England.

Unfortunately for France, there were grave differences between the power exercised by Napoleon in the earlier years of the Empire and the power which he wielded in 1815. On his return from Elba Napoleon hesitated for some time before he reintro-

duced ' Conscription ', and not until early in June was Marshal
Davout ordered to send out the instructions for levying the class
for 1815. As it happened France was resigned to war and there
was no difficulty in collecting the conscripts.

There was another serious difference between the Emperor of
1815 and the Napoleon of 1805, or even of 1809. No longer were
Napoleon and the State synonymous terms. Within a very short
space of time the Chamber virtually became the State ; and a
further weakness lay in the fact that France did not stand united
behind the Emperor.

NAPOLEON'S PLAN FOR THE DEFENCE OF FRANCE IN 1815
(Maps 1 and 2)

Even up to the beginning of June the Emperor could still
choose between acting offensively or defensively. He might adopt
the same general plan which he had used so brilliantly when he
stood at bay in 1814 : operating defensively from a central
position, throwing himself against Army after Army, and defeating them in succession. In 1815, however, this would only
delay the end. If the Allies were well handled and speed was
not allowed to destroy size, the Emperor would be pressed back
remorselessly and driven to make his last stand in front of Paris.
Then he would be forced to deliver a decisive pitched battle to
cover his capital with all the odds of numbers and even of *moral*
against him.

The Emperor calculated that the Allies would only open the
invasion of France on the 1st July and would not reach the
vicinity of Paris before the 15th August. By that time Napoleon,
if he decided to wait in front of Paris, would probably be able to
collect a field army of 240,000 men. Even if the Armies of the
Seventh Coalition dropped 150,000 men to mask the French
fortresses on the northern and eastern frontiers, yet the Allies
would be able to bring up to Paris at least half a million men and
ensure a numerical superiority of two to one in the decisive
battle of the campaign. If Napoleon then suffered a defeat in
front of his capital, either he would be chased away in flight,
leaving Paris at the mercy of the invader, or he would be flung
back into the city. To await the onslaught would ensure defeat.

Cunctator strategy, such as Russia employed in 1812 and Wellington used in the Peninsula, would not save France in 1815.

There was another alternative for a Great Captain to choose. The time to strike had come ; and Napoleon decided to take the offensive himself and attack Wellington and Blücher in Belgium, before Schwartzenberg and the remainder of the Allied Armies could intervene. The plan was feasible because the Allies could not undertake a general offensive until the 1st July. By destroying the two most renowned Army Commanders of the Seventh Coalition Napoleon hoped to strike terror into the Allies and restore confidence to his own Nation.

Napoleon knew, from spies and reports from officers, that the dispersed cantonments of the Anglo-Prussian forces stretched from Ghent to Liége. If, unknown to the Allies, he could mass the *Armée du Nord* opposite to Charleroi, he could break the front and then beat Wellington and Blücher in detail. Napoleon probably believed that, if he defeated Wellington and Blücher, Belgium would openly declare for France and her troops would augment the strength of the Grand Army. In this the Emperor may have been over-confident. The Army of the Netherlands fought loyally enough for the Allies in 1815, and, although some 2,000 of its officers and men had been decorated with the *Légion d'Honneur*, not one deserted to the *Armée du Nord*. On the other hand, Napoleon probably estimated correctly when he considered that, if Wellington was overthrown, the British Ministry would fall and a strong peace party would be returned to power. Moreover, if the war continued and the Seventh Coalition survived this first disaster, the *Armée du Nord*, flushed with the successes gained in Belgium, reinforced by the V Corps (Rapp) from Alsace, and by reinforcements despatched to it from the depots and fortresses, would gather strength as it went, like an avalanche in movement. Passing through the Vosges the Emperor would oppose the Russian and Austrian advance. A mere threat at Vienna would probably chain Schwartzenberg in the vicinity of his capital. Meanwhile Barclay de Tolly could be destroyed, and 1812 would have been avenged at last. With Austria alone left in the field the campaign would have been over. Napoleon would have won all along the line, overcoming vast numerical superiority by superior mobility and, above all, by superior leadership.

The advantages of this plan were numerous and striking. It involved no surrender of territory whatever, there was the chance of immediate and decisive success, and of dissolving the Coalition with a thunderbolt—the destruction of Wellington's and Blücher's forces. By invading Belgium Napoleon covered the most open and most vulnerable section of the French frontier, ensuring for himself greater freedom and more time in which to strike the decisive blow. The conception was perfect; everything depended on execution.

As the situation unfolded itself, Napoleon learned that the Anglo-Prussian forces numbered at least 210,000 men and 550 guns. The question naturally arose whether it was possible, within the available time-limit, to defeat them decisively with 125,000 men accompanied by 370 guns. At this critical stage it was necessary to throw for complete success, any lesser result must ensure France's ruin quite as certainly as a defeat would do. Fortunately it was not really just a question of pitting 125,000 men against 210,000, because the 210,000 were composed of troops of varying quality. Although the British and King's German Legion Troops possessed the finest fighting qualities, yet in Blücher's force there was little real homogeneity, though the proportion of veteran troops was higher than in Wellington's Army. More important still, the Allies were commanded by different, and independent generals, they possessed divided interests, and they had separate and divergent lines of operation. As in all wars of coalitions, Napoleon hoped that suspicion, doubt, and even blundering would weaken the effectiveness of the Allies in line of battle. But, just as they had in the wars of Liberation and Conquest in 1813 and 1814, so in 1815 the Allies had one common object, strong enough to bind them together— fear of Napoleon.

On the French side the state of affairs was very different. Only one Army was involved. It had been led for years by a man who was acknowledged to be not only the greatest captain of his own, but of all time; he was not only head of the Army but also head of the State, and thus combined supreme military and political power. His appearance in the field ensured that all ranks would put forth all their energies in the furtherance of the selected plan. His personality inspired those whom he led with unswerving and unsurpassed devotion, and his presence on the battle-field was calculated to stimulate his own troops to perform feats of unparalleled valour. The French Army, too, was perfectly homogeneous. It spoke one language, possessed one creed of military loyalty ; and every man in it had been hardened in the furnace of war.

But for some serious defects the Grand Army of 1815 might have taken precedence after that which fought at Jena. Although in 1815 the Grand Army was composed of devoted veterans, led and commanded by officers of experience, yet the larger organizations had not been exercised together for sufficient time, before they took the field, for all ranks to have gained the necessary mutual confidence in their commanders and to have got used to working together. In this respect the Grand Army of 1815 was inferior to the Grand Armies of 1805 and of 1806. Another inherent weakness in the Grand Army of 1815 lay in the fact that many of its superior leaders took the field tainted with acts of treachery to the Bourbons, which lay heavy on their consciences. These officers realized that, in the event of defeat, their betrayal of the Royalist cause might foreshadow a felon's doom. Although such a presentiment might induce them to expose themselves more than ever in battle, yet in times of stress such thoughts would not tend to fortify and strengthen their judgment. To sum up, the Army led out by the Emperor was a Napoleonic rather than a national or French Army ; and, in a disaster, this difference might lead to its disappearance. Formidable though it would be if all went reasonably well, yet the Army might prove too fragile to withstand the agony of a defeat.

The other great defect of the *Armée du Nord* was one of quantity. That it was too small for the task in hand was a sign of decadence in Napoleon's military character. Although he led out 125,000 men for the campaign in Belgium, yet he left 56,500 locked up in purely secondary theatres. Had this latter number been reduced, as it might have been, to 19,500, then the strength available for the Grand Army would have been increased to 162,000 men. With such a force, handled as the Emperor alone could handle it, nothing would have been left to chance and decisive success in Belgium would have been certain.

To show that the suggestion is not a mere visionary project the following example will suffice : Rapp with the V Corps (20,000) was left at Strasbourg to cover Alsace, though a force of this size was quite useless to stem the advance of the Russian and Austrian Armies, totalling 350,000 men. A small mobile detachment of 5,000 would have been large enough to get touch with this hostile advance as it closed on the Rhine, and then have delayed that advance by employing rear-guard expedients, such as breaking down bridges, breaking up and blocking roads, etc. In any case, if closely pressed, whatever its size 20,000 or 5,000, Rapp's force eventually would be compelled to retire under the shelter of the guns and bastions of the fortress of Strasbourg. But a force of 20,000 would prove a severe drain on the limited amount of provisions available, and cause the place to fall at an earlier date than Napoleon had calculated. Whereas a mobile detachment of 5,000, if driven to take refuge, would be a welcome increase to the strength of the garrison, and their horses would provide a useful addition to the supplies in the magazines, if necessity demanded their destruction. Napoleon fully appreciated that no pressing danger could threaten the Alsatian frontier until the beginning of July, consequently the other 15,000 men of the V Corps could have been used to swell the ranks of the *Armée du Nord*. All the other detachments could have been shorn of superfluous men in an analogous manner.

The nice adjustment of her defensive means was vital to France in 1815. If he had still been the General of Austerlitz, Napoleon's disposition of his soldiers on the theatre of war would have been very different. He would have launched against Wellington and Blücher a perfectly compacted Army of veteran troops over 160,000 strong, and success in Belgium would have relieved the pressure on all the other frontiers. The Napoleon who failed to concentrate every available man for the stroke was assuredly not the Napoleon of Austerlitz and Jena. In 1815, the Emperor's correct appreciation of the real measure of his offensive means, and his disposal of his forces at the opening of the campaign, seem to have fallen short of his great reputation as a strategist. The fate of France was jeopardized before a shot was fired.

When Napoleon decided that he would strike Wellington and Blücher in Belgium, he had the choice of four directions for his advance.

Map 1.—In 1815 Belgium presented a practically open frontier to France and the country was divided naturally by the rivers

which traversed it. The first natural partition, or gap, lay between the northern seaboard and the Lys, the next was between
the Lys and Schelde. Between the North Sea and the Schelde,
however, the country was low-lying, intersected by numerous
canals, and unfavourable to rapid military operations. The third
gap was between the Schelde and Sambre (near Charleroi the
Sambre was perhaps 30 yards broad) ; and the fourth gap was
between the Sambre and Meuse.

Belgium had so often been one of the cockpits of Europe
that many fortresses and strong places had come into existence.
Between the coast and the Lys there were the fortresses of Ostend,
Nieuport, and Ypres. To close the gap between the Lys and
Schelde there were the strong places of Courtrai and Oudenarde,
and the western half of the gap between the Schelde and Sambre
was strengthened by the fortresses of Tournai and Mons. In the
centre was the old-time strong place of Charleroi, covering the
bridge over the Sambre, but its defensive value was negligible.
In the right, or eastern, gap one dilapidated fortress, the historic
one of Namur, alone confronted an invader. Thus the centre
of the gap, between the Schelde and Sambre, lay peculiarly open.
This part of Belgium had other striking advantages. It was
entirely suitable for military operations on a large scale, the
ground was undulating, there were numerous good roads, and
there were three passages over the Sambre in the immediate
vicinity of Charleroi.

The country was a rich one (although the harvest was not
yet in), and Belgium favoured swift operations and Napoleon's
procedure of living on the country, by making war support war.
The condition of the *pavés* admitted rapid marching even in wet
weather ; and the by-roads were traversable in good weather,
though in heavy weather their condition was apt to become
deplorable.

The one grave defect of this centre section lay in the fact
that there was no extensive, natural screen to cloak Napoleon's
preliminary concentration. Nevertheless, the limited view, owing
to the rolling nature of the country and the existence of large
woods, assisted to make good the lack of better means for screen-
ing the first offensive moves of the *Armée du Nord*. Charleroi
also possessed an additional advantage, it was the ganglion of two
main roads which, as they left the Sambre, pointed respectively

at Wellington's and Blücher's cantonments. The capture of Charleroi by the French would allow forces to be pushed at once up both roads to locate the Allies ; and if the reserve was held at Charleroi, it would be centrally situated between its covering forces and would be able to advance rapidly in either direction, directly definite information came to hand. Hence, geographically speaking, Charleroi and attack by the centre line had much to recommend it.

If Napoleon had based his Army on Lille and struck straight at Brussels through Ath he would have ensured the concentration and co-operation of the Allies, which he did nothing to hinder and everything to assist, by driving Wellington back on to Blücher. Certainly such a stroke would cut Wellington's line with Ostend. But command of the sea gave great freedom of base ; the Anglo-Dutch base would be changed to Antwerp, the line of communications would be altered accordingly, and with a certain allied victory all inconveniences would disappear. To advance into Belgium from the east had little to recommend it. Although such a stroke would threaten, and might temporarily sever Blücher's line with the Rhine, yet again the result would be a concentration of the Allies and the speedy termination of the campaign. An early disaster must befall the Grand Army under such conditions. Such a stroke also would be singularly ineffective, as Blücher's Army was by no means tied to a line of communications through Namur and Liége and so back to the Rhine at Coblentz. A new line could have been opened without great trouble through Louvain and Maestricht, and the Prussian base could be shifted from Coblentz to the more convenient Cologne somewhat lower down the Rhine. Further, an invasion on this front would be immensely impeded by the rough, broken country of the Forest of the Ardennes, a natural obstacle which would prove troublesome to cross with a large army and would delay the movement so much as to rob it of the element of surprise. On debouching the Grand Army might easily find the two Allied Armies concentrated and drawn up ready to accept battle.

Sketches A, B, and C.—Another variant was to select Wellington's Army as the sole objective and concentrate the *Armée du Nord* at Valenciennes, Bavai, and Maubeuge. The Grand Army would then advance northwards, closing in to a narrowed front—Braine le Comte, Soignies, and Lens. Pushing on into the heart of Wellington's scattered cantonments, before Blücher could intervene, the *Armée du Nord* would destroy the Anglo-Dutch Army piecemeal as it attempted to concentrate. By advancing in this way Napoleon could be sure that he would only encounter one of the Allied Armies in the first battle. Wellington had envisaged just such an irruption, consequently he would have attempted to concentrate just as he did, and disaster would have swiftly overtaken him. Be that as it may, Napoleon decided to advance on Charleroi, and for this reason the place had to be mastered in force and by surprise. This initial success must be followed up at once, and each Ally must be pushed back towards his base, so as to allow the Grand Army to penetrate between the Allies and have sufficient elbow-room to swing on to each in turn.

Map 1.—Napoleon's calculations were based on the fact that the Allies were dispersed over an area whose front measured 90 miles and the mean depth (Brussels–Charleroi) 30 miles. Consequently the Emperor considered that it would take the Allies six days to concentrate on either flank, or three days to mass on the common centre—Gosselies–Fleurus. To be given a chance of success, therefore, the Grand Army must effect its concentration unsuspected, and within gun-range of the Allied outposts on the Franco-Belgian boundary to the south of Charleroi, and do so before the Allied Armies had made a single defensive move. The task seemed impossible. The Grand Army was strung out in an extended line of cantonments from Lille to Metz, a stretch of 175 miles, and its rearmost troops were in Paris, 125 miles from the frontier opposite to Charleroi. Save the Forest of Ardennes on the right flank, there was no natural obstacle to cloak the manœuvre and shroud it in the necessary secrecy. Nature would have to be supplemented by the Emperor's skill.

After weighing the pros and cons, Napoleon decided to mass the *Armée du Nord* on the French side of the Frontier opposite Charleroi. The Emperor would then advance against the Allied junction-point, push back the Allies, and drive them apart. Into the gap thus formed the *Armée du Nord* would be thrust, ready for all eventualities.

The Allied Plan for 1815

The time has come to consider briefly the plan formed by the Seventh Coalition for the Invasion of France.

The Allied project was an ambitious one. It contemplated no less than a great and well-articulated advance on Paris to begin on the 1st July. This invasion was to be carried out by all the Armies of the Seventh Coalition. Three of the Allied Armies—those under Wellington, Blücher, and Schwartzenberg—were to enter France and advance rapidly towards Paris, moving *via* Péronne, Laon, and Langres, respectively. It was decided that whatever befell a first-line Army, whether it fought or not, or was beaten or not, the remaining two generals would press on regardless of its fate. In the second line would follow the Fourth Army, the Russians under Barclay de Tolly. The Russian Army was to make good all reverses sustained in the invasion by any of the first-line Armies. If Napoleon fought and beat one of the three first-line Armies and proceeded to open a pursuit of the broken Army, it was arranged that the other two leading Armies, paying no attention to what had befallen their Ally, would continue their uninterrupted advance and make good part of the road to the French capital. Meanwhile, to safeguard the beaten force from annihilation, Barclay de Tolly would move the Reserve Army to its rescue.

The plan (so far as conception went) had much to recommend it. It was both bold and sound. It would, however, have required a master-mind to carry it through—without vacillation.

It is well known that the Duke of Wellington often expressed the opinion that Napoleon was wrong to take the offensive. The Duke considered that the land of France was much exhausted by the 1814 campaign; and in 1815 four Allied Armies were to open the invasion before the harvest, consequently supply difficulties would probably have arisen and hampered the rapidity of the Allied advance. The Duke thought that Napoleon should have stationed himself with some 300,000 men on the Meuse, manœuvring from one invading Army to the other, and attacking each separately. In other words, playing over again the campaign of 1814. Nevertheless, Napoleon decided wisely when he determined to forestall the Allies by launching a bold offensive in June against Wellington and Blücher. Of course, after the disastrous failure which befell the *Armée du Nord* in Belgium all the risks attendant on the Allied plan of invasion naturally disappeared. It is unnecessary, therefore, to consider this plan more fully.

NOTE.—*The Napoleonic Strategy*

It is necessary to give a brief explanation of the system of advancing in mass and of manœuvring, which was used by the Emperor in all his later campaigns. Herein lies the key to Napoleon's strategy in 1815.

In 1800, as a direct result of the Marengo campaign, Napoleon realized the necessity of wide reconnaissance. The Ulm Campaign of 1805 brought home to Napoleon that cavalry, acting alone, was incapable of gripping and holding a hostile army in position, after it had accurately located the foe. These were some of the difficulties with which Napoleon was faced. The problem which he had to solve was complicated to a certain extent by the fact that he was usually at war with a Coalition, so he had to ensure beating one army before the other could strike in. It became, therefore, imperative for him to devise some strategical system which should find, grip, and hold fast his enemy, in order that the battle could be brought on at once before any help could reach the foe ; and the tactical methods employed must ensure his enemy's decisive defeat in the short time-limit left at the disposal of the Emperor.

The system which he devised was inaugurated in the Jena campaign, when he advanced in the celebrated ' battalion square of 200,000 men '. In this campaign (1806) the eight Corps of the Grand Army were divided into four parts. Six Corps were charged with the duty of strategical protection, and acted as strategical covering forces. Two Corps acted as Strategical Right Flank Guard, two more were Strategical Advanced Guard, and two were Strategical Left Flank Guard. The remaining two Corps (one being the Guard) acted as the Reserve (*la masse offensive*, or *la masse de manœuvre*) which was centrally placed and retained under the immediate command of the Emperor. In 1806 the underlying idea was to march heading for Berlin. This would compel the Prussians to offer battle, because a proud nation would not surrender its capital without striking a blow in its defence. Then the Prussian Army could be dealt with decisively before the arrival of their Russian Ally, at the time far away over the Polish frontier. The formation, used by Napoleon, in his advance across Prussia, ensured that whenever and wherever the Prussian Army was encountered it would be held up by one of the covering detachments attacking it furiously and immobilizing it. The attack of some 40,000 French troops, with freedom to manœuvre, could not be disregarded; and the Prussian Army would be gripped and held fast for a sufficient time to allow the Emperor to manœuvre the other free masses so as to deliver a ' knock-out ' blow. Further, either of the other covering forces was well placed to hold up and contain, far from the decisive field, any other bodies of hostile troops which might be located near at hand, or might desire to intervene at the crisis.

The Emperor relied on his covering forces being fought out to the utmost limits of human endurance. This would ensure at least a day's fighting. Hence, after the enemy was first gripped, the Emperor could always calculate on having twenty-four hours in which to mass and deliver the death-blow. In twenty-four hours his masterful mind and tremendous driving energy could accomplish great results. Napoleon only aimed at economy of force on the whole transaction, and the fate of a detachment was of little moment and did not cause him any uneasiness. The Emperor, when he took the field, always aspired to win a campaign in the shortest possible time. He did not economize in the lives of his men, or endeavour to keep them out of hospital by skirmishing around the country-side, achieving nothing.

Then, in 1807, Napoleon introduced ' the case-shot attack ', and thereby added to the certainty of rapid success, once he had gripped and immobilized his foe. This development of artillery tactics was made the most of by the Emperor in later actions. When he judged his battle was ripe for the decisive blow, he ordered his reserve batteries to be galloped forward, and brought into action at such a range that they could tear a breach in the living wall of the enemy's battle-line with their concentrated point-blank discharges of grape. At the crisis of a battle these guns galloped up to within 400–500 yards from the enemy's position and opened a tremendous fire of grape (or case-shot) against his shaken line, already worn out in a prolonged fire-fight. A few minutes of this hail of death usually tore the requisite breach for the horse and foot of the Guard to storm; and the enemy, his equilibrium gone, his line sundered, his reserves already engaged, was speedily overpowered and crushed. As the infantry of the Grand Army deteriorated during the long never-ending wars, this procedure (evolved by Senarmont at Friedland) became increasingly important; because ' the case-shot attack ' ensured that the foe was crushed in the time available.

Maps 1 and 2. By 1815 the advance in ' battalion square ' (or the use of Strategical Advanced Guards, or covering masses) had passed out of the experimental stage. This system was peculiarly adapted to meet the critical needs of the strategical outlook in 1815, when a decision had to be forced on the Allies in Belgium, and obtained from them at the earliest moment. If the *Armée du Nord*, organized in two Wings with a centrally placed Reserve, was pushed into Belgium from Beaumont through Charleroi, its two Wings could be trusted to locate and grip any forces of the enemy which they might encounter, and then hold the hostile forces fast until the Emperor swung in the Reserve to obtain the decision from the immobilized foe whom he had selected to destroy. The covering Corps would perform effectively the services of exploration, intelligence, location of the enemy's principal force, and local protection of the *Armée du Nord*; in addition, they would hold fast the enemy until the Emperor could mass superior numbers to deal with him.

The idea, underlying this system of advancing in mass, was that the information gained by the covering forces furnished the basis on which Napoleon could and did manœuvre the Grand Army. By engaging and pinning their immediate opponents (and by their own powers of resistance) the covering forces constituted the adversary a ' fixed point '. Around this point the Emperor could then manœuvre and swing in his Reserve. Thus the covering masses gave Napoleon the power of developing his operations, and the chance to deal a swift and sure death-blow to his immobilized and heavily engaged foe.

If the handling of a Strategical (or Tactical) Advanced Guard is compared to the various phases of a duel with rapiers, or sabres, it will be seen that, in each case, the procedure is always the same against an adversary who is mobile and free to manœuvre :

The Duel.	Handling a Strategical (or Tactical) Advanced Guard.	Underlying Idea.
Standing on guard.	Placing an advanced guard in position.	To cover oneself.
Engage or cross weapons.	Contact of advanced patrols.	To establish contact.
Thrust.	Attack of advanced guard.	To threaten the adversary by a direct menace, so as to fix his attention, and allow the assailant to be free to manœuvre.
Double, or disengagement, with lunge.	Offensive stroke by the main body, or *masse de manœuvre*.	To deal the decisive and deadly stroke.

Map 2.—Probably no campaign illustrates the use and handling of Strategical Advanced Guards better than this, the Waterloo Campaign. But, like all systems, it required application to meet the especial and peculiar circumstances of the particular case. In the Waterloo Campaign there were two enemies in the field lying in contact with each other, and the Emperor was only at the head of six Corps. Consequently the ' battalion square ' of eight Corps, used in the Jena campaign, required practical adaptation so that the means at hand might attain the end in view. Hence, as one foe lay away to Napoleon's left front and the other to his right front (from Beaumont), the centre covering mass could be safely discarded. The available force could then be disposed in two Strategical Advanced Guards, or Wings, with a centrally placed Reserve ; so that each foe might be sought, fixed, and then prepared for the stroke of the Reserve. The containing Wing, not implicated in the decisive battle, would place itself inside the other Ally and be able to keep him away. This containing Wing would not only grip and neutralize the foe opposed to it, but it would prepare him for the blow which would be delivered on the morrow by the Reserve, when it was free to swing across and strike in on this other flank. The advance in two Wings and a Reserve was admirably suited to the situation and to the organization of the *Armée du Nord* in 1815. Two Corps could be used to form each Wing, whilst two (including the Guard) would act as the Reserve under Napoleon. Thus the Emperor arranged his Army for his last campaign.

CHAPTER II

THE DISPOSITIONS OF THE ALLIES IN BELGIUM IN MID-JUNE

(Maps 1 and 2; Sketch 1)

Map 1, *Sketch* 1.—In mid-June the disposition of the *Anglo-Dutch Army*,[1] 93,000 (including 14,000 horse) and 196 guns, was as follows:

I Corps (30,000), commanded by the Prince of Orange (Constant de Rebecque, Chief of the Staff), head-quarters Braine le Comte, with—

   1st (British) Division (Cooke), head-quarters Enghien,
   3rd (British) Division (Alten), head-quarters Soignies,
   2nd (Dutch-Belgian) Division (Perponcher), head-quarters Nivelles,
   3rd (Dutch-Belgian) Division (Chassé), head-quarters Roeulx.

II Corps (27,000), commanded by Lieut.-General Lord Hill, head-quarters Ath, with—

   2nd (British) Division (Clinton), head-quarters Ath,
   4th (British) Division (Colville), head-quarters Oudenarde,
   1st (Dutch-Belgian) Division (Stedman), Grammont-Ghent,
   Dutch-Belgian Indian Brigade (Anthing), head-quarters east of Ghent.

Since no surprise attack was apprehended and to facilitate the supply of forage, the *Heavy Cavalry and Horse Artillery* (10,000), under Lord Uxbridge, were cantoned in the valley of the Dendre between Ninove and Grammont.[2]

The Reserve (25,000), under the Duke of Wellington, was cantoned around Wellington's head-quarters at Brussels—

---

[1] For detailed Order of Battle see Appendix I (C).
[2] Whilst the British Horse Artillery was in Belgium, Lieut.-Colonel Sir A. Frazer, C.R.H.A., had three of the Troops rearmed with 9-pounders, and one Troop rearmed with heavy 5½-inch howitzers.

24

5th (British) Division (Picton),
6th (British) Division,
Brunswick Corps (Duke of Brunswick).
The Nassau Contingent (Kruse) was between Brussels and
Louvain.

Sketch 1.—The cantonments of the Reserve were immune from
surprise, and they were more concentrated than those of the other
Corps. The Reserve could be massed at short notice and moved
rapidly in any required direction. It could then support either
of the other two Corps and assist in checking a French invasion
for sufficient time to allow the Allies to concentrate their men
and concert their plans. The weak points of the Duke's dispositions were the wide dispersion of the two forward Corps and
the lack of suitable arrangements for covering the scattered
cantonments strategically. A sudden surprise attack might sweep
away one of the scattered Corps before the Reserve could reach
the front ; and Wellington's Army, arriving piecemeal, would
suffer defeat in detail.

The frontier from *Bonne Espérance* (in front of Binche) to a
point in front of Leuze was watched by two Brigades of Dutch-
Belgian Light Cavalry, with a Brigade of Dutch-Belgian Carabiniers placed centrally at Roeulx to support the outpost troops.
In addition, that part of the frontier for which the Duke was
especially nervous (from Leuze to Menin) was covered by two
British Brigades (Vivian and Grant), and in support was Arents-
child's Brigade placed behind Tournai. The Duke's outpost line
ran from Menin to *Bonne Espérance*, blocking all the main lines
of approach from that part of France. It is beyond question that
a proper system of posts, connecting the outpost line with Brussels
as well as with Blücher's inner flank, should have been organized,
so as to ensure that the earliest news of French movements could
be sent back rapidly. This was necessary because Wellington's
head-quarters were situated at some distance from the frontier,
and the Anglo-Dutch troops were so widely disseminated that
ample warning was essential to enable them to concentrate
forward. More important still, in Wellington's arrangements for
Couverture no troops were placed so as to secure his concentration
point—Gosselies. The Duke calculated that, within twenty-four
hours after the first warning, he could collect his Reserve and
one out of his remaining Corps at any place within the area of

his cantonments. That is, if no accident occurred, he could mass about 60,000 men at either Nivelles or Quatre Bras. But to the twenty-four hours necessary to effect this concentration must be added the time requisite to transmit news, from the outposts, of a French irruption into Belgium, as well as the time for formulating and despatching the necessary orders and issuing them to the troops. Opposed to any other general of this era Wellington's arrangements might not have been unduly hazardous. Opposed to Napoleon the risk was too great. The Duke relied too much on the luck of obtaining timely information, and not enough on the certainty of gaining time by the action of a strategical covering force such as Blücher used.

Map 1.—The Anglo-Dutch Army was extended over a tract of country of greater length than that protected by the Prussian Army, and Wellington's entire front ran along the French border. This part of the Allied front, traversed by excellent paved roads leading from one or other of the French fortresses, was considered by the Duke to require for its protection a different system of occupation to that adopted by the Prussian Army.

In comparing the arrangements made by Wellington and Blücher for the occupation of their areas and the security of their cantonments, due weight must necessarily be given to Wellington's considered opinion. Even so, realizing as he did that his front was far more dangerously exposed and open than Blücher's, the Duke made no special arrangements to ensure gaining the time and space necessary for concentration at any given point. Wellington appreciated the risk which he ran. He was content, however, to rely on his secret service and a cavalry screen.

In mid-June the disposition of the Prussian Army,[1] 117,000 (with 12,000 horse) and 296 guns, was as follows :

Map 1, *Sketch* 1.—*I Corps* (Zieten, 31,000), with head-quarters at Charleroi, was in contact with the extreme left of the Anglo-Dutch Army.

The I Corps was disposed as follows :

1st Brigade (Steinmetz), head-quarters Fontaine l'Évêque,
2nd Brigade (Pirch II), head-quarters Marchienne,
3rd Brigade (Jägow), head-quarters Fleurus,
4th Brigade (Henckel), head-quarters Moustier.

---

[1] For detailed Order of Battle see Appendix I (B).

The Reserve Cavalry (Röder) was at Sombreffe, and the Reserve Artillery at Gembloux.

The I Corps outpost line ran from *Bonne Espérance* along the frontier through Lobbes, Thuin, Gerpinnes, and Sossoye. The disposition of Zieten's Corps shows Blücher's arrangements for *Couverture*.

Map 1.—*II Corps* (Pirch I, 31,500) had its head-quarters at Namur, and the head-quarters of the Prussian Army were also located in this fortress. The II Corps was disposed as follows :

5th Brigade (Tippelskirch), head-quarters Namur,
6th Brigade (Krafft), head-quarters Thorembey,
7th Brigade (Brause), head-quarters Héron,
8th Brigade (Langen), head-quarters Huy.

The Cavalry Reserve was at Hannut, and the Reserve Artillery was along the Louvain road. The outpost line ran from Sossoye to Dinant.

III Corps (Thielemann, 24,000, with Clausewitz as Chief of the Staff) had its head-quarters at Ciney, and was located as follows :

9th Brigade (Borcke), head-quarters Asserre,
10th Brigade (Kemphen), head-quarters Ciney,
11th Brigade (Luck), head-quarters Dinant,
12th Brigade (Stülpnagel), head-quarters Huy.

The Cavalry Reserve was between Ciney and Dinant, and the Reserve Artillery at Ciney. The outpost line ran from Dinant to Rochefort.

IV Corps (Bülow, 30,800) had its head-quarters at Liége, and was placed as follows :

13th Brigade (Hake), head-quarters Liége,
14th Brigade (Rijssel), head-quarters Waremme,
15th Brigade (Losthin), head-quarters Hologne,
16th Brigade (Hiller), head-quarters Liers.

The Reserve Artillery was between Glons and Dalhem (northeast of Liége), and the Cavalry Reserve was around Tongres and Looz.

Sketch 1.—Blücher had cantoned his Army so as to ensure that each Corps could concentrate unhindered at Corps head-quarters within twelve hours. He had also made adequate arrangements to cover the concentration of his Army at Fleurus, should Napoleon effect a surprise and strike between the Allies. The concentration point of the Prussian Army was covered by Zieten's Corps holding the line of the Sambre from Fontaine l'Évêque to Moustier.   The I Corps was placed so as to gain early intelligence of a French advance, and it was disposed so as to gain sufficient time for Blücher to collect his three other Corps at Fleurus.

As late as mid-June the Allies still remained dispersed to live. Even in so rich a country as Belgium, dispersion facilitated the supply question ; and by covering Belgium the Allies hoped to prevent the leakage of information.

Napoleon knew that the cantonments of the Anglo-Dutch and Prussian Armies were widely dispersed over Belgium and that the lines of operation of the two Armies met almost at right angles at Charleroi.   It was reasonable, therefore, to suppose that, if the *Armée du Nord* effected a surprise and irrupted into Belgium at the junction-point—Charleroi, the Allies would fall back along their respective lines of operations so as to ensure unhampered concentration.   It was unlikely that they would attempt a forward concentration within supporting distance of each other.

As it happened the Allies had foreseen this plan for invasion. In the event of its occurrence, they had decided to concentrate southwards so as to offer immediate battle to Napoleon directly he debouched on the left bank of the Sambre.   The Anglo-Dutch Army would then form up at Gosselies and the Prussian Army at Fleurus.   This plan for a joint concentration, however, presumed that Wellington and Blücher received due warning of Napoleon's advance, and secured the time necessary (about three days) to enable them to effect their concentration before Napoleon forced the Sambre.   The Allies never expected that Napoleon would surprise them whilst they were still ' dispersed to live '.   It does not appear that they had made any adequate arrangements to ensure concentration in such circumstances, so that nothing would be left to fortune in a moment of confusion whilst they were assembling and arranging for mutual co-operation.   It was this omission which caused the Allies to run such fearful risks at the opening of hostilities in Belgium, offering Napoleon the chance of finishing the campaign with two swift and heavy blows.

The great dissimilarity between the terrain of Northern Italy and that of Belgium renders a comparison of the campaigns of 1796 and 1815 more fancied than real.   Even though General

Bonaparte in 1796 did hold the Sardinians with a detachment whilst he forced away the Austrians, and then turned back on the Sardinians and finished with them, yet in this, his first, campaign the Apennines assisted Bonaparte's strategy.   In his last campaign, in the plains of Belgium, there was no defile or gorge in which a detachment could hold at bay either Blücher or Wellington.   Consequently the opening stroke across the Sambre in 1815 was far more dangerous to deliver than the blow at Montenotte in 1796.

CHAPTER III

FIRST PHASE OF THE CAMPAIGN: ASSEMBLY OF THE *ARMÉE DU NORD*, 7th–13th JUNE

(Map 1)

NAPOLEON had to consider how he could mass the *Armée du Nord* within gunshot of the Franco-Belgian frontier without unduly alarming Wellington and Blücher. The moves which would naturally put the Allies on their guard were the marches which the flank Corps must make as they closed in to mass on the common centre at Beaumont. On the other hand pushing up the centre Corps, nearer to the frontier, would almost pass unnoticed. It would be looked on as a natural precaution for Napoleon to move forward a force in order to oppose Wellington's and Blücher's threatened irruption.

To distract the attention of the Allies, demonstrations were made from Lille and Dunkirk to alarm Wellington for his communications with the sea, and rumours were spread about a French movement towards Lille and an advance therefrom. As an additional precaution, to prevent any leakage of news, the frontier was closely guarded from the 7th June, all coastal traffic was interrupted, boats were ordered to remain at anchor, and false information was disseminated.

Orders for the assembly of the *Armée du Nord* were sent out early in June. Gérard and the IV Corps from Metz, forming the Right Wing, were ordered to start first and move on Philippeville. The IV Corps began to move on the *6th June*. Gérard's exposed right flank was covered by the difficult country of the Forest of Ardennes which screened his northward march from Thielemann's outposts. Gérard reached Philippeville on the *14th/15th June*.

The Imperial Guard moved to Laon from Compiègne on the *8th June*, and then advanced to Beaumont. Lobau and the

VI Corps left Laon on the 8*th* and preceded the Guard to Beaumont; and Reille collected the II Corps at Avesnes.

On the 9*th June*, D'Erlon with the I Corps marched for Avesnes, and Reille left Avesnes on the 11*th* for Maubeuge, so as to screen D'Erlon's flank march. These two Corps were to form the Left Wing at Solre-sur-Sambre.

On the 11*th* Vandamme and the III Corps moved from Rocroi to Beaumont. This Corps was to screen the Centre and Right Wing whilst the concentration was effected at Beaumont and Philippeville. On the same day (the 11*th*) Marshal Ney was informed that he must be at Avesnes on the 14*th*, if he wished to be in time for the opening of the campaign.

By the 12*th June* the *Armée du Nord* was well on the move. To prevent any hint of the concentration reaching the Allied advanced outpost screen, the places vacated by the troops marching to the various *rendez-vous* were taken over by bodies of the National Guard.

Napoleon left Paris on the 12*th*, reached Laon on the same day, and Avesnes on the 13*th*. The Emperor had delayed his departure to the last moment so as to avoid arousing suspicion and the dissemination of rumours.

As a result of these arrangements it was only on the 13*th June* that the Prussian outposts, in front of Charleroi, detected bivouac fires on the French side of the frontier, and Zieten reported two large bivouacs at Beaumont and Solre. This disquieting news reached Blücher at Namur on the 14*th June*, and the Field-Marshal directed Zieten to send off his heavy baggage to Gembloux. Zieten's Corps was ordered by Blücher to give ground in front of a French advance in force and then make a stand in front of Fleurus, so as to cover the Prussian concentration point as well as the line of connection with Wellington along the Namur–Nivelles road. Meanwhile the three other Prussian Corps would concentrate and advance to Fleurus. By a deplorable oversight no orders were issued to destroy the Sambre bridges.

Since Blücher received warning on the 14*th* of the proximity of a considerable enemy force, he was given time to effect his concentration at Fleurus, and thereafter to co-operate with Wellington on the arranged line Quatre Bras–Sombreffe. But, as the French manœuvre was not as yet definitely pronounced, inadequate arrangements were made and Napoleon succeeded in gaining a start which might have proved decisive.

Sketch 1.—Up to the 15th June it is difficult to admire Wellington's attitude. Unlike Blücher, the Duke had not made really adequate arrangements to cover his forward strategical concentration. He had no troops on the Brussels road between the Sambre and Gosselies, nor was the disposition of his troops in their cantonments calculated to ensure for him the time and space in which to concentrate undisturbed at Gosselies. From a political point of view the Duke's choice of Brussels as his head-quarters is understandable. Strategically Nivelles or even Mons was far preferable. Both places were connected by road with Blücher's head-quarters, and both were within an easy ride of the frontier.

In any case, there is no gainsaying that Wellington and Blücher were surprised in their dispersed cantonments when not expecting an attack. Shortly before (on the 3rd) Blücher had written to his wife that the invasion of France would soon begin, because Bonaparte would never dare to attack them. This comfortable feeling also existed at Wellington's head-quarters. As late as the 13th the Duke wrote to Lord Lynedoch that the Allied strength in Belgium precluded any idea of a French attack. On this same night Napoleon in his travelling carriage dashed into Avesnes, and the storm so little expected was about to burst. Even on the 15th Wellington stated in a letter to the Czar that he hoped to take the offensive at the end of June. Indeed, at 1 p.m. on the same day, the very day on which Napoleon entered Belgium, the Duke wrote to the commander of the 2nd Division (General Clinton) suggesting the renumbering of the Divisions, so as to return to the old Peninsular numbers. Had the Duke possessed even the faintest inkling of what had actually taken place he would never have made this proposal at such a time. In addition the Duke had arranged to give a ball on the 21st June, the anniversary of Vittoria ; this is still one more indication that Napoleon's secret had been kept from his foes.

On the 13th June, when the Emperor reached Avesnes, the French concentration had been almost effected. With the exception of Gérard's IV Corps, all the troops had reached their allotted positions. It is true that Soult had neglected to issue orders to Marshal Grouchy to move the Cavalry Reserve to the front, and up to the time when the Emperor entered Laon (at 2 p.m. on the 12th) Grouchy had not moved. Napoleon sent for Grouchy and learned that he had received no orders. Soult reached Avesnes before he remembered Grouchy, and only on the 12th did he send back the necessary orders to the Cavalry Reserve. But, after his interview with the Emperor, Grouchy anticipated the orders which Soult was sending to him so tardily and started off at once with the Cavalry to the concentration area. So much energy was put into this manœuvre that the whole Cavalry Reserve cleared Avesnes by the next night, though all the regiments had to make a tiring forced march, and some actually covered 60 miles in about thirty-six hours.

Map 1.—On reaching Avesnes the Emperor proceeded to issue orders for the 14th. The arrangements he now made for the grouping of the Corps in the final phase of the concentration were as follows : Reille with the II Corps was to lead the Left Wing and bivouac in mass at Leers, as close to the frontier as possible without crossing it. The Corps Cavalry was to watch the *débouchés* across the frontier, but not to cross it ; and Reille's bivouacs were to be arranged so that the glare of the fires was screened from observation by the low hills and woods. D'Erlon's I Corps completed the Left Wing. D'Erlon's Corps was to follow Reille, bivouac in mass at Solre, and take the same precautions as Reille. Both Left Wing Corps were to be ready to move at dawn on the 15th.

Gérard and the IV Corps were ordered to reach Philippeville on the 14th and be ready to set off on the 15th at 3 a.m., so as to co-operate with the III Corps which bivouacked at the head of the Centre. Gérard was to secure the safety of his exposed right flank as he advanced to the Sambre.

The Centre of the *Armée du Nord* was to bivouac around Beaumont on the night of the 14th/15th. Vandamme and the III Corps were to bivouac 3 miles north of Beaumont and as close as possible to the frontier which was not to be passed by the troops, and no one of any description was to be allowed to cross it. The III Corps was to be ready to advance at 3 a.m. on the 15th.

Lobau and the VI Corps were to bivouac behind Vandamme. The Infantry of the Guard was to bivouac in front of Beaumont with the Guard Cavalry in rear of the town. In Beaumont were the Imperial head-quarters and the 1st Grenadiers acting as escort to the Emperor. The town itself was to be kept clear of other troops.

Marshal Grouchy was to bivouac with his four Corps of Reserve Cavalry between Beaumont and Valcourt, he was to conceal his fires and prevent anyone crossing the frontier. Grouchy was to be ready to move on Charleroi at 3 a.m. on the 15th and act as advanced guard.

That night, the 13*th*, the *Armée du Nord* halted as follows :
II Corps, Maubeuge ; I Corps, Pont-sur-Sambre.
III Corps, Philippeville ; VI Corps near Beaumont ; Guard and Imperial head-quarters, Beaumont ; and the Emperor at Avesnes.
Reserve Cavalry, Beaumont.
IV Corps, Marienburg.
The preliminary operations were at an end. A short forward march on the 14th would bring all the Corps into the positions they were to occupy in the strategical concentration, and leave them ready to open the campaign at dawn on the 15th.

Many writers have blamed the French subordinates for their failures in this campaign ; so we may pause to consider who were the principal subordinates in the *Armée du Nord*, and whether any other officers might have been preferred to those actually selected.

In the first place, Marshal Berthier, Prince of Wagram, that indefatigable amanuensis, was no longer available to take the field as Napoleon's Chief of the Staff (or *Major-Général*). Berthier died on the 1st June ; but even before this (on the 9th May) his place had been filled by the appointment of Marshal Soult, Duke of Dalmatia. Soult was above all a man of action. He had held an active command for so long that naturally he was without the necessary practice as Chief of the Staff, but his temperament did allow him to give that passive obedience which Napoleon always expected from his *Major-Général*. On the other hand, Marshal Suchet, Duke of Albufera, might have been selected to fill this appointment, for which he was well qualified. Had Suchet been appointed Chief of the Staff for the campaign in Belgium, Soult would have been set free for high command in the field. Advantage could then have been taken of Soult's previous experience against Wellington and the British, by appointing him to command the Left Wing of the *Armée du Nord*, the Wing which was destined to operate against and contain Wellington. This appointment would have released Marshal Ney (to whom the post was given), and the Prince of the Moskowa would have become available to act immediately under the Emperor on the decisive field and to command the main attacks. No leader of men excelled Marshal Ney on a battle-field. His energy, courage, and utter contempt for danger always inspired the troops whom he led to the assault. His quick, sure grasp of tactical situations fitted him admirably for any task, however desperate. In an obscure strategical situation, however, Ney's temperament required that the orders which he received should make his line of action absolutely and unequivocally clear to him. Then with his mind at ease and at the head of officers and men whom he knew and trusted ' *le brave des braves* ' would face and triumph over every difficulty.

In 1815 Soult perpetrated some serious mistakes as Chief of the Staff. At more than one difficult moment the orders which he drew up and issued were too laconic and lacked precision, consequently he cannot avoid criticism. Certainly Berthier's work had not always been above suspicion, because in 1807, 1809, 1813, Berthier's orders had occasionally given rise to doubt and hesitancy. So it was with Soult in 1815. Both Ney and Grouchy were faced—Ney on the 16th and 17th and Grouchy on the 17th and 18th—with critical situations which were both obscure and perplexing. Both Marshals needed the clearest orders, stating quite simply the essential tasks which they had to perform. On each occasion Soult failed to furnish them with such orders.

The Emperor's decision, condemning Murat to remain in idleness, was truly regrettable. At that time France possessed no cavalry leader who could handle masses of horsemen on the battlefield with the skill and dash of Murat. Nor had she any other leader of horse who possessed Murat's power to inspire his foes with terror and his own men with that enthusiasm which would make them attempt the impossible itself. When the Emperor decided to include a Cavalry Reserve of 13,000 veteran horsemen in the *Armée du Nord*, Murat's presence at their head was indispensable. On the slopes of Mont St. Jean Murat might have turned the fortunes of the day. Kellermann was as brave and as determined, possibly even a more skilful tactician than the King of Naples ; but Murat possessed brilliancy which no other cavalry leader of his epoch could equal. As it was, on the 18th June, the magnificent French cavalry became entangled among the squares and were then destroyed by the infantry who stood so steadfast and so still.

To replace Murat the Emperor selected Marshal Grouchy, who had been given his *bâton* on the 17th April, at the conclusion of his successful operations in the South of France.[1] Grouchy's record as a soldier was a long and honourable one. On many a field he had proved his worth and capabilities as a leader of horse, but he was only a faint shadow of Murat. Instead, however, of accompanying the Emperor to handle the masses of horsemen Marshal Grouchy was entrusted with the command of the Right Wing of the *Armée du Nord*, which was destined to neutralize Blücher until Wellington was destroyed. The Marshal was given a mission which neither his character nor his previous achievements justified.

Was there no Marshal available to take charge of the operations against Blücher whilst the Emperor was busy with the Anglo-Dutch Army ? There was one—Marshal Davout, Duke of Auerstädt and Prince of Eckmühl. His record, personality, and character alike demanded that he should be given a high command when France's existence was at stake. Marshal Davout was a brilliant general, a bold and resolute leader. Unfortunately for France Napoleon appointed Davout Minister of War, Governor of Paris, Commander-in-Chief of the National Guard and of all troops in Paris. Davout requested repeatedly to be given active employment, but Napoleon answered : ' I can entrust Paris to no one but you.' It is difficult to understand what useful purpose in 1815 Davout could fulfil in Paris. If he was to guard against underground plotting, then he was unlikely to succeed. Davout was a great soldier, but he was no politician. If he was to safeguard Paris from the Allies, then that presupposed Napoleon's overthrow in the field. In such circumstances even Davout could not have averted France's defeat. Perchance did Napoleon leave Davout behind because he felt he had no real need of him

[1] Grouchy was removed from the Marshalate on the 1st August 1815 and he was not reinstated until the 19th November 1831. Grouchy died in 1847, aged 81.

in 1815 ? Was the Emperor already belittling the task which confronted him in Belgium ?

If this was so, then Napoleon had forgotten Blücher and the Prussian Army, and the necessity of taking out with the *Armée du Nord* a Marshal, to whom could be entrusted the task of neutralizing this able and bitter foe. Davout's record naturally pointed to him as the one man who was most fitted for this task. At Auerstädt (1806) the Marshal had won a great victory over Blücher and the main army of Prussia, whilst Napoleon was crushing Hohenlohe's Saxons at Jena. In 1815 victory in the field was the essential, and then Paris would be safe enough ; but when disaster overtook the Grand Army even Davout could not prevent the final collapse. By including Marshals Murat and Davout in the *Armée du Nord*, Marshal Grouchy would have been set free to replace Marshal Suchet at the head of ' the Army of the Alps ', to which Marshal Grouchy had been originally appointed, before he was recalled to Paris to take up his post as Commander of the Reserve Cavalry. Paris could have been entrusted to General Clausel, as the Army of the Western Pyrenees might have been given to an officer of far less experience and ability than Clausel.

The Emperor selected the subordinates who were to fill the chief commands, therefore primarily on the shoulders of the Emperor must rest the responsibility for the mistakes which these subordinates perpetrated. In this particular, as in his personal responsibility for the organization and grouping of his available armed forces at the outbreak of hostilities, Napoleon must bear the greater part of the burden of censure. The Emperor deliberately selected merely good generals to fill posts for which in reality great generals were required, and for which great generals were available. For this reason the talons of the Eagle were by no means so formidable in 1815 as they had been in earlier campaigns. This was immeasurably unfortunate, because the strategic outlook had never been so black as it was when France for the last time confronted Europe in arms.

CHAPTER IV

THE FRENCH ASSEMBLY AROUND BEAUMONT: 14TH JUNE

(Map 1)

ON the 14th June, the anniversary of Marengo and of Friedland, Napoleon, by skilful dispositions and making use of natural cover as well as of the screen afforded by the French frontier fortresses, completed his concentration of the *Armée du Nord* behind the line of the Sambre, almost unknown to the Allies. On the morrow the Emperor intended to advance on Charleroi and penetrate between the unsuspecting Allies at their junction point. By rapid manœuvring he would separate Wellington from Blücher with the armoured wedge which he would drive between them, then, holding them apart, he would beat them in detail. To achieve this, Napoleon planned to organize the *Armée du Nord* in two Wings and a Reserve ; and he intended to push a Wing up each of the arms of the so-called ' Fleurus triangle ', which reach from Charleroi to Quatre Bras and to Sombreffe. In due course the Wings would establish contact with and grip both Wellington and Blücher. Thereafter, according to the information which he received, the Emperor would move up from Charleroi with the Reserve and throw in the weight of this force against whichever Ally had assembled an Army large enough to be crushed. It was no time to throw for half-successes, or to expend the energies of the *Armée du Nord* on a mere screen. One of the hostile Armies must be located in strength as soon as possible, held to its position, and speedily destroyed.

Meanwhile the other Wing would have established contact with the other Ally. A part of this containing Wing should suffice to neutralize its foe for twenty-four hours, and this containing Wing should be able to detach a considerable force to move across and co-operate in the decisive battle, in which the other Wing and the Reserve were already engaged, under the Emperor's command.

It is with this underlying idea that Napoleon's distribution of the *Armée du Nord* on the 14th should be studied. Already the formation was taking definite shape, and the organization of the French Army for its advance into Belgium was almost completed. The only developments required were the strengthening of the Right Wing (which could easily be done by attaching to it the leading Corps from those bivouacked in the centre) and the final distribution of the four Corps of Reserve Cavalry. The strengthening of the Right Wing would come about naturally as the *Armée du Nord* advanced into Belgium across the Sambre. The allotment of the Reserve Cavalry would be decided on when the situation had cleared up sufficiently to allow definite plans to be made.

Each Wing would have two Corps allotted to it, giving it a strength of 40,000 to 45,000 men ; and the Emperor would have a similar force in hand, including the VI Corps, the Guard, and such of the Cavalry as had not been attached to either Wing. This force would act as the Reserve and it would be engaged on either Wing according to circumstances. As events dictated Napoleon intended to weaken one (the containing) Wing so as to strengthen the Reserve. The Emperor had no idea of gaining a decisive victory on both Wings on the same day. He was obviously too weak even to dream of such a consummation.

A great French victory obtained over one of the Allies must neutralize any success achieved by the other Ally in a secondary action on the other flank. Indeed such local success would have placed the victorious Ally in a dangerous position. By gaining ground in the secondary action, the successful Ally's inner flank and rear would have become fully exposed to the weight of Napoleon's next blow, and the French Wing confronting him would attack early next day and prevent him decamping. This method of advancing, and the possibilities resulting from this advance, in ' battalion square ', must be understood if the strategy of the Emperor in the Waterloo campaign is to be appreciated.

In 1815 Napoleon considered that the Prussian Army would first concentrate a force which it would be worth his while to crush. The dispositions of the two Allied Armies, as well as the very different characters of their commanders—the strategically circumspect Wellington and the dashing Blücher—went far to confirm him in this view. Unfortunately the Emperor's estimation of Blücher's character did not go deep enough. He did not weigh sufficiently the Prussian Field-Marshal's hatred of himself, loyalty to Wellington, and unswerving adherence to the essential end—Napoleon's overthrow. Never having confronted Wellington personally, the Emperor seems to have underrated the Duke's great tactical skill, admirable obstinacy in battle, capability for taking punishment, and refusal to admit that he was beaten. These underestimations had a vital bearing on the campaign.

Napoleon probably considered that the Prussian Army would move to support the Anglo-Dutch Army with far greater celerity and mobility than the latter would exhibit in bringing help to Field-Marshal Blücher ; and Napoleon's plans were based on the hypothesis that the Prussian Army would first offer him the target which his perfect man-killing machine could destroy in the short time-limit at his disposal. On the other hand, even if things so turned out that Wellington was found ready and Blücher through a tardy concentration had not come up, yet the decision could be obtained, owing to the simple but very comprehensive formation used by the Emperor when he burst into Belgium. Nothing would require alteration, since the means at hand, as he used them, were perfectly and easily adaptable to meet any situations which might arise.

Before leaving Avesnes the Emperor issued his last orders to some of the detachments employed in the secondary theatres. Rapp was ordered to defend Alsace as long as possible, so as to keep the right of the Grand Army free and delay an invader's progress towards Paris. If he had to fall back, Rapp was to dispute the passages of the Vosges, and finally hold in turn the river lines of the Meurthe, Moselle, Meuse, and Marne. Suchet was ordered to defend Lyon and the river lines of the Saône and Rhone. Lecourbe was to dispute the passage of the Rhine. If pressed back, he would hold the passes of the Vosges and Jura and the Belfort position, later on Langres and the Saône, then the Aube and the Seine, and lastly the river line of the Yonne. After issuing these final orders Napoleon was ready to open his invasion of Belgium.

Map 1.—By nightfall on the 14th the first phase of the campaign concluded with the completion of the French concentration.

The *Armée du Nord* (except Gérard's Corps, which was still coming up) now occupied the following positions :

Right Wing, 16,000 men—Gérard and the IV Corps assembling at Philippeville.

Left Wing, 44,000 men—Reille and the II Corps bivouacked at Leers, with Bachelu's Division in front at Thuin ; and (behind Reille) D'Erlon with the I Corps was around Solre-sur-Sambre.

Centre, 65,000 men, around Beaumont. Vandamme (III Corps) was in front, then came Lobau (VI Corps), and in rear the Guard. The Emperor and Imperial Head-Quarters were in Beaumont. The Centre, at Beaumont, was covered by the Reserve Cavalry.

The *Armée du Nord* was halted within easy gun-shot of the frontier and the Allied outpost line. Its front, from Philippeville through Beaumont to Leers, was less than 20 miles. Meanwhile Wellington and Blücher had heard only the vaguest rumours. The Allies had not moved a single man to meet the enemy already assembled around Beaumont and about to open hostilities by forcing the passage of the Sambre at Charleroi. Further, the French Wings were magnificently placed to broaden the front of the attack by carrying the bridges at Marchienne and Châtelet, on either side of Charleroi.

The strategical advantage lay entirely with Napoleon. Originally the French Corps had been strung out on a front of 175 miles (from Lille to Metz) whereas the Allied frontage had never exceeded 90 miles (from Ghent to Liége). Napoleon had now drawn in his scattered Corps until, at nightfall on the 14th they were massed on a front of 20 miles. Even this would decrease as they closed in on Charleroi.

During the night of the 12th/13th Steinmetz reported to Zieten that a French concentration was in progress. A deserting drum-major had given Steinmetz this news and stated that an attack would be delivered on the 14th or 15th. Zieten only sent this important information to Namur on the morning of the 14th.

At 3 p.m. on the 14th General von Dörnberg, in command of Wellington's cavalry screen, sent a message to Brussels that a French concentration at Maubeuge, Beaumont, and Philippeville was in progress, and he estimated the strength of the hostile gathering to be 100,000. Dörnberg drew attention to the *Paris Journal*, which stated that Napoleon had left his capital for the frontier on the night of the 11th/12th June. Had Wellington's and Blücher's head-quarters been in telephonic communication with each other these reports could have been compared. At that era and distant 40 miles from each other by road, a conference, so desirable in the circumstances, was out of the question. Even if Zieten and Dörnberg had arranged to exchange immediately all reports which they received, a different result might have been chronicled. Although Müffling had received news at Brussels on the 14th, from Zieten at Charleroi, that the French were concentrating in front of the Prussian outposts and an attack on the I Corps appeared to be impending, yet the Duke stated that his first intimation of Napoleon's attack on the I Prussian Corps was received between 3 and 5 p.m. on the 15th from the Prince of Orange in person. Wellington admitted that ' he had known for some days of the augmentation of the enemy's force on the frontier and even of the arrival of Bonaparte at the Army ', but the Duke still considered that a strong French column would be pushed along the *pavé* through Mons to Brussels. Despite the warnings which the Allies received, Napoleon succeeded in surprising them and catching them off their guard.

Towards midnight on the 14th Gneisenau at last heard definitely that an important enemy concentration in front of Charleroi was in progress. Only thirty-six hours later, however, Napoleon fought and won from Blücher the Battle of Ligny.

The Emperor had gained over the Allies a three-days' start in strategical concentration—the essential prelude to a successful campaign in Belgium. In a commanding central position he had assembled (*réuni*) the Grand Army, organized in two Wings and a Reserve, whilst the two Allied Armies still lay scattered over Belgium. Thus the campaign was nearly won at the outset before a shot was fired, since Blücher and Wellington had failed to foresee the impending French concentration opposite Charleroi. As matters stood, the end of the first phase found the assembled *Armée du Nord* merely waiting for the dawn to close with its unready foes across the Sambre.

Au vrai courage, rien impossible !

CHAPTER V

SECOND PHASE: THE PASSAGE OF THE SAMBRE AND THE SEPARATION OF THE ALLIES

15TH JUNE.—THE PASSAGE OF THE SAMBRE

(Maps 1 and 2 and Sketch A)

ON the evening of the 14th the Emperor drew up his March Orders for the 15th. All the Corps having been warned to be ready to start at dawn, it would suffice if this order reached them as they paraded. The order (*Correspondance*, No. 22053) was very long, as no detail was overlooked. Many things—sounding of *réveillé*, orders for the baggage, etc.—were repeated again and again. In the later wars, however, great negligence had often been shown in matters which should have been mere routine. Some of the officers had not had sufficient experience for the positions which they filled, and they, as well as some of the generals and marshals, had to be reminded of details which should have been instinctively carried out. When he wrote orders for Marshals like Davout and Soult the Emperor could be terse enough.

Unfortunately, long as the order was, there was no mention in it of the essential task for the 15th : the envelopment and annihilation of that hostile force which covered and held the Charleroi bridgehead (the I Prussian Corps under Zieten). Nor was any mention made in the order of any objective for the day's operation. On the other hand, the harmony of the previous concentration was not disturbed since the order arranged for the advance of the *Armée du Nord* in its three columns.

In the Centre, tactical protection by light cavalry was ensured, horse artillery and engineers were placed near the head of the central force, and the various columns were ordered to time their advance so as to arrive in front of Charleroi together.

43

Domon and Vandamme's Light Cavalry, with Pajol's Corps of Hussars, were to move ahead of the *Centre* and start at 2.30 a.m.

Vandamme was to follow at 3 a.m. ; behind would come Lobau (at 4 a.m.), then the Guard (starting at 5 a.m.), and the rearmost troops (the Grenadiers) were to move off at 6 a.m. This column was to advance to Charleroi. The Cavalry Reserve, starting at 5.30 a.m., would also move on Charleroi using cross-country and lateral roads.

Reille was to lead the *Left Wing*, which would advance from Solre sur Sambre at 3 a.m., march *via* Thuin, and reach the bridge at Marchienne by 9 a.m. D'Erlon was to follow Reille and support the latter if need arose. D'Erlon was to push patrols towards Mons and Binche and was responsible for occupying Thuin with one Division.

Gérard formed the *Right Wing*. The IV Corps was to start at 5 a.m., move on Charleroi, and reach it simultaneously with Vandamme.

In this advance the *Armée du Nord* converged as it neared the Sambre so as to cross the river on a front of less than 5 miles. After crossing, the two Wings would be pushed forward towards Fleurus and Frasnes, and the Centre would concentrate at Charleroi. The Grand Army would then be in hand and assembled, ready for any eventuality on the 16th. There was no idea of seizing Sombreffe and Quatre Bras on the 15th. It was never part of Napoleon's plan to prevent Blücher and Wellington from committing the vital mistake of attempting a forward concentration.

Perfection, however, was not attained in the execution of this march order. Soult made an elementary mistake by neglecting to send it out in duplicate. As it happened, Vandamme had quitted the bivouac of his Corps so that he might pass the night under a roof, and no responsible officer with the III Corps knew his whereabouts. The orderly carrying the despatch had to search for the General in the darkness, and whilst he was doing so the horse fell and broke its rider's leg. As an immediate consequence Vandamme did not receive his orders, and he learned no details of the forward movement until Lobau, closing up in his rear, began to collide with the III Corps. Vandamme's conduct was especially culpable, because the Emperor's orders (issued on the 13th) had instructed him to be ready to march off at 3 a.m. The General appears to have taken very little trouble to ensure that this order was complied with.

Too much importance, however, must not be attached to this incident. The Emperor merely dubbed it ' *un funeste contre-temps* ', which exactly described it. Napoleon's strategical covering forces nullified the result of such accidents ; and on the 15th June the advance in two Wings and a Reserve proceeded undisturbed by this misadventure. By the end of this day the Sambre bridges had been seized, the junction-point captured, and the Allies driven apart.

Nevertheless the accident did cause some delay. Pajol and Domon were unsupported when they reached the Sambre at Charleroi, and Zieten's resolute bearing imposed on Pajol. The barricaded and strongly held bridge was unassailable by cavalry alone. Some hours were wasted, and the Sambre passage was not secured by 9 a.m. as Napoleon expected. At 11 a.m. Pajol was still before Charleroi when the Emperor arrived at the head of the Marines and Sappers of the Guard, followed by Duhesme's Division of the Young Guard. Having learned of Vandamme's delay, the Emperor promptly hurried these troops to the front along a cross-road, and Charleroi and its intact bridge fell to the Guard just after midday. The Emperor personally directed this assault.

There had been delay also on the left. Steinmetz's Brigade at Marchienne fought truculently to gain the hours necessary to enable Blücher to concentrate, and it was noon when this passage was mastered by the French. Had Marchienne fallen at 9 a.m., a column pushed across and down the left bank of the Sambre would have effectually outflanked and cleared Charleroi for Pajol. Before Steinmetz withdrew he sent to inform Chassé and Merlen of the French attack on his outposts and that his Brigade was withdrawing. This important information was reported to Mons, and General Behr passed it on to Braine le Comte. Despite Merlen's Cavalry Brigade being well placed on the flank of Reille's advance, Merlen made no attempt to reconnoitre the French column and ascertain its strength. When the time came for Zieten to draw back, two Brigades retired through Charleroi along the Fleurus road, whilst Steinmetz's Brigade halted and prepared to hold Gosselies to delay Reille's farther advance.

On the Right Wing, Gérard's IV Corps only completed its concentration in the morning and was late in taking the road to Charleroi. The march had not been long in progress when the commander of the leading division—General de Bourmont—deserted to the Prussians with five officers of his staff. De Bourmont took with him the operation order which Napoleon had directed him to treat as confidential. Blücher received the traitor characteristically. When he was reminded by Gneisenau that the French General sported the Bourbon badge—the white cockade—the old Field-Marshal remarked quite audibly : ' Cockade be hanged ! A cur (*Hundsfott*) is always a cur ! '

De Bourmont's open desertion occasioned some consternation in Gérard's column. It necessitated further delay whilst a report was made to the Emperor ; thus it was late when Gérard reached the river line at Châtelet. Gérard advanced on this place, and not on Charleroi, in compliance with an after-order, which Soult had sent to the General at 3.15 p.m., directing him to support the right and cross the Sambre at Châtelet (below Charleroi). Owing to his late arrival, Gérard was unable to co-operate in the affair of Gilly, although, had he crossed, he would have been magnificently placed to drive in Pirch II's left flank. This co-operation would have saved several hours and have enabled the whole of the *Armée du Nord* to cross the Sambre on the 15th. As it was, Gérard's Corps halted astride the Sambre, instead of bivouacking on the left bank, and only its leading Division (under General Hulot) crossed the river. In consequence the Corps was late in concentrating at Ligny on the 16th, and the opening of that battle was delayed. This delay contributed partly to the late hour at which the Battle of Ligny ended, and to the consequent impossibility in the darkness of recognizing the true direction of the Prussian retreat. Gérard's late arrival on the Sambre had unfortunate and far-reaching results.

CHAPTER VI

15TH JUNE: THE SEPARATION OF THE ALLIES

(Map 2 ; Sketches B and C)

By surprise and with little delay the line of the Sambre had been mastered. Napoleon was in possession of Charleroi, the three Sambre bridges, and the junction of the two main roads to the north of Charleroi. His Army was well placed, it could advance along either or both of the roads leading towards Wellington's and Blücher's cantonments ; and, as there were no signs of large Allied concentrations, the time had come to separate the two Allied Armies, preparatory to defeating each in turn. To ensure this separation the Namur–Nivelles road had to be reached before Wellington and Blücher came up in force ; and the dispositions of the *Armée du Nord* must make certain that, on the 16th, either Quatre Bras or Sombreffe was seized. Then, if no forward concentration of the Allies took place, Napoleon could advance and stand between the Prussians and the Anglo-Dutch.

After the capture of the bridge at Charleroi, the Emperor passed through the town acclaimed by the inhabitants. He halted on the far side of the place, dismounted, and sat in a chair whilst his troops defiled past him. Soon, however, he dropped into a doze and even the shouts of his soldiers failed to wake him.

It was 2 p.m. when news reached the Emperor that the Prussians had made a stand at Gosselies in front of the 1st Hussars who led the advance of the Left Wing. The Emperor at once ordered Reille to push on rapidly towards Gosselies and D'Erlon was to support the II Corps ; at the same time Lefebvre-Desnoëttes was ordered to take the Light Horse of the Guard and co-operate with the 1st Hussars.

Napoleon urgently required a commander for this Left Wing ; and, just when he was wanted shouts announced that Marshal Ney was at hand. As he rode past the marching columns, he was recognized and saluted with cries of ' *Voilà le Rougeot!* ' and between 3 and 3.15 p.m. Marshal Ney, Prince de la Moskowa, Duc d'Elchingen, reached the northern outskirts of Charleroi and reported to the Emperor.

Napoleon received the Marshal frankly and gave him the command of the Left Wing, consisting of Reille's and D'Erlon's Corps and the Cavalry of Lefebvre-Desnoëttes. The orders given to Ney, ' Go and drive the enemy before you along the Brussels road! ' were verbal, consequently they have been hotly disputed. As the Marshal had only just reached the front, Napoleon must have said something more to Ney about the general plan of campaign as well as explaining the situation. The fact that no written orders were sent after the Marshal showed that Napoleon had explained matters sufficiently to ·Ney, before the latter left him. Whether Ney was, or was not, ordered to seize Quatre Bras is immaterial. Ney's advance would obviously depend on the progress made by the Right Wing. If Quatre Bras was mentioned it was probably made use of by Napoleon so as to give the Marshal an objective to aim at, but which he could hardly reach. Riding forward, Ney arrived at the front about 4 p.m., and he took over command just before Reille attacked Gosselies.

Hardly had the Emperor finished giving his instructions to Ney when Marshal Grouchy came up. Grouchy had returned from the front to report that the Prussians had taken up a position at Gilly, and he wished to receive the Emperor's instructions. It was on this side that Napoleon apprehended most danger, because the Fleurus road led directly to the centre of Blücher's cantonments. The Emperor therefore accompanied Grouchy back to Gilly.

Grouchy had considered that the strength of the opposing force was about 20,000. Napoleon, however, after a brief personal reconnaissance estimated the enemy at not more than 10,000. (Grouchy was only confronted by Pirch II's Brigade.) But the Emperor saw at once that infantry co-operation was needful to drive the Prussians back from Gilly. Although Gérard was still too far away to co-operate from Châtelet, yet Vandamme's Corps was now advancing through Charleroi. The Emperor, at once, handed over the command of the Right Wing to Marshal Grouchy and suggested a plan of attack, in which Pajol's Cavalry and one of Vandamme's Divisions were to pin the Prussians to their ground, whilst Exelmans' Horse outflanked them and threatened their line of retreat.   Once Pirch II gave ground he was to be pressed back relentlessly to Sombreffe, where Grouchy and the head of his advance would halt for the night.   As it was already 4 p.m. the impossible, Sombreffe, was indicated, so as to ensure that the possible, Fleurus, was attained.   Having arranged matters on this flank the Emperor returned to Charleroi so as to hasten the onward flow of the Centre of his Army across the Sambre.

Unfortunately, Vandamme gave no ready obedience to the Marshal under whose orders he had been placed, as he regarded him merely as the ' Commander of the Cavalry '.   Two hours were wasted whilst Grouchy and Vandamme talked over and perfected their arrangements for the attack of Pirch II's position.

It is now time to consider what the Allies were doing.

On receiving a definite report from Zieten, confirmed by information extracted from two deserters, that a great French concentration was in progress, Blücher directed Bülow, during the night of the 14th/15th, to collect the IV Corps at Hannut. But the order was not imperative, and Bülow saw no reason for hurry.   Fortunately the other Corps were more vigorously handled.   Blücher ordered Zieten's Corps to fall back fighting towards Fleurus, and then Zieten was to hold the place for a long enough time to allow the other three Corps to come up.   Pirch I was ordered to concentrate his Corps at le Mazy at nightfall on the 15th, and Thielemann was ordered to reach Namur by the same time.   Consequently on the 16th both the II and III Corps would be able to reach Fleurus in time for the battle.   Blücher sent a second order to Zieten (which reached the General about 4 p.m.) directing Zieten to hold on to Fleurus and cover the concentration of the Prussian Army at Sombreffe.   After issuing his orders Blücher proceeded to the front and he arrived at Sombreffe about 4 p.m. on the 15th.   Blücher's situation could hardly be described as satisfactory, since it was unlikely, on the 16th, that he would be able to put in line of battle more than 80,000 men.   Wellington's situation, however, was not only unsatisfactory, it bordered on the hazardous.

The first news of the French invasion reached Wellington at

Brussels about 3 p.m. on the 15th. It was the Prince of Orange who, coming in from the outposts of the Anglo-Dutch Army, reported that the French had attacked the Prussians at Thuin. Soon afterwards General von Müffling, the Prussian *Attaché* on the Duke's staff, arrived and confirmed the fact that Thuin had been attacked. Thuin was attacked soon after dawn on the 15th so the news took overlong to reach Müffling ; and Zieten's report had only stated that he had heard (at 4.30 a.m.) heavy musketry and gun-fire at his outpost positions. If the Duke had been at Mons or Nivelles he must have heard the gun-thunder long before Zieten's belated despatch reached his head-quarters.

It was noon when Gneisenau wrote from Namur to Müffling to inform him that serious hostilities had opened and the Prussian Army was concentrating at Sombreffe, covered by Zieten's Corps. Gneisenau added that Blücher had determined to accept battle at Sombreffe on the 16th. Müffling was also told that Blücher's head-quarters were to be shifted to Sombreffe, where the Prussian Field-Marshal would await information about Wellington's arrangements for concentration and the plan which the Duke had formed.

Even so the Duke did not feel justified in issuing orders to concentrate on his inner flank, as Blücher had done. It was now certain, however, that the troops would have to concentrate and all that was uncertain was the place of concentration. So as to avoid any delay, once the Duke had satisfied himself of Napoleon's real line of advance, Wellington ordered his troops (preparatory to receiving other orders) to assemble as follows :

Sketch B. I Corps—1st Division, Enghien ; 3rd Division, Braine le Comte. (Both Divisions were to hold themselves in readiness to hasten to Nivelles when it was certain that the Allied centre was the French objective.) Perponcher's and Chassé's Divisions were to collect at Nivelles.

II Corps—2nd Division, Ath ; 4th Division, Grammont ; Stedman's and Anthing's Dutch-Belgians (under command of Prince Frederick of Orange) were to mass at Sotteghem.

Reserve.—5th and 6th Divisions, to be ready to move from Brussels at a moment's notice ; Brunswick's Corps to collect between Brussels and Vilvorde ; and the Nassau contingent to mass between Brussels and Louvain.

Cavalry Reserve—To collect at Ninove.

These orders show that the Duke ran a grave risk, even if he did eventually decide on a forward concentration. It would now be almost impossible on the 16th for him to bring even one-half of his Army into action ; and it would have been safer to have sent immediately to Blücher suggesting that the Allied concentration should be made at Waterloo and Wavre. Such a manœuvre was simple, feasible, practical, and eminently safe. It covered Brussels adequately ; and, most important of all, Napoleon could not prevent it. As matters were, no troops were ordered to collect eastward of Nivelles, so the Brussels road was left open for Ney's advance ; and Ney would only meet the Reserve from Brussels as it pushed southwards on the 16th.

For timely information about Napoleon's movements the Duke had relied on Colonel Colquhoun Grant, an officer who, in the Peninsular War, had performed extraordinary feats in the collection of secret intelligence. Colonel Grant himself never acted as a spy but invariably wore uniform. He always trusted to quickness and resolution to get himself out of the enemy's clutches. In 1815 Grant selected two reliable secret agents, a man and his wife, whom he despatched to Paris to act as spies, and through them he obtained accurate intelligence of all that was afoot. Grant himself was also in advance of the Allied outpost line. To ensure a rapid transmission of Grant's reports the Duke appointed General von Dörnberg to act as intermediary. On the 15th, Grant's agent reported that ' the roads were encumbered with men and vehicles and that officers of all ranks spoke freely of a great battle being fought within three days '. This information Grant immediately sent back for transmission to the Duke. General von Dörnberg, however, arrogated to himself the right to select those messages which he considered worth sending on to the Duke ; and the General returned the message to Grant with the remark that, far from convincing him that the Emperor was advancing to give battle, it assured him the contrary was the case. Grant instantly arranged to send the message straight to the Duke, but it was impossible to get it through in time and it only reached Wellington at 11 a.m. on the 18th at Waterloo, too late to be of the slightest service. Dörnberg's presumptuous folly was responsible for keeping Wellington in the dark during the 15th and 16th. Had this news come to hand in time, Napoleon's plan would have been far clearer to

Wellington and it would have prevented some of the delay which occurred on the 15th and early 16th, at any rate so far as the destination of the Reserve was concerned. Considering the confidence which the Duke reposed in Grant's ability to collect information, the non-arrival of Grant's report must have tended to still the Duke's misgivings and made him mistrust the full significance of the first news of the invasion which arrived at his head-quarters.

It was late on the 15th before Wellington's doubts were resolved. Realizing at last that a concentration on the inner flank was indicated, about 10 p.m. he issued and sent out the necessary after-orders :

Sketch C. I Corps.—1st Division, to Braine le Comte ; 3rd Division, to Nivelles.

II Corps.—2nd and 4th Divisions, to Enghien.

Reserve.—To leave Brussels at daybreak on the 16th and move southwards on the Mt. St. Jean–Charleroi road. (On reaching Mt. St. Jean the Reserve halted for some time at the fork of the Nivelles and Quatre Bras roads, because Wellington desired to be sure before he committed it in either direction. Had the Duke only been at the front on the 15th he would have caused the Reserve to make a night march from Brussels to Quatre Bras, and, instead of leaving Brussels at dawn, the Reserve would have reached Quatre Bras at that hour.)

Cavalry Reserve.—To Enghien.

Fortunately the Duke had been well served in the meantime. In the absence of the Prince of Orange, his Chief of the Staff (de Constant Rebecque) about 2 p.m. issued instructions to General Perponcher to concentrate one of his Brigades (Bijlandt's) at Nivelles, and one (Prince Bernard's) at Quatre Bras. Further-more de Constant Rebecque, after interviewing an officer who had come in from Quatre Bras, issued orders about 10.30 p.m. to General Perponcher to move his remaining Brigade to Quatre Bras, so as to support Prince Bernard. Wellington was deeply indebted on this day to the initiative of de Constant Rebecque and to the intrepidity of Prince Bernard. Without their ready acceptance of responsibility the Anglo-Dutch Army must have lost Quatre Bras.

To allow the Duke to keep touch with Blücher, render eventual co-operation secure, and stay the French advance, the position of Quatre Bras, covering the important road junction, had to remain in Wellington's hands. De Constant Rebecque considered this essential was more important than the wording of the order : 'collect at Nivelles'. Rebecque's prompt action went far to retrieve what was rapidly becoming a desperate situation, due to Wellington's slowness and misconceptions. The initial danger to which the Allies exposed themselves was the grave risk of defeat in detail. This was much enhanced because, until after the 16th, they did not obey the fundamental rules that the two Armies should keep as close to one another as possible, neither Army should accept or deliver a pitched battle before the joint concentration was absolutely completed, and neither Army should move without letting its Ally know where it was moving to, when the march would begin, and the necessity for the manœuvre. A settled understanding between the Allies to this effect and absolute loyalty in the execution of it were essential.

To return to the French.

On the *left* Ney reached the front just before the attack on Gosselies. The Prussians held the place as long as they could, and then, to escape being cut off, they withdrew in a north-easterly direction. Wellington's concentration point was in Napoleon's hands, and so far the Duke had made no move.

Ney at once detached Girard's Division (II Corps) to follow the Prussians. This Division, whilst keeping the Marshal's right flank clear, was also to connect Ney with Grouchy. Girard pressed slowly forward and on reaching Wangenies he halted for the night.

Meanwhile Ney pushed on. In the van was Lefebvre-Desnoëttes' Cavalry, the Lancers and Chasseurs of the Guard. On reaching Frasnes, towards 6.30 p.m., the Guard Cavalry came under the fire of the first Anglo-Dutch troops so far encountered. Lefebvre-Desnoëttes had struck into a battalion of Prince Bernard's Nassau Brigade accompanied by Bijleveld's Dutch horse artillery battery. Of the 8 guns, 2 were unlimbered on the road, 3 guns on the right of the road, and 3 on the left. The battalion and the horse artillery at Frasnes barred the road to Lefebvre-Desnoëttes, and the Dutch-Belgian troops boldly stood their ground until they were nearly enveloped. Then, faced by the large mass of hostile cavalry, Prince Bernard slowly drew back his small force towards the main body which was in position along the Bossu Wood, 1½ miles south of Quatre Bras. Prince Bernard's whole available force only numbered about 4,000 infantry and 8 guns ; but his situation was never really critical, because he was only threatened by 2,000 French horsemen unaccompanied by horse artillery. In this brush with the enemy Prince Bernard encouraged heavy firing. He knew that the sounds of a brisk cannonade and musketry engagement would spread the news abroad quicker than any other means at his disposal and would draw attention to the critical point. Owing to the height of the corn the Prince had been unable to gauge the strength of the force with which he was in touch. The crops, too, had also embarrassed Lefebvre-Desnoëttes in his advance and prevented the French general from estimating with any accuracy the force which was opposing him, except the number of enemy guns. The columns of smoke which they emitted on discharge disclosed both their number and position.

Map 2. To dislodge Prince Bernard, Lefebvre-Desnoëttes asked Ney to send him some infantry to co-operate with his Lancers and Chasseurs. Ney promptly sent up one battalion, but that was not sufficient. The day was drawing on, the men were fatigued, and about 8 p.m. Ney determined to halt for the night.[1] The Marshal's decision was wise. The Left Wing was strung out and the situation was obscure ; further, only four hours earlier, Ney had taken over the command of two Corps and two Cavalry Divisions which were operating on ground he had never seen. Engaged in front with an enemy of unknown strength, hearing the cannon at Gilly away to the south-east, and with the day coming to an end, it would indeed be surprising if so experienced a Commander had not adopted a prudent course of action.

On deciding to halt Ney made the following arrangements : he drew back his vanguard, the *Light Cavalry*, to Frasnes ; placed *Piré's Lancers* at Heppignies ; ordered *Bachelu's Division* to halt at Mellet and form the main guard of his tactical Advanced Guard ; and covered his right with *Girard*, at Wangenies. The remainder

[1] Lefebvre-Desnoëttes' Report to Marshal Ney is given in Appendix II, No. 1.

of *Reille's Corps* (Divisions of *Foy* and *Prince Jérôme*) halted at Gosselies, where *Marshal Ney* established his head-quarters. *D'Erlon's Corps* stretched right back to the Sambre. *Durutte's* and *Donzelot's Divisions* were between Jumet and Gosselies, *Marcognet's Divison* was at Marchienne, *Alix's Division* at Thuin, and *Jacquinot's Cavalry Division* at Jumet.

The general disposition of Ney's Strategic Advanced Guard is interesting. It moved with a tactical advanced guard thrown sufficiently far to the front to safeguard it whilst in column of route, but there was no wide strategical reconnaissance. The cavalry were not worn out on this duty, nor the enemy forewarned. The mounted troops were kept fresh for the battle and for pursuit. In this campaign a wide strategical reconnaissance would have been a mistake, since it would certainly have warned the Allies of their impending danger.

It was 11 p.m. when Ney wrote to the Emperor reporting that he was in touch, on the Brussels road, with an uncertain number of Wellington's troops who were inclined to stand. Prince Bernard had handled his small force with rare skill; he had imposed on the experienced French officers by whom he was confronted, and he had secured for the Duke of Wellington the strategic point of Quatre Bras. But, so far as the French were concerned, nothing had been compromised on the Left Wing.

Meanwhile, on the Right Wing, Grouchy and Vandamme had spent two hours in elaborating their plan of attack. About 5.30 p.m. the Emperor, at Charleroi, became uneasy at hearing no sounds of battle on the right, and he hastened to the front to take charge of affairs. The Emperor rode to Gilly escorted by the four squadrons who were on duty round his person (*Escadrons de service*). On arrival he surveyed the scene and immediately came to the conclusion that Grouchy was only confronted by a small force. This was no time to proceed with deliberation. The old fiery energy blazed up. There was a brief preparatory cannonade and then Pirch II was chased away by the bayonets of Vandamme's Infantry and kept on the run by the long swords of Letort's Dragoons. The Emperor himself gave the order to Letort: ' *Letort, prenez mes escadrons, chargez et enfoncez tout cela !* ' In this charge Lieut.-General Letort was mortally wounded. Brave Letort! happy in the time of his death. He passed with victory in his imagination.

The retiring Prussians were heavily pressed as they withdrew. Pajol co-operated, Exelmans came up on the French right, and the Prussian retreat only ended at Fleurus. Despite the failing light Grouchy wished to storm Fleurus, which was weakly garrisoned, and then he could reach Sombreffe as the Emperor had directed. The Marshal called on Vandamme to support him with some infantry. Vandamme flatly refused to do this. The III Corps were shaking down into bivouacs near the Soleilmont Wood, and Vandamme said he would take no orders from the Commander of the Cavalry. Grouchy's advance came to a standstill; and, placing Pajol and Exelmans to cover the III Corps, the Marshal called a halt in front of Fleurus.

Faced by superior forces Zieten had shown great skill. Owing to the short distance over which he had to manœuvre, Zieten had to fight several times to regulate the French advance, and he was skilful enough to gain the necessary time and space for Blücher without having the I Corps destroyed.

Map 2.—Grouchy's night dispositions were as follows :

Pajol and *Exelmans* bivouacked between Lambusart and Campinaire, with Grouchy's head-quarters at Campinaire.

Vandamme's Corps was across the Fleurus road. Its right was at Winage and its left on the Soleilmont Wood.

Gérard's Corps was astride the Sambre at Châtelet. Only *Hulot's Division* (late De Bourmont's) was on the left bank.

Grouchy arranged for the adequate tactical protection of his Strategic Advanced Guard, by pushing his cavalry far enough ahead to cover the French advance and ensure tactical security. Marshal Grouchy's night dispositions furnished an additional reason for Marshal Ney not to push on to Quatre Bras on the 15th, because Ney would only be safe at Quatre Bras when Grouchy was master of Sombreffe. In the existing circumstances, if Ney had advanced beyond Frasnes his right flank would have been open and exposed to a Prussian attack.

By halting short of Quatre Bras and Sombreffe, Napoleon had still left the Allies a chance to attempt a forward concentration. All the Emperor desired to effect on the 15th was to place the *Armée du Nord* so that it could carry out the decisive manœuvre which he had planned for the 16th ; and when Sombreffe and Quatre Bras had been seized the two Wings would be only 8 miles apart. Napoleon had postponed the capture of the Namur–Nivelles road until the morrow ; but its retention by the Allies induced them to make a very serious mistake on the 16th.

Map 2.—The Centre (or *Masse de Manœuvre*), under Napoleon, halted for the night around Charleroi :

Young Guard (Duhesme) at Gilly ; *Middle Guard* (Morand), *Old Guard* (Friant), and *Heavy Cavalry of the Guard* (Guyot) between Gilly and Charleroi. The *I Grenadiers* and *I Chasseurs* acted as escort to *Imperial Head-quarters* in Charleroi. The *VI Corps* (Lobau) halted on the right bank of the Sambre, as well as *Milhaud's Cuirassiers* and the *Grand Park* of the Army. *Kellermann's Cuirassiers* bivouacked near the leading Division of Gérard's Corps, to the north of Châtelet.

One other stroke of bad fortune had befallen the Grand Army on this day. Marshal Mortier, Duke of Treviso, commanding the Imperial Guard, had fallen sick and been left behind at Beaumont. Thenceforward all orders for the Guard passed through General Count Drouot (*Aide-Major* of the Guard). Thus, from the outset of the campaign, Drouot was given duties to perform which kept him from being available to handle the massed artillery in battle, and at Waterloo this was disastrous.

Despite all the delays, by evening the *Armée du Nord* was bivouacked in a square whose sides measured about 10 miles each. The Grand Army was massed to fight ; and it was disposed so that it could manœuvre against Wellington or against Blücher. It was already placed between them.

As the opening events seemed to indicate that the Prussian Army would be the first objective, Napoleon concentrated his Centre so that, on the 16th, it could take the Fleurus road and strike in at Sombreffe with the least delay. No considerable body of hostile troops could now move between the French Army and the Dyle-head without running the risk of destruction.

The Emperor's opening advance fell short of the conception in one important particular ; no less than 30,000–35,000 men were on the south side of the Sambre when darkness fell. In Gérard's case the failure was serious, because on the morrow the IV Corps might be wanted to co-operate with Vandamme and Grouchy at an early hour, so as to engage and fix whatever force Blücher presented in front of Fleurus.

It was essential, on the 16th, to make sure that the Allies were not allowed to slip away unobserved and unbeaten. If Napoleon lost contact on the 16th he would be once more in the dark, and, whilst he was groping about trying to regain touch, the Allied concentration would be perfected. On the other hand, if the Allies had determined to attempt a forward concentration, the earlier the decision could be reached on the 16th the better, so that more time would be available for the pursuit immediately after the victory. Already the enemy had been strongly gripped. This grip must not be relaxed but tightened up on the 16th.

Although Napoleon's position was not perfect, yet there is no gainsaying that it was dominating ; that of the Allies, however, was extremely unpromising. The French were in possession of all the ground on which Wellington was to have met them, and of most of that on which Blücher was to have stood. Further, when night fell on the 15th, the Prussian Field-Marshal (who had ordered his concentration to take place at Sombreffe) had on the intended ground only one Corps (Zieten's), and this Corps had suffered severely in the day's fighting. Two of the other Corps (Pirch I's and Thielemann's) were close at hand, but the fourth (Bülow's) could not co-operate for two days at least, owing to Gneisenau's failure to make the critical situation clear to its commander. On this same day Wellington had not moved one man to meet the enemy. The small body of his troops holding Quatre Bras so gallantly were there contrary to his orders which had directed them to collect at Nivelles. Wellington himself had remained at Brussels, and he went to the Duchess of Richmond's ball at night ; whereas Blücher hastened forward at the first warning of serious danger and reached the front during the afternoon.

Prince Bernard's Brigade at Quatre Bras and the other Brigade (Bijlandt's) of Perponcher's Division at Nivelles were the only available troops of Wellington's Army who were at hand. Only this force was ready to fill the widening gap as Napoleon drove back Zieten to the north-eastward ; and, if it was strictly adhered to, the concentration which Wellington had ordered at Nivelles must leave open the Brussels road and surrender Quatre Bras to Ney.

Sketches B and C.—Had Wellington hastened to Nivelles when he received Dörnberg's first message (sent from Mons at 3 p.m. on the 14th), reporting that Napoleon had taken the field and a

French concentration was in progress, the Duke must have made different arrangements. He would have ordered all his Divisions to assemble on the 14th at their concentration centres and moved the Reserve to Mt. St. Jean, ready to advance to Nivelles or to Quatre Bras. Then, on the 15th, directly the Duke heard the sounds of engagement along Zieten's outpost line, he would have ordered a concentration on his inner (eastern) flank. When the long day drew to a close the bivouac fires of the concentrated Anglo-Dutch Army would have glowed within the triangle included by Quatre Bras–Frasnes–Nivelles. Müffling correctly remarked, ' Napoleon's fate depended on the trifling circumstance of the Duke leaving Brussels on the 14th. In that case Napoleon would have fallen into the Caudine Forks on the 16th.' There would have been no Waterloo.

The news that the Emperor was behind the Sambre did not lead to any concentration worthy of note, though immediately the Allies effected a safe concentration, within a short day's march of one another, the risk of defeat in detail would disappear. By allowing themselves to be surprised, and by their slowness on the 15th and 16th, the Allies offered Napoleon the very opportunity which he sought.

CHAPTER VII

16TH JUNE: FEELING FOR THE ALLIES
AND PRELIMINARY ARRANGEMENTS;
NAPOLEON'S PLAN OF CAMPAIGN IN
BELGIUM

(Maps 2 and 3 ; Sketch D)

AFTER the Left Wing halted on the 15th Ney rode back to Charleroi to report to the Emperor. It was 2 a.m. before the Marshal
returned to Gosselies, but so far Ney had received no orders for the
next day. Napoleon only decided on his course of action at
6 a.m. on the 16th, after receiving the information which had
come in during the night.

In no direction had British troops been sighted by the French.
Although part of Wellington's Army, the troops which had held
up Ney's advance were not British, and even this force had not
been struck into until late on the 15th and to the northward of
Gosselies. Napoleon concluded that Wellington, acting with
circumspection, had fallen back on Brussels so as to cover Antwerp and Ostend, secure his line to the sea, and keep within
distance of his base ; and the Emperor decided that a rapid
advance on Brussels would hasten Wellington's strategic concentration to the rear, increase the distance between the Allies, and
broaden the area on which the campaign was to be fought out.
He also thought that the capture of the Belgian capital and the
triumphant entry of the *Armée du Nord*, would produce a great
moral effect. Napoleon did not select Brussels because it was a
geographical point whose capture could end the war. Brussels
was to be merely a stepping-stone to the destruction in turn of
Wellington's and Blücher's Armies. Once at Brussels the
Emperor could move against Wellington and force him to fight
single-handed or embark his red-coats, leaving his Dutch-Belgian
Allies to their fate. Then the French Army would be free to
turn at once on Blücher, and ensure the latter's destruction

before the Austrians and Russians reached the Rhine frontier. Put tersely Napoleon's plan was : general direction for the advance—Brussels ; objective—the Allied Armies, as soon as they were located.

The Emperor decided to push boldly into the gap which so obviously existed between the Allies, and he would then engage and crush whichever Allied Army first presented itself. To carry out this project, the Prussians must be pushed away beyond Gembloux, so as to deny to Blücher the use of the Namur–Wavre–Brussels road. Even if the Allies lost the Namur–Sombreffe–Quatre Bras–Nivelles highway, yet the Wavre road would be still available for the use of the Allied generals when concerting their plans and operations.

Towards 8 a.m. the Emperor sent General Count de la Bédoyère with a personal letter of instructions (*Correspondance* 22059) to Grouchy, commanding the 45,000 men forming the Right Wing. The Marshal was ordered to advance against the Prussians who were holding Sombreffe and Grouchy was informed that the IV Corps was moving up to join him, but this Corps was to keep Fleurus clear as the Emperor was moving his head-quarters to that town. All the generals of Grouchy's Wing were placed under the Marshal, and the Emperor explained that he would only issue orders directly to those corps commanders who were at the place where he was himself. (This statement, which was repeated to Ney, has a considerable bearing on the D'Erlon incident.) Grouchy was also informed that the Emperor was moving the Guard up to Fleurus, but he would only push the Guard on as far as Sombreffe if essential, that is, if the enemy was at Sombreffe. In this case the Emperor would attack. Even if the Prussians were at Gembloux the Emperor would attack them and occupy Gembloux. In possession of Gembloux further active operations against the Prussians could be stopped, and the Emperor would swing across with his Reserve and co-operate with Ney against the Anglo-Dutch Army. This letter made clear that the Emperor believed the Allies were falling back to secure concentration.

Between 8 and 9 a.m. the Emperor sent General Count de Flahault to Ney with a most important letter (*Correspondance* 22058).[1] In this letter Ney was told that Grouchy was moving

[1] This letter is given in Appendix II, No. 2.

to Sombreffe, and the Emperor and the Guard were following in that direction. If the Prussians stood Napoleon intended to drive them back beyond Gembloux, and then he would decide on his course of action. Ney was to hold the Left Wing in readiness to move on Brussels after the Emperor had mastered Gembloux, so that the Left Wing could reach Brussels early on the 17th. To be ready for this, Ney was to push one Division 5 miles along the Brussels road to the north of Quatre Bras, hold six Divisions at Quatre Bras, and push one Division to Marbais for intercommunication purposes. These arrangements would ensure holding Quatre Bras, prevent co-operation between Wellington and Blücher, and keep the Nivelles–Namur highway under French control.

Kellerman's Cuirassiers were to be attached to the Left Wing to replace the Light Cavalry of the Guard, whom Napoleon desired to husband, as there was no need for them on the Right Wing. Ney was directed to keep Lefebvre-Desnoëttes' horsemen in hand and to cover them with the Cavalry of the Line.

Then Napoleon wrote : '. . . I have adopted for this campaign the following general principle, to divide my Army into two Wings and a Reserve . . . The Guard will form the Reserve ; and I shall bring it into action on either Wing just as the actual circumstances may dictate . . . Also, according to circumstances, I shall draw troops from one Wing to strengthen my Reserve . . .'

These sentences cannot be considered too carefully as they are the basis of the whole strategical plan for the campaign. In the clearest manner they show Napoleon's organization of the *Armée du Nord* for the invasion of Belgium, in face of the two Allied Armies. They describe in the simplest way how the Army was to be arranged so that it could pass from a marching to a fighting formation without any waste of time. The sentences emphasize that the functions of one Wing were merely to contain, or to hold up, one of the Allies, whilst the decision was obtained on the other Wing. The Emperor made clear that for this ' containing rôle ' part of a Wing would suffice. This would leave the other part free to march across and swell the Reserve. Then, engaging together on the decisive flank, a shattering blow would be struck.

Flahault reached Ney about 11 a.m. After handing over the letter, he gave the Marshal orders ' as from the Emperor, to move to Quatre Bras, to hold this important point in strength, and (should the enemy allow him to do so) to support with every man at his disposal the Emperor's offensive against the Prussian Army '. Flahault stayed with the Left Wing all day, had supper with Marshal Ney at night, and did not rejoin Imperial Head-Quarters at Fleurus until 6 a.m. on the 17th.

To be in a position to support Grouchy the Emperor proposed to move the Guard and Milhaud to Fleurus, so as to be able to intervene and settle the affair if Blücher massed any serious force on the 16th. For the present Lobau was ordered to remain at Charleroi, as the situation was not yet clear enough for Napoleon to decide on which Wing Lobau's Corps would be needed. The Corps was a small one and it would suffice if Lobau received orders by midday on the 16th. Napoleon thought that the Prussian forces, which the French advance might encounter, would be driven beyond Gembloux by Grouchy's command alone, and Lobau would not be required at all on the Fleurus side of the triangle. In this eventuality the VI Corps could join Ney direct and thus save a tiresome counter-march. Should Wellington manage to concentrate superior forces early in the day and threaten to overwhelm Ney, then Lobau at Charleroi was well placed to reinforce Ney, and assist him in pinning Wellington until the Emperor could bring across his Reserve—the Guard—and destroy the Anglo-Dutch.

Napoleon's early arrangements on the 16th were made for an advance, nevertheless he won a great pitched battle on that same afternoon. He was able to do so because he had disposed the *Armée du Nord* in depth, and he could change from a marching to a fighting formation directly he was offered the chance of destroying the Prussians at Ligny. His plan did not depend for success on mere good luck, or on fortune. ' In making preparations against an enemy it must always be assumed that they have taken the best counsel. It would be madness to build hopes on the mistakes they may possibly make.'

Sketch D.—To return to the Allies. Blücher's plan for the 16th was to collect his Army and accept battle at Ligny. To carry this out he closed up his two nearest Corps, Pirch I from Le Mazy and Thielemann from Namur ; and the Field-Marshal believed that Bülow was moving from Hannut to Sombreffe and would arrive in time for the battle. Unfortunately for the Prussians this was impossible, and on the 16th the head of the IV Corps only reached Baudeset (north-north-east of Gembloux).

Wellington's latest orders had commanded a concentration at Nivelles, and to this place his troops were hurrying to the utmost of their ability. Fortunately, on his return from Brussels, the Prince of Orange realized the importance of holding on to Quatre Bras and he determined to support Prince Bernard. Consequently the remaining Brigade (Bijlandt's) of General Perponcher's Division was ordered to move to Quatre Bras, as soon as any other troops reached Nivelles and assured the safety of that place. As a result Prince Bernard, ' towards morning on the 16th, was reinforced by a battalion of Dutch Jägers and a Militia Battalion '. Shortly afterwards General Perponcher and the Prince of Orange rode up, and the latter then assumed the chief command.

Ney, with Reille and Lefebvre-Desnoëttes (21,000 men and 50 guns) available at dawn near Frasnes, could have crushed Prince Bernard's force ; and, even by 9 a.m., the latter only numbered 6,500 and 8 guns. The cross-roads could have passed into French possession by noon. But by 2 p.m., owing to the initiative of the Prince of Orange, de Constant Rebecque, and Perponcher, Prince Bernard had available a force of 8,000 and 16 guns to defend a front of 2 miles. Not having been given sufficiently clear orders, Ney had missed a chance.

Sketches B, C, and D.—About 7 a.m. Sir William de Lancey (the Duke's Chief of the Staff) drew up the celebrated Memorandum which bears his name.[1] This purported to give the places towards which the various Divisions were marching, and the destinations which they had been ordered to reach. A consideration of the previous orders, a study of this Memorandum, a glance at the map, and a recollection of the overnight positions, show that not more than 50,000 of Wellington's troops were within a 25 miles' march of Quatre Bras. These were the only troops which could reach the place before night fell and put an end to the battle. Over 40,000 troops were outside the 25-mile radius, and they were too far away to reach the concentration point in time to be of the least use on the 16th June.

On the French side Napoleon could oppose Wellington with

---

[1] Only a copy of a copy compiled from memory exists. De Lancey died of injuries received at Waterloo.

his Left Wing of 45,000 men ; whilst Blücher, who could only put 85,000 in line of battle at Sombreffe, would be confronted by the Emperor at the head of 80,000 men, a force ample to ensure a decisive French victory. On the first critical day of the campaign Napoleon, by effecting an initial surprise and by his manœuvres, had lessened the advantage which their great numerical superiority had conferred on the Allies. If the Emperor decided to hold Wellington with 20,000 men, then he could concentrate superior numbers against Blücher. This concentration would take place on the battle-field, and the blow struck should be deadly.

Sketch C.—On the Anglo-Dutch side the Reserve, with Picton's Division leading, left Brussels at 2 a.m. and marched southwards. The after-orders, issued at 10 p.m. on the 15th, had directed this column to march from Brussels by the Namur road to the point at Mt. St. Jean where the road to Nivelles branched off. The real danger had not yet been appreciated at the Duke's headquarters. Evidently Wellington had not determined whether his Reserve should march for Quatre Bras, or Nivelles. This explains the selection of the Mt. St. Jean fork roads as the first objective. The Brunswick Contingent followed Picton's Division somewhat later, and the Brunswickers were followed by Kruse's Nassau Brigade.

Wellington left Brussels about 6 a.m. and rode to Quatre Bras, which he reached between 9 and 9.30 a.m. On arrival he approved the dispositions made by Perponcher and the Prince of Orange. The French were inactive in front of the position, and the spasmodic firing did not suggest the presence of large hostile numbers. As it was reported, however, that the French were showing large masses in front of Blücher's Prussians, Wellington at last sent back orders to Picton and Brunswick to advance to Quatre Bras.

The Reserve had remained halted from 11 a.m. to 1 p.m. at Mt. St. Jean, waiting for the situation to clear up sufficiently for Wellington to decide in which direction the Reserve was required. It was only when the Duke was convinced that the French were not attacking in the direction of Mons, as he had apprehended, that he ordered the Reserve to advance to Quatre Bras, which it reached at 3 p.m. The delay in the arrival of Picton's Division at Quatre Bras is accounted for by the halt at Mt. St. Jean. On a good road, starting early in the morning, unmolested by the enemy, and marching to meet the foe, no body of British troops under an officer of Picton's known characteristics could have taken thirteen hours to march from Brussels to Quatre Bras.

After sending his orders to the Reserve, the Duke wrote to Blücher to inform him that Quatre Bras was held by a Division of the Anglo-Dutch Army and the remainder of the Army was also concentrating there.[1] Wellington concluded by remarking that no body of hostile troops of any strength was visible in front of him, and he awaited news from the Prussians. About noon, however, as he did not anticipate an immediate attack on Quatre Bras, Wellington wisely decided to visit Blücher so as to arrange personally about co-operation. Accompanied by two of his staff and a small escort he rode over to Sombreffe.

On the French side : Napoleon ordered Kellermann to report to Ney, told Drouot to move the Guard to Fleurus, and directed Lobau to cross the Sambre and form up beyond Charleroi. At the same time Vandamme and Gérard were directed to place themselves under Grouchy's orders, and the Right Wing was ordered to advance to Sombreffe and occupy Gembloux with an advanced guard.

Ney had previously been ordered to seize Quatre Bras. The Marshal was to cover himself by pushing a Division to Genappe, and connect with the Right Wing by placing another Division at Marbais. The Marshal was also told to reconnoitre to the north and west and ascertain if Wellington was concentrating his Army.

It was after Grouchy had reported strong hostile bodies marching up from Namur and others visible near St. Amand, that Napoleon wrote to Ney and Grouchy the letters which were carried by Generals de Flahault and de la Bédoyère. A perusal of these letters makes clear that the Emperor had not yet decided on the course which he would adopt on the 16th. At 10 a.m., just as Napoleon was ready to start from Charleroi, a lancer officer reported that hostile troops were in sight at Quatre Bras, and Girard, at Wangenies, had seen Prussian masses forming up beyond Fleurus. This latter news, taken in conjunction with

[1] Given in Appendix II, No. 3. The letter was written in French.

Grouchy's, indicated that the Prussian Army was not retreating towards the Meuse. Perhaps the critical day had come, since the Prussians seemed to be undertaking a forward concentration. The Emperor determined to hasten to Fleurus ; and he sent fresh orders to Ney, urging the Marshal to concentrate his command, capture Quatre Bras, and send all further reports to Fleurus.

Lobau was still halted at the northern edge of Charleroi. But the time had come for the VI Corps to move to some central position nearer to the front, where Lobau would be within easy reach of either side, would have no counter-marching to do, and would be able to cover the inner flanks of Ney and Grouchy. If centrally placed the VI Corps could engage on the 16th either at Quatre Bras or Sombreffe, and be magnificently placed to strike against the inner flank of either enemy. Napoleon, however, left the VI Corps at Charleroi, merely directing Lobau to send his Assistant Chief of the Staff (Janin) to Frasnes, to report on the situation on the Left Wing.

Napoleon reached Fleurus about 11 a.m. Orders, however, had not reached the IV Corps until 9 a.m., and the Emperor found Grouchy waiting for Gérard's arrival before pushing on. Napoleon's usual superabundant energy was lacking, or he would have undertaken a personal reconnaissance of Blücher's position by 8 a.m. at latest. As it was the delay did not save Blücher from a severe defeat, but it postponed the hour of the French victory until there was no longer any light available in which to reap the fruits of that victory.

In previous campaigns Napoleon had usually rested about 7 p.m., rising again at 1 a.m. to receive the reports which had come in and to issue his operation orders, and these orders had then reached the troops soon after daybreak. Had this procedure been followed on the 16th then nothing could have saved Blücher from destruction. The Prussian Army have to thank Napoleon's impaired physical powers for the chance given to them to escape from Ligny.

Map 3.—Napoleon intently reconnoitred Blücher's position from the Naveau Mill at Fleurus. As yet only one Corps was in position. The other two Corps, with the heads of their columns at Sombreffe, were covered by folds of the ground. Napoleon accurately estimated the force in front of him as not more than one Corps, though its disposition must have struck him as peculiar. The Corps was not drawn up at right-angles to the Namur and Gembloux roads, as a rearguard would have been, or as the Corps would have been if it was covering a rearward Prussian concentration. On the contrary, Zieten's troops held the villages of St. Amand and Ligny and were formed parallel to the Sombreffe–Quatre Bras road. To Napoleon it was at once apparent that the Corps was there to cover the arrival of other Prussian troops, as well as to protect the road along which Wellington and the Anglo-Dutch troops could march from Quatre Bras. At last the situation was clear. Blücher was attempting a forward concentration and expected help from Wellington.

A closer examination of Blücher's position showed that his right flank was in the air and well placed for the delivery of a death-stroke. This was the correct flank to drive in. It was Blücher's inner wing and its destruction would ensure the disorganized flight of the rest of the Army towards the Meuse, the Allies would be driven asunder, and Wellington's inner flank exposed. But at the moment only Girard's Division, Vandamme's Corps, and Pajol's and Exelmans' Cavalry Corps were available ; and Napoleon had to wait for the belated arrival of the IV Corps. It was 1 p.m. before Gérard began to form on Vandamme's right.

Gérard, accompanied by a small escort, rode on ahead of his Corps and went up to the advanced French posts. Whilst looking for the Emperor, he ventured too close to some Prussian Cavalry who promptly charged. The General was unhorsed and narrowly escaped capture, and he was rescued by one of his aides-de-camp. Gérard then joined the Emperor at the Naveau Windmill.

Napoleon decided to attack and wear down the Prussians with the Cavalry of Pajol and Exelmans and the Corps of Vandamme and Gérard, whilst he held in reserve the Guard and Milhaud ; and he counted on part of Ney's force becoming available to envelop the exposed Prussian right flank. At 2 p.m. the Emperor ordered Ney (this letter is in Soult's register) to drive away any force which was in front of the Left Wing. The Marshal was then to turn eastward, so as to co-operate at Ligny and ensure the destruction of the Prussian Army. Ney was also informed that, if the Prussians were rapidly overcome, the Emperor would manœuvre in Ney's direction, so as to deal a decisive blow to any force which might be opposed to the Left Wing. This last sentence showed that Napoleon had not yet gauged the strength of the Prussians at Ligny. Had he done so, he would have ordered Ney to neutralize Wellington with Reille and Kellermann, and without delay send D'Erlon and Lefebvre-Desnoëttes to Bry to outflank Blücher's right.

Whilst Napoleon was reconnoitring the Prussian position he would have been surprised to know that Blücher and Wellington were concerting their plan of action on the high ground near Bry Windmill, from which a fine view of the battle-field was obtainable. (Bry Windmill was pulled down in 1895.)

After examining the ground and Blücher's dispositions, Wellington realized at once the exposed situation of the Prussian troops. Turning to Blücher and Gneisenau he said : ' Everyone knows his own Army best ; but if I were to fight with mine here, I should expect to be beat.' Blücher promptly rejoined : ' My lads like to see their enemy.' Wellington remarked afterwards (probably on his homeward ride) that the Prussians would get ' damnably mauled '.

Between Blücher's choice and occupation of a position and the defensive measures which Wellington usually took there was real dissimilarity, based on the fighting characteristics of the two Nations. Wellington knew that British troops could be trusted to stand steady on the reverse slope of a hill. Such a position was valuable, because of the protection it afforded to the troops from the heavy point-blank case-shot discharges from massed French batteries at the crisis of an action.

To return to the Allied conference which took place at Bry Windmill. Gneisenau suggested that the Anglo-Dutch Army should move eastward, and form a reserve in rear of the Prussian troops. But Wellington's dispersed Army could not carry out this manœuvre on the 16th. Fortunately Müffling had accompanied the Duke and he came to the rescue. Müffling suggested that the Anglo-Dutch Army should concentrate in front of Quatre Bras, then advance and wheel to their left, and co-operate in the impending battle by coming up on Blücher's right. Wellington jumped at this proposal, as it kept Brussels covered.

It is evident that both Wellington and Blücher took the French troops in front of them for the whole of the *Armée du Nord*, and estimated that not more than one Division was in front of Quatre Bras. This reconnaissance was a poor one ; because at 1 p.m. nearly half of the *Armée du Nord* : D'Erlon, Reille, Lobau, Kellermann, and Lefebvre-Desnoëttes were either invisible or miles away. Be that as it may, Gneisenau would not acquiesce in Müffling's suggestion and persisted in adhering to his original plan. Blücher's Chief of the Staff obviously supposed that Wellington could assemble his whole Army at Quatre Bras in very few hours, the Anglo-Dutch Army would reach Blücher's battle-field before Napoleon gained the decision, and no French detachment was placed to prevent Wellington's flank march from Quatre Bras to Bry. These hypotheses, however, were all incorrect. The troops on Wellington's right could not reach Quatre Bras before nightfall, and the strength of the French force opposite to Quatre Bras was quite unknown. On the other hand the value of Müffling's suggestion was considerable. The Prussian Attaché had skilfully glossed over Wellington's actual situation and the Duke's miscalculations connected with the concentration of his troops, as well as Gneisenau's erroneous calculation with reference to the arrival of the Anglo-Dutch Army at Bry. But Gneisenau negatived the proposition. He declared it was too long and insecure. The Duke then replied with decision : ' Well, I will come ; provided I am not attacked myself.' This conditional promise terminated the discussion ; and Wellington, with his staff and escort, left Blücher and rode back to Quatre Bras.

The Allied plan was by no means ideal. Despite his fiery zeal Blücher could not be compared to the Duke as a tactician. The latter, indeed, was unsurpassed as a commander in a defensive battle fought on a position which he had carefully selected. To accept a pitched battle with Napoleon, with the idea of wearing out the *Armée du Nord* and preparing it for the death-blow, the Anglo-Dutch Army should have been selected if possible. The Allies should have made the most of the mobility and manœuvring power of the Prussian Army by relying on Blücher to come up at the psychological moment and deal Napoleon a fatal blow. Two days later these arrangements worked most admirably at Waterloo. On the 16th, however, Blücher's Army had to accept battle, and on Wellington's Army devolved the duty of General

Reserve. The points to consider were : Had Blücher's Army sufficient resisting power to carry out the rôle assigned to it ? Was Wellington's Army sufficiently in hand, and had it sufficient mobility and manœuvring power to carry through its task in time ? Lastly, if the Allies failed at Ligny, would Napoleon give them a second chance ?

CHAPTER VIII

THIRD PHASE; THE OFFENSIVE AGAINST THE PRUSSIAN ARMY: MARSHAL NEY'S ADVANCE AND THE ACTION OF QUATRE BRAS

(Map 3 ; Sketch D)

The Goddess of Battle requires not only that men shall die like heroes, but that they shall also think like heroes.

FRITZ HOENIG.

To be able to destroy the Prussians Napoleon had to feel secure during the battle from any interference by Wellington, and he also required the co-operation of Marshal Ney. The possession of Quatre Bras would facilitate both these ends. Consequently Ney had been urged to seize the cross-roads ; his manœuvres, therefore, were subsidiary on the 16th, so his operations shall be considered first.

Ney could have destroyed Perponcher's Division at Quatre Bras and secured the cross-roads by 2 p.m. Even at that hour Ney could have engaged over 20,000 men and 50 to 60 guns against 8,000 and 16 guns, and still have had in reserve D'Erlon's Corps, another 20,000. But the orders which he had so far received had not impressed on Ney the necessity for early and vigorous action ; and the Marshal, who required clear and definite orders at this turning-point, hesitated. Ney set off for the front at 8 a.m. At this hour the head of Reille's Corps was in its overnight halting-place at Frasnes and the tail of D'Erlon's Corps was still on the Sambre. The Marshal, however, did not warn the Left Wing to stand to arms, and merely directed Reille to carry out any orders which arrived from the Emperor and to pass them on to D'Erlon. If at 6 a.m. Ney had ordered each Corps to close up on its leading Division, then by 8 a.m. Reille would have concentrated at Frasnes and D'Erlon just to the south of Gosselies.

Map 2.—When Ney reached Frasnes he heard that the foe had been reinforced and had pushed back the French outpost troops. This activity seemed to indicate that the Anglo-Dutch meant to retain their position covering the important cross-roads, but Ney still thought he had only a handful of Germans to deal with.

Then at 11 a.m. General de Flahault reached Frasnes and handed the Emperor's letter to Ney.[1] Although he had assembled his Divisions, Reille had not moved northward. He was uneasy at the presence of Prussian masses beyond Fleurus, and he had decided to wait for Ney's orders. This caused another hour's delay.

It was only at 11 a.m. that Ney issued his march orders, directing Reille to halt at Quatre Bras and push one Division forward to Genappe, D'Erlon to mass three Divisions at Frasnes and move one Division and his Cavalry to Marbais, Kellermann to form up at Liberchies and Frasnes, and Lefebvre-Desnoëttes to collect at Frasnes. At the hour when he issued these orders Ney had learned in general outline the Emperor's plan of campaign.[2] The Marshal's duty was clear, he had to attack and master Quatre Bras. He was confronted by only a small force and he had crushing strength available for this task. Any further delay was needless and might be dangerous.

It was high noon before Reille's Corps began to move northwards. Piré and Bachelu led the advance, and they were followed by Foy and Prince Jérôme. The van cleared Frasnes at 1.30 p.m., though Foy did not reach it until 2 p.m. Meanwhile the Emperor's 10 a.m. letter had reached Ney. In this letter the Marshal was directed to seize Quatre Bras, but to carry out this order Ney had to wait for Reille's belated arrival.

The position held by the Prince of Orange at Quatre Bras was not unfavourable for defence. It lay along rolling ground, and combined farm-buildings, large woods, and thickets ; but, although the Bossu Wood was dense and intricate, there were no hedges or obstacles to impede troops on the field itself. The small group of houses comprising the hamlet of Quatre Bras consisted of a large farm, an inn, and a few smaller buildings grouped around the cross-roads. The hamlet was placed on the top of a ridge which formed the skyline when viewed from the

[1] Appendix II, No. 2.   [2] Appendix II, No. 2.

south, and from this ridge Frasnes and its church could be seen. All the ground was covered with rye of a considerable height and this prevented a good view over the battle-field. Nevertheless Wellington owed a debt of gratitude to this rye, as the weakness of the defenders was concealed from the French by the tall corn. Even so, favourable or unfavourable, the position had to be held. There was no choice in the matter, and the Prince of Orange, knowing that supports were hastening up and could not be far distant, determined to impose on the French by a bold display of force.

Map 3.—Eleven guns were unlimbered in the centre of the front line. Bijleveld's Battery had 2 guns on the road to the south of Gémioncourt and 3 to the east of the road ; whilst Stevenart's Battery had 6 guns in action to the west of the Brussels road, between Gémioncourt and the Bossu Wood. Bijleveld's remaining 3 guns were on the Namur road, reinforcing the left ; and Stevenart's other 2 guns were placed in front of the south-west corner of the Bossu Wood. All the artillery wagons and spare vehicles were formed up to the north of Quatre Bras.

To protect the guns one Chasseur Company was deployed to the east of Bijleveld's left gun. Two Nassau companies held the south-east angle of the Bossu Wood, with the remainder of the battalion in reserve in the wood. The Chasseur battalion was deployed on a thousand yards front from Gémioncourt to Pirau-mont, with two companies in reserve.

One militia battalion had a company in Gémioncourt, with the rest of the battalion on the spur to the west of the road. Three other battalions held the southern edge of the Bossu Wood —a Nassau Battalion and an Orange-Nassau Battalion of Prince Bernard's Brigade, and a militia battalion of Bijlandt's Brigade. In front of the Bossu Wood, the two Farms of Pierrepont were both held by detachments from the Orange-Nassau Battalion ; and a detachment of Nassau Chasseurs was on the extreme right, to the west of Stevenart's detached section. Three battalions were held in reserve and placed south of the cross-roads. Another battalion, which came up at 3 p.m. from Nivelles, was posted on the road in front of Quatre Bras, though later on it was pushed (as a militia battalion from the Reserve had been) into the Bossu Wood to reinforce the defence against the assault made by Jérôme's Division.

The Prince of Orange had made skilful use of the natural cover available, and the Bossu Wood concealed the weakness of its garrison. The Prince's dispositions, as well as the wide extent of ground he took up, were calculated to impose on Marshal Ney and induce him to waste valuable hours in reconnaissance and in concentrating sufficient troops for an attack. The very natural desire of the Prince of Orange was to safeguard the Brussels and Nivelles roads along which the Anglo-Dutch reinforcements would march up. His dispositions, however, offered Ney an easy chance of smashing in the weak left flank, and gaining the vital Namur highway which led to the rear of Blücher's position. Nor did the Duke alter these dispositions or issue any orders to secure the section from Gémioncourt to the Namur road. He also feared for his right.

The deployment of Perponcher's Division was as significant as that of Zieten's Corps at Ligny. The Dutch-Belgian troops were formed parallel to the Nivelles–Namur road and in front of the road-junction, covering the *débouché* of the Brussels road. These troops were undisguisedly disposed to protect a forward concentration at Quatre Bras and to cover the connection with Blücher.

It was 1.30 p.m. when Reille, marching with his advanced troops, joined Ney. The Marshal informed Reille that the Bossu Wood, to their left front, was weakly held and must be captured immediately. Reille suggested that this might be another of those disastrous Spanish battles. This ill-omened remark recalled to Ney his experiences in the Iberian Peninsula where it had always been the Duke's custom not to make a display of force. In Spain, Wellington had often used a strong skirmishing line and a few light guns to mask the main body of his Army, which would be formed out of sight behind a convenient ridge whilst far-flung flanks prohibited any closer reconnaissance. Confronted by a Wellingtonian position, the French Marshals had to take the bull by the horns and attack. But the repulses had been so numerous and bloody that the Marshals gradually lost confidence, and the troops began to believe they lacked the ability and power to beat Wellington. Well might Ney reflect. In front of him was a position which showed none of the usual signs of serious occupation. Yet Wellington's main Army might be concealed in the valleys and behind the wood, merely waiting for the moment, when the Marshal was compromised, to strike in and effect his destruction. It was at this critical juncture that Ney required complete and precise instructions, emphasizing the Marshal's duty on the 16th and detailing the help he was to render to the Emperor during the day. So far the Emperor had vouchsafed no such guidance to Ney, and the Marshal was left to sort out for himself, as best he could, the essential in the situation with which he was confronted.

The position at 1 p.m. on the 16th was very different to what it had been at 5 p.m. on the 15th. The sooner the Marshal mastered Quatre Bras and the Namur–Nivelles highway the more certain would be Wellington's severance from Blücher, and the more sure would be Ney's communication with the Emperor, and the co-operation of the Left Wing in the battle at Fleurus. Any force which Ney despatched down the Namur road must strike into Blücher's right rear and settle the fate of the Prussian Army, if it offered battle at Ligny. Nor was there any risk in mastering Quatre Bras. An attack would impose on Wellington, and he would certainly wait until he had concentrated a considerable force about Nivelles, before he moved to reopen his direct communication with his Ally. It would be too late then for the Duke to effect anything on the 16th. Even if by nightfall he had forced Ney to yield some ground, yet he could not interpose between the two French Wings, or prevent Ney's detachment reaching the Emperor's battle-field and striking a deadly blow. Nor would the mastery of Quatre Bras by the French Left Wing at 1 p.m. give Blücher timely warning of the impending danger, or cause him to slip away before the blow fell ; because, by 1 p.m., Napoleon had sufficient forces in front of Fleurus to grip the Prussian Army and immobilize it. After 1 p.m., the sooner Ney mastered Quatre Bras the better placed the *Armée du Nord* must be, in case Fortune deigned to smile on Napoleon and offer him the chance of fighting a decisive battle thus early in the campaign.

Ney brushed aside Reille's ominous admonition but the reference to Spain remained in his mind. The dangerous weakness of Perponcher's Division was hidden by the tall standing corn, and Ney waited until Bachelu's and Foy's Divisions marched up at 2 p.m. and joined Piré's Cavalry and a Brigade (Guiton's Cuirassiers) of Kellermann's Cavalry Corps. The Marshal, however, considered that he did not yet stand in sufficient strength to attack the whole of the enemy's front, and he determined to concentrate against the weak left flank. He moved the leading Division (Bachelu's) to the east of the Brussels road, between the main road and the Delhutte Wood, formed one of Foy's Brigades in column on the road abreast of Bachelu, and held the other Brigade in reserve. Piré's Chasseurs covered Bachelu's right flank, and his Lancers formed in rear of the interval between Foy's and Bachelu's Divisions. The Light Horse of the Guard formed in column on the main road and Guiton's Cuirassiers deployed to the left of the road. Kellermann's three other Brigades (2,700 and 12 guns) remained at Liberchies, covering the left flank.

Map 3.—At 2 p.m. Ney's 14 guns opened a brief but heavy preparatory cannonade against the 11 Dutch-Belgian guns. The Marshal directed his opening attack against the eastern flank of the Dutch-Belgian position, as it was obvious that this flank was in the air and the whole section to the east of the highway was dangerously denuded of troops. Without further delay Bachelu attacked and stormed Piraumont, and Perponcher's left was driven in. To mitigate the losses caused by the heavy cannonade, the Prince of Orange led forward a militia battalion to deliver a counter-stroke ; but Piré, who was moving in support of Bachelu, seized the chance to charge the battalion in flank, scattered it, and the Prince had to thank his horse's speed for his own escape. Three other battalions moved up to the assistance of the routed troops, but Foy's Brigade was on the move and advanced to meet them. The Dutch troops were outnumbered and they recoiled. Foy then seized the farm of Gémioncourt. Within an hour the whole Allied line of defence, to the east of the Brussels road, had crumpled up ; but, so far, no attack had been delivered to the west of the road. Jérôme's Division was now drawing near, and Foy's other Brigade launched an attack on Prince Bernard's five battalions which held the Bossu Wood and Pierrepont Farm. This attack was unsuccessful.

It was after 3 p.m. when Jérôme's Division (8,000 and 8 guns) debouched on to the battle-field, and Ney at once launched them against Pierrepont Farm and the Bossu Wood. The French drove the defenders from the farm and forced them to retire into the wood, where a stubborn resistance was offered. The situation was rapidly growing desperate, Foy was advancing against Quatre Bras from the south and Bachelu from the east. Under this concentric attack Perponcher's Division would have dissolved, but reinforcements arrived in the nick of time. From east, from north, and from west they reached the stricken Division and proceeded to readjust the fight.

First to arrive was Wellington, fresh from his interview with Blücher ; a most opportune arrival as the Duke's handling of troops at the crisis of a fight never lacked resolution. Shortly afterwards, Merlen's Cavalry Brigade (Dutch Hussars and Belgian Dragoons, 1,000 and 2 guns) rode in from Nivelles ; and at 3.30 p.m., after a 20-mile march, Picton's Division (8 British and 4 Hanoverian battalions, 7,700 strong with 12 guns) reached the field by the Brussels road. At once the proportion of the opposing forces changed considerably. Ney's 25,000 were now confronted by Wellington with 17,000 men and 30 guns.

Merlen formed up near the cross-roads. Picton, to strengthen the left, was ordered to deploy along the Nivelles–Namur road to the east of Quatre Bras. The General placed Kempt's and Pack's Brigades in the first line, hidden by the standing corn, and Best's Hanoverian Brigade in the second line, behind the road embankment. Rettberg's Hanoverian Battery unlimbered on Picton's right, and Rogers's (British) Field Brigade of 9-pdr. guns came into action on the left of the Division. Picton at once launched the 1/95th against Piraumont, to wrest the buildings from the French and to keep open the Namur road. The French garrison was too strong, and all that the 1/95th could achieve was to secure a wood on the left. The roar of the guns at Ligny was distinctly audible, ' but the intervening higher ground prevented us from seeing any part of it '.

Whilst Picton was deploying, the Prince of Orange dashed his Cavalry, the Hussars followed by the Dragoons, against Foy's Infantry who were approaching Quatre Bras. Before the horsemen reached the infantry Piré's Lancers charged and overthrew them, and the routed horsemen retired beyond Quatre Bras. Piré was indefatigable ; he pressed on, rode over a battalion of militia, charged the 6 field guns in the front line, and after a sharp fight captured them. To the south of Gémioncourt a regiment of French Chasseurs found itself face to face with one of Belgian Dragoons. The two regiments closed and a bitter struggle en-

sued, until a French Lancer Regiment came to the aid of the
Chasseurs and the outnumbered Dragoons were driven back.   As
they went one of Pack's battalions mistook the Belgians for French
horsemen, owing to the similarity of uniform, and poured in a
telling volley.   The unfortunate regiment rallied behind Quatre
Bras.   Immediately after this the Brunswick Corps (about 4,000)
reached the field and brought Wellington's strength up to 21,000,
placing the Duke nearly on an equality with Marshal Ney.

It was 4 p.m. when Ney received Soult's 2 p.m. letter, which
ordered the Marshal to close with whatever force occupied Quatre
Bras, press it vigorously and push it back, so that Ney might be
free to carry out the decisive manœuvre of closing round the
Prussians at Bry, ensuring their destruction.   Naturally this order
was supplementary to the letter which Flahault had delivered.
The 2 p.m. letter did not definitely state that, on the 16th, the
decision was to be gained at Ligny, nevertheless the Marshal
might have realized that the essential on this day was not that he
should concentrate his two Corps and defeat Wellington, but
he should manœuvre so as to hold Wellington in check until
darkness fell, and do this with the minimum force, Reille's Corps
and Kellermann's Cuirassiers ; leaving D'Erlon and Lefebvre-
Desnoëttes free to move to Ligny, directly Napoleon should
demand their co-operation.

To overpower and force back Wellington and his well-handled,
tenacious troops would take too long, and prohibit any co-operation at Ligny.   As long as Wellington was nailed to his position
at Quatre Bras, the despatch of one Corps to Sombreffe would
ensure Blücher's annihilation whatever forces he concentrated
on the 16th.   Unfortunately Ney, who was without precise
instructions from the Emperor, still thought it impossible to carry
out his orders until D'Erlon's Corps came up.

Meanwhile the Brunswick Corps, having passed Quatre Bras,
moved southward between the Bossu Wood and the main road.
At the same time, to carry out the 2 p.m. order, Ney ordered a
general forward movement so as to capture the road-junction
and the Namur–Nivelles highway.   To achieve this, Bachelu
pressed forward against Wellington's left, Foy advanced against
Quatre Bras, Jérôme pushed one Brigade through the Bossu
Wood to clear it of its defenders, and moved the other northward
between the wood and the road.   The progress of the struggle

in the Bossu Wood was marked by the rattle of musketry. The defenders, except one battalion which maintained a grasp on the northern corner, were driven out by the French and retired towards Nivelles. While this was going on, Brunswick's advance collided with Foy's Division and Jérôme's Brigade, and the Brunswickers were driven back. The Duke of Brunswick led a charge of his cavalry, but this broke on the wall of steel presented by the 1st Light Infantry and the Duke received a mortal wound.

Bachelu had been less fortunate than Foy and Jérôme. Whilst his Division was climbing the slope up to the Namur road it came under the close-range fire of Picton's deployed battalions, concealed by the high corn. Bachelu's men halted, wavered. Impetuous old Picton flung Kempt's Brigade upon them with the bayonet, routed them, and drove them back to Piraumont. The French guns and Bachelu's Reserve then checked the victors, who retired to their original position. This seemed an opportune moment for cavalry to intervene, and two of Piré's Regiments charged the British. Some skirmishers were cut up, but the battalions formed square and resisted all attacks. The square of the 28th was attacked all round and appeared in jeopardy, but it regained its *moral* on Picton's timely, steadying shout, ' Twenty-eighth, Remember Egypt ! '

At the same time, Pack's Brigade was tested in a similar fashion and came out of the ordeal as favourably. Piré's victorious Lancers, galloping after the retreating Brunswickers, suddenly caught sight of the red-coats near the road-junction. This acted on them much in the same way as the sight of a red rag infuriates a bull, they turned, and charged Pack's right. The 42nd, caught reforming square, were partly broken by a furious rush ; but the men closed in, and bayonets and lances clashed in a hideous *mêlée*, in which the infantry were victorious. The 2/44th, on the left of the 42nd, most gallantly withstood a very unexpected trial. The officer commanding the 2/44th considered there was no time to form square. As the Lancers dashed round and came against his rear, he turned the rear-rank about ; then, as the horsemen closed, the men poured in a smashing volley which emptied many saddles. Some of the Lancers then attempted to seize the flag of the 44th, but, foiled in this, they drew off pursued by a dropping fire as they retired towards the French line. The feat of withstanding this onslaught in line and with the rear-rank faced about redounds greatly to the credit of the undaunted 2/44th. The battalion can look back with pride to that stubborn fight.

Whilst the British Infantry was repelling Piré's onslaught, one of his regiments of Lancers dashed through to the Namur road and cut to pieces a Hanoverian battalion. Fortunately, however, more reinforcements came streaming up to Wellington's battlefield. The new-comers included the Nassau Contingent, as well as Sir C. Halkett's (British) and Count Kielmansegge's (Hanoverian) Brigades of Alten's (3rd) Division, and Lloyd's Field Brigade, R.A., and Cleeves's K.G.L. Battery (12 guns in all). At 5 p.m., with the arrival of this force, the numerical advantage passed over to Wellington. The Duke now had 26,000 men and 42 guns to withstand Ney's 22,000 and 42 guns. At once the Marshal's task became really difficult. At this crisis, even a slip might mar the Emperor's offensive against Blücher.

The Duke sent Kielmansegge's Brigade to form on the extreme left, but he retained Halkett's Brigade close to Quatre Bras. This reinforcement for the centre was timely. Pack's ammunition was running low, and had support not been available he must have abandoned his position. Halkett ordered the 69th Regiment to support Pack and the remainder to rally the Brunswickers. Lloyd's Field Brigade of six 9-pdrs. came into action on an open space between the Brussels road and the Bossu Wood. After suffering severely from the heavy fire of two French batteries, Lloyd's guns gradually gained the mastery and silenced their opponents. Finding that the position of his Field Brigade was too exposed, Lloyd withdrew it, temporarily abandoning 2 guns which he recovered at the close of the day's fighting.

Naturally Ney expected D'Erlon's arrival, but the Marshal was destined to be disappointed. After concentrating the I Corps at Jumet, D'Erlon waited for Reille's advance. About 11 a.m. Reille warned D'Erlon that the I Corps must be prepared to follow the II Corps as soon as the latter moved forward. Shortly after midday D'Erlon received Ney's order to advance to Frasnes ; but he could not move until the II Corps had defiled and, delayed by Jérôme's dilatoriness in taking his place in the marching column, it was nearly 2 p.m. when D'Erlon passed through Gosselies. Another delay then occurred. False intelligence, about the presence of some Anglo-Dutch troops on his left flank, caused D'Erlon to halt at Gosselies whilst he reconnoitred towards the north-west. Having at last discovered that his outer flank was not menaced, D'Erlon again moved on. It was after 4 p.m., however, when the I Corps approached Frasnes. At this time the centre of the I Corps was abreast of the junction of the Roman road and the Charleroi–Brussels highway.

General Count de la Bédoyère, one of the General Aides-de-Camp of the Emperor, reached the head of the marching column as it drew near to Frasnes. D'Erlon had ridden forward to reconnoitre the battlefield before the I Corps arrived ; and, in the absence of the Corps Commander, de la Bédoyère, as he passed the head of the column, ordered the I Corps to move eastward at once. Unfortunately the direction was a blunder, because the I Corps, on arrival on the Emperor's battlefield, would merely prolong the French left and not deploy behind Blücher's right flank as Napoleon desired.

Whilst D'Erlon was talking to the Generals of the Guard Cavalry near Frasnes, de la Bédoyère joined them ; and the A.D.C. showed D'Erlon a note, written in pencil, which he was taking to Marshal Ney. The note ordered the Marshal to send D'Erlon's Corps to Ligny ; and de la Bédoyère informed D'Erlon that he had already swung the head of the Corps in the required direction, and he told D'Erlon where he would be likely to overtake his Corps. Filled with misgivings, D'Erlon sent his Chief of the Staff (General Delcambre) to Ney, to apprise the Marshal fully of what had occurred. Then with a heavy heart D'Erlon set out to rejoin his Corps.

How had it happened that direct orders from the Emperor had been given to the I Corps ? No trace of this ' pencil note ' exists, nor is this note recorded in Soult's register. It did exist, however, on the 16th, since it was shown, certainly to D'Erlon and possibly to Ney. It was left, however, in no one's hands. Is it not probable that it was a fabrication ? The General A.D.C., bearing a duplicate of one of the earlier authentic orders and being fully conversant with the Emperor's plan and the situation at Ligny, overtook the I Corps. Here, and available, was the needed reinforcement ; but it marched north and not eastward. How could he turn it ? Two lines scrawled in pencil and substituted for the duplicate which he carried, and the curt command : ' Order of the Emperor ' ; and the deed was done. He risked all to gain all. But D'Erlon's fruitless counter-march and Napoleon's failure to destroy Blücher at Ligny were directly due to this thoughtless, but well-intentioned, fabrication. The swift over-throw of the Empire and de la Bédoyère's execution on the 19th August probably explain why this ' pencil note ' was not detected as a fabrication.

From this audacious act sprang all the subsequent troubles and failures on this critical day. The Emperor, never expecting the arrival of the I Corps at so early an hour or that it would debouch on the prolongation of his left, considered Ney had made some mistake. Ney, furious at the withdrawal of the I Corps at the moment when he had counted on its intervention at Quatre Bras, thought the Emperor was responsible for weakening the Left Wing just as the Marshal was preparing to smash Wellington. The bearer of the note would have given the Marshal this impression when he said : ' Order of the Emperor.'

Somewhat earlier, as he feared that Ney, who commanded nearly half the Army, might remain on the defensive for the rest of the day, the Emperor had called up Colonel Forbin-Janson (who was about to carry the original of the 3.15 p.m. order) and told him to ride rapidly to Quatre Bras and order Ney to seize and hold the cross-roads. He was to inform the Marshal that all was going well at Ligny, and in Ney's hands lay ' the Fate of France '. On receiving this verbal message, Ney said to Forbin-Janson : ' Tell the Emperor what you have seen. I am opposed by the whole of Wellington's Army. I will hold on where I am ; but, as D'Erlon has not arrived, I cannot promise any more.' Forbin-Janson returned to the Emperor ; but Napoleon interrupted the report, and, shrugging his shoulders, said : ' The Marshal does not know what he is talking about. I am fighting the whole Prussian Army, Ney's affair is only with Wellington's Advanced Guard. Go back at once and tell him he is at any cost to over-throw all opposition and to seize Quatre Bras. Tell him the Fate of France lies in his hands.' Napoleon said nothing to Forbin-Janson about having issued orders to D'Erlon to march to Ligny, obviously he still knew nothing about it ; but his orders to Ney were definite so far as they went. Forbin-Janson set off again with this fresh message, but it was very late when he arrived.

It was about 5.15 p.m. when General Delcambre reported to Marshal Ney that D'Erlon's Corps had been moved towards the Emperor. At this very moment Ney was anxiously awaiting the arrival of the I Corps to drive back Wellington, prior to swinging eastward with his whole force so as to ensure Blücher's destruction at Ligny. Ney realized immediately that it was hopeless to think of mastering Quatre Bras, indeed he would need all his skill to contain the hostile forces which were rapidly gathering along his front. Unfortunately the Marshal did not appreciate that matters were still advantageous, so long as D'Erlon was allowed to continue his eastward march and Ney with the rest of the Left Wing held Wellington fast at Quatre Bras, thus preventing the Duke from sending any troops to Blücher's help on the 16th.

In a crisis how rare is it for a subordinate to keep the essential steadily in front of him. Ney, worried by Forbin-Janson's message, saying the ' Fate of France ' lay in the Marshal's hands, and maddened by Delcambre's report, abruptly told Delcambre to return to the I Corps and order D'Erlon to march back at speed to Quatre Bras. In his rage Ney could not have reflected that D'Erlon could not possibly regain Frasnes before nightfall, and only on the Right Wing could the I Corps come into action.

Almost immediately after Ney had decided to recall D'Erlon's Corps, Colonel Laurent arrived and delivered the duplicate of Soult's despatch, timed 3.15 p.m., which ordered Ney to manœuvre so that he could be sure of enveloping Blücher's right and striking the Prussian rear. The severe nature of the fight at Ligny was mentioned, and the Marshal again learned, this time in writing, that the ' Fate of France ' lay in his hands. Ney, however, did not attempt to modify the peremptory order of recall which he had just despatched to D'Erlon.

This 3.15 p.m. order was not intended to be read by itself as it was merely a continuation of the previous correspondence. The Emperor in his original letter to Marshal Ney stated that he would strive to gain a decision on one flank, but not on both at the same time ; and he would reduce the strength of one Wing so as to augment his Reserve and thus compel the decision on the selected flank. Ney should have read this 3.15 p.m. order in this light. It implied clearly enough that, on the 16th, the essential was to crush and destroy Blücher. For this task half of Ney's force would be ample. Since Ney realized that he could not beat Wellington, he should have made sure of neutralizing all the troops which Wellington concentrated at Quatre Bras on the 16th, and meanwhile have allowed D'Erlon to proceed to the Emperor's battle-field. A French victory on the right flank would relieve Ney of any inconvenient pressure, supposing Wellington did gain the upper hand by nightfall. But, inasmuch as the ' Fate of France ' was in the balance, Napoleon might have taken the precaution of indicating the *rôle* Ney was to play, and laid down precisely the general lines of procedure to be followed. As it was, Soult in labouring to be brief became obscure. This gave Fortune a chance to stab Napoleon in the back.

At 5.30 p.m. D'Erlon received Ney's order of recall. The General promptly ordered his Corps to wheel about and march back to Quatre Bras, although, after an hour's easterly march, the I Corps had reached the edge of the Ligny battle-field. The question may fairly be asked why D'Erlon who, earlier in the day, had rightly gone forward to reconnoitre a forming-up place for his Corps at Quatre Bras, did not send on ahead two responsible staff-officers : the senior to warn the Emperor of the approach of the I Corps and to receive his order for its employment, and the other officer to warn the French left of the approach of a friendly column. For some reason, however, these precautions were not taken. In such an obscure situation D'Erlon himself naturally could not leave his Corps. Even so on receiving Ney's order of recall, D'Erlon, a very experienced officer, might surely have weighed up the probability of counter-marching the I Corps and reaching Quatre Bras in time to be of use on the 16th. It was highly improbable that he could do so, but he was well placed to co-operate at Ligny. In the circumstances, despite Ney's order of recall, as a decisive success on the Right Wing must overweigh and annul any temporary set-back on the Left Wing, D'Erlon, would have acted wisely to report his arrival to the Emperor, and, in anticipation of orders, form up his Corps to deal Blücher his death-blow.

D'Erlon decided otherwise. But, to fill the gap between the two Wings, he left behind Durutte's Division and three regiments of Jacquinot's Cavalry with the divisional horse battery. Unhappily he gave Durutte the paralysing order to ' be prudent ', instead of ordering him to report personally to the Emperor and inform Napoleon of what had happened. This was not done. Only after reiterated orders from the Emperor did Durutte tamely engage his force and crawl forward as far as Wagnelée, although he was well placed to strike the retreating Prussians a telling blow. In a crisis ' True wisdom lies in energetic resolution '.

To return to Quatre Bras.

Ney was uneasy. Haunted by Napoleon's repeated admonition, ' the Fate of France is in your hands ', the Marshal determined to force a decision with his heavy cavalry and back the blow with his whole available force. In this way he might carry Quatre Bras, drive back Wellington, be free to go to the Emperor's aid in the thick of the fight at Ligny, and complete the decisive manœuvre planned for the 16th. Consequently the Marshal ordered Kellermann to bring up from Frasnes Guiton's Brigade of Cuirassiers (8th and 11th Cuirassiers) of Lhéritier's Division.

Ney met Kellermann as soon as the General arrived at the head of his two regiments, and the Marshal pointed out the plateau in front of Quatre Bras, on which the thin lines of Wellington's infantry loomed like a long red wall barring the way to Brussels and standing between the Marshal and his desires. Turning to Kellermann, Ney said : ' General, a supreme effort is necessary. That mass of hostile infantry must be overthrown. The Fate of France is in your hands. Take your cavalry and ride them down. I will support you with all the cavalry I have.'

No task on the battle-field could daunt the bold heart of Kellermann ; but now he must have mistrusted his ears. He was ordered to lead his Brigade against a force of all arms over 20,000 strong, holding a fairly dominant position and ready to receive a charge, and well leavened by the obstinate British infantry. That it was to be a death-ride mattered nothing to Kellermann, but he felt bound to make certain that the Marshal was in earnest before he led his Brigade to its destruction. He pointed out the real nature of the task and that he had only one brigade present out of his four. Ney angrily rejoined, finishing up the outburst with the stinging words : ' Go, I tell you ! Go on ! ' (' *Partez ! Mais partez donc !* ') Kellermann could only obey ; but Ney's last words had infuriated him. Never waiting for the Marshal to make the necessary arrangements to support him with Piré's squadrons, Kellermann returned to his Cuirassiers and at once led them forward at a sharp trot up the southern slope of the plateau on which the British stood. On reaching the crest of the ridge (south of Quatre Bras) the ' Gallop ' and the ' Charge ' rang out almost together, and the Cuirassiers spurred at full speed against Halkett's Brigade. Kellermann stated afterwards in his written report to Ney, ' I used great speed so as to prevent my men shirking, or even perceiving the full extent of the danger which confronted them.' Amid a shower of turf-clods this blaze of steel swept down on the devoted infantry like a whirlwind, gathering pace and energy as it went. Ahead of all rode the dauntless Kellermann.

The high rye prevented Halkett's Infantry from seeing much of the French movements, or even realizing, until the last moment, that Kellermann and his Cuirassiers were advancing to charge. The 30th and 33rd promptly formed square. Whilst the 69th were doing so (they had been warned by the Brigadier that a French cavalry charge was impending) the Prince of Orange rode up, and remarking that there was no chance of cavalry appearing he ordered the battalion to deploy into line. Hardly had this order been carried out when Kellermann and his Cuirassiers suddenly appeared and closed with the 69th. The regiment stood firm, showed a fine front, and reserved their fire until the cavalry reached point-blank range. The 8th Cuirassiers were within 30 yards of the 69th when the volley rang out. An avalanche cannot be stopped in full career by stones discharged from a catapult, nor could the fire of the British line stop the galloping French horsemen. The Cuirassiers swept on through the hail of bullets, burst through the ranks, and seized the King's Colour of the 69th Regiment.[1]

The 30th, in square, were subjected to a like test which they were in far better case to resist. The Cuirassiers dashed against the 30th ; but the square beat off all attacks and the waves of horsemen lapped the firm, unyielding sides which they could not throw down. The 33rd was unfortunate. This square was on rising ground and formed a prominent mark. French guns opened on it at short range and inflicted fearful loss, and the regiment had to be deployed and moved to a more sheltered position. It had been tried too high, and it rushed in disorder into the Bossu Wood and was reformed there. By this time the Cuirassiers themselves were out of hand. They swept on in their

---

[1] In 1909 Captain J. W. G. P. Jeffcock, (late) 6th (Inniskilling) Dragoons, saw the King's Colour of the 69th Regt. for sale for 600 francs at Azay le Rideau. Captain Jeffcock bought the flag.

mad career, sabreing all whom they passed, until they reached
the houses of Quatre Bras.

Kellermann had achieved a wonderful performance. His two
regiments of Cuirassiers had torn a bloody breach in the centre of
Wellington's battle-line. The situation was as follows : To the
east of the Brussels–Charleroi highway, Picton's troops maintained
their ground ; farther off, Bachelu's Infantry was working forward
towards the Namur high-road. In the centre, on the Brussels
road, Kellermann's breathless Cuirassiers had reached Quatre
Bras. To the west of the high road Jérôme's Division was
fighting in the Bossu Wood, wresting it step by step from its
defenders, and had almost reached the Nivelles road.

Fortunately for the Duke a welcome diversion occurred.
Kühlmann's Horse Artillery Troop, of the King's German Legion
(attached to Cooke's Division), had hastened forward and reached
the field in time to unlimber in front of Quatre Bras and open
fire on the Cuirassiers, who were still carrying all before them.
Two guns came into action on some rising ground close to the
cross-roads, behind the Lüneburg (Landwehr) Battalion who
were lining a ditch. When the French horsemen were a few
paces away the 2 guns poured in salvos of round-shot and grape.
This close range fire strewed the ground with dead and wounded
and went far towards stopping Kellermann's victorious thrust.

The gallant horsemen who carried out this death-ride had not
been supported. Kellermann had launched his Cuirassiers before adequate arrangements to back the blow could be made by
Marshal Ney. Ney, still boiling with rage at the D'Erlon incident, did not manage this supreme effort with his usual masterly
skill. Since he had determined to throw for complete success at
Quatre Bras, before turning eastward, he would have been justified in using the Light Horse of the Guard (still halted at Frasnes)
to compel the decision. These troops, however, were out of
sight and it is probable that, in his anger, Ney overlooked them.

In the existing circumstances no small cavalry force, however
boldly handled, could expect to achieve a permanent success ; and
close support had to be given to Kellermann before the Allied
Infantry could be rallied and reformed. Ney should have
arranged to follow up Kellermann's charge with a mass of infantry,
who would drive back the Allied infantry over whom this furious
cavalry storm had just burst, and then capture the exposed

batteries and fasten with an iron grip on that part of the position which his cavalry had broken through. Some French horse batteries, held ' like greyhounds on the leash ', should have been slipped when the Allied line was pierced and sent to the front at full speed to open on the Allied infantry a heavy, devastating fire at short range, and clinch the victory.

Kellermann's Cuirassiers, having driven a way into the heart of Wellington's position, found themselves reduced to half their strength, broken by their furious ride, and with their chargers out of breath. At this supreme moment the promised support was only just advancing and the critical period for Wellington had passed.

Moreover Kellermann's regiments, subjected to heavy artillery and infantry fire from all sides, were suffering heavy casualties. Then Kellermann's horse was shot and fell on top of the General. This was the signal for a wild rush back to the French lines. Kellermann scrambled to his feet and vainly tried to rally his men, but they were out of hand. Facing about, the mob galloped back the way they had come. Notwithstanding, they were a dangerous mob. They burst a way to safety through a perfect hail of bullets, carrying with them the flag of the 69th, which ' extraordinarily disappeared '. By now the Cuirassiers were quite out of control. Colliding with Foy's advance, they got entangled with the infantry and hustled it rearward, and their wild career was only stopped by the Light Horse of the Guard at Frasnes. Not until then was order gradually re-established.

Bachelu, from afar, saw the confusion on the French left and halted. Piré alone pressed on and dashed against Kempt's Brigade. The British formed square to receive the horsemen and opposed them with a murderous flank fire, and Piré's Lancers and Chasseurs drew off, baffled.

This dramatic episode was over by 6.30 p.m. ; and at this moment Major Baudus arrived from Napoleon with explicit orders. Ney was told, whatever his situation might be, he was to allow the I Corps to co-operate at Ligny. This was imperative and urgent. Baudus' message made clear, but too late, that whatever happened on the Left Wing mattered nothing, as at all costs the Emperor intended on this day to settle matters with Blücher, this alone was the essential. It would suffice, there-fore, if Ney contained Wellington, so long as D'Erlon was left free to bring his Corps to join in the Emperor's decisive battle at

Ligny. Ney, however, was still excited and he refused to pay serious attention to the order which Baudus carried, though he did make clear to Baudus that he had recalled D'Erlon and ordered him to march back to Frasnes. Baudus' remonstrances were in vain. The Marshal refused to reconsider his decision, and the discussion was abruptly terminated by Ney rushing off on foot into the midst of Foy's disorganized battalions. Ney rallied the infantry and led it against Pack's Brigade, which was advancing. Unhappily the Marshal had become a mere *Sergent de bataille*. Fighting like a grenadier, he courted a soldier's death so as to end all his embarrassments and perplexities.

Sketch D.—Whilst Ney was rallying his men, fresh reinforcements were pouring in for Wellington. Brunswick's guns reached the field from Brussels, and Cooke's Division of the British Guards (Maitland's and Byng's Brigades) came marching up along the Nivelles road from Enghien, more than 20 miles away. These fresh troops brought Wellington's force up to 36,000 men and 70 guns. The Duke was now too strong to be denied and he took the offensive along the whole line. He intended to drive back Ney and establish himself in position to the south of the Namur–Nivelles road, then early on the morrow he could assist Blücher, if the Prussians had succeeded in holding off Napoleon on the 16th. The sounds of heavy firing at Ligny showed that the battle was still fiercely contested.

To carry out the Duke's project, Maitland's and Byng's Brigades were launched into the Bossu Wood and they pressed forward with a cheer. Halkett's and Pack's Brigades, supported by Brunswickers and Nassauers, advanced against Gémioncourt astride the Brussels highway. At the same time Kempt's Brigade, with the Hanoverians and Kielmansegge's Brigade, converged on Piraumont. The French fought sternly. Gradually, however, weight of numbers told and Ney's Wing was pushed back. For more than an hour the incessant rattle of musketry indicated the grim nature of the fight for the Bossu Wood. At last the British Guards drove Jérôme out of its friendly shelter, just as Foy was rallying his exhausted men around Gémioncourt and Bachelu, after a fierce fight, had been driven from Piraumont.

It was past 8 p.m. when one of Maitland's battalions broke out from the southern border of the Bossu Wood and advanced to storm Pierrepont. Woods, never very difficult to get into, are proverbially hard to get out of. As the Guards attempted to make ground to the southward they were pounded in their advance by Foy's divisional artillery, and Piré slipped his tireless Lancers at them and pushed them back into the wood. Owing to the confusion and the fire of the French guns, it was not possible for the Guards to form square to resist the cavalry. Having regained the shelter of the wood, the Guards extended along its edge and beat off the horsemen with a heavy and destructive fire. Then the same scene was re-enacted ; but on this occasion the withdrawal of the Guards into the wood was partly covered by some Brunswick infantry. Simultaneously the French gained their last success, when the 7th Cuirassiers charged and routed a Dutch-Belgian battalion close to Pierrepont. Before the day closed the French were pressed back ; and, although some troops clung to Gémioncourt, Ney's main line withdrew towards Frasnes.

Wellington hoped that the two Allied Armies would assume the offensive on the next day, consequently it was a question whether the assault of Gémioncourt should be postponed until the morrow, or whether it should be stormed forthwith. Everything was in favour of an immediate assault, particularly as the French were dispirited. If the attack was postponed the farm would be strengthened during the night, and the storm might be a more costly operation. The Duke therefore ordered the assault, and the farm fell after a feeble resistance.

By 9 p.m. the struggle was over. Once more the Duke of Wellington had triumphed over a Marshal of France. Possibly the juster view, from the purely tactical standpoint, is to look on the affair as an inconclusive one, since darkness had stopped the fight before the French had been driven from their morning positions. The value, however, of Ney's achievement must not be judged solely by its tactical merits. Ney had been placed in command of an important detachment and his duty was to neutralize Wellington's force. When necessary the Marshal was to detach a large portion of his Wing to co-operate on the decisive field at the critical time ; he was never intended to gain a great victory. Judged by this standard, Ney had justified his detachment, so far as containing Wellington at Quatre Bras was concerned. He had neutralized very superior hostile forces and he had prevented the Duke from giving any assistance to Blücher in his hour of need. Had Ney failed in this duty, Ligny would hardly have been the great French victory that it was, and the campaign would probably have come to an end on the 16th. As matters had turned out no evil results did or could possibly spring from Ney's repulse. Wellington had advanced to the southward of the cross-roads, consequently the Duke was better placed, than at the opening of the fight, to be dealt a death-blow by Napoleon's Reserve on the 17th.

The evils which had arisen were the result of very different causes. Trouble sprang from Marshal Ney's late advance and his hesitation to open the action. Even more important and far-reaching were his misappreciation of the strategic situation and of the secondary rôle which he was intended to perform. These grievous shortcomings can all be traced to the orders which he received on the 16th not being definite and explicit enough on the essential points. These faulty orders were responsible for Ney's failure in the all-important duty of co-operation at Ligny. The Marshal never appreciated the real significance of Napoleon's plan until it was too late. Further, as a result of de la Bédoyère's ' pencil note ' and Marshal Ney's ill-judged counter-order to D'Erlon, half of the French Left Wing oscillated between the Action of Quatre Bras and the Battle of Ligny and ended by taking part in neither. Had the I Corps been thrown into the wavering balance at Quatre Bras, Wellington would have been overpowered. Had D'Erlon's Corps been allowed to engage in the Battle of Ligny, Blücher would have been destroyed. As it was D'Erlon's Corps was wasted on the first critical day of the campaign. At 9 p.m., after the decision at Quatre Bras had been reached, the I Corps marched into Frasnes, dejected and disappointed at not having been employed on this eventful day. D'Erlon then relieved Reille on the outpost line.

The French bivouacked in front of Frasnes and the Anglo-Dutch between Pierrepont and Piraumont, with Wellington's head-quarters at Genappe ; but spasmodic firing went on for some time by moonlight.

Both sides had suffered severely and the thickly strewn battlefield bore eloquent testimony to the bitter nature of the fight. The French lost about 4,000 men and the Allies about 4,800, including about 2,400 British casualties.

Wellington's artillery, although inferior in numbers, had been well placed, well handled, and well fought at Quatre Bras. ' It had performed its duty.' It had supported the other arms, beaten off the enemy's attacks by fire, prepared the foe for the final assault, and assisted its infantry to conquer by increasing its fire whenever the infantry met with any obstacle, or were engaged too heavily.

It cannot be overlooked that by the end of the day the Duke had only concentrated at Quatre Bras about one-half of his infantry, one-third of his artillery, and one-seventh of his cavalry. No British cavalry or British horse artillery took part in the fighting on the 16th ; though, as an artillery officer remarked, ' Had we had a couple of brigades of British cavalry, we should have gained a decided advantage.'

Wellington's troops, who had not been actively engaged at Quatre Bras on the 16th, halted that night as follows :

Sketch D.—Colville's (4th) Division at Braine-le-Comte ;
Clinton's (2nd) Division, and
Chassé's 1st Dutch-Belgian Division, at Nivelles ; and Prince Frederick, with Stedman's Dutch-Belgian Division and Anthing's Dutch-Indian Brigade, at Enghien.

The cavalry and horse artillery reached Quatre Bras during the night ; and by the morning of the 17th Wellington had concentrated a large force. The Duke's position would now have been quite satisfactory if it had not been twenty-four hours too late, and had Blücher not already suffered a heavy defeat at Ligny and uncovered the left flank of the Anglo-Dutch Army.

At the Duke's head-quarters the situation at Ligny was still obscure, even at 9 p.m. Müffling heard after dark that a Prussian officer had been wounded and unhorsed on the Namur highway, and the officer had said that he was charged with a message for General von Müffling. (This officer, Major Winterfeldt, was the bearer of the news of the result of Ligny.) But Müffling took no steps to unravel the matter, which he considered ' somewhat confused '. During the night nothing further was heard from the Prussians, and Müffling thought the French skirmishers had probably rendered the Namur highway too insecure for the passage of messengers. The distance (7 miles), the smoke, the dim light, and the restricted view which the Duke had of Blücher's battle-field, made it impossible for Wellington to follow and appreciate (from personal observation) the various phases of the bitter battle at Ligny. Although Wellington might have been able to distinguish the dim outline of some of the Prussian masses, yet the picture which he could obtain was too blurred and confused for it to be of any great value to him, in arriving at any conclusion about the fate of the day on the Allied Left. Naturally, therefore, the Duke awaited a report from Blücher with some impatience and anxiety.

At 10 p.m., when Quatre Bras was over, Ney wrote a brief report to Marshal Soult,[1] minimizing the result and making no mention of his recall order to D'Erlon, but stating definitely that everyone had done his duty except the I Corps. Whilst Ney was at supper Colonel Forbin-Janson reported to him for the second time that day. The second verbal order which he bore had obviously ceased to be appropriate, so Forbin-Janson handed to the Marshal the original copy of the 3.15 p.m. order ! Forbin-Janson had been entrusted with (and never delivered) this order when he carried for the Emperor the first verbal message to Marshal Ney. Colonel Forbin-Janson's was a casual and haphazard performance.

Had Ney mastered Quatre Bras at an early hour on the 16th and taken up a good position covering the cross-roads and the Namur highway, the Marshal, with Reille and Piré, could have held off until dark any force which the Duke could possibly engage. In this case Wellington might easily have been imposed upon and have taken the whole day to effect a safe concentration out of striking distance. When he heard the firing near Fleurus, Ney would have detached D'Erlon and Kellermann to move down the Namur road with orders to smash into Blücher's right rear at Ligny. If this had happened, Blücher's destruction would have been assured. Even by acting boldly Ney ran no very great risk ; and there was a chance of obtaining a great success, in the event of the Allies attempting a forward concentration. Despite his repulse Ney had attracted and held Wellington, and he was well placed to perform the same office on the morrow until such time as Napoleon could come up and co-operate on the Left Wing. In accordance with the general plan, outlined in the Flahault letter, Ney's duty at daybreak on the 17th was to attack the Anglo-Dutch Army promptly and so vigorously that it became ' a fixed point ', around which the Emperor could then manœuvre and deal Wellington his death-blow.

[1] Given in Appendix II, No. 4.

CHAPTER IX

THE BATTLE OF LIGNY

THE BATTLEFIELD ; AND PRELIMINARY DISPOSITIONS
(Map 3)

In one and a quarter centuries the French three times gained a victory near Fleurus over troops of the German powers. The scene of these triumphs, like the field of Quatre Bras, lies on the watershed which divides the basins of the Meuse and Schelde.

Map 3.—The battlefield of Ligny, the last of the three French victories, is traversed by numerous streams. The principal one, the Ligny, winds across the field past the villages of St. Amand, Ligny, Sombreffe, Tongrinelle, Boignée, and Balâtre, until to the south of Mazy it joins the Orneau (a tributary of the Sambre). Although not more than 10 feet broad near Ligny village, the marshy banks of the Ligny gave considerable value to the bridges at St. Amand, Ligny, and Tongrinelle ; and between St. Amand and Sombreffe the right bank commanded the left, favouring the powerful French artillery. In the hamlet of St. Amand la Haye the houses clustered round the solid buildings of an old farm ; and well-built farmhouses, surrounded by strong enclosures and outbuildings, became small fortresses with loopholed walls. The houses in the villages were also suitable for defence. But the numerous forest and fruit trees gave the villages the appearance of a dense wood, and houses, placed in the middle of orchards, were discerned with difficulty. Much of the remainder of the battle-field was under cultivation, and the rye was 4 feet high.

Just to the east of Sombreffe the Namur–Nivelles road and the Charleroi–Gembloux road crossed. The continuation of the latter from Tongrinelle was merely a branch leading to the hamlet of Point-du-Jour, and only a field-road ran on to Gembloux. A Roman road (sometimes called the Brünhild Way) ran north-eastward past the west of the battle-field, cutting obliquely across the Namur road at Trois Burettes, and then ran on past Gembloux to Liége. The field-roads to Wavre joined at Mt. St. Guibert. The windmill at Bry was situated on a knoll to the south-west of the highest ground on the battlefield, and Blücher's head-quarters were near this mill. Its top was probably the highest object on the Prussian right flank, and during the battle Prussian officers climbed to the top to see if any reinforcements were coming from Wellington. Even from the upper part of the mill, however, only the higher parts of the battle-field of Quatre Bras could have been visible, and we do not know what belts of trees may have been in existence in 1815. In any case, the whole of the Quatre Bras battle-field was not visible. Owing to the distance, the smoke and the bad light at the end of the day, only a most confused view of what occurred at Quatre Bras could have been obtained by Prussian officers reconnoitring from the top of Bry Mill.

Bry Windmill no longer exists, but the Naveau Windmill is still standing to the north of Fleurus, near the Gembloux road. Napoleon used this latter mill as his observatory. From its summit he made his preliminary reconnaissance of the Prussian Army and the ground on which he was about to engage, and attached to his staff, as a guide, he had Simon of Fleurus, a local surveyor. From the Naveau Mill the Emperor was able to keep the whole battle in view and to control his general reserve when the time was ripe for the decisive stroke.

PRELIMINARY DISPOSITIONS

Map 3.—After Wellington's departure, Blücher, observing the French deployment, moved forward part of the II and III Corps to support the I Corps, and his Army then formed up with the I Corps in the front line and the II Corps in Reserve, whilst the III Corps covered the left as well as the roads to Gembloux and Namur.

The I Corps was disposed as follows : Steinmetz's Brigade had three battalions in Bry and six battalions behind St. Amand ; whilst Jägow's Brigade had three battalions in St. Amand and the other six formed a second line to the north of Ligny. In any case village fighting will always lead to great confusion and Zieten's arrangements were likely to accentuate the intermingling of the Prussian Brigades. Ligny was held by four battalions of Henckel's Brigade with two battalions to the north of the village, Pirch II's Brigade (8 battalions) formed a second line between Bry and Ligny, and the Corps Reserve Cavalry formed up behind the 3rd Brigade. The right flank of the line was refused and well placed.

The II Corps, held in General Reserve, formed up in two lines (Brigades side by side) in front of the Namur highway, between Les Trois Burettes and Sombreffe, with the artillery close to its own Brigades. Three heavy batteries unlimbered between Ligny and St. Amand, whilst two heavy batteries and two batteries of horse artillery were kept in reserve near Sombreffe.

Thielemann's four Brigades (III Corps) formed Blücher's left wing. Borcke's Brigade held Sombreffe, Kemphen's Brigade garrisoned Tongrinne, Luck's was between these two, and in reserve to this wing were Stülpnagel's Brigade and Hobe's Cavalry at Point du Jour.

Blücher held a position 7 miles long with only 84,000 men. Probably he had extended his front because he expected Wellington's arrival later in the afternoon, and he had to reach westward as far as he could and cover as much as possible of the Nivelles highway. On the 16th June Blücher's rôle was to retain his position, Wellington's fresh troops would strike the deathblow. Blücher also expected Bülow to arrive and he had to cover the roads by which this large reinforcement would debouch. So, in the circumstances, Blücher's dispositions were reasonable.

The villages of St. Amand and Ligny were regarded as an advanced line, intended to break the force of the French attack, and an offensive return would be delivered against the assailants when they debouched disordered and exhausted from the villages. Wellington, however, considered the villages were rather far to the front. Bry, St. Amand, and Ligny were only within gunshot of the mass of Blücher's reserves and could not be supported by the musketry fire of the Prussian reserve. It was also most unfortunate that the Prussian reserves were carefully arranged so as to act as stop-butts to the enemy's ' overs ', thus preventing any stray French round-shot from being wasted. On the long, upward slopes behind the villages the French projectiles would ricochet into the exposed Prussian masses, consequently the fire of the French batteries was bound to be very destructive. On the other hand the French supports were in many cases out of effective gun-range, and the French reserves, sheltered in hollows, were protected from the Prussian artillery.

All dissimulation was at an end when Blücher deployed. Directly the Prussian reserves formed up on the slopes above the villages, the Emperor recognized at once that he was opposed by the bulk of Blücher's Army. It was no longer needful to think of pushing on to Brussels on the 16th. The first decisive day of the campaign had come and it was essential to take every advantage from so favourable a situation. Blücher, caught in the act of concentrating his Army, must be crushed before more than the heads of Wellington's columns could reach Quatre Bras and become dangerous. The Emperor would have liked to begin at once the task of exterminating the Prussians, but he was bound to wait for the opening of Ney's cannonade, which would inform him that Wellington's Army was held fast at Quatre Bras ; also it was 1 p.m. before Gérard's Corps reached Fleurus. These reasons explain why it was as late as 2.30 p.m. when the battle opened, thus decreasing the time available for Blücher's annihilation.

Whilst the Emperor surveyed the scene he matured and formed his plan of action. He saw that the Prussian front stretched from Bry, through St. Amand and Ligny, to Balâtre, and the Emperor decided to neutralize the Prussian left, and to concentrate all his efforts, and the mass of his troops, on smashing the Prussian centre and right at St. Amand and Ligny. Behind Blücher's right he would call up part of Ney's Wing, and this force would form the anvil on which the sledge of his attacking columns and the mass of the Guard would pound to pieces the Prussian right wing. The plan was perfect. By destroying Blücher's right the Allies would be completely sundered ; and, once the two jaws of the French vice closed, the only line of retreat left to the débris of the Prussians was to the north-eastward. An Allied concentration then became impossible, since Wellington would not be able to keep the field alone for sufficient time to allow Blücher to return. The strategical situation made it imperative for a decision to be obtained at Ligny.

To carry out his plan, Napoleon determined to fix the Prussian Army by a tremendous frontal attack so as to wear down all resistance and force Blücher to engage his reserves. Then, when

Blücher had thrown in his last closed body of troops, the Prussian Army would be a ' fixed point ', around which Napoleon could manœuvre his masses and deal the knock-out blow. Inevitably Blücher's left would become involved and entangled in the rout of his broken centre and right, and the Army, a mere horde of fugitives, would be driven away towards the Meuse. Thus Napoleon planned it. Turning to Gérard he remarked : ' In three hours the fate of the campaign will be decided. If Ney carries out his orders thoroughly, not a gun of this army in front of us will get away.' But Ney—failed. The whole Waterloo Campaign, particularly the French manœuvres of the 16th and 17th June, proved the wisdom of the valiant words spoken by Jeanne d'Arc nearly four centuries earlier : ' *Plutôt maintenant que demain, plutôt demain qu'après.*'

To carry out his attack the Emperor arranged his troops as follows :

Map 3.—On the left was Domon's Cavalry. Then in the first line, destined for the assault of St. Amand, were the infantry Divisions of Lefol and Berthézène, of Vandamme's Corps. Habert's Division (III Corps) and Girard's Division (II Corps) were on the flanks, to act as local reserves to this wing. Vandamme commanded in this part of the field.

Gérard was to attack Ligny, and his Corps (facing westward) was at right-angles to Vandamme. For the storm of Ligny, Gérard deployed the Divisions of Pécheux and Vichéry, keeping Hulot's Division in reserve. Hulot's Division was also available to support the French right, and eventually it was used to assist Grouchy.

Grouchy's two Cavalry Corps (Exelmans and Pajol) were on the extreme French right. They formed up perpendicular to the Fleurus–Tongrinne road and at right-angles to Gérard's right.

In General Reserve, in the valley west of Fleurus, were the Imperial Guard, horse (less Lefebvre-Desnoëttes), foot, and artillery. From this central position not only could the veterans move to the critical point at the decisive moment, but they were also available to cover the gap which existed between Gérard and Vandamme, and take the Prussians in flank if they forced a way in between the III and IV Corps. Also in reserve, formed up on the hillside to the east of Fleurus, were Milhaud's Cuirassiers, a splendid body of steel-clad squadrons, 3,000 strong.

Napoleon's dispositions were suitable and simple. For the separate tasks, separate and appropriate units were assigned. Meanwhile the Emperor kept in hand his choicest troops ; and he reserved for himself the signal for the opening of the action and for the engagement of his General Reserve.

The opposing Armies numbered :

French, 68,000 (including 12,500 horse) and 210 guns (after Lobau's arrival at 7 p.m. the French numbered 78,000 and 242 guns) ;

Prussians, 84,000 (including 8,000 sabres) and 224 guns. But, as he arranged to neutralize Thielemann with Grouchy's Horse, Napoleon could engage 60,000 Frenchmen against the 61,000 Prussians at Ligny and St. Amand.

We may pause here to consider the arrangements which the Emperor made to ensure Ney's co-operation and the rôle which he desired Lobau to play.

The Emperor realized that his 2 p.m. order to Ney might not be pressing enough to make the Marshal turn against the Prussians, and at 3.15 p.m. he ordered Soult to send another and far more urgent despatch to Ney (Soult's register). To stimulate Ney to even greater exertions he sent the Marshal a verbal message by Colonel Forbin-Janson, who was taking the original copy of the 3.15 p.m. order.

Ney could hardly receive this 3.15 p.m. order for more than an hour after the arrival of the 2 p.m. order, and he had already been commanded to seize Quatre Bras. Consequently, when Ney received the 3.15 p.m. despatch he would be heavily engaged with the Anglo-Dutch troops at Quatre Bras. In these circumstances the Marshal might find it more than difficult to discontinue and break off the action, and impossible to move the whole of the Left Wing behind Blücher's right, so as to deal the Prussians their *coup de grâce*. Hence it was essential, in the 3.15 p.m. order, to state very clearly that it was unnecessary for Ney to drive back Wellington's troops ; but he must contain any Allied troops which reached Quatre Bras with the minimum French force, leaving free the greatest possible proportion of the Left Wing to be driven against the right flank and rear of Blücher's Prussians. It was essential to emphasize to Marshal Ney that Wellington's overthrow on the 16th was not of primary importance, and to make certain that Ney did not assign a secondary rôle to the higher duty of co-operation at Ligny. But this detailed explanation of the plan is not to be found in the 3.15 p.m. order, or even in the verbal message entrusted to Forbin-Janson. At this crisis it was the plan, as well as the course to be followed and the desired end, which should have been stated in firm, simple, and direct language, admitting no possibility of doubt and impossible to be misunderstood at this critical time.

The other difficulty (in those pre-electric telegraph days) was the distance which Ney was from Imperial Head-Quarters. It was 7 miles, even by the most direct road from Fleurus (through Mellet) to Frasnes, and it was nearly 5 miles from Frasnes to St. Amand (*via* Villers-Perwin and Wagnelée). Unless Ney could send at once, directly he received the 3.15 p.m. order, his reinforcement would not reach the battle-field of Ligny till darkness fell, and Napoleon's great combination would be of no avail. Probably Napoleon was revolving this problem when he heard from Lobau, at Charleroi, stating that Janin (his assistant chief of the staff who had been sent, on the Emperor's own order, to report on the situation confronting Ney) had just returned, and Janin reported that Ney was opposed by 20,000 men. The Emperor reflected. Faced by such a force as this and handled as it would be by Wellington, Ney might be engaged all day at Quatre Bras ; and the Emperor began to fear that Soult's 3.15 p.m. order was neither clear enough, nor pressing enough, to induce the Marshal to detach a part of his force to assist at Ligny, and to do so before he had mastered Quatre Bras. It was already about 5 p.m., so Napoleon sent off Major Baudus with explicit orders to Marshal Ney that he was to allow the I Corps to co-operate at Ligny. Baudus only reached the Marshal about 6.30 p.m. when (as we have already seen) orders had been sent to the I Corps to return to Quatre Bras, and the plan for the 16th had been ruined. If only the Emperor had made his desires as clear to the Marshal at 8 a.m., instead of at 6.30 p.m., then Blücher's Army would have been annihilated.

Meanwhile, at 3.30 p.m., the Emperor sent an order to Lobau to march at once with the VI Corps to Fleurus (Soult's register). Seeing that Napoleon's plan was to crush Blücher's right, it is strange that Lobau was not directed to form on Vandamme's left. So placed, the VI Corps would have been in a better position to back the decisive blow, connect with any troops

which Ney might detach to co-operate at Ligny, and act in conjunction with them in enveloping and destroying Blücher's right.
Had Lobau come up on the French left, then Lobau's Corps, not
being engaged, would have been free to reconnoitre the oncoming
troops when D'Erlon was first sighted ; and Lobau's men, being
fresh, would have been less liable to panic when the strange
Corps was seen.   If the new-comers were foes, Lobau possessed
just that undaunted and fearless personality which fitted him
admirably for the task of blocking a hostile advance against
Napoleon's left at Ligny.   On the other hand, if the new-comers
were friends, touch would have been established early, connection made between D'Erlon and the Emperor, and all mis-
understandings avoided.   Blücher's destruction would have been
certain.

CHAPTER X

THE BATTLE OF LIGNY

1st PHASE : *LE COMBAT D'USURE* OR PREPARATORY
COMBAT : 2.30 P.M.–5 P.M.

THE FRENCH ATTACK THE VILLAGES

(Map 3)

DIRECTLY Gérard's Corps had taken up its allotted position
and the noise of the action to the westward proclaimed that
Ney had engaged the Anglo-Dutch troops at Quatre Bras, Napoleon decided to begin the battle of Ligny.

The day was insufferably hot and very still. Half-past two
had just been struck by the church clock of St. Amand when a
battery of the Guard, near Fleurus, fired three rounds in quick
succession. As the echoes died away Vandamme launched
Lefol's Division against St. Amand. With bands playing and
colours spread Lefol's Division advanced in three columns
covered by skirmishers. The first round fired from the Prussian
guns against Lefol fell in a company and killed eight men ; but,
undeterred by this grim salute, the French infantry dashed forward. Point-blank discharges of musketry and cannon failed to
stop the rush of the French, and Lefol at the head of his men
forced his way into St. Amand. After fifteen minutes' desperate
fighting the Prussians were driven from the orchards and houses
and had to evacuate the cemetery and the church. Steinmetz sent
forward four of his battalions to support Jägow, and concentrated
the fire of his divisional battery on the place. Once more the
village changed hands.

Vandamme renewed the struggle by deploying Berthézène's
Division on Lefol's left. To support this fresh attack, he directed
Girard's Division to carry the two hamlets of St. Amand. A
long and bitter fight ensued. Once more the village was wrested

from the Prussians who lost nearly 2,500 men in its defence. But Steinmetz was unwilling to admit defeat, he counter-attacked once more, and his endeavour was in part successful, though on this occasion the French succeeded in keeping a foothold in the place.

It was about 4 p.m. when Girard advanced against the two hamlets. He soon mastered them and then Blücher's right was endangered. To readjust the situation Zieten's reserves were called upon, and Pirch's Brigade was directed to retake St. Amand la Haye. A furious fight broke out and the hamlet changed hands four times. In a supreme effort the dauntless Girard received a mortal wound whilst leading on his men. But his loss was speedily avenged by the French and the Prussians were driven from the hamlet.

Meanwhile Blücher moved up Jürgass's Cavalry and Tippelskirch's Brigade to Wagnelée, to attack the French left and make sure of securing the road by which Wellington would debouch. Fortunately Vandamme had previously moved up Berthézène between Lefol and Girard, placed Habert on Girard's left, and Domon and Subervie on the extreme left. Habert's skirmishers, hidden in the corn, surprised Tippelskirch's Brigade whilst in column of route. Disorder broke out. Habert saw his chance, charged the enemy and flung them back into Wagnelée, whilst Domon's horsemen neutralized Jürgass.

Blücher left his observatory to direct the attack in person, and he was within gunshot of St. Amand when Girard's men drove Pirch II headlong from the hamlet. Blücher promptly issued orders for the immediate renewal of the assault by the same troops. The Prussians, inspired by the fiery old Field-Marshal, advanced again to storm the village with the bayonet ; but the gallant defenders, reduced to 2,500, fought to the last party wall, and after that fell back and rallied in ' le Hameau ', leaving the Prussians in possession of La Haye. Battalion after battalion was thrown in and used up against Girard's Division, a testimony to its gallantry and resolute handling. As well as Girard, the Division lost both its brigadiers, and the leadership finally devolved on a regimental commander.

At 5 p.m. the Prussians still held St. Amand, St. Amand la Haye, and Wagnelée, but all their efforts to debouch to the southward of these villages had proved abortive.

A little later than Vandamme Gérard had advanced to storm Ligny, and the fight for this village has become historic. Pécheux, advancing in three columns, at once came under heavy fire from the guns on the high ground above the brook. The two left columns gained the outskirts of the village, but were then driven back by the fire of the garrisons of the houses and the *château*. The right column, however, burst in, then, on reaching the church, it came under fire from all sides. The carnage was fearful. In a little time 20 officers and 500 men fell, the head of the column was crushed, and, falling back in disorder, it reformed in its original position.

Gérard twice more renewed his attack. Twice more he failed. At this juncture Napoleon sent some 12-pounder batteries from the Guard to co-operate with Gérard's artillery. Shortly after the 12-pounders opened fire on the village, the buildings were shattered and numerous fires broke out. Gérard promptly attacked again. This time he supported Pécheux with one of Vichéry's Brigades, and the whole mass advanced against the village. After a house-to-house fight the French succeeded in mastering the upper part of the village, and the Prussians rallied around the church and the cemetery. Pécheux renewed his attack, but his men became disordered by their efforts and were charged by a mass of Prussians. A furious *mêlée* resulted, in which quarter was neither asked nor given. At last victory declared for the French and the disordered Prussians retired over the two bridges, pressed by the victors who flung some of the vanquished into the muddy stream. Reinforcements then reached the Prussians and they again showed front. But the French, spurred on by their previous success, were not to be denied, and two regiments stormed the bridges and drove in the Prussian light troops who were lining the banks of the brook. Then four of Jägow's battalions came up to Henckel's support. The Prussians promptly retook the offensive and drove back the French from the left bank of the stream. Once more a tremendous fight broke out. Only separated by the small stream the two forces engaged in a heavy and murderous musketry duel. Above the roar and rattle of the musketry rose the shrieks and cries of the wounded as they burned to death in the flaming houses. That anyone lived at all must be ascribed to the dense pall of smoke which enshrouded the troops engaged in this terrific struggle in the streets, houses, stables, and gardens of Ligny. At 5 p.m. the fight was raging from Ligny to St. Amand. Over the Ligny brook slowly rose clouds and banks of smoke, until the little stream resembled one of those burning rivers in Hades which Dante has immortalized.

In this furious village fighting Blücher was swiftly worn down. He was compelled to engage reserve after reserve and throw them into the fiery furnaces of the villages, where they just melted away as gold does in a crucible.

*   *   *   *   *   *   *

All this time, on the extreme French right, Grouchy was engaged in neutralizing Thielemann's Corps. By 4 p.m. he had pushed back the Prussians from Boignée, and then Hulot unsuccessfully attacked Tongrinelle. A little later in the battle, Thielemann was ordered to despatch Marwitz's Cavalry Brigade to the Prussian right, where it would come under Jürgass and be ready to connect with Wellington, if the Duke came to his Ally's assistance on that Friday afternoon.

CHAPTER XI

THE BATTLE OF LIGNY

2ND PHASE: D'ERLON APPROACHES THE BATTLE-FIELD
AND THEN WITHDRAWS. BLÜCHER'S COUNTER-ATTACK:
5 P.M.–7.30 P.M.

(Map 3)

SOON after 5 p.m. Blücher decided to make a further effort by engaging the fresh II Corps (Pirch I) which he ordered to move to the south of Bry. Without delay the Emperor made arrangements to meet this new danger. Subervie's Cavalry was already with Domon on the French left, and now the Young Guard and half of the Middle Guard were moved to support Vandamme, and the remainder of the Middle Guard was ordered to assist Gérard. It was at this time Major Baudus was sent to inform Marshal Ney that nothing should be allowed to retard the arrival of D'Erlon's Corps.

Shortly after, at 5.15 p.m., there was a dramatic incident. Vandamme suddenly saw, near Villers-Perwin, a column of all arms, 20,000 strong, and apparently hostile, advancing in the direction of Fleurus (towards the French left rear). Vandamme at once reported the approach of this strange column to the Emperor, and the General added that its effect on the III Corps was so bad that, as a temporary measure, Girard's Division had been drawn back to cover Fleurus. Probably Vandamme had not forgotten his own disaster at Kulm in 1813.

Meanwhile the Emperor had been watching the progress of the battle. About 5.30 p.m., considering that the Prussians were ready for the final stroke, he deemed it would be wise to have his Reserve ready to engage directly D'Erlon arrived from Quatre Bras, probably towards 6.30 p.m. Lobau, however, could not reach Fleurus before 6.30, consequently the Emperor only had available the Old Guard (the ' Invincibles '), the Heavy

Horse of the Guard, and Milhaud's Cuirassiers ; and it was
with these picked troops that he decided to smash in Blücher's
centre directly D'Erlon was in position. This onslaught, delivered in co-operation with D'Erlon, would shatter the two
Corps forming the Prussian right and centre ; and, if the advantage was immediately pushed home, the Corps on the Prussian
left must be involved in the ruin of the other two.

On the French side all was ready, and Napoleon merely waited
for the signal to drive home the blow. That signal would be
the deep-throated roar of D'Erlon's guns booming the Prussian
death-knell. Caught between D'Erlon's murderous fire and the
deadly steel of Vandamme, Gérard, and the Guard, not a Prussian
would escape, not a gun would get away.

Napoleon was still thinking of this final combination, when an
orderly officer rode up from Vandamme and reported that the
French left was threatened by a hostile column, 20,000 strong,
advancing from the westward ; and disorder was showing itself
in some of Vandamme's battalions. The Emperor paused. He
was undoubtedly perplexed to account for these troops who had
come into sight so inopportunely. He did not expect D'Erlon's
Corps to appear from this direction, nor would the I Corps reach
the Ligny battle-field for at least another hour. This column,
therefore, could not be D'Erlon's Corps.

Undoubtedly if Napoleon had sent the ' pencil note ', the
Emperor would have answered Vandamme's orderly officer somewhat as follows : ' Tell your General from me there is no cause
for uneasiness. The strange column is D'Erlon's Corps. I
ordered it to co-operate at Ligny.' Inasmuch as Napoleon did
not answer in this way, it is strong presumptive proof that he
knew nothing of the ' pencil note ' ; and, as Soult's register
ignores its existence, it was probably fabricated by de la Bédoyère.
Consequently Napoleon's state of mind when he first heard of the
arrival of the strange Corps was, in the circumstances, quite
natural.

This column was certainly not the division which Ney had been
directed to push out to Marbais to connect the two Wings, since
no division in the *Armée du Nord* numbered 20,000 men. Nor had
General de la Bédoyère rejoined Imperial Head-Quarters at
5.30 p.m., or he would have exclaimed : ' It is D'Erlon. I
overtook the I Corps near Frasnes and headed it at once for St.

Amand.' Nor could de la Bédoyère have returned to Fleurus before General Dejean came back (after having identified the column), because until Dejean's return Napoleon did not realize that the new-comers were D'Erlon's Corps.

Be all that as it may, Napoleon decided at once that Vandamme must be supported, the final manœuvre must be postponed, and the approaching Corps must be reconnoitred so that its nationality and intentions could be penetrated. By that time Lobau and the VI Corps should have arrived and the Emperor could then decide on his further plan of action. Meanwhile the reinforcements, already moving to Vandamme, would serve to rally the French left until the situation became less obscure. To reconnoitre the hostile column, Napoleon sent off General Dejean. But the Emperor did not entrust the General with any orders for D'Erlon, should the column turn out to be the I Corps. The Emperor could hardly be expected to solve the identity of this body of troops by deduction, and certainly he could not do so by knowledge. Knowledge never entered into this matter at all, it was a case for intuition, inspiration, or penetration. A sudden flash of genius might have given the solution to Napoleon. By no possibility could it be deduced by his unaided reason from the facts known to him at 5.30 p.m. The identity of the column was of first importance at the moment, and General Dejean was only directed to reconnoitre it. It is by no means certain that Dejean went right up to D'Erlon. Naturally, knowing the uneasy state of the Emperor's mind, Dejean would have executed his task as rapidly as possible. Having galloped near enough to the Corps to ascertain its identity, he would have returned at speed to report to the Emperor that the column was D'Erlon's Corps.

It was 6.30 p.m. before the Emperor learned this reassuring piece of news. Even then he was unaware that D'Erlon had counter-marched, and, still believing that the I Corps was coming up to take a hand in the battle, Napoleon sent orders to D'Erlon to move through Wagnelée and attack the Prussians. But the aide-de-camp bearing these orders found only Durutte's Division, which had been left behind by D'Erlon to connect the two Wings.

Surely D'Erlon should have ordered Durutte to send at once to Napoleon and report what had happened. Even at 5 p.m., when D'Erlon was only 2 miles from the Ligny battle-field, he did nothing to establish contact with the troops of the III Corps, or even with Domon's Cavalry on their outer flank. Even his behaviour, as he drew near, led to his troops being taken for a hostile column. Moreover, when he received his order of recall from Ney, he must have realized that he was only about 2 miles from Imperial Head-Quarters and more than double that distance from Ney's. Nevertheless D'Erlon did nothing to inform the Emperor of the quandary into which he was plunged by the contradictory orders which the I Corps had received. The delay in time, whilst he reported to the Emperor, was immaterial at such a juncture ; since the simplest time and space calculation would have shown him that, on the 16th, there was only one battle-field on which he could bring his Corps effectively into action—and that field was Ligny. Nor was the problem complicated for D'Erlon, his Corps was not engaged and his mind was free to grapple with the emergency. Despite his own explanation, it is extraordinary why so experienced a general did not behave as he had done when his Corps was originally wheeled to the eastward. D'Erlon failed to realize the essential at this moment, and his decision to withdraw from the decisive field of Ligny to the secondary one of Quatre Bras was immeasurably unfortunate for France.

Again, surely it was not too much to expect of a General Aide-de-Camp of the Emperor, who had just acted in so high-handed a fashion, that, after he had left Marshal Ney, he would catch up the I Corps as rapidly as possible, gallop ahead of it, warn the French Left at Ligny of its approach, and then rejoin the Emperor at Fleurus. Had de la Bédoyère done this, then, despite the 'pencil note', Blücher would have fought his last fight at Ligny.

Admitted that D'Erlon had arrived at the wrong place yet he was an hour ahead of time. This rectified his mistake in direction, and the Emperor could have issued orders to the I Corps to head for Bry, moving past Wagnelée. Certainly this would not have been so effective as an advance down the Nivelles–Namur road, nevertheless it would have sufficed ; and, combined with the advance of the Guard and Milhaud through Ligny, the Prussian right would have been crushed and the connection with Wellington severed.

It is time to consider how Blücher profited by his hour's respite and the slackening of the French attacks.

Just before 6 p.m. the Prussian reserve artillery came into action to prepare the way for their infantry, and the Prussians surged forward. Jürgass's Squadrons covered the right, whilst Tippelskirch advanced against Le Hameau, and Pirch II with Brause (II Corps) and part of Krafft (II Corps) closed on St. Amand on three sides. Another fierce fight ensued and at first it went in favour of the Prussians. The French were driven from the hamlet by the 1st Pomeranian Regiment; then, after mastering St. Amand, the Prussians began to debouch to the southward of the villages and Lefol had to turn his guns on the French fugitives to stiffen their *moral*. From his observatory Blücher saw the great advantage gained by his troops. Luckily at this critical moment assistance reached Vandamme. Duhesme with the Young Guard hurried to the front and with irresistible *élan* furiously attacked the Prussians. Tippelskirch was checked, roughly handled, and driven back into Wagnelée; and Jürgass's Squadrons had to content themselves with covering the retreat of this Brigade, as they had been neutralized previously by Domon's horsemen and Colbert's Lancers whom the Emperor had sent up to the left. Everywhere on this part of the front this French success had great effect. Girard's heroic Division turned round and drove back all the attacks delivered on Le Hameau; whilst Lefol and Berthézène drove Pirch II out of St. Amand, and the French regained possession of all the ground which they had previously won. Well might an *émigré* exclaim that the French troops had changed since 1814, for in 1815 they fought like heroes or like devils.

At Ligny and Waterloo the Emperor's presence never failed to kindle enthusiasm, even among the severely wounded of his Army; and from many a throat the

> . . . dying shout was heard
> Blessing him they served so well.

At 7 p.m. the situation was as follows : on the right, Grouchy's troops were in possession of Tongrinelle and Hulot was attacking Potriaux. In the right centre, troops were still melting away in the Ligny furnace, which had just absorbed Gérard's last available reserve—Vichéry's second Brigade. Blücher also had been

compelled to add fresh men on his side, and he sent into the
inferno of the blazing village the bulk of Krafft's Brigade. Fed
in this way the fight raged on as fiercely as ever for this smouldering
rubbish-heap. Krafft very soon reported that he had little
chance of maintaining his grip on the place. At the same time
as this report came to hand, a despatch arrived from Müffling
stating that the Anglo-Dutch were hotly engaged at Quatre Bras
with a large French force, and it was out of the question for the
Duke to send even a single squadron to assist Blücher.

It is to Blücher's credit that this serious news failed to daunt
him. His Prussians still held on to their positions and were
not physically incapacitated from further efforts, consequently
the battle had not been lost; and, since Wellington was confronting a heavy force, it was certain that Blücher had not got the
whole of the *Armée du Nord* on his hands. The French attacks
were moderating, and the Guard, after its success, had been withdrawn. Perhaps the French had shot their bolt. At any rate,
if victory was to be attained the time had come to strike boldly
for it; so Blücher decided to keep to his former plan and driving
in the French left wing he would roll it up on their centre. He
resolved to lead this great attack in person; but it was a deplorable
resolution, because only Blücher could ensure that the Prussians
continued to act in concert with Wellington's Army. Should the
chief command devolve on Gneisenau it was by no means certain
he would place co-operation with Wellington before everything
else, although neither Ally could hope for a single-handed success
against Napoleon, and it was vital for them to combine their
operations. At this crisis in their affairs, Blücher was doubly
wrong to run a great personal risk by heading a general attack.

Before launching this attack, Blücher placed two battalions
at the Windmill at Bry, sent a few troops to reinforce the exhausted garrison of Ligny, and commanded Thielemann to send
Stülpnagel's Brigade to the same place. Then at 7 p.m., dis-
regarding the risk, he placed himself at the head of his last Reserve,
Langen's four remaining battalions and the rallied and reorganized
remnants of Steinmetz's Brigade, and the Field-Marshal led them
forward towards St. Amand. On the way Blücher collected
around him all the stragglers and fugitives he met, thus swelling
his force to some eight battalions. When he reached the front
he swept together the exhausted débris of the Brigades of Tippel-

skirch, Brause, and Pirch II, although Pirch II reported his ammunition was all spent. Blücher was inexorable, he shouted out : ' Use your bayonets ! ' and spurring forward he led onward his reanimated soldiers. A momentary success crowned this supreme but expiring effort, for the Prussians did recapture Le Hameau. Then they dashed in vain against the rampart of steel which was opposed to them by the Chasseurs of the Guard waiting beyond St. Amand. The Prussian attack was over-powered, and the beaten troops retired in disorder to La Haye. It was not, however, at St. Amand that the fate of this battle was to be decided. Ligny was the scene of the heaviest fighting and the decisive act was played out close to the smoking ruins of that village.

As late as 7.30 p.m. Blücher still hoped to cling to his positions through the night, so as to be able to co-operate with Wellington on the morrow, and the rapidly failing light, caused by a gathering thunderstorm, encouraged his belief that darkness was at hand. Then the storm burst and flashes of lightning dimmed the flashes from the guns, though not for long did Nature have the mastery.

Napoleon had noticed the small force which Blücher launched in his last desperate effort to gain a decision and the Emperor determined to crush Blücher's exhausted Army forthwith, so as to be able to turn on Wellington on the next day. But so fierce had been the fighting that, to prevent his first line from being broken up, Napoleon had been compelled to part with some of his picked troops. Nevertheless he had kept in hand the flower of his Army for the death-blow ; and, as he knew Lobau's fresh VI Corps was close to Fleurus, the time had come to destroy the ' damnably mauled ' Prussian Army. So the final phase opened of what was destined to be the Emperor's last victory.

CHAPTER XII

THE BATTLE OF LIGNY

3RD PHASE: NAPOLEON'S DECISIVE ATTACK AND THE DEFEAT OF THE PRUSSIANS: 7.30 P.M.–9 P.M.

THE ATTACK OF THE GUARD

NOTE.—*Napoleon and D'Erlon's Corps on the 16th June*

(Map 3)

UNFORTUNATELY for Napoleon the golden moments were flying past. D'Erlon's inopportune arrival had wasted a full hour as well as giving Blücher a breathing space in which to reorganize his defences, and a thunderstorm at the critical moment had further decreased the available daylight. But at last the time had come to give the *coup de grâce* to Blücher's sorely wounded Army and the Emperor determined to finish the battle that evening, cost what it might. He would drive away Blücher's Army so as to be free of all Prussian interference when he turned against Wellington on the 17th. In accordance with his final orders, Friant with the Grenadiers of the Old and Middle Guard and the 1st Chasseurs, followed by Guyot's Heavy Cavalry and Milhaud's Cuirassiers, moved off in the direction of Ligny. On the right was a column of sixty guns, marching on a front of two batteries.

The Prussian guns opened on the Guard, but the veterans carried through their advance as they would have carried out a parade evolution. This approach march, lasting twenty minutes, was accompanied by a continual rattle of musketry and the unceasing boom of more than 200 guns. Having reached assaulting distance, the Infantry of the Guard formed up under a hail of bullets, grape, and round-shot, and the Artillery of the Guard unlimbered at case-shot range. With truth the Emperor said, ' It is the Artillery of my Guard which decides most of my battles, because I can bring it into action whenever and wherever I wish.'

At 7.30 p.m., just as the French guns opened a tremendous cannonade, drowning even the crashes of thunder, Lobau's Corps came streaming through Fleurus and began forming up on the heights to the east.

At this crisis, the spirit permeating the *Armée du Nord* at Ligny is shown by the speech made by Lieut.-General Count Roguet to the Grenadiers of the Old Guard : ' Gentlemen, warn the Grenadiers that I am going to shoot the first one of them who brings me a prisoner.'

At 7.45 p.m. the Guard was ready to attack. The Emperor rode on to an adjacent knoll, and the Guard Artillery saluted the doomed Prussian Army with a deafening salvo from 60 guns. This was the signal for the assault. As they passed their Emperor the soldiers thundered out their well-known war-cry. Then the Old Guard closed, the guns ceased firing, and in place of their incessant roar rose the roll of the drums beating the charge.

The Guard advanced in two columns of double-companies. The left column (2nd, 3rd, and 4th Grenadiers) struck the western half of Ligny ; the right column (1st Grenadiers, 1st Chasseurs, and the Sappers and Marines of the Guard) attacked the eastern part of the village. Gérard still held that part which lay on the right bank of the Ligny stream, and, placing himself at the head of Pécheux's Division, with a desperate effort Gérard drove out the Prussians. As Gérard issued from the village the Grenadiers and Milhaud's squadrons followed him. On the left the Emperor rode at the head of the Head-Quarter Squadrons and the Heavy Horse of the Guard. The defence collapsed. This tremendous impact of veteran troops swept away the Prussians, as shrubs are whirled away by a torrent. The finish of the great battle was Napoleonic, a mere half-hour turned the fate of the day.

It was 8 p.m. Even though the retiring squares withstood some furious charges yet the Prussian centre was pierced ; and in the rays of the setting sun Blücher perceived ruin everywhere. He saw the disastrous retreat of his troops and the wide breach cleft in his line of defence, the breach which was being filled by the bearskins of the Guard. Even now, he would not own defeat. Determined to stop the advance of the French he galloped up from La Haye to the point of danger, expecting to find part of Henckel's Brigade and Stülpnagel's and Borcke's Brigades as well as Röder's squadrons. But Henckel had withdrawn to Sombreffe, Stülpnagel was nowhere near Ligny, and Thielemann found himself too hotly pressed by Grouchy to spare Borcke's Brigade. The only troops available were Röder's squadrons. These five regiments charged, but failed to make any impression on the squares of the Old Guard. As the Prussian cavalry closed the French poured in point-blank volleys which strewed the ground around with dead and dying men and horses. The failing light hampered the horsemen, who also fought with Milhaud's Cuirassiers and the Dragoons of the Guard around and in front of the French squares, which continued their steady advance towards Bry Windmill.

Blücher himself charged at the head of his last remaining squadrons; but his horse was shot, and in falling it rolled over the old Field-Marshal. Immediately afterwards the 9th Cuirassiers rode over the place where the Marshal lay, attended only by his aide-de-camp, Major Nostitz, who had dismounted to assist him. In the dim light, it was 9 p.m., the Cuirassiers failed to notice the Prussian Commander-in-Chief; and a few minutes later, after being repulsed, the Cuirassiers recrossed the ground but again failed to recognize the prize which lay within their grasp. Major Nostitz hailed some Prussian Uhlans. Together they hauled out the Field-Marshal from under his charger, placed him on a non-commissioned officer's horse of the 6th Uhlans, and led him from the battle-field surrounded by a flood of fugitives. Although covered with bruises, Blücher was not actually wounded. Even so, considering his advanced age (72), the fall alone might have been fatal. His good fortune was the misfortune of the French, because if Blücher had been captured by Napoleon the campaign might have had a different termination.

Blücher had acted foolishly when he led his general counter-stroke earlier in the fight, but to risk himself again in the hour of defeat, by taking part in a cavalry charge which could not turn the fortune of the day, was unwarrantable. It was at this moment that a Commander-in-Chief was wanted to let Wellington know what had happened and what moves his beaten Army intended to make. In particular, he was required to arrange and order those moves so as to ensure co-operation with Wellington on the 17th and 18th. Yet it was at this moment that Blücher jeopardized the campaign by fighting like a mere dragoon. Blücher being temporarily incapacitated, Gneisenau assumed the executive command.

The well-timed devotion of Röder's squadrons had gained sufficient time for their infantry to draw off and for most of the Prussian guns to be got away. The broken centre fell back northward and began to rally just to the south of the Roman road. Then later in the night a panic broke out and about 8,000 Prussians fled in all directions.

When Napoleon's final blow shore through the Prussian centre the wings were better placed. Both Zieten and Thielemann managed to maintain their positions until they learned that Ligny was in the enemy's hands, when their situation became impossible and they drew off at once in good order. Zieten fell back past Bry, but his troops continually turned round to check Vandamme's pursuit and at sunrise the rearguard was still holding Bry. At the same time Thielemann withdrew past Sombreffe, though he continued to hold the place with a strong detachment. It was lucky for Gneisenau that he could rely on Thielemann's fairly fresh Corps to take up the duties of rearguard and hold back the French, should they attempt any immediate or vigorous pursuit of the shaken Prussian Army.

Before the day ended the *Armée du Nord* crossed the Ligny stream and bivouacked beyond it, and Lobau's Corps moved up into the front line near Bry Windmill. The French outposts faced the Prussians from Bry to Sombreffe, and battalions of the Guard bivouacked in squares in the closest proximity to the enemy. Firing continued as late as 9.30 p.m., though spasmodic outbursts of gun and musketry fire occurred until 11 p.m. In the *Armée du Nord* shouts and music proclaimed the great victory, until gradually silence reigned and the moon shed a pale light on the horrors of the battle-field. Then, about midnight, everyone was disturbed by heavy musketry fire. This outbreak was occasioned by a collision between two French regiments. Fortunately matters were quickly readjusted and sleep once more claimed the tired soldiers.

At 11 p.m. the Emperor returned to Fleurus for the night; and when Grouchy came to head-quarters to receive orders he

was told they would be issued on the morrow.   During the night
Napoleon seems to have been in considerable physical pain.

The Prussian losses were 16,000 and 21 guns, and the French
lost over 11,000.   The 27,000 dead and wounded lay piled on
two square miles of country and sufficiently indicated the nature
of the fighting.   The ferocity of the conflict is described by an
eye-witness, Captain de Mauduit of the Grenadiers of the Old
Guard : ' Ligny and Waterloo consisted in hand-to-hand fighting which lasted for hours together ;   and with this was combined,
not a fusillade and cannonade carried on at ranges of some four
to six hundred yards, as occurred in most of the other battles,
but point-blank discharges of musketry and grape-shot salvoes
fired at fifty-yards range.   At Ligny, more than 4,000 dead were
piled on an area less in measurement than the Tuileries garden
[300 or 400 yards square]. . . .   The aspect of the cemetery at
St. Amand was not less terrible. . . .   The gallant 82nd of the
Line (Girard's Division), lay here, almost to a man.'

*   *   *   *   *   *   *

In 1815, as in 1813 and 1814, mere victories could not save
Napoleon ;   and the result of this day, the first critical day of the
campaign, was by no means decisive.   Wellington and Blücher
were not separated and Blücher had not been crushed.   Even
so the Emperor's failure to gain a decisive success at Ligny
was not due to anything which the Allies did.   Owing to the
delay which had been caused by D'Erlon's appearance, the decision
was not obtained until nightfall ;   and then merciful darkness
enshrouded the Prussians, spared them the rigours of an immediate pursuit, and enabled them to draw off to the northward
almost unnoticed.   Had the battle ended in daylight, Napoleon
would have pursued at once, so as to reap the fruits of his victory ;
and the beaten Army, under this extreme and final pressure, might
have dissolved into a rabble.   The direction of the final stroke
did not sever the line joining the two Allies, consequently future
co-operation, though difficult, was not made impossible.   If
D'Erlon had participated in the final scene, Blücher would have
been sundered completely from Wellington.   Such Prussian
troops as escaped must have retired rapidly to the north-eastward,
that is away from Wellington.   Had this been achieved, Ligny
would have been a decisive battle.   As it was, both execution and

result fell short of Napoleon's conception. Nevertheless, the Emperor still remained in possession of the winning chance.

At Ligny Napoleon triumphed over very superior numbers in a hard-fought fight, apparently falsifying his aphorism : ' Providence sides with the big battalions.' He had engaged at Ligny with a general numerical inferiority, because he knew that he could ensure the requisite superiority at the decisive point and at the psychological moment. By exercising a rigid economy of force in the preliminary fighting, he wore down Blücher in a bitter struggle ; and Blücher (relying on Wellington's advent) was compelled to engage his last formed body of troops before the Emperor had brought into action either the Old Guard, Guyot, Milhaud, or Lobau. Thus the Emperor stood in overwhelming superiority at the right place and at the critical moment. This is the real meaning of his aphorism anent ' the big battalions '.

In one respect, however, the Emperor failed. At 2 p.m. the conditions were most favourable to him and the Allies were unable to dispose of any greater force than the *Armée du Nord*, consequently the Emperor should at least have smashed Blücher. Napoleon had rightly refrained from crushing Zieten early on the 16th. Such action would have compelled Blücher to draw back and concentrate out of striking distance, and then Napoleon could not have aimed that stroke at Blücher's rear which he planned that Ney should deliver at Ligny. The Emperor was also justified in waiting before he opened the battle, so as to give Blücher time to concentrate at Sombreffe a force which it would be worth the Emperor's while to destroy within the time available.

What a victory Napoleon would have won had D'Erlon only come up in rear of Bry at the moment when the Guard cleared Ligny. The news of such a victory would have shaken Europe to its foundations, and have raised France to a pitch of enthusiasm which must have carried Napoleon on to ultimate triumph. Owing, however, to the mishandling of D'Erlon's Corps in the complicated manœuvre which was attempted with it, Napoleon had to rest content with bivouacking on the battle-field which he had wrested from Blücher. He had failed in his great object to throw at the first opportunity and at all hazards for complete and absolute success. But, owing to the formation used for the advance, the campaign was far from lost. The advance in two Wings and a Reserve was not even seriously affected. Fortune was again smiling. Within Ney's grasp lay the Army of Wellington. The Marshal could engage it on the morrow and hold it at Quatre Bras, until Napoleon swung in with the Reserve and sealed its doom. Alternatively Ney, with D'Erlon, could keep Wellington in play on the 17th, whilst the Emperor closed on Blücher's hammered Army, rounded it up, and finally destroyed it. Which alternative would Napoleon choose?

The Prussian Army immediately after the Decision

Just before Blücher headed the cavalry charge at Ligny, the Field-Marshal had despatched one of his aides-de-camp (Major Winterfeldt) to the Anglo-Dutch head-quarters to inform the Duke that the Prussians were obliged to retire. Unfortunately Major Winterfeldt insisted on riding too close to the French skirmishers near Piraumont, was badly wounded by their fire, and fell from his horse. He lay on the road for some time between the French and Nassauers, until the latter managed to bring him in. Even then Winterfeldt would not trust the Nassauer officer with the delivery of his very important message, and merely requested that his condition should be communicated to the nearest officer of general's rank in the vicinity. Winterfeldt would not communicate to a subordinate the alarming, but urgent, news which he carried. No general, however, was near at hand and the verbal message remained undelivered. It will be recalled that a rumour of Major Winterfeldt's fate duly reached Müffling, but the Attaché gave no particular attention to the matter.

Such a pressing message should have been sent in triplicate and by different routes. In any case Winterfeldt should not have run any unnecessary risk, but he should have concentrated on the safe delivery of the message which he carried. A crisis had been reached. If under a misapprehension Wellington remained at Quatre Bras and bore the full weight of Napoleon's blow on the 17th, the campaign was virtually over. It was imperative to warn the Duke of the Prussian withdrawal which exposed the Anglo-Dutch inner flank and left Napoleon free to act.

At the close of Ligny, Lieut.-Colonel Sir H. Hardinge, Wellington's representative on Blücher's Staff, had his left hand shattered by a round shot. The British Attaché remained with the Field-Marshal and did not have his hand operated on until about midnight. Immediately afterwards, however, this gallant officer despatched his brother—Lieut. R. Hardinge, R.H.A.—to report the result of the Battle of Ligny to the Duke of Wellington. The report was to the effect that the Prussians, although they had been beaten, were not dispersed and were ready to show fight again. Undoubtedly the report was too optimistic. It was impossible for Blücher's Army to remain any longer in the neighbourhood of Sombreffe, or to oppose Napoleon before it (the Prussian Army) had been rallied and reformed, and reinforced by Bülow's Corps. Nor did the report make clear that Blücher was withdrawing northward to Wavre, and probably Wellington was slightly misled by it. Nevertheless, although the report was not quite clear on all points, it is greatly to Hardinge's credit that, under such disadvantages, he should have remembered to send a report at all.

Not only had Napoleon been disappointed and deprived of reinforcements on which he calculated, but Blücher had also experienced a double disappointment, since neither Wellington nor Bülow had co-operated at Ligny.

By 9 p.m. it was clear that neither Wellington nor Bülow would reach Ligny during the night, and the only course open to Gneisenau was to order an immediate retreat. The pregnant question was, in which direction should he retire ? As the battle gradually went against the Prussians, Blücher and his Staff must have spent some anxious moments in considering the direction of their eventual withdrawal. The most prudent course was to withdraw down the communications in the direction of Liége. But this withdrawal would mean the abandonment of all idea of concentrating with Wellington and bringing the campaign in Belgium to an end, by delivering a pitched battle in which the two Allies would combine to ensure Napoleon's overthrow. Even to attempt this eastward retreat might prove dangerous, since the defeated Prussian Army had been driven north of the Nivelles–Namur highway and it would have to draw off across the front of the *Armée du Nord*.

As matters stood the Prussians could have retired to Quatre Bras during the night, although this would necessarily entail abandoning Bülow. This westward retreat, however, could only have been ordered if the Prussian Staff was certain that Wellington was victorious at Quatre Bras ; but this was just what Gneisenau did not know. In all probability Wellington had got the worst of the fighting, as he had been unable to send even a single squadron to his Ally's aid. In consequence the westward retreat was too risky to contemplate.

Considering, however, the actual situation, there was another course to adopt which met the needs of the emergency. The Prussian Army having been driven to the north of the main road, the easiest and safest way to open the retirement was undoubtedly northward. Principally for this reason the Staff selected this line of retreat. By retiring northward the Prussians would ensure picking up the wandering IV Corps, whose reinforcement would be most welcome and opportune ; further, to move off in this direction would place between vanquished and victors the greatest distance in the least time, and Thielemann's comparatively fresh Corps could cover this withdrawal. Furthermore, several roads existed and the retirement could be begun on a broad front, thus saving time. Another advantage was that the northward retreat might take Napoleon by surprise. He would expect a force, after losing such a hard-fought fight, to retire directly down its communications so as to refit and recuperate. Hence a start might be obtained which, if improved on, would become valuable should Napoleon desire to finish off the Prussians on the 17th, seeing that he might not come up with them until it was too late for him to gain a decision. Meanwhile ample intelligence about Wellington's plans and situation would have been obtained.

Even if the Prussian Army retreated northward it could soon reopen a fresh line of communications which would run back across the Meuse at Maestricht and thence to a new base on the Rhine at Cologne. Most important of all, by retiring northward the Prussians would be moving parallel to the road by which Wellington must draw off his exposed force on the 17th if he wished to cover Brussels, and the Allies after uniting to the south of Brussels might then make up for the opportunity they had lost in front of Fleurus.

In coming to a conclusion on this weighty matter, Blücher and his Quarter-Master-General (Grölmann) appear to have been influenced by different motives to those which swayed Gneisenau.

In selecting a northward retreat, Blücher and Grölmann desired at all costs to keep in touch with the Anglo-Dutch Army so as to ensure eventual co-operation, and only by moving northward could this end be attained. The more circumspect Gneisenau selected the course for more prudent reasons : the withdrawal was easier and safer at first, and Bülow could be picked up. Then, having concentrated the Prussian Army to the northward, Gneisenau could make sure of the northern line of communications with the Rhine. But it does not appear that Gneisenau ordered the retreat northward with the idea of aiding Wellington. This great strategic manœuvre was certainly ordered by Gneisenau, but in all probability he did so to secure the safety of the Prussian communications.

Fortunately Blücher was soon again in the saddle and at the head of his Army, otherwise concerted action between the Allies would have been unlikely. It was not until the 17th that the Prussian Staff decided to keep in touch with Wellington at all costs, and ensure the co-operation of the Allies on the selected battle-field. Then, in a lengthy discussion, Blücher and Grölmann carried the day and overcame Gneisenau, who was still in favour of falling back to Liége, securing the Prussian communications, thereby abandoning Wellington. Gneisenau evidently feared that the Anglo-Dutch Army would be destroyed before the Prussians reached the battle-field, and then the fate of the Prussian Army, executing a hazardous flank march within striking distance of the enemy, would be a foregone conclusion.

Once the northward retreat was decided on it was necessary to select some place to head for. The little town of Wavre at once suggested itself. It was the ganglion of numerous roads which converged there on the Dyle bridges, the town was within easy marching distance of the present positions of the Corps, and Bülow, who was halted on the road to it, could join the Prussian Army as it trudged northward. After massing his Army at Wavre Blücher should find himself within easy supporting distance of Wellington, if the latter used the Brussels road for his retreat as it seemed probable he would do. By halting at Wavre Blücher would be able to move to Wellington's support on the 18th, should the latter elect to fight on that day to the south of the Forest of Soignes ; or the Prussians could move on to Brussels and join the Anglo-Dutch Army there. In each case the Dyle

would be a useful obstacle to hold with a detaining force, so as
to delay any French troops who might be following the retiring
columns. Even if the Prussian retreat was to be continued it
was not a long march from Wavre to Louvain, and the Army
could carry this out on the 18th.

Probably Wavre was selected for some such reasons as these.
At any rate it appears to have been decided on before Blücher
became a casualty ; as a little later when Gneisenau, seated on
his horse behind Bry with his map spread out in front of him,
was surrounded by officers who came to him asking for orders,
he merely glanced at his map in the moonlight and uttered the
historic words, ' Retreat on Tilly and Wavre ! ' (' *Rückzug nach
Tilly und Wavre !* ') These five words led to the great Allied
Victory at Waterloo.

Directly Gneisenau decided that the Prussian Army could
remain no longer in the neighbourhood of the Ligny battle-field
and he had ordered an immediate retreat, Wellington's position at
Quatre Bras became exposed, owing to the Anglo-Dutch left
becoming uncovered directly the Prussians drew off. It was
vital, a real matter of life and death to the Allies, for Wellington
not to run any risk of being crushed unsupported on the 17th,
since, if that occurred, the fate of the Prussians would then be
settled within a few more hours. On the 16th the Prussians had
been most fortunate in escaping annihilation, and it was to
Gneisenau's advantage to assist Wellington to escape on the 17th.
Directly this retreat to Wavre was decided on it was imperative
to send several staff officers to Wellington. These officers would
have warned the Duke that, at dawn on the 17th, the Prussians
were retiring to Wavre, because they were too shattered to
re-engage on that day and wished to ensure taking the field again
on the 18th, after reorganizing and collecting Bülow. At the
same time Wellington should have been asked what he intended
to do.

By drawing off and leaving his Ally in an exposed and critical
situation for some hours and without any warning, Gneisenau
failed to read the situation aright and he made clear that he was
playing solely for the Prussian hand. Although the Duke was
most anxious to conform with his Ally's movements yet it was
impossible for him to do so, unless he was informed accurately
of the precise position of the Prussian Army, any movements

which it made, and the necessity for making them. Gneisenau neither maintained nor arranged any proper system of inter-communication between the Allies, and Wellington's lack of knowledge about the Prussian movements was most marked at this crisis of the campaign, when Gneisenau was in charge. With Wellington absolutely ready to co-operate, everything hung on Blücher's recuperative powers. It was fortunate for the Allies that the old Field-Marshal was sufficiently himself on the 17th to protest at once against Gneisenau's desire to retreat towards the Prussian communications and abandon Wellington, and that Blücher proved mentally strong enough (supported by Grölmann) to override Gneisenau. Providentially, on the 18th, Blücher was also physically strong enough to lead his troops to the direct support of his loyal Ally at Waterloo.

*   *   *   *   *   *   *

The short night was spent by the bulk of the Prussian I and II Corps between Mellery, Tilly, and Gentinnes, on two of the roads which ran to Wavre. Thielemann, near Sombreffe, was ready to cover the retirement of the I and II Corps, and afterwards withdraw the III Corps to Wavre, *via* Gembloux.

NOTE.—*Napoleon and D'Erlon's Corps on the* 16*th June*

It may be considered that Napoleon's genius showed signs of decadence when he failed to employ D'Erlon's Corps on the 16th ; but this was not the first body of troops which had missed the decisive battle-field in the Napoleonic Campaigns. Although D'Erlon's Corps spent the 16th in oscillating between two battles and taking part in neither, yet this in itself was not an especial sign of any decline in Napoleon's powers. An earlier instance may be recalled for which Napoleon himself was responsible. On the 14th June 1800, the day of Marengo, an important part of the *Armée de Réserve*—Lapoype's Division—was neutralized by the issue of counter-orders. Despite that Napoleon gained the glorious triumph of Marengo, without the help of the missing Division which never debouched on the battle-field. It is beyond dispute that in 1800 Napoleon's genius was waxing, and not waning.

A parity of reasoning can be applied to the Allied Commanders in 1815. Was it a special mark of decadence in Blücher that he missed the co-operation of Bülow's Corps at Ligny ? Was it a mark of deterioration in Wellington's powers that he left 17,000 men on the Hal road during the Battle of Waterloo, only two days later ? These happenings are inseparable from war and the hurry and confusion associated with a battle-field, but not one of these cases showed any especial mark of degeneracy.

The handling, however, of D'Erlon's Corps by the Emperor on the 16th did show signs of decadence in Napoleon's procedure. The Emperor had evolved certain maxims to which he held fast in practice. One of these great truths ran : ' An enemy should be outflanked without separating one's Army.' Nevertheless, at Ligny, Napoleon disregarded his own maxim, which had lost none of its force or appropriateness, nor was this the first time he acted in a like manner.

This same risky manœuvre had been tried at Bautzen in May 1813. Indeed the likeness stretches further. At Bautzen Ney was the commander of the left wing. Being isolated, the Marshal failed to rise to the height of a critical occasion ; and, instead of the destruction of the Allied Army which Napoleon had planned, only an incomplete victory was gained. Could any parallel be closer ? In both cases Ney was the Marshal at fault ; both at Bautzen and at Ligny, Ney was isolated and not under the immediate personal control of the Emperor ; in each case an immediate decisive result was required, because in each case a crisis in the campaign had been reached. In neither case would half-measures or a barren victory save the situation. In both cases Ney failed in the higher duty of co-operation. But, in both cases, the responsibility for failure rested principally on the Emperor, because he was riding rough-shod over his own maxim by attempting an extremely difficult combination. Further, in both cases, Napoleon had selected for his subordinate, on the outer wing, a Marshal, who, although he was as brave as a lion and a great leader of men, did require the clearest and most detailed orders to enable him to realize his paramount duty in a critical and difficult situation. At any rate, remembering his dolorous experience at Bautzen, Napoleon on the day of Ligny might have recognized that Ney could hardly achieve what was required of him without definite and precise indication being given to the Marshal in the earliest orders which were issued for his guidance. At Bautzen, and later at Ligny, this clear guidance was lacking. In both cases, at these critical times, the orders sent by Napoleon to Ney were too curt and laconic. In labouring to be brief the Emperor became obscure, consequently the Marshal failed to discern what was in the Emperor's mind. Napoleon's orders did not state in full and precise terms, impossible to misread even in the excitement of action, the exact duty which the Emperor desired his Marshal to perform. Engaged on a risky manœuvre, Napoleon did not take all the necessary precautions to control Fortune. She retaliated by stabbing him in the back.

A study of history and the campaigns of previous Great Captains furnish examples which act as a guide to the procedure which Napoleon might have adopted. In Frederick the Great's *chef d'œuvre*—Leuthen (1757)—the Prussian King marched round Prince Charles's force, which stood rooted to the hills on which it was placed, and, smashing in its left flank, rolled up and routed the huge Austrian Army. The great King's victory was the direct result of movement, manœuvre, and resolution. The circumstances, however, at Leuthen and Ligny were dissimilar.

On the other hand, on this very ground in front of Fleurus, the Marshal Duke of Luxembourg's handling of the French Army, in his great victory in 1690 over the Prince of Waldeck and his Austrian Army, is very instructive. Luxembourg attacked the Prince of Waldeck in front, engaged his attention, and held his Army to its ground. Meanwhile the French Marshal boldly led a large proportion of his force, undetected, around the Austrian left, and then proceeded to form up in rear of his unsuspecting enemies. The two jaws of the vice closed and the Austrians were destroyed. The hunchbacked Marshal's arrangements were perfect. He left nothing whatever to chance, and ensured that a decisive result was obtained. Luxembourg's manœuvre was in accord with Napoleon's maxim.

Napoleon, who possessed in a very exceptional degree all the qualities which are required in a Commander-in-Chief : broad and correct conception, clear and precise direction of events, an admirable obstinacy, and a character of steel-like coldness, which no emergencies of a battle-field could influence in the least, also possessed perfectly formed ideas about the principles of the art of war, and his strength of character allowed nothing to intervene and make him false to himself. Above all else Napoleon believed in the maxim, ' March together, strike together ! ' In general he held true to the principle of keeping his Army concentrated and striking with it in this fashion. Bautzen and Ligny showed, however, that he deviated occasionally from his own great maxim. Bitterly he paid for his deviation in both these battles.

There is no analogy between Ney at Bautzen (1813), or at Quatre Bras (1815), and Davout at Auerstädt (1806). The battles of Jena and Auerstädt were two separate battles (from the tactical point of view) and the results achieved on these two fields were totally independent of one another. It was not so at Bautzen, where Ney's attack was a main factor in deciding the enemy's retreat. So in 1815 it was no part of the Emperor's plan to fight two battles on the 16th and he intended to fight only one decisive engagement, merely neutralizing the Ally on the other wing.

Judging the Emperor by his own maxim it would appear that, if Napoleon wished to outflank Blücher, it would have been far better to have held D'Erlon under his own hand until the decisive flank had been made clear, and not have subordinated the I Corps to Marshal Ney. In this case, D'Erlon would have been ordered to concentrate his Corps early in the afternoon of the 16th at some central position—say, near Heppignies—where, without any unnecessary counter-marching, the I Corps could be brought into action on either flank directly the tactical situation had cleared up. Heppignies could have been easily reached by D'Erlon, who would have left the Brussels road at Jumet (where the head of the I Corps had halted at night), and D'Erlon's advance would not then have been delayed by Reille's tardy start. Once at Heppignies, the I Corps would have been magnificently placed to manœuvre against either Wellington's or Blücher's inner flank, as circumstances should decide. The I Corps in this case would belong to the Reserve and it would receive orders direct from the Emperor himself, until he decided where to engage it. The obvious lateness of Wellington's concentration was an additional argument for cutting Ney's Wing down to one Corps only.

If it is urged that such a course was impossible, because Napoleon did not and could not know early enough that Blücher had concentrated for battle, then the Emperor might have made arrangements to move over to the left flank directly he sent the 3.15 p.m. order to Ney, so as to be in touch with D'Erlon from the first moment when he headed eastward from the Brussels road ; and he might have contrived that he himself should meet and lead the I Corps, as Luxembourg had done in 1690. Some such plan would have met even the situation created by the ' pencil note ', and must have ensured a decision-compelling stroke. By 3.15 p.m. the frontal battle had been well started and Soult could have been entrusted with its execution ; leaving the Emperor free to handle the Guard and D'Erlon's Corps.

After all is said, the original omission to include every available man in the *Armée du Nord* for the campaign in Belgium lay at the root of Napoleon's failure. Had the Emperor, on the 16th, possessed the other 30,000–35,000 men (as has been suggested) then D'Erlon's failure to strike in on this day would not have mattered overmuch. The Emperor would have had such a force available under his own hand that Blücher's utter destruction would have been assured ; and undoubtedly Blücher would have offered battle, just as he did. Napoleon, however, in possession of crushing superiority, would have held the Prussians to their position and passed a force round Blücher's right. Then, when the battle was ripe, Blücher's inner flank would have been crushed by the hammerstroke of the Guard on the anvil which Napoleon himself would have placed so carefully in position. As a fighting machine the Prussian Army in Belgium would have ceased to exist. It was not to be. Napoleon neglected the observance of his own maxims, and his distribution of his soldiers on the theatre of war was inferior to that of the immortal campaign of 1805.

CHAPTER XIII

17TH JUNE: EARLY DISPOSITIONS

(Sketch E)

AT dawn the general situation was as follows :

The Emperor with Vandamme, Gérard, Lobau, the Guard, Pajol, Exelmans, and Milhaud—nearly 70,000 men—were at Sombreffe. In front of Napoleon, but temporarily out of touch, was *Blücher's Army*, about 70,000 strong. This Army was retiring towards Wavre along the Tilly, Gentinnes, and Gembloux roads. Bülow's Corps, which had reached Baudeset (near Gembloux) on the previous evening, was in touch with Blücher.

At this same hour, *Wellington* had concentrated at Quatre Bras, the 1st British Division, 5th British Division, 5th British Brigade, 1st Hanoverian Brigade, 2nd Dutch-Belgian Division, Brunswick and Nassau Contingents, and most of the Cavalry, a force about 40,000 strong. At Nivelles, 8 miles away, were the 2nd British Division, and 4th British Brigade, another 10,000. At Arquennes (between Nivelles and Seneffe) lay the 2nd Brigade, K.G.L., Ditmer's Brigade of Chassé's Division, and 1st and 2nd Dutch-Belgian Cavalry Brigades, nearly 7,500. If he was forced to fight at Quatre Bras on the 17th, Wellington could collect nearly 60,000 men, a force well worth Napoleon's while to destroy.

Lying farther away, at Braine-le-Comte, were the 6th British Brigade and 6th Hanoverian Brigade, as well as two regiments of the 1st Hanoverian Cavalry Brigade, about 7,000. The 1st Dutch-Belgian Division and Anthing's Dutch-Indian Brigade, another 10,000 had reached Enghien. At Hal, some 8 miles distant from Mt. St. Jean, was the remaining Brigade of Chassé's Dutch-Belgian Division, 3,500 strong ; and at Brussels and in the vicinity lay the 6th British Division and the Reserve Artillery, about 7,500. During the 17th Wellington could have concentrated 90,000 men to cover Brussels, although at dawn less than one-half was available at Quatre Bras.

At 9 a.m. the Brunswick, Belgian, and Nassau troops, which had all been to the east of the Bois de Bossu on the 16th, were moved to the west of the wood ; Maitland's Brigade occupied the wood with light troops, holding its reserves in rear ; Byng's Brigade formed up close to Quatre Bras ; and the 3rd and 5th Divisions formed to the east of the cross-roads. Piraumont was occupied by an advanced post, and the Cavalry took post behind the other troops. These positions were maintained until the retreat to Waterloo was opened about 10 a.m.

The *French Left Wing* near Frasnes was not far away from Wellington, and Ney's force comprised the fresh I Corps, II Corps (less Girard), Light Cavalry of the Guard, and Kellermann's Cavalry Corps. Allowing for the losses suffered on the 16th, Ney had nearly 42,000 men available.

On the 17th Ney's immediate duty was to attack Wellington promptly and vigorously, and to attract to and hold about Quatre Bras as much of the Anglo-Dutch Army as possible. Then Napoleon would have been given the chance of destroying Wellington with the French Reserve.

At daybreak, hearing Prussian troops were withdrawing towards Namur, Grouchy pushed one of Pajol's Cavalry Divisions in pursuit and backed it with a Dragoon Brigade from Exelmans' Corps. In reality the Prussian troops retiring along the Namur road were in disorder and they had used, unintelligently, the first convenient road. Nevertheless they served one useful purpose as they laid a false scent which for some time directed the French attention away from Blücher's main Army. All day Pajol remained on this flank.

Meanwhile Grouchy reported at Imperial head-quarters. But the Emperor was still asleep and no one would take the responsibility of waking him, so the Marshal had to wait until 7.30 a.m.

This delay was important. If Blücher was to be pursued, rounded up, and destroyed on the 17th, then the Right Wing must start not later than 5 a.m. or the decision would have to be sought on the other Wing. In this latter case, Wellington had to be held at Quatre Bras by Ney, until Napoleon and the Reserve could close round the Anglo-Dutch Army and annihilate it. This must be done on the 17th, whilst Blücher was out of the game for twenty-four hours. To-morrow would not do. Hence, after 5 a.m., as Napoleon was still asleep, it devolved on Soult and Ney to arrange to have Wellington fixed and the Reserve made ready to march westward at the shortest notice. This action would have prevented this fresh delay from having disastrous consequences. In Flahault's opinion, ' Our Army could not be expected to start off again at dawn,' and the considered opinion of this officer cannot be brushed aside. Consequently it devolved on Soult to make the requisite arrangements for Ney to grip and hold Wellington at Quatre Bras.

Both Marshals, each supreme for the moment on their respective Wings, could have made all the necessary preparations for an early move. They could have established intercommunication between the two battle-fields, reconnoitred widely to their fronts and flanks ; and Ney, directly he found Wellington in strength in front of the French Left Wing at Quatre Bras, should have attacked the British Marshal and held him to his position, reporting to the Emperor the action he had taken. Neither Soult nor Ney rose to the occasion. Neither Marshal made any arrangements to prepare for the forthcoming operations. Whereas up to nightfall on the 16th the hours had been precious, on the morning of the 17th the very minutes were golden.

Certainly the situation was obscure. During the night only Ney's brief report on the state of affairs at Quatre Bras had been received. Even at 7.30 a.m. obscurity enshrouded what had befallen the Left Wing, and Napoleon could not be sure whether Ney had engaged Wellington's rearguard or the whole Anglo-Dutch Army. The recall of D'Erlon suggested that Wellington had collected an important force by late in the day ; and overnight the Emperor, before he rested, would have done well to send detailed instructions to Ney. In these instructions the Emperor would have made clear to the Marshal the rôle which the Left Wing was to adopt. He would have emphasized that, if Wellington had concentrated his whole Army at Quatre Bras, the Anglo-Dutch Army was to be attacked as soon as possible and held fast, so that it might be destroyed on the 17th before Blücher could rally and turn round. In this case Ney need not have reported what he was doing, because the opening of a violent action at daybreak would have caused the Emperor to start off westward with Lobau, Milhaud's Cuirassiers, and the Guard. These troops were fresh, their ammunition supply was adequate for the occasion, and for them an early start was quite possible, as Pajol proved by the dash he made at break of day along the Namur road.

Unfortunately Ney did nothing; and General de Flahaut only reached Fleurus at 8 a.m. and made a detailed report of the fight at Quatre Bras. Soult had also been remiss. He had failed to warn Ney of the victory obtained at Ligny and he did not repair this omission until 8 a.m.

In the twenty-four hours from 5 p.m. on the 16th to 5 p.m. on the 17th the campaign was lost. Twice on these two days Fortune, usually so chary of her bounties, offered Napoleon the opportunity of destroying the Allies in turn. Only when the second chance had been allowed to slip away unutilized did she turn her back on her former favourite for ever and transfer her fickle smiles to his adversaries.

*　　　*　　　*　　　*　　　*　　　*　　　*

Soon after 7 a.m. Pajol reported that he was following hostile troops, retiring towards Namur, and he had captured prisoners and cannon. Pajol's report, however, did not answer the following all-important questions : what was the strength of the body which sought safety in this direction ? was it the whole of Blücher's Army ? or perhaps his left Corps ? or merely stragglers, who were withdrawing eastward ? The pressing need was to clear up this situation at once, since the plan for the 17th depended on its correct solution.

COURSES OPEN TO NAPOLEON ON THE 17TH

If, on the 16th, Wellington had got the better of Ney at Quatre Bras, as D'Erlon's withdrawal from Ligny seemed to indicate, and Blücher's Army had retired northward after Ligny and not eastward, then danger to the *Armée du Nord* was imminent, because an immediate Allied concentration became possible. This would nullify the Emperor's brilliant opening moves, unless he could destroy one or other of the Allied Armies on the 17th June. It was now of paramount importance to throw for complete and instant success, no lesser bid could save France ; and, at this crisis, three courses were open to Napoleon.

I. Napoleon could leave Ney to contain Wellington as best he could on the 17th, whilst the Emperor, at the earliest hour, led forward the whole of the rest of the *Armée du Nord* to seek out the vanquished Prussian Army, and then and there forced a decision from Blücher.

II. Napoleon could follow Blücher with the squadrons of Pajol and Exelmans (stiffened by a division of infantry say, Hulot's, or even by Gérard's Corps). Meanwhile the Emperor would have led the whole of the rest of the Right Wing and Reserve to combine with Ney against Wellington, and then fought a decisive battle with the Anglo-Dutch on the 17th, whilst the Prussians were too distant and too disorganized to turn round and come to their Ally's aid in the thick of the fight.

III. Napoleon could follow Blücher with a strong detachment (the Right Wing), consisting of Pajol's and Exelmans' Horse, and the Corps of Vandamme and Gérard, placed under a suitable officer whose duty it would be to locate Blücher, interpose between him and the Emperor (whilst the latter was dealing with Wellington), and neutralize the Field-Marshal until the crisis on the left was past. Meanwhile the Emperor, ensured against Prussian intervention on the 17th, would move the rest of the force (Lobau, Milhaud, and the Guard) and throw them against Wellington, whom Ney would have attacked and held about Quatre Bras until the Emperor swung in and dealt the Anglo-Dutch Army a deadly blow.

These three courses of action require careful consideration, because the fate of the campaign was at stake. There is no doubt that if the First Course had been adopted and was successful a decision must have been obtained. Blücher could hardly avoid offering battle on the 17th ; and he would have had to fight in an unselected position, provided Napoleon moved forward with the whole of the Right Wing and Reserve at a very early hour, located the Prussian Army, and then promptly engaged it. Even a relentless pursuit would probably have cost the Prussians another 20,000 men, and have so crippled Blücher that all idea of coming up to Wellington's assistance would have been out of the question. On the other flank, Ney could have contained the Anglo-Dutch Army. As matters turned out Ney would have run very little risk, because Wellington would have simplified the French situation considerably when he decided to fall back to Mt. St. Jean ; although, at daybreak, Napoleon could not have known Wellington's decision. Even if the Duke did engage Ney in an attempt to draw Napoleon off Blücher, yet, with D'Erlon's fresh Corps at his disposal, Ney could have contained the Duke at Quatre Bras. Ney would thus have secured for Napoleon the time in which to annihilate the Prussian Army, provided the Emperor overtook Blücher early enough to complete the Prussian rout.

The result of an immediate second battle with the Prussians was certain. Blücher's Army would never have stood the strain of another defeat and would have gone to pieces and streamed away to the Rhine in hopeless confusion. By ceaseless repetition the strokes would have gained in power, as Marshal Foch proved in the Advance to Victory in 1918. By pursuing Blücher's Army and giving it no time to rally, the next sledge-hammer blow would have caused its disintegration. Once the Prussian Army was destroyed it would be a mere matter of days before Wellington was compelled to take refuge on his transports. This course of action, if undertaken betimes, seemed likely to ensure the decision which was desired by Napoleon, and which it was essential to obtain at once. Even if Ney was forced back, Wellington would be even better placed for destruction when the time came for the Emperor to turn on the Anglo-Dutch. The pursuit of Blücher would have enabled Napoleon to open a new line back to France, running through Namur and up the Meuse valley. Even if Wellington got the better of Ney the Duke could not cut Napoleon's new line of communications, or seriously threaten it.

The disadvantages, however, were serious : Blücher had disappeared in the darkness at the close of the fighting, and the tracks would have to be picked up. Unless he was followed at daybreak he would not be found in time to force him to fight a decisive battle on the 17th ; and, if the blow struck the air, Wellington would have to be reckoned with. In the early morning the situation was too obscure to justify Napoleon in launching his whole available force in the pursuit of Blücher. He had to pause so as to learn about his other adversary. One of the disadvantages, inherent to all operations undertaken from a central position, is that a ground pursuit can rarely be carried out by the victor. The first course of action, correct in theory, was impracticable when the strategical situation was considered.

As for the Second Course. It avoided anything in the nature of half-measures and aimed at effecting a decision. Pajol and Exelmans would be able to pick up Blücher's line of withdrawal and keep the Emperor informed of the Prussian movements. Nor, on the 17th, would Blücher be likely to discover that he was only being followed by cavalry. In the meantime, by leading every man, every horse, and every gun against Wellington, Napoleon might gain at Quatre Bras the decision so necessary to the success of the campaign.

Was it possible, however, to force Wellington to fight at Quatre Bras on the 17th, since it seemed that the Duke had got the mastery over Ney on the 16th? If Wellington succeeded in evading the blow there would be no adequate force in position to neutralize Blücher, and the Prussians might become very dangerous on the 18th. Nor could Napoleon ensure that Wellington remained for sufficient time at Quatre Bras so as to allow the exhausted Corps of Vandamme and Gérard to be brought up to the Left Wing, as these two Corps were by no means ready to move at daybreak. If Napoleon waited for Vandamme and Gérard, Wellington might shake off Ney and withdraw before the Emperor arrived. Whereas if Napoleon went on with Lobau, Milhaud, and the Guard, Vandamme and Gérard would reach Quatre Bras after the decision had been gained and their assistance would not be wanted. It must be wiser to make certain that these two Corps were not wasted on the 17th. Also this second course involved the whole Right Wing being swung across and engaged against Wellington, which would be a change of the strategic plan. For these various reasons the second course can be dismissed.

Lastly, there is the Third Course. This was the one which the Emperor adopted, so it is necessary to appreciate the reasons which prompted him to come to this decision, and not to make the easy criticism that he was wrong because he did not succeed.

If this course was adopted it was essential to send the clearest orders to Ney, either overnight or at a very early hour, explaining to him the general situation and detailing precisely the action which he was to take. Then soon after daybreak Milhaud, Lobau, and the Guard should have started marching westward along the Quatre Bras road. If Wellington had slipped away this blow would fall in the air ; or if he had retired to another position, farther northward, the decision would not be gained on the 17th and then Blücher would have to be reckoned with. Hence the need for detaching a force sufficiently strong to neutralize and ward off Blücher on the 17th and 18th, and thus give Napoleon ample time to deal with the Anglo-Dutch Army. This explains why Napoleon detached 30,000 under Grouchy, just when he turned against the Anglo-Dutch. In the circumstances, Grouchy with a force of 30,000 was sufficient to neutralize Blücher and his 70,000. For pursuit of a beaten army ' brigades are not necessary, battalions will suffice '. But no smaller force could have ensured for Napoleon the time and space in which to deal with Wellington.

Unfortunately, Davout had been left in Paris and only Grouchy was available to command this detachment, and Grouchy exercised little control over Vandamme or Gérard. So as to insure against failure, Grouchy should have been given the most detailed orders defining the duty which he was expected to perform, and emphasizing the necessity of exploring thoroughly the whole Dyle valley, as far northward as Louvain, before he attempted to move eastward through Gembloux. Then news of any threatening move on Blücher's part would be forthcomng in time for the Emperor to arrange to meet it.

To prevent the Prussian Army rallying it must be followed immediately by cavalry and as soon as possible by a considerable detachment. If Blücher was allowed to rally and Wellington managed to slip away from Ney, then the Emperor would be in the Caudine forks by the evening of the 17th. The first requisite was to reconnoitre rapidly along every route which the retiring Prussians could have used, meanwhile keeping the bulk of the Right Wing in hand so as to launch it on the heels of the Prussians directly their main line of withdrawal was established. A short delay, whilst accurate information was gained, would avoid moving the main body of the pursuing detachment in a wrong direction.

No doubt this third course especially recommended itself to Napoleon because it was in accord with the idea which underlay his plan for the campaign in Belgium : to manœuvre in two Wings and to engage the Reserve alternately on either Wing, as circumstances demanded. Ney was magnificently placed to grip and hold Wellington fast, and the Reserve was ready to move up and engage decisively once Wellington was fastened upon and constituted a fixed point. So as to prevent the enemy decamping at a critical moment, Napoleon had invaded Belgium with his Army organized in two Wings and a Reserve. Wellington's position was known and an adequate force lay immediately to his front, so this third course was undoubtedly the one to pursue.

Napoleon knew what he was about on the 17th when he selected the course of action which required no disarrangement of his general plan, and he adopted the wisest course at this crisis of the campaign. If only his manœuvre had been made thoroughly clear to the *Major-Général* (who had to write the orders) and to the Marshals who held the two independent commands, then only chance, or a miracle, could have saved Wellington.

Unfortunately chance was given an opening. It was 8 a.m. before any instructions were sent to Ney ; and no detailed news had as yet reached Fleurus about what was happening at Quatre Bras, consequently the Reserve had not begun its westerly march. This delay was due partly to Napoleon's state of health.

It has been argued that to swing from Blücher on to Wellington was unsound, because Blücher would be given time to rally. This, however, is just what Napoleon intended the Prussians should not be allowed to do. The Emperor sent a Marshal of France with 30,000 victorious troops to keep the vanquished on the run, and interpose between the Prussians and the *Armée du Nord*. Secure from Blücher's intervention, Napoleon would rain ceaseless blows on Wellington until he succumbed.

In truth it matters not in war so much what is done, as that what is done, is done betimes, with proper unity, and with proper strength. Probably any of these three plans was capable of ensuring a decision. The third, however, was in accord with the Napoleonic principles of the art of war, and it resulted naturally from ' the advance in two Wings and a Reserve ', without any regroupings, rearrangements, or counter-orders.

As a result of a report that the Prussians were in strength at Gembloux, Exelmans collected his Cavalry Corps and moved in that direction, though Pajol still remained at le Mazy on the Namur road.

About 8 a.m., the Emperor directed Soult to send Ney the result of the Battle of Ligny. In this letter the Marshal was criticized for not keeping his force concentrated on the 16th (another proof that Napoleon never sent the ' pencil note ' to D'Erlon). The Emperor blamed Ney for recalling D'Erlon, thus preventing a decision from being gained on either flank. Napoleon also remarked that if Ney had used all his available force (45,000) he must have overpowered Wellington. The letter went on to say that in Napoleon's opinion it was unlikely that Wellington would take the offensive against Ney ; but, should the Duke attack, the Emperor would move at once with the Reserve along the Namur–Nivelles highway, and caught between two fires the Anglo-Dutch Army would be annihilated.

Once more there is the same lack of sufficient clearness in the letter, because Ney's paramount duty on that vital morning was neither emphasized nor even indicated. The Emperor was temporarily free of Blücher and could march westward at once, consequently Ney should have been ordered to hold the Anglo-Dutch Army at Quatre Bras, so that the decision which had not been gained on the 16th, owing to D'Erlon's wanderings, would be obtained on the 17th. In the letter no stress was laid on the essential duty which Ney had to perform at once, and left without clear guidance at the crisis of the campaign, Ney failed to realize the part he had to play and his responsibility. Nor did the conclusion of the letter do anything to dispel the fog of war which was gathering around the Marshal at Quatre Bras, since it finished by saying that the day was required for Ney to complete the occupation of Quatre Bras, and, if this was impossible, the Marshal was to inform the Emperor who would march at once and co-operate with the Left Wing. The day was to be used for collecting stragglers, replacing ammunition, etc.

Napoleon was no longer the victor of Austerlitz, who issued the peremptory order : ' In the position in which we are there is only one order to issue, namely, to inflict as great losses upon the enemy as possible, and to improve our victory in every way. In war nothing is done so long as anything remains to be done. No victory is complete so long as there is an enemy in the field.' Analogous instructions applied and with far greater cogency to the situation on the early morning of the 17th.

Superior skill and energy in the conduct of his operations had placed Napoleon within sight of ultimate victory. On the 17th a mere continuance of that skill and energy must have ensured decisive success. But the driving power lay temporarily dormant, because Napoleon's astonishing physical strength was no longer boundless ; otherwise at dawn he would have been with his outposts and he would have urged Grouchy to extend the radius of his reconnaissances. Gallopers would have sought Ney as soon as it was light, so as to learn what had happened on the 16th and what was happening on the 17th. At an early hour the Emperor himself would have sent Ney full instructions about his procedure ; and the Reserve would have been ready to move off at a moment's notice.

On the 17th the delay was occasioned partly by the obscure nature of the strategical situation, but more particularly by Napoleon's ill-health and by the Emperor believing that Blücher had been so disastrously defeated that he was out of the campaign for two or three days at least. In the Emperor's opinion there was no need for hurry—and he dallied.

General Monthyon was instructed to push out reconnaissances towards Wavre. But, as it was expected that only stragglers would be encountered, the reconnaissances were conducted conventionally and they were late in reporting their efforts.

Far from acting with energy, Napoleon received Grouchy at a late hour and did not send him at once to superintend the reconnaissances on which Pajol and Exelmans were engaged. Indeed, at 9 a.m., the Emperor took Grouchy to Ligny. Here the Emperor reviewed his troops in their bivouacs and was received with wild acclaim. He then rode over the battle-field, and in passing through St. Amand he was delayed for fifteen minutes. The heap of corpses in the village was so large that considerable time was required to make a way through this shambles. Having traversed the field, the Emperor talked with his Staff about the situation in Paris.

At 11 a.m. one of the reconnaissances returned from Quatre Bras and reported the English were still there. Napoleon now rapidly decided on his further procedure. Blücher was out of the way, but Wellington lay within striking distance ; so the time had come to combine with the Left Wing and obtain among the woods and fields of Quatre Bras that decision which yesterday he had failed to wrest from Blücher upon the bare, open slopes of the Bry plateau. The Emperor ordered Lobau to move his Corps (less Teste) to Marbais. Lobau was to be accompanied by Subervie's Light Cavalry and Drouot would follow closely with the Guard. This reinforcement would raise the Left Wing to 74,000 men and 240 guns, a force ample to effect Wellington's destruction so long as Blücher was prevented from co-operating with his Ally. After he had made the necessary arrangements to hold off Blücher, the Emperor would be ready to ride over to Quatre Bras.

Having used his Right Wing and Reserve to give battle to Blücher, Napoleon arranged to employ his Reserve and his Left Wing to destroy Wellington. So began the fourth, the final, phase of this Great Campaign.

CHAPTER XIV

FOURTH PHASE: THE ARRANGEMENTS MADE TO FIND AND NEUTRALIZE BLÜCHER; AND THE OFFENSIVE AGAINST THE ANGLO-DUTCH ARMY

(Sketch E)

'In War, opportunities will not wait.'—THUCYDIDES.

HAVING decided to turn against Wellington, Napoleon wrote at noon to Ney ordering the Marshal to attack whatever force was at Quatre Bras and he would be supported by the troops at Marbais. At the same time the Emperor entrusted Marshal Grouchy with the command of the detachment which was to locate the Prussian Army, pursue it, and keep it away from the Anglo-Dutch Army. Had the Prussian line of withdrawal been foreseen, or discovered, then the Emperor's instructions to Grouchy would have been more complete, definite, and satisfactory.

Marshal Grouchy may have wished to refuse a task so difficult and so embarrassing. But, to the Master who dominated him, Grouchy merely pointed out that the Prussians had gained a long start. Napoleon cut him short, and then indicated Namur as the direction probably taken by the Prussians. Just as Grouchy left, the Emperor exhorted him with words which remained graven on Flahault's memory: '*Allons, Grouchy, poursuivez les Prussiens l'épée dans les reins ; mais communiquez toujours avec moi par votre gauche.*'

At this moment France wanted a Masséna, a Lannes, or a Davout to command the detachment sent in pursuit of Blücher. But it was the Emperor who left Davout in Paris, and so it is the Emperor who must bear the principal responsibility for Grouchy's terrible failure.

Hardly had Grouchy left when the Emperor decided to give

143

the Marshal his orders in writing, and Napoleon wished to stress some news which he had just obtained. Consequently between 11.30 and noon, Soult being still at Fleurus, the Emperor dictated to the Grand-Marshal, General Bertrand, the following order :

'*17th June, 1815.*

' *Marshal,*
　' *Proceed to Gembloux with the Cavalry Corps of Generals Pajol and Exelmans, the Light Cavalry of the IV Corps, General Teste's Infantry Division (and of this division you will be especially careful, as it is detached from its own Corps), and the III and IV Infantry Corps. You will reconnoitre towards Namur and Maestricht, and you will pursue the enemy. Observe his march and inform me of his movements, that I may penetrate his intentions. I shall move my head-quarters to Quatre Bras, where the English still were this morning ; our communications will then be direct by the Namur highway. Should the enemy have evacuated Namur, write to the General in command of the 2nd Military Division, at Charlemont, to occupy the former place with some battalions of the National Guard and some guns, at present at Charlemont. The command at Namur will be given to a Major-General* (un maréchal de camp).
　' *It is important to discover what the enemy intend doing, whether Blücher is separating himself from Wellington, or whether they meditate uniting to cover Brussels and Liége by risking the fate of another battle. At all events, keep your two infantry Corps continually together within the limits of a league of ground ; and occupy each evening a good military position which has several avenues of retreat. Place cavalry detachments between us, so as to keep up communication with head-quarters.*
　' *Dictated by the Emperor in the absence of the* Major-Général,
　　　　　　　　' *GRAND-MARSHAL BERTRAND.*'

When Grouchy wrote his book in 1818 he overlooked this order. The Marshal only remembered it and unearthed it in 1840, twenty-two years later and a quarter of a century after it was written. One must conclude that the Marshal's memory was a convenient one because the order is undoubtedly important.

This ' Bertrand Order ' (as it is often called) required careful reading. It clearly implied that Grouchy was to act as a shield to the right flank of the *Armée du Nord* ; but, lacking sufficient precision, the order was capable of being misread and Grouchy misread it, or rather he read part of it quite literally. ' To Gembloux ' he was ordered to go and as far as Gembloux he went. On the 17th Grouchy remembered only the first part of the order, ' *Rendezvous à Gembloux* ' ; but he forgot how the order continued, ' *et vous poursuivrez l'ennemi* '. Would that the Emperor himself had added to this ' Bertrand Order ' the exhortation : ' *Activité, Activité, Vitesse ! Je me recommande à vous. Napoléon.*' Just as on the 18th April 1809 he had added these words as a postscript to a letter which he sent to Masséna.

Somewhat earlier in the day, Exelmans' Cavalry (Berton's Brigade) had obtained touch with some Prussians near Gembloux, and Exelmans reported this to Grouchy. The Marshal passed on the information to the Emperor but at the moment Napoleon seems to have attached little importance to the message. After Grouchy had left, either his Staff called Napoleon's attention to the presence of Prussians at Gembloux, or he himself recalled it ; and, wishing to direct the Marshal's attention especially to Gembloux, the place figured in the opening sentence of the ' Bertrand Order '. It was obvious that if Grouchy drove the Prussians to the eastward of Gembloux, then Blücher would lose the easiest means of reaching Wavre and communicating with Wellington ; whilst Grouchy, at Gembloux, would then be between Blücher and Napoleon and able to cover the open flank of the *Armée du Nord*. Thus placed the Marshal could forestall the Prussians anywhere on the left bank of the Dyle and interpose the deep muddy ditch of the little river between the French Right Wing and the Prussians. Grouchy had to be given a direction for starting his march, and Gembloux combined all the necessary requisites. Even in moving to Gembloux Grouchy would cut across both eastern lines of retirement which remained open to the Prussians after Ligny. If Blücher had used either the Namur or Liége roads, the Marshal must hear of it at once and note the obvious signs of retirement ; and, on the way to Gembloux, Grouchy would learn of any dangerous development, such as a Prussian withdrawal northward. If Blücher had gone to Wavre, and the Emperor

was able to act in conjunction with Ney against Wellington at
Quatre Bras, then Grouchy, at Gembloux, would be well placed
to prevent any attempt which Blücher might make to advance
to Wellington's assistance.   The Emperor chose wisely in selecting Gembloux as the place where Grouchy was bound to glean
the necessary information on which the Marshal could mould
his further plans and report to Napoleon about them.   Napoleon,
however, did mean that Grouchy should reach Gembloux with
all reasonable speed.   On his arrival at Gembloux, the Marshal
was intended to reconnoitre in all directions for traces of Blücher,
and gain sufficient information to enable Napoleon to decide on
his future course of action.   What Napoleon did not mean was
that Grouchy, after arriving at Gembloux, should then be satisfied with his day's work and forget that he had been told em-
phatically: ' *poursuivez les Prussiens l'epée dans les reins* '.

At first, Grouchy and the Emperor would move in divergent
directions and would draw away from one another.   It behoved
the Marshal to gain Gembloux as rapidly as possible and reconnoitre widely to the northward, because if Blücher had retreated
towards Wavre the Allies would be drawing together whilst
Grouchy and Napoleon were marching apart.   In this event
serious danger threatened, and Grouchy could not halt for the
night until his force lay inside Blücher's ; otherwise he could
not ensure neutralizing Blücher on the 18th when the Emperor
might still be engaged with Wellington.

The force entrusted to Grouchy was adequate for the duty
required of it and it was thoroughly well suited to the needs
of the situation, since, of the 33,000 men, 5,000 were cavalry
and the Right Wing had been given 96 guns.   It is true that
Grouchy's reputation rested on his ability as a tactician, and his
renown was that of a successful leader of horse.   Nevertheless
was it asking too much of a Marshal of France, who was entrusted with clearing up an obscure and critical situation, to
assume that his opponent had adopted the most far-sighted
project ?   In this case the Prussians would have to be sought for
northward, and not eastward.   If the Prussian movements were
based on correct methods, then the dispositions taken to thwart
them would avail against Blücher if he had made a bad mistake,
whereas the contrary did not hold true.   Hence Grouchy might
have decided to flood the whole Dyle head and valley with his

squadrons, and merely use officers' patrols for reconnoitring to
the eastward. In this way and advancing as rapidly as possible,
the Marshal must have obtained early and authentic news that
a Prussian concentration around Wavre was actually in progress.
If he had then reported this news immediately to the Emperor,
the solution of the problem could have been left in Napoleon's
hands.

NAPOLEON'S AND NEY'S ADVANCE

Sketch E.—On the morning of the 17th, the war of masses
which Napoleon practised demanded imperiously that the Marshal commanding the Left Wing should take the initiative, and
attack Wellington strenuously with every man he could lay hands
on. Only by acting in this way could he immobilize the Anglo-
Dutch Army until Napoleon could close and deal it a knock-
out blow. The force under Marshal Ney's hand was strong
enough for the purpose and the enemy at dawn was suitably
placed to be attacked. The situation called for prompt and
vigorous action.

Ney had in hand, besides Reille's somewhat exhausted Corps,
the comparatively fresh I Corps, Kellermann's Cuirassier Corps,
of which three Brigades had not been in action, as well as the
Light Horse of the Guard and Jacquinot's Lancers, neither of
which had been seriously engaged. The force at Ney's disposal
numbered 40,000, and until 9 a.m. Wellington lay inviting an
attack. Had Ney made a resolute onslaught soon after dawn
he could have ensured that Wellington was no longer a free
agent, and he could have prevented the Duke's retirement before
the Emperor arrived and struck in with the Reserve. Had Ney
acted in this fashion there would have been no Waterloo.

It is not very much to the point to quote the somewhat
homely, and very English, proverb, ' The proof of the pudding
is in the eating.' The appreciation of what should have happened in this campaign must be based on a close study of
the previous Napoleonic Campaigns from 1806 onwards. If this
is done and so long as the subject is not approached in a
Chauvinistic frame of mind, it will be realized that Napoleon's
system of advancing in mass almost worked itself, leaving the

minimum loophole by which Fortune could intervene. This system had often produced the results expected of it by the Emperor and, but for Ney's failure on the 17th, it would have done so in Belgium. Napoleon's Plan of Campaign, outlined in the letter which Marshal Ney had received on the previous day, showed that blows would be struck alternatively on either flank. It had become Ney's turn to arrange on his flank for the stroke of the Emperor's Reserve.

Until 7.30 a.m. the French Left Wing and the Anglo-Dutch Army remained in their overnight positions. Both sides were resting after the heavy fighting of the previous day, added to which most of Wellington's troops had made a long and harassing march to reach the battle-field. Wellington, after passing the night at Genappe, had returned to Quatre Bras about 5 a.m. To ascertain what had happened on the previous day at Ligny and to learn precisely where the Prussians were and what they intended doing, Wellington at an early hour despatched a reconnaissance eastward under one of his staff officers (Lieut.-Colonel Hon. Sir A. Gordon), escorted by Captain J. Grey's Troop of the 10th Hussars. Gordon rejoined the Duke about 7.30 a.m. and reported that Blücher had been severely defeated by Napoleon and the Prussian Army lay to the north of the Nivelles–Namur road. Gordon also reported that Zieten, commanding the Prussian rear-guard about Tilly, had told him that the withdrawal was northward towards Wavre.

Wellington realized at once the insecurity of his own position. There was nothing to prevent Napoleon from descending on the exposed left of the Anglo-Dutch Army if it remained at Quatre Bras, and Wellington would have to reckon also with Ney, who luckily was still inactive. The Duke decided to retire whilst there was yet time, and he resolved so to direct his retreat as to ensure co-operation with the Prussians. It was fortunate that there was in command at Quatre Bras a loyal ally and a great soldier.

The Duke determined to make everything subserve one end, keeping in touch with the Prussians and acting in combination with them. Thus could disaster be averted, thus alone could victory be won. Blücher and Grölmann also held these sound views, so these three Generals must be given the principal credit for carrying through the great strategic plan which, on Sunday the 18th, overwhelmed Napoleon and the *Armée du Nord* on the field of La Belle Alliance.

About 9 a.m. a Prussian officer reached Müffling from Gneisenau. Müffling and the Duke were at the time sitting together on the ground whilst the troops were having their early morning meal. Knowing that Gneisenau's orderly officer spoke both French and English, Müffling signed to him to state direct to the Duke what he had been ordered to report to the Prussian Attaché. Accordingly the orderly officer informed the Duke of Wellington that the Prussians were withdrawing northward, so as to concentrate that night at Wavre, and Gneisenau was anxious to know what Wellington intended doing. Wellington replied that he was about to fall back and take up a position on the plateau in front of Mt. St. Jean, to the south of the Forest of Soignes ; and he would offer a defensive battle there if he was promised the support of one of Blücher's Army Corps. On receiving the Duke's message the Prussian officer rode off to rejoin head-quarters. (It was 2 a.m., on the 18th, before Wellington received Blücher's reply.)

At 10 a.m. Wellington's withdrawal to Mt. St. Jean was begun, and the 40,000 men retiring from Quatre Bras used all available roads on both sides of the *chaussée*. Lord Hill withdrew the force at Nivelles (20,000), using the road which joined the Charleroi–Brussels highway at Mt. St. Jean. The 4th British Division remained at Braine le Comte, to block the Mons–Hal–Brussels road ; whilst the troops immediately under Prince Frederick of Orange (Stedman and Anthing) were ordered to march from Enghien to Hal (7–8 miles to the west of the Anglo-Dutch Army at Mt. St. Jean).

To cover his withdrawal from Ney, Wellington left Uxbridge's Cavalry and two British horse artillery Troops (Gardiner's and Mercer's), and Alten's Division remained in support of this screen. At noon Alten's Division began to move back, and until then the Duke had cast many anxious glances to the front. But when Alten took the road the Duke said : ' Well, there is the last of the infantry gone, and I don't care now.' So as to cover the movement as long as possible, Lord Uxbridge and the mounted troops still remained in position and Wellington remained with them.

Ney, without explicit and detailed orders from Napoleon, had done nothing whatever to hinder Wellington's withdrawal. The Emperor's first orders merely directed the Marshal to take up a position at Quatre Bras, and, if that was impossible, he was to report and the Emperor would arrange to combine in the operation. On the other hand, if Ney was only confronted by a rear-guard he was to drive it off and occupy the position. Ney did nothing. At noon the Emperor reiterated his first order, but the despatch was shorter and more peremptory. In it he informed Ney that a corps of French infantry had been placed at Marbais. He ordered Ney to attack Quatre Bras at once, adding that he himself was going to Marbais and he awaited a report from Ney.

About 1 p.m. Napoleon reached Marbais and halted there for a short time. He expected to hear the thunder of Ney's cannon, or at any rate to receive a report from the Marshal. Hearing nothing and receiving no report, the Emperor became impatient and rode on towards Quatre Bras. There he learned disastrous news. The Anglo-Dutch Army had slipped out of their compromising situation and were already far along the Brussels road. Only Uxbridge's horsemen and two horse artillery troops remained on the position. The main danger was over so far as Wellington was concerned.

The Emperor reached Quatre Bras about 2 p.m. On meeting Ney he expressed great surprise at the delay exhibited by the Marshal in attacking Wellington. D'Erlon's account of the arrival of the Emperor depicts Napoleon's feelings : ' The Emperor . . . marched . . . to rejoin Marshal Ney at Quatre Bras, which had already been partly evacuated by the English.

' The Emperor found me (D'Erlon) in front of this position, and, in a displeased tone, said to me the following words which have remained engraved on my memory : " *On a perdu la France ! Allons, mon cher général, mettez-vous à la tête de cette cavalerie, et poussez fortement l'arrière-garde anglaise !* " '

Napoleon realized at once that the Anglo-Dutch Army had escaped from the toils which should have fastened around it at Quatre Bras. This fault, at this vital moment in the campaign, probably rendered abortive the advance in ' two Wings and a Reserve '. This was no ' *funeste contretemps* ', it was a blunder likely to ruin France.

It is time to review the three mistakes which Napoleon criti-

cized immediately he learned of them, and to appreciate the
language which he used about them. The incident of Vandamme's orderly, on the 15th, was merely ' *un funeste contre-
temps* '. It was one of those pieces of bad staff work which
' his advance in two Wings and a Reserve ' absorbed and nullified.
Ney's recall of D'Erlon, on the 16th, grieved the Emperor and
only caused him regret. This internal friction did not throw
the whole machinery out of gear. On the contrary, the machine
continued almost to work itself; and on the morning of the
17th Napoleon still had the game in his hands. Ney's blunder
on the 17th was very different. The Emperor at once stigma-
tized it as ruinous, and ruinous it was. In the attendant circumstances not even the ' Strategical Plan for 1815 ' could rectify
the misfortune of such abstinence from action.

Despite Napoleon's anger, this was no time for words ; and
at the end of his career, his eagerness to close with the British
spurred him on to give one more demonstration of the ruthless
vigour with which he could pursue a retreating foe. The old
well-known energy blazed up again. Placing himself at the
head of his cavalry he opened a headlong pursuit. Almost at
once he came on Uxbridge's cavalry in position across the
Brussels road.

To the eastward of the highway was Vivian's Hussar Brigade
with E Troop, R.H.A. (Captain and Bt.-Lieut.-Colonel Sir R.
Gardiner). In the centre, G Troop, R.H.A. (2nd-Captain A. C.
Mercer)¯had been in action on a small ridge near the farm of
Quatre Bras, its ammunition wagons having started northward
so that the retirement should be encumbered as little as possible. Vandeleur's Light Dragoon Brigade was some 300 yards
in rear of Mercer's Troop, with scouts pushed southward towards
Frasnes, as Lord Uxbridge had definite orders to avoid a cavalry
action.

Though an affair seemed inevitable yet for a time all was
quiet. Then French vedettes worked up through the wood and
fired on Vivian's front line. To keep them back, Gardiner's
guns opened on the French and the cannonade was replied to.
The French pushed on. At the last moment, the order to retire
was given, and Vivian's Brigade and Gardiner's Troop drew
off in three columns, just as the great thunderstorm burst and
transformed the ground into ' a complete puddle '.

In the meantime, Milhaud's Cuirassiers and some Light Cavalry came in sight to the eastward, and directly afterwards Ney's force began to move forward. Thereupon Captain Mercer withdrew his Troop and unlimbered again just in front of Vandeleur's Brigade. Mercer intended to loose off a round of grape at the French as they rose the little hill on which his guns had first been in action, and the Troop would then retire as quickly as possible. The gunners loaded the guns and waited for a suitable target. The target they got had not been foreseen by anyone.

Gradually the sky darkened. Suddenly a single horseman, followed closely by others, galloped on to the little hill in front of Mercer's guns and pulled up regarding the foe intently. As the small party sat on their horses in clear silhouette against a background still bathed in sunshine, the leading horseman was recognized at once—the Emperor ! A lucky round might end the campaign. If Napoleon was removed the *Armée du Nord* would come to a standstill. There was little time to dally. Several French squadrons could be seen approaching, and Lord Uxbridge, in his excitement, yelled out : ' Fire ! Fire ! ' A salvo crashed from Mercer's guns which then limbered up under cover of the smoke. It was well they did so, for the French dashed forward and two of their horse artillery batteries opened fire. At the first discharge, the heavy thunder-clouds broke and a deluge of rain poured down. Flash succeeded flash, and peal after peal of thunder roared and rumbled.

The French pursuit began in deadly earnest. Napoleon had conquered his earlier lassitude and flung his horsemen furiously against Wellington's rapidly retreating rear-guard, hoping to compromise the rearmost troops so seriously that Wellington must turn about to succour them. In this way a chance might come to strike a telling blow on the 17th.

Wellington's left column, which Gardiner's Troop accompanied, retired at a hard gallop for some 6 miles, until the Waterloo position was reached. But, owing to the sodden state of the ground, the French were unable to press the pursuit on this cross-road. In fact when one of the gun-horses lost a shoe Lieut. W. B. Ingilby halted the gun and had the shoe put on. Our skirmishers easily kept back the French by forming as if to charge. On Wellington's right, however, matters were very different. Here, with some picked squadrons and a horse artillery battery, the Emperor galloped at the head of the pursuit. He was followed closely by Jacquinot's Lancers, Subervie's Cavalry, and the Horse Artillery of the Guard. Then came Milhaud's Cuirassiers and D'Erlon's Corps, followed by Reille's Corps, Lobau's Corps, Kellermann's Cavalry, and, in rear of all, the Guard.

Fate was against the Emperor. Rarely has this violent storm been credited with sufficient importance for the part it played in thwarting the Emperor's fiery, if tardy, pursuit. The sodden roads and fields immeasurably delayed the French advance. Given good weather Napoleon could have attacked towards evening, and by 8 a.m. on the 18th the great battle would have begun. It might have been as bloody as Eylau, but it would have been far more decisive and a French victory.

By the time Genappe was reached the thunderstorm was over though the heavy rain continued. Even despite the drenching rain the pursuit was carried out ' at the pace of a fox-hunt '; and at Genappe the Anglo-Dutch rear-guard had to make a stand to check the onrushing flood of French horsemen. The 7th Hussars awaited the arrival of the French Lancers on the northern side of the town. As the Lancers debouched, the 7th charged and a fluctuating fight ensued. To assist the 7th, Mercer brought his guns into action and fired until he had exhausted the ammunition in his gun-limbers. At last Uxbridge flung two squadrons of the 1st Life Guards into the *mêlée*, and the heavy horsemen, driving back the French Lancers, chased them into the town inflicting severe casualties. After this check at Genappe the pace of the pursuit slackened.

It was getting dusk when Napoleon and the head of the French column reached the ridge near La Belle Alliance. This ridge was separated by a shallow valley from a lower and almost parallel range of heights, stretching from east to west in front of the junction of the Nivelles and Charleroi highways. It was behind this second ridge that Wellington's Army had already begun forming up when the rain started. In the valley beneath him, the Emperor saw signs of the effect of his relentless pursuit. Disordered Brunswicker infantry were crossing the valley bottom, throwing away arms and knapsacks in their flight. In rear of them came the British cavalry screen, covered by

Mercer's guns in action on the top of an old gravel pit.   Marbot's
Hussars (of Jacquinot's Division) followed the English screen.
But most of the French cavalry halted on the heights about La
Belle Alliance, 1,200 to 1,300 yards from Mercer's guns which
began to blaze away at the masses of French horse as they formed
up.   It was about 6.30 p.m.

Napoleon scanned the Allied position.   In the damp, misty
light it was very difficult to appreciate Wellington's dispositions,
but the Emperor's searching glance detected signs which suggested the presence of a large force.   Before bivouacking for
the night, the Emperor determined to wring the truth from
Wellington and compel him to disclose whether he had taken
up a battle-position with his whole Army, or whether he had
merely dropped a strong rear-guard to cover a further withdrawal through the Forest of Soignes.   By the Emperor's orders
four French horse artillery batteries opened rapid fire on the
Anglo-Dutch position.   Under cover of this cannonade Milhaud's
Cuirassiers deployed for a smashing charge at Wellington's line.
Swiftly came the reply, bellowed by 60 guns.   The situation
was resolved.

Napoleon's beloved guns had unmasked Wellington.   It was
the whole Anglo-Dutch Army which lay within easy gun-shot
of La Belle Alliance.   At long last the red-coats were within
the Emperor's grasp.   But the light was dying fast ; and realizing the chance which had been missed through his own lassitude and Ney's delay, the bitter cry escaped Napoleon : ' Would
to God I had Joshua's power to stop the sun for two hours.'

About 9 p.m., a report reached the Emperor that Milhaud's
patrols (during the march to Quatre Bras) had sighted a Prussian
column retiring from Géry towards Wavre ; but no importance
was attached to this somewhat startling information.

The rain stopped at nightfall, nevertheless the troops had
miserable night-bivouacs, their cloaks and uniforms were
drenched and the fields were sodden.   On the French side
the troops, widely scattered by the long and rapid pursuit, were
short of food and lacked dry wood both for fires and shelters.
To make things worse, later in the night the rain again came
down in torrents.

The Anglo-Dutch Army bivouacked largely on open cornfields, in which the rye was 7 feet high.   The ground every-

where was churned into mud, the cold excessive, and fires scarce. The men, allowed to pile arms but forbidden to leave their places, gathered bundles of the standing corn and with this and their knapsacks they made improvised seats, and then held their blankets over their heads to keep off the rain.

Wellington had massed at Mt. St. Jean a formidable Army, 67,000 strong with 156 guns. In addition, as he still feared for his right flank, another 17,000 and 30 guns, under Prince Frederick of the Netherlands, halted between Braine-le-Comte and Hal. That night Wellington's head-quarters were in the village of Waterloo.

Map 4.—In the *Armée du Nord* the Corps of Lobau and D'Erlon lay astride the Brussels–Charleroi road between Plancenoit and Mon Plaisir, and behind them were Milhaud's and Kellermann's Cuirassiers. Owing to darkness, Reille's Corps halted near Genappe and the Guard bivouacked at Glabais. Imperial Head-Quarters, covered by the 1st Chasseurs of the Guard, were at Le Caillou on the Charleroi road. The Emperor had available for his battle with Wellington, 74,000 men (including 15,000 cavalry) and 260 guns.

Napoleon was determined to settle matters on the morrow with the Anglo-Dutch Army. His main anxiety was that Wellington might decamp under cover of darkness. Consequently, about 1 a.m. the Emperor and General Bertrand left Le Caillou and went round the French outposts. All was quiet in the Anglo-Dutch position, and the Emperor concluded that his foe must fight on the morrow, because Wellington's bivouacs would already have been astir had he intended to slip back into the Forest of Soignes.

About daybreak Napoleon returned to his head-quarters and found a letter from Marshal Grouchy, which, leaving Gembloux about 10 p.m., had reached Le Caillou about 2 a.m. Grouchy reported that the Prussians were retiring in three columns : *via* Perwez, Wavre, and Namur ; and on the 18th, when he had definite intelligence of the whereabouts of the Prussian main body, he would arrange to follow it. It was 10 a.m. on the 18th when the Emperor answered this report, and drew Grouchy's attention to a strong body of Prussian troops who were reported to have moved on Wavre past Géry (the column sighted and reported by Milhaud). The Emperor added that he was about to attack the English Army which was in position in front of the Forest of Soignes. The Marshal was told to reach Wavre as rapidly as possible so as to draw near to the Emperor; and, pushing the Prussians before his advance, Grouchy was to report continuously.

This despatch was important. It showed that Napoleon was preparing for a decisive battle with Wellington; and, inasmuch as Grouchy was to reach Wavre and connect with the Emperor, it implied that he must gain the left bank of the Dyle as early as possible. Unfortunately this despatch could not reach Grouchy before he was fully committed to his advance along the right bank of the Dyle. Napoleon, however, was not at all uneasy, though the situation was an anxious one. Grouchy was at Gembloux, 15 miles from Le Caillou; but if the Prussian mass at Wavre turned out to be Blücher's main body, then the Prussians had gained an important start as they were halted within easy supporting distance of Wellington, and Grouchy was outside this mass. Napoleon would not admit, either the possibility of danger, or that Blücher need be reckoned with only two days after Ligny. It is clear that he treated his adversaries with contempt and the situation with carelessness, foreign to his nature when he was in his prime.

Nevertheless Napoleon's situation was growing critical. The incessant downpour had turned the ground into a sea of mud and the French Army was not ready to open an action at daybreak. At the earliest it would be 9 a.m. before the battle could begin, consequently extra time would be given to the Prussians to make their presence felt (and according to Grouchy's report some were already at Wavre).

*   *   *   *   *   *   *

Meanwhile Wellington was anxiously awaiting tidings from Blücher. If the Prussians could not pledge their assistance, all Wellington's skill would be required to extricate his force. He would have to deal with Napoleon himself not merely with Ney, and this difference would be vital if Blücher failed to arrive. At 2 a.m. all Wellington's doubts were at last set at rest. A letter arrived from Blücher, and the Duke learned: ' Bülow's Corps will set off marching at daybreak to-morrow in your direction. It will be followed immediately by the Corps of Pirch I. The I and III Corps will also hold themselves in readiness to proceed in your direction. The exhaustion of the troops, some of whom have not yet arrived, does not allow of my beginning my movement any earlier.' Thus Blücher pledged himself to send two Corps to Mt. St. Jean, or double the force Wellington had asked for.

If Blücher had sent only one Corps, as he was asked to do, this reinforcement would simply have shared in Wellington's rout and contributed to the magnitude of the disaster. Fortunately for the Allies Blücher realized that the task, which Wellington had consented to undertake, was far more formidable than the Duke conceived. It was no time to run any further risk, a decision must be obtained and as soon as possible ; and Blücher, rising to the height of the situation, determined to send every available man to co-operate at Mt. St. Jean. Despite his injuries, the old Field-Marshal intended to lead his men to Mt. St. Jean and drive his Corps against Napoleon's open and exposed right flank, when the Emperor attacked Wellington on the 18th. Blücher also suggested (through Müffling) that, if the 18th passed without any fighting, the two combined Armies should attack the French on the 19th. Such invincible determination on the part of the commander of a beaten army requires no comment.

The plan for the co-operation of the Allies in the decisive battle was eminently feasible and adequate. It was marred, however, by the selection of Bülow's Corps to lead the advance. The IV Corps had bivouacked at Dion le Mont, on the right bank of the Dyle, consequently it lay farthest away from Wellington. Its selection meant unnecessary delay at a most critical time in the campaign.

CHAPTER XV

MARSHAL GROUCHY ON THE 17TH JUNE

(Map 5 and Sketch E)

THE events of the 16th June had proved that the Allies were ready and willing to fight, thus the risk on the 17th was increased. Grouchy's duty was clear, he had to ascertain where the Prussian Army was, pursue it, and keep the Emperor well supplied with information. So far no more bodies of Prussian troops had been reported from the Namur side, consequently Blücher must have retreated westward or northward. If the Prussian retirement was westward then the Emperor would gain news of it and it was Grouchy's duty to guard against the other eventuality. Either Blücher would move through Gembloux to Liége and his magazines, or retire northward towards Brussels, moving past Wavre. The Marshal's orders alluded to the possibility of this latter course, and Grouchy had to examine the situation and come to a decision. If Blücher was moving on Liége, the Prussian Field-Marshal ceased to be a threatening factor. Every mile he covered in this direction widened the gap between the Allies, and no immediate danger need be expected. Nor was it expedient for Grouchy to follow Blücher towards Liége, because it was essential that the containing Wing should be placed so that it could swell the numbers of the Reserve, directly it was required to do so. The position, which suited this plan, was on the Dyle's left bank near Wavre, so that the Dyle could be used by Grouchy to hold up the Prussian advance, the Marshal's communications with the *Armée du Nord* would be short and secure, and co-operation a simple matter. Had the Marshal strained every nerve to reach Wavre on the 17th, he would have been in a position to cope with the critical danger which from that night threatened the *Armée du Nord*. To reach Wavre before dark a rapid march was essential, and the detachment would have to advance in two columns. Gérard (covered by Pajol) would move *via* Gembloux, Nil Pierreux, and La Baraque to Wavre, and use officers' patrols to reconnoitre eastward past Mazy, Grand Leez, and Perwez ; whilst Vandamme, together with Teste's Division (VI Corps) and Exelmans' Dragoons, would march *via* Sombreffe and Gentinnes to Mt. St. Guibert, cross the Dyle at Mousty, and move down the left bank to Limal. Directly the Dyle was crossed Exelmans would get in touch with the right of the *Armée du Nord*. Advancing in this way, the whole countryside would be flooded with cavalry and swept for information of the Prussians, nor were the country people unfriendly to the French.

In the existing circumstances Grouchy could not have reached Wavre on the 17th, but at any rate he would have discovered that the Prussian Army had concentrated around that town, astride the Dyle, from Bierges to Dion le Mont. The Marshal would have located Blücher. The secret of the latter's manœuvre would have been a secret no longer, and Napoleon, with this information in his possession, would have had no further doubts.

Grouchy acted very differently. When every moment was golden he displayed no energy whatever, used only one road for his advance, the direct one from Sombreffe to Gembloux, and ordered Vandamme, whose Corps was farthest from the starting-point, to lead the marching column. Gérard had perforce to sit still and watch the III Corps defile before he could take the road.

Previously Berton's Dragoon Brigade (Exelmans' Corps) had followed Pajol along the Namur road. But Berton hearing of a mass of Prussians retreating to Gembloux reported this intelligence to Exelmans, although he did not trouble to inform Pajol who was only a short mile ahead of him on the Namur road. Berton's report finally reached the Emperor, after passing through Exelmans' and Grouchy's hands, and it probably caused the mention of Gembloux in the ' Bertrand Order '.

Exelmans ordered Berton to move to Gembloux. The Brigade reached the place at 9 a.m., and beyond the village saw large masses of the enemy resting (mainly Thielemann's III Corps). Shortly afterwards Exelmans himself rode up with his three other Dragoon Brigades. Exelmans had 3,000 sabres and two horse batteries, and within 4 miles was Pajol at the head of 1,400 sabres and two horse batteries, as well as Teste's Division (VI

Corps) numbering 3,000 muskets. Exelmans made no effort to secure Pajol's co-operation in any attack on the enemy, whose strength he estimated to be 20,000. It was even more unpardonable that Exelmans did not send in an urgent report to Grouchy for transmission to the Emperor, stating he was in touch with one of Blücher's beaten Corps. Nor did Exelmans make any effort to harass the foe. So peaceful was he that the Prussians mistook one of his brigades of dragoons for part of the Corps Cavalry of Pirch's Corps ! Unfortunately Exelmans did not even open fire on the Prussians, because the noise of a cannonade at Gembloux would have quickly informed the Emperor of the real state of affairs.

Meanwhile Marshal Grouchy ordered Vandamme to march from his overnight bivouac (near St. Amand) to the starting-point at Point du Jour, and the Marshal sent one of his orderly officers to find Exelmans to learn the latest news. Grouchy ordered Gérard (at Ligny) to follow Vandamme to Gembloux. Vandamme was over a mile from Ligny, which he had to pass so as to reach Point du Jour, and his Advanced Guard only arrived at 3 p.m. It had taken over one hour to crawl 1¼ miles.

In the meantime Pajol reported that the Prussians on the Namur road were moving northward towards the Namur–Louvain road, followed by guns and wagons from Namur. Then, at 3 p.m., Grouchy, at Point du Jour, received Exelmans' report which stated that a mass of Prussians was at Gembloux. The difficult duty of obtaining contact was completed, and the Marshal was now free to concentrate on the other two essentials : the pursuit of the Prussians, and the penetration of Blücher's intentions. If the Prussians remained at Gembloux, Grouchy could engage them immediately Vandamme reached the front. If they drew off, by following closely on their heels he would have been in contact that night with the main Prussian Army to the south of Wavre. At daybreak Grouchy could have arranged to prevent any westerly movement of the Prussians, the only dangerous move which Blücher could make. Action, however, had to be taken to-day, to-morrow would be too late. It was to-morrow Grouchy chose.

Exelmans' news was important enough to have caused the Marshal to gallop on to Gembloux and at the same time recall Pajol, ordering him to move at once to Gembloux so as to be ready to co-operate. But the Marshal, overburdened with his task, merely accompanied Vandamme to Gembloux which he reached at 7 p.m., followed by Gérard at 9 p.m. The long column, winding along the sodden road under drenching rain, took four hours to cover 4½ miles. Vile though the weather was, it was insufficient to account for this dilatoriness. Nor need the rain have interfered with the bold handling of Exelmans' Dragoons or Pajol's Hussars, who had apparently taken root in the mud of Belgium.

The loose grip which Exelmans kept of the Prussians allowed Thielemann to slip away unnoticed about 2 p.m. An hour passed by before Chastel's Dragoon Brigade moved through Gembloux. The Brigade then halted at Sauvenière only 2 miles farther on. After Thielemann left Gembloux, nearly twenty-four hours passed before touch with any large body of the Prussians was regained by Grouchy's horsemen. On reaching Gembloux Grouchy felt so satisfied that he decided to halt there for the night, and thus he allowed the Prussians to obtain a start which on the morrow he was never able to catch up.

At 6 p.m. Exelmans pushed out two reconnaissances, to Tour-innes and towards Perwez. It was after 9 p.m. before they returned and reported news of a Prussian concentration at Wavre. This most important information only reached Grouchy con-siderably later. By this time it should have been evident to Grouchy that, whatever course Blücher was adopting, at any rate the Field-Marshal was not retiring to Namur ; and the alternatives were a withdrawal to Liége, to Louvain, or to Wavre. On the evidence to hand Wavre was the most likely, and it was by far the most dangerous for the French. Even as late as 8 p.m. it was still possible for Grouchy to prepare for the morrow's manœuvres, based on a sounder plan. He might have pushed on Exelmans to Walhain, moved Vandamme through Gembloux to Ernage, wheeled Gérard to the left before he reached Gembloux, and halted the IV Corps at Gentinnes. Pajol could have been ordered to move to Grand Leez.

With the Right Wing thus placed, at 5 a.m. on the 18th the Marshal could have started on two roads ; and, at an early hour, seizing the Dyle passages at Mousty and Ottignies, he could have moved part of his force to the left bank without delay. Then he could have closed on Wavre on both banks of the river, clearing and opening each passage as he moved down-stream.

Sketch E.—Grouchy did nothing of the kind, but he settled down to pass a comfortable night at Gembloux. When Exelmans' information reached him, he wrote at 10 p.m. to the Emperor, stating that on the morrow he could march either on Wavre or Perwez, according to the intelligence which he obtained. A glance at his map should have shown the Marshal that Wavre lay on the direct road from Gembloux to Brussels. If Blücher was at Wavre, then, by advancing direct on Wavre, Grouchy could not separate Blücher and Wellington, as he would drive the Allies together, the very thing which Napoleon had been doing his utmost to prevent all through the campaign. Not only was Grouchy halted outside Blücher, but the French Right Wing was farther from the decisive battle-field than the Prussian Army. Even if Wellington retired to a position covering Brussels to await his Ally's arrival, Grouchy was just as badly placed to prevent this concentration. Notwithstanding this, the orders which Grouchy issued for the 18th showed clearly that it was not at Wavre he would expect to discover Blücher but in the direction of Liége, since, in his evening orders to his subordinates, no mention was made of Wavre and Perwez appeared several times.

In these orders Exelmans and Vandamme were directed to proceed to Sart à Walhain. (The hachuring on the map which Grouchy used obscured the name ' Walhain,' though ' Sart à Walhain ' happened to be easily legible. Probably for this reason, on more than one occasion, Grouchy confused the hamlet with the village.) Once more Gérard was to follow Vandamme, whilst Pajol was to advance to Grand Leez. Grouchy was carefully arranging for Blücher to outmanœuvre him.

THE PRUSSIAN MOVEMENTS

Gneisenau had decided to abandon the Prussian line of communications *via* Namur and Liége, preferring to change to Louvain, Maestricht, and Cologne. This would not necessarily result in abandoning Wellington and all chance of the Allies combining and crushing Napoleon ; because, after concentrating at Wavre, the Prussians could reopen a new line of communications and also co-operate with Wellington. Even though

Gneisenau thought more about his communications yet Blücher and Grölmann always kept before them the duty of working in conjunction with Wellington. It was their inflexible determination to combine against Napoleon which, on the 18th, drove the Prussian masses to Waterloo, enabling them to deal a deadly blow to the *Armée du Nord*.

Sketch E.—The Prussian retirement from Ligny was carried out on a broad front. The two most shattered Corps (I and II) withdrew more rapidly than the III, which covered their retreat. At 10 a.m. Zieten and Pirch I were both clear of Mt. St. Guibert. At noon the two Corps concentrated at Wavre, whilst Bülow moved north through Walhain, and Thielemann halted at Gembloux. By nightfall Blücher's Army was concentrated around Wavre with Zieten at Bierges and Pirch I near Aisemont. After Thielemann left Gembloux about 2 p.m. he marched to Wavre, and the III Corps then crossed the Dyle and halted for the night near La Bavette ; and Bülow halted at Dion le Mont to the southeast of Wavre.

At last Blücher's concentrated Army lay within striking distance of Napoleon and within easy supporting distance of his Ally. That night Gneisenau issued orders for Bülow's Corps to lead the westward march on the 18th and Pirch I was to follow Bülow, although these two Corps were on the right bank of the Dyle and farthest from Wellington. It is true that Bülow had not been engaged on the 16th, yet that reason was inadequate. Even if Zieten had suffered heavily, Thielemann was fairly fresh and the III Corps was better placed to lead the movement when every moment was golden. The III Corps might have been ordered to march to Wellington's support at 6 a.m., *via* Ohain, whilst, at the same hour, the I Corps moved from Bierges, *via* Chapelle St. Lambert, against Napoleon's right. Starting as suggested, Zieten should have reached the Lasne before 11 a.m., and by noon Thielemann would have been close up to Wellington's left. Bülow could have followed Zieten and supported the I Corps ; whilst Pirch I remained at Wavre to hold up Grouchy on the line of the Dyle. This, or some similar plan, would have ensured timely Prussian co-operation at Waterloo. But Gneisenau's arrangements involved unnecessary delay and ran a risk of Wellington losing the battle before the Prussians engaged.

Was Gneisenau still uncertain whether Wellington would

be true to his word and stand at Waterloo ? or, after his experience at Ligny, was he doubtful whether Wellington's troops could hold a position against Napoleon for sufficient time to allow the Prussians to arrive ? If, on the 18th, Wellington continued to retire, or the Anglo-Dutch Army was swiftly shattered by Napoleon, then the fate of the Prussian Army moving to Waterloo was certain, and Grouchy would complete the encircling net. But if Bülow, followed by Pirch I, led the advance, then, before these two Corps were so compromised that they could no longer retire, the Prussian Head-Quarters would have ascertained Wellington's intentions and his situation. Was this the reason which caused Gneisenau to select Bülow to lead the advance on the 18th ?

* * * * * * *

On the 17th darkness found the combatants within sword's thrust of each other. On the morrow would the Eagles soar triumphant over a field more glorious than Austerlitz, or would Fate raise to France's lips. a cup more bitter than Leipzig, and compel her to drain it to the dregs ?

CHAPTER XVI

NAPOLEON'S PLANS FOR THE 18TH JUNE

(Map 4)

WHEN light broke and it became certain that Wellington's Army had not decamped, Napoleon exclaimed : ' *Je les tiens donc, ces Anglais.*'

Napoleon wished to open the battle at 6 a.m., but he soon decided that the fields were still too soaked for artillery and cavalry to manœuvre, and his troops not only required a meal but they were too strung out by the rapid pursuit to be able to form up for battle at 6 a.m. In consequence the attack was postponed until 9 a.m. to allow the sodden ground to dry, and permit the Army to cook a meal, close up, clean their arms, and form for battle. Even during the battle the ground was still so soft that it smothered the shell bursts, and prevented the round-shot ricochetting and doing incalculable mischief as they had at Ligny.

Map 4.—The *Armée du Nord* gradually deployed in three lines, resembling three W's. The First Line, D'Erlon's Corps and Reille's Corps formed to right and left of the Charleroi road, with Light Cavalry on the outer flanks. In the Second Line, Kellermann's Cuirassiers were behind Reille, and Milhaud's Cuirassiers behind D'Erlon ; and in the centre, astride the highway, Lobau's incomplete Infantry Corps was to the west, with Domon and Subervie to the east. The Third Line was composed of the ' Invincibles,' horse, foot, and artillery. The Heavy Cavalry of the Guard (Guyot) was behind Kellermann, the Light Horse of the Guard (Lefebvre-Desnoëttes) was behind Milhaud, and, behind the centre, the Infantry and Artillery of the Guard formed in a huge and imposing mass across the Charleroi road. The Infantry of the Guard deployed in six lines of four battalions each, Young Guard (Duhesme) in front, Middle Guard

(Morand) in the centre, and the Old Guard (Friant) in rear. Behind this mass of veteran infantry were the horse and field batteries of the Guard Artillery. Otherwise the horse artillery batteries were with their respective cavalry organizations, and the divisional field artillery was in front of the infantry of each division.

The array of the *Armée du Nord* was undoubtedly intended to impress any wavering contingents in Wellington's Army, as every single man was visible from the Anglo-Dutch position. Never before had the Emperor massed his troops on so short a front (2¾ miles), except at Borodino where the 138,000 men and 584 guns of the Grand Army formed for battle on a front of 4¼ miles. Borodino was a barren victory, dearly bought, yet the same general plan was followed at La Belle Alliance.

The two first-line Corps, D'Erlon and Reille, were available to attack Wellington all along his front and wear down his powers of resistance, and the cavalry were placed to co-operate with the infantry. Then at the critical moment Lobau would launch his Corps against Wellington, so as to compel the Duke to engage his last reserve to save his line from being broken ; but Napoleon would still have in hand the Guard. At this moment batteries of the Guard Artillery would gallop to the front, unlimber within case-shot range of Wellington's line, and with their grape tear the requisite breach for the veteran infantry to storm and then deal the finishing stroke. Certainly Napoleon's formation for battle did not arrange for Blücher's intervention—but that was Grouchy's business. To Napoleon it was inconceivable that if Grouchy failed to find and hold Blücher, the Marshal would also fail to render direct aid to his Emperor in the thick of the fight at Mt. St. Jean. Napoleon would have been equally justified in assuming that the Marshal might be swallowed by an earthquake.

On the 18th Napoleon calculated on having only Wellington to deal with. Nevertheless his plan of attack was almost too simple. He intended to take the bull by the horns and smash in Wellington's centre by a tremendous frontal attack. Napoleon may have feared that Wellington, once the pressure became extreme, would draw off through the Forest of Soignes and unite with Blücher to the north of the wood. For this reason Napoleon meant to hold and wear down Wellington by an attack all along his front ; and, at the crisis, the VI Corps would break through the centre, seize the village of Mt. St. Jean, and block the principal line of withdrawal.

This frontal attack against Wellington's position promised to be murderous enough, if any conclusions could be drawn from the disastrous battles in Spain. Whereas an attack against Wellington's left flank not only promised to be less bloody than a purely frontal attack, but it might be more effective and far-reaching. In this case the same central plan would be followed, tactically and strategically. Strategically Napoleon had planned to penetrate between the Allies, drive them asunder, and beat them in detail. The plan for Ligny was to outflank and crush Blücher's right, and ensure an eastward retreat of the beaten rabble. This failed, because Ney had not co-operated. The plan for the 17th placed Grouchy as a protection to Napoleon's right flank, whilst Wellington's left was to be beaten in at Quatre Bras ; but Ney let Wellington decamp. So on the 18th, if Wellington's left was driven in the Allies would be separated. Whereas if the centre was pierced Wellington's left might succeed in rallying on Blücher, and if the right joined the force at Hal the immediate result would not be decisive. Nor can the proximity of the Prussians be urged as a reason for not adopting this plan, because Napoleon never considered this danger. As matters turned out the arrival of the Prussians would have had one of two results : either it must have precipitated the French attack, or it would have caused it to be postponed indefinitely. In the latter case the impending battle must have been put off, a procedure which was unlikely to have led to the disaster which did occur.

It was of vital importance to obtain a decisive victory over Wellington at the earliest moment and drive him as far away from his Ally as possible, seeing that the Ligny losses had been so heavy that four or five more actions of that description would ruin the *Armée du Nord* by attrition. On the 18th a decisive result had to be obtained without any further delay, and ' The Fate of France ' lay in Napoleon's hands at La Belle Alliance. By delivering a frontal attack Napoleon sensibly diminished the chances of overthrowing the Anglo-Dutch Army before Blücher could intervene.

If, however, the French Artillery had been well handled, even

a frontal attack might have succeeded.   La Haye Sainte appeared
to be the key of Wellington's centre, at any rate this large farm
had to be reduced before the centre could be assailed.   This
required a large artillery concentration.   Consequently, at 10 a.m.
at latest, the selected batteries (including 12-pounders and
howitzers) should have advanced up the Brussels road, deployed
astride it, and unlimbered along the spur in front of the farm.
Within an hour of the guns and howitzers opening fire on the
farm, it would have been smashed and reduced to a smoking heap
of débris.   Then, as the range of the 12-pounders was 2,000 yards
and that of the 8-pounders about 1,600 yards, destructive fire
could have been opened on Wellington's main position so as to
prepare it for assault.   At 1 p.m., after having been deluged by an
inferno of fire, Wellington's centre could have been riven by the
combined and successive efforts of D'Erlon, Lobau, and the
Guard, before Bülow was in any position to co-operate and take
off the pressure.   Thus the last chance which Fate offered to her
favourite depended on the handling of his favourite arm, the
Artillery.   In no other battle of this era did artillery, so numeric-
ally superior, fail to produce a far greater effect than the French
guns obtained in the battle against Wellington.   *Un grand artilleur*
was required.   Senarmont, however, was dead, though Drouot
was on the field, but he was otherwise employed and no other
artillery officer of his calibre was available.

About 9 a.m. some of the French Generals met the Emperor
at Le Caillou.   Definite anxiety was shown about the outcome
of a battle with Wellington, owing to the dismal results which
had been achieved in Spain.   Some of the Generals openly
advocated the recall of the bulk of Grouchy's force, to enable
it to take part in the impending action.   On the other hand,
the Emperor realized this was no time for half-measures, his
demeanour, too, was calculated to allay anxiety and inspire his
chiefs with the certain hope of victory.   He said : ' The enemy's
Army is superior to ours by more than one-fourth.   Yet we have
ninety chances in our favour, and not ten against us.'   As he
spoke, Marshal Ney came in, fresh from a visit to the French outpost line.   Whilst he was there Ney had noticed a movement
among the Anglo-Dutch troops which he thought was the beginning of a retirement on Brussels, and he observed : ' Doubtless,
Sire, provided Wellington is so simple as to wait for you.   But

I must inform you that his retreat has begun ; and, if you do not hasten to attack, the enemy is about to escape from you, as his columns are in full retreat and are disappearing in the forest [of Soignes].'

The Emperor replied : ' You are mistaken, for it is too late now, as Wellington would expose himself to certain loss. He has thrown the dice, and they are in our favour.'

Marshal Soult, who had good cause to appreciate Wellington's skill, next ventured a suggestion. He advocated the recall of Grouchy's troops ; not because he thought Blücher would join Wellington on the 18th, but he considered the pursuit of the beaten Prussians could be carried out with a weaker force, and the assistance of the troops recalled would be very helpful in the great battle with Wellington. He knew the tenacious courage of the British infantry and he did not think that the *Armée du Nord* could be too strong for the impending battle. But Napoleon never took counsel of his fears. Indomitable as ever, he was filled with self-confidence and a tremendous scorn for his foes. Stung by such ill-omened croakings, he turned sharply on Soult and answered him :

' Because you have been beaten by Wellington you consider him a good General. But I tell you that Wellington is a bad General and the English are bad troops. This whole affair will not be more serious than swallowing one's breakfast.'

' I hope so sincerely,' rejoined Soult, manifestly unconvinced.

The Emperor's words must not be taken too literally. Obviously he wished to check all exaggerated opinions of the enemy's strength, and thus prevent every man in the *Armée du Nord* from looking on the attempt as hopeless. Before a battle it was always Napoleon's custom to make his troops consider themselves irresistible ; and he showed his art by rarely calling on them to endure more punishment than they could bear. Thus he served his purpose, without diminishing their glory.

Soon afterwards Reille and Prince Jérôme reached Imperial Head-Quarters. Reille had often encountered the British in Spain, so Napoleon asked him for his opinion of the British Army. Reille spoke out and said : ' Well posted, as Wellington knows how to place it, and frontally attacked, I consider the English Army to be impregnable, through its quiet tenacity and its superior fire-action. Before crossing bayonets with it one may expect half of the assailants to be shot down. But the English Army is less agile, less supple, and not so expert in manœuvring as ours. If we cannot defeat it by a direct frontal attack, we may accomplish its overthrow by manœuvring.' Reille's opinion was valuable, but it was given too freely to suit Napoleon. The Emperor considered it as wanting in tact for Reille to speak so unguardedly before the other Generals. Showing most unmistakably that he attached no great importance to Reille's outspoken comment, he stopped any further remarks by an expression of incredulity.

Prince Jérôme then gave the Emperor some information which had been obtained from a waiter who, having served the Prince with supper on the 17th, had previously waited on Wellington at breakfast. This waiter reported that one of Wellington's A.D.C.s had mentioned an Allied concentration which was to be effected in front of the Forest of Soignes, and the waiter had said that the Prussians were at Wavre. The Emperor ridiculed the idea: ' After such a battle as Fleurus, the junction between the Allies is impossible for at least two days ; besides, the Prussians are pressed by Grouchy's detachment, who are at their heels.' Napoleon then added : ' We are only too pleased that the English wish to remain and accept battle. The battle which we are about to deliver will save France, and will become celebrated in the annals of the world. I shall make use of my numerous artillery, I shall launch my horsemen to compel the enemy to unmask ; and, as soon as I am certain of the position held by the English, I shall advance straight against them with my Old Guard.'

Until Bülow was actually in sight near Chapelle St. Lambert, the Emperor scouted any idea of the Prussian Army co-operating effectively on the 18th. Nevertheless, despite Napoleon's answer to Prince Jérôme, surely the knowledge already in the Emperor's possession negatived his assertion. He knew the relative position of three of the Armies, and he knew some Prussians were at Wavre. Hence it must have been clear that Grouchy, if he followed directly on the heels of the Prussians, would not be able to prevent an Allied concentration, but he would drive the Prussian force at Wavre towards Wellington's Army. It the Marshal was blind, so alas ! was the Emperor.

The time had nearly come for action, the ground was drying rapidly, and the artillery would soon be able to manœuvre. But

an officer, who somewhat earlier had been sent forward to the
French outposts, came back and reported to the Emperor that
Wellington was continuing his retrograde movement, and Napoleon promptly ordered D'Erlon to advance with the I Corps
and relentlessly pursue the Anglo-Dutch Army.   D'Erlon, however, was an experienced officer, and his personal observation
inclined him to take a precisely opposite view of Wellington's
situation.   He sent back General Delcambre, his Chief of the
Staff, to inform the Emperor that in his (D'Erlon's) opinion the
Anglo-Dutch Army was in position and ready to accept battle.
The Emperor then mounted and proceeded to the front to carry
out a close personal reconnaissance of Wellington's line, whilst
the *Armée du Nord* was taking up its allotted stations.   Napoleon
could see little because the crest of the low ridge completely
masked Wellington's dispositions, but he at once agreed with
D'Erlon that Wellington's Army was still in position waiting for
the French onslaught.   Before the Emperor returned to write
his attack orders, he sent forward General Haxo, of the Engineers,
to ascertain whether Wellington's troops had strengthened their
positions.   On his return the General was content to furnish the
insufficient report that Wellington had not entrenched his front.
Haxo must have been blind or very unobservant.   Serious signs
of occupation were only too visible.   There was a barricade on
the Brussels–Charleroi highway, an *abatis* on the Nivelles road,
the advanced posts of Hougoumont and La Haye Sainte were
evidently occupied, hostile troops held the farms of La Haye and
Papelotte, troops were in the Sand-Pit opposite to La Haye Sainte,
numerous gun muzzles should have been detected peering over the
brow, and at this time a whole Dutch-Belgian Brigade (Bijlandt's)
was deployed south of the ridge.   Naturally Wellington
had done nothing to discourage a frontal attack.   There was
no long line of entrenchment visible from the forward slope,
because the Duke knew that his men could be trusted to stand
steady behind the ridge where entrenchments were not required.
But the garrisons of the advanced posts had strengthened them
as far as time and means were available, and so experienced an
officer as General Haxo should not have overlooked the numerous
signs of serious occupation.

It is true that Bijlandt's Brigade, massed on the forward slope,
might have been the rear echelon of a rear-guard.   The number

of gun muzzles, however, directly refuted the idea that only a covering force had been left on the position. On the 17th, Wellington had left only two horse artillery troops with his rear screen ; but, on the 18th, Haxo could have counted more than five times twelve gun muzzles. This, together with Wellington's known weakness in artillery, and the fact that field artillery in 1815 was not suitable for rear-guard work (as, before the introduction of axle-tree seats, the dismounted gun detachments could not be withdrawn rapidly) proved that the Duke, for some reason or other, had determined to accept battle to the south of the Forest of Soignes. The glaring inconsistency, which could not be fitted into the idea of a rear-guard, was, even if some were invisible, there were far too many guns in sight for the force to be Wellington's rear-guard.

After receiving General Haxo's report, the Emperor spent a quarter of an hour in serious thought and then proceeded to dictate his orders for a general action.[1] By this time Napoleon had no doubt that he was confronted by Wellington's main Army, nor did he pause to consider the possibility of Blücher's intervention on the 18th, because the Field-Marshal would be accounted for by Grouchy. Here was Wellington offering himself for the blow and the Emperor determined to finish the Anglo-Dutch Army. Unfortunately, Napoleon saw no need to hurry on the decisive attack. He considered it was impossible for Wellington to decamp, and a few short hours of the long summer day would suffice for the task in hand. It was convenient to give time for the fields to dry, so as to allow the powerful French artillery to manœuvre freely. Until now Wellington's troops had never been properly handled by the French Marshals. At La Belle Alliance the British should be subjected to a pitiless bombardment, followed up by the terrible case-shot attack which would render them powerless to mete out that punishment at the critical moment which the Grand Army could not endure. With the centre shattered, the sundered wings could be crushed in detail.

Napoleon, however, had miscalculated seriously ; not by underestimating Wellington's strength on this Sunday morning, but by belittling Wellington's firmness and tactical skill as well as the admirable, unyielding spirit of the British and King's

---

[1] These orders are given in Appendix II, No. 5.

German Legion Troops, and Blücher's unswerving loyalty to his Ally.   These miscalculations and his late opening of the battle sealed his doom.   Wellington's personal endurance and the resolute tenacity of his troops extended the time-limit beyond its available and intended bounds.   Further, the position which Wellington had selected was skilfully calculated to render difficult, if it did not neutralize, Napoleon's ' case-shot attack '.   In this way the Emperor was deprived of his one great chance of forcing on the crisis and the decision at an earlier hour than the Allies had allowed for.

Before the battle opened Napoleon held his last review of the *Armée du Nord*, and his soldiers received the God of Modern War with clamorous cheering.   The Infantry raised their shakos on their muskets in salutation of their Emperor, the horsemen elevated their casques on their uplifted sabres, whilst the War God's name was volleyed forth by regiment after regiment.   The thunder of the cheering rolled far away into space, across hill and dale, past farmsteads, and over woods.   Thus his troops honoured the Victor of Ligny and showed him the place which he held in their hearts.

CHAPTER XVII

THE PLANS OF THE ALLIES FOR THE 18TH JUNE

(A) WELLINGTON'S PLANS

(Map 4)

AFTER dawn the weather improved. Fires were lighted along the Anglo-Dutch position and an irregular fusillade proclaimed the cleaning and drying of muskets.

Fortified by the promised co-operation of the Prussians, Wellington determined to accept battle at Mt. St. Jean. The Duke showed the trust which he placed in his troops when he took up his main infantry position along the reverse slope of the low ridge, so that the crest masked his strength and dispositions, screened his defensive moves, and prevented the thorough bombardment of his line by Napoleon's powerful artillery (*vide* section on Map 4). The position, although very dissimilar to the famous one at Bussaco, was, nevertheless, one after Wellington's own heart, although at first sight it did not appear to be even a good defensive position. But closer inspection showed how admirably suited it was for Wellington's troops to hold, since the steepish glacis sloping down to the French was combined with a moderate slope on our side.

Here in Belgium, as in the Peninsular War, the French would have to move forward under a vexatious gun and musketry fire, which would shake their formations, though, as they climbed the slope, they would not be offered any definite, compensating target to engage. Immediately on reaching the crest, the French would find Wellington's deployed battalions ready to pour in a smashing volley before the assailants could deploy their columns and develop their fire-power. Directly afterwards the red-coats would be on them with the bayonet, whilst the welkin rang with British cheers.

The position Wellington selected was quite unlike that usually chosen by commanders of this period. Continental generals preferred to draw up their troops on the forward slope so that they could see their enemies, and be seen by them, like Blücher had done at Ligny. By holding the advanced posts—the Sand-Pit, La Haye Sainte, and Hougoumont [1]—in front, and down the forward slope of the hill, the Duke expected to gain further time and to embarrass the attack. Until these advanced posts were mastered a serious attack on the main position could not be delivered. Always fearful for his right, Wellington considered that Hougoumont was the most important, and he garrisoned the post with the Light Companies of the 2nd Guards Brigade under Lieut.-Colonel J. Macdonell, the Light Companies of the 1st Guards Brigade under Lieut.-Colonel Lord Saltoun, together with a company of Hanoverians, a battalion of the Nassau Regiment, and 100 men from the Lüneburg Battalion. Macdonell was placed in command of this advanced post.

In point of fact, in a frontal action, the key of the position was the farm of La Haye Sainte. It lay only a short distance in front of the Allied centre and afforded a covered way to within 100 yards of the crest of the ridge. The farm, a large and important one, would have accommodated quite 1,000 men ; but only Major George Baring with the 2nd Light Battalion, King's German Legion (376 men) were allotted for its garrison. Baring placed three companies in the orchard, two in the buildings, and one in the garden. The mule with the entrenching tools had been lost on the previous day and Baring was ordered to send off his pioneers to Hougoumont, so he had not a single tool handy. Although La Haye Sainte was reinforced continually during the action, the place eventually fell and that was the really serious moment for the Anglo-Dutch Army.

On the opposite side of the road to La Haye Sainte was the Sand-Pit which was held by three companies of the 95th Rifles. The farms of Papelotte, La Haye, etc., on the Duke's left were held by Prince Bernard of Saxe-Weimar's troops. No defensive works were constructed on the main position owing to Nature providing the rampart in front of Wellington's main line at Waterloo.

[1] The spelling which is usually employed to-day. It is also found on a map of 1777.

' The whole battle-field was covered with the finest wheat, the soil was strong and luxuriant, consequently, from the rain which had fallen, it was deep, heavy for the transport and moving of artillery, and difficult for the quick co-operation of cavalry. The heavy ground was in favour of our cavalry from the superiority of our horses. Likewise, in any charge down the face of the position, we had the advantage of moving downhill, yet we felt the inconvenience in returning up the hill with distressed horses after a charge.' The foregoing explains the comparatively slow pace at which the French cavalry charges were delivered. Even a month after the battle, in many places the holes made by the horses' hoofs still measured 12 to 18 inches in depth.

Early in the morning Müffling drew out his proposal for the co-operation of the Prussian Army, and he provided for three different cases :

1. If Napoleon attacked Wellington's right, the Prussians would march to Ohain and support the Duke with a force equal in strength to his own ;

2. If Napoleon attacked Wellington's centre and left, one Prussian Corps would advance *via* St. Lambert and Lasne and attack the French right, whilst another would move *via* Ohain and support Wellington's left ;

3. If Napoleon advanced to St. Lambert and threatened to interpose between the Allies, the Prussians would stand fast and receive his attack whilst the Anglo-Dutch Army took the offensive and closed round the Emperor's left flank and rear.

Wellington at once signified his approval, on hearing Müffling's suggestions for the co-operation of the Prussian Army.

To anticipate, directly it was clear that the centre of Wellington's line was to be Napoleon's objective, Müffling sent word to Blücher that the second case was occurring ; and, knowing that Bülow led the advance, Müffling gave the A.D.C. an open letter, desiring him to show it to Bülow as he passed. As it turned out Blücher himself was in front and the old Field-Marshal took the necessary steps to provide the agreed co-operation.

Müffling had always been convinced that ' if fortune so far favoured us in a battle that the English Army could act on the defensive while the Prussian Army acted simultaneously on the offensive, we should obtain a brilliant victory over Napoleon '. At Waterloo Napoleon offered to the Allies a battle on the very lines desired by General von Müffling, who earlier in the campaign had said to Wellington : ' You may depend upon this, when the Prince [Blücher] has agreed to any operation in common, he will keep his word, should even the whole Prussian Army be exterminated in executing the manœuvre. But do not expect from us more than we are able to perform, we will always assist you as far as we can. The Prince will be perfectly satisfied if you do the same.' It was the close bond existing between the Allies, and the effective arrangements Müffling made for their co-operation at Waterloo, which enabled Wellington and Blücher to secure so signal a triumph on the 18th June.

The preliminary arrangements having been concluded, Wellington ordered his generals to ' form in the usual way '. This formation, however, had to be adapted, so that the battalions could pass from line to a formation capable of resisting cavalry and then reform line again as quickly as possible. In the 3rd Division, which was behind La Haye Sainte, holding the most important part of Wellington's battle line, Alten's A.-Q.-M.-G. (Captain James Shaw, 43rd Regt.) solved the difficulty by forming the 3rd Division in nine ' oblongs ' (five in the first line and four in the second line), the oblongs in the second line being placed so as to cover the gaps in the first line. During the cannonade, Alten's Division lay down in line.

In the case of Bijlandt's Brigade Wellington's order was quite literally interpreted, and, according to the continental practice, the Brigade formed up on the forward slope to the east of the Sand-Pit where it was fully exposed to the French guns. Otherwise all the troops were admirably disposed ; and Wellington arranged that the foreign troops were chequered all along the line with the British and K.G.L., as he had done in the organization of his Army Corps. The usual swarm of skirmishers were in front of the ridge ; and the guns, in action on the ridge, had their muzzles just showing, so that the front slope could be swept with fire.

One thing, however, was most noticeable. The mass of men was behind the right. Even though Blücher was the real support to the left wing, the bulk of the reserve would have been better placed behind the centre.

Wellington divided his $3\frac{1}{2}$-mile front into three parts. Lord Hill was entrusted with the right, to the west of the Nivelles road ; the Prince of Orange commanded in the centre, between the Nivelles and Charleroi roads ; and Sir Thomas Picton was in charge of the left, east of the Charleroi road. To hold his position Wellington had 67,000 men (including 12,000 cavalry) and 156 guns. Of this force not more than 15,000 were British and less than 5,000 belonged to the King's German Legion. Slender as was this leaven, Wellington remarked during the morning to Lord Uxbridge : ' It will take some hours to kill them all, and I know that they will not run.'

Lambert's 10th (British) Brigade of the 6th Division (2,000 bayonets) only arrived after the battle opened. It formed up at first near Mt. St. Jean Farm, but later on it was pushed into the front line between Kempt's Brigade and the Charleroi–Brussels road.

The French infantry balanced the Anglo-Dutch foot in numbers, the French horse outnumbered their opponents by one-fourth, and the French guns were in a superiority of five to three. In his Army at Waterloo the Duke had five British Field Brigades (or batteries) and eight British Horse Artillery Troops, a strange proportion ; whereas in the *Armée du Nord* there were thirty-five field batteries to fifteen batteries of horse artillery. The fine work performed by the gallant British Horse Artillery Troops at Waterloo was beyond all praise, but Wellington's Artillery would have been compacted far more satisfactorily if the number of Field Brigades had been at least doubled. Fortunately, whilst it had been waiting in Belgium, the armament of the British Horse Artillery had been changed as far as possible. In three of the Troops 9-pounder guns were substituted for the 6-pounders, and one Troop was rearmed with heavy $5\frac{1}{2}$-inch howitzers. This change was due entirely to the officer commanding Royal Horse Artillery—Lieut.-Colonel Sir A. Frazer. He wrote on the 20th June, ' the English Horse Artillery did great execution ; and I must be allowed to express my satisfaction, that, contrary to the opinion of most, I ventured to change (and under discouraging circumstances of partial want of means) the Ordnance of the Horse Artillery. Had the Troops continued with light guns (6-pounders) I do not hesitate to say the day had been lost.' Three days later he wrote, ' the more

I reflect, the more I bless my stars that I had obstinacy enough to persist in changing the guns of the Horse Artillery. . . .'

To occupy a position in Napoleonic times usually required 20,000 troops to the mile, and this allowed one-quarter of the force to be held in reserve. The Anglo-Dutch main position from Smohain to Hougoumont, measuring 4,200 yards, was held by 50,000 men, consequently Wellington had deployed twelve men to the yard. This force should prove sufficient to entangle the *Armée du Nord* whilst Blücher closed round the French right and dealt the death-blow as arranged. On the 18th June Blücher's Army was the General Reserve. Wellington merely had to maintain his position until the battle was ripe for the decisive act, consequently he should have had a considerable margin of safety. As the Duke could have concentrated an even larger force at Mt. St. Jean, it is necessary to consider why he did not do so.

Wellington's Detachment at Hal

(Sketch E)

On the 18th, Wellington left out on the Mons–Brussels road, under Prince Frederick of the Netherlands, a detachment which included Colville's 4th (British) Division (5,000 strong) together with Stedman's Division and Anthing's Brigade, a total of 17,000 men and 30 guns, or nearly one-fifth of his available strength. That part of Colville's Division which had spent the night at Braine le Comte was drawn back to Tubize ($2\frac{1}{2}$ miles SSW of Hal) during the morning of the 18th. The force under Prince Frederick remained all day around Hal and Tubize, yet it was never engaged, nor did it encounter any enemy. Why was it left at Hal?

The force at Hal was never intended to act as a strategic reserve. Had the Duke desired to fall back across the Schelde and cover Ostend, then a force at Hal, prepared to hold its position to the last, might have been able to cover such a retreat. But when Wellington offered battle to Napoleon on the 18th and was heavily engaged in front, the most he could have done, if the battle went against him, would have been to retreat northward, since any oblique withdrawal was impossible. From early in the afternoon of the 18th, it was clear that the Hal Detachment was not required to cover any retreat towards Ostend.

It is obvious that no French force could strike at Brussels through Hal without having advanced *via* Mons or Nivelles. No such force had been heard of, and Colville's troops, who had occupied Braine le Comte, must have learned of its presence and overnight position. Nor would Napoleon, when he wished to fight a decisive battle with Wellington, ever have allowed himself to be distracted by a side-issue. The Emperor knew that the key of the country lay not in Brussels, but in the Allied Field Armies.

The real reason for the Hal Detachment was that Wellington thought in 1815, and still thought in 1845, that Napoleon, after Ligny and Quatre Bras, ought to have manœuvred towards Hal with the idea of drawing Wellington westward, away from Blücher. If this occurred, Prince Frederick and his 17,000 men would hold Marlborough's old position at Hal, covering the roads from Ath and Mons, until the Duke could come up. Nevertheless such a manœuvre could never have obtained an immediate decisive result, because it ensured the Allied junction, the very thing which Napoleon, on the 16th June, had fought to prevent. Moreover such a manœuvre would abandon Grouchy to his fate unsupported, as it would have allowed the Allies to interpose between Napoleon and his Marshal.

The Hal Detachment did not contain superior forces of the enemy, it did not hold a point of strategic importance, and it seems that Wellington left it out to parry an imaginary danger. At any rate, whatever he thought, Wellington might have given directions to Prince Frederick that, if no enemy had been heard of between Hal and Mons by 10 a.m., he was then to march at once to Mt. St. Jean with Colville's Division leading and form up behind the centre of the Anglo-Dutch Army. This would have ensured that the Hal Detachment, in place of being wasted, would have arrived to swell Wellington's reserves by 3 p.m., and have been available to strengthen the centre. Prince Frederick, however, was left severely alone, although the Duke had one of Colville's A.D.C.s with him all day. Once battle had been joined the Hal Detachment was forgotten and it remained inactive at Hal and Tubize. Curiously enough it did not even hear the firing. Prince Frederick's position lay in the valley of the Senne ; the woods, a light westerly wind, and the 5 miles which separated the inner wings of the forces, may account for the Hal Detachment not hearing the thunder of the guns at Waterloo.

The Hal Detachment was a grave and might have been a disastrous error of judgment if the troops engaged at Mt. St Jean had not possessed such fine fighting qualities, if their commander, the Iron Duke, had not shown such invincible resolution and skill in directing the storm which raged around him, and if Wellington had not been supported by so staunch and true an Ally as the indomitable Blücher.

THE WATERLOO BATTLE-FIELD

NOTE.—Anyone who desires to gain a correct appreciation of the contour of the Waterloo battle-field, as it was in 1815, should study Captain Siborne's magnificent model (begun in 1831) which is on view in the Banqueting Hall of the Royal United Service Institution. On this superb model the ground is shown at a scale of 9 feet to the mile. Points of visibility can be solved, the shape of the ground appreciated, and the advanced posts, houses, crops, and trees can be seen. Probably most students will agree that the representation of smoke has no useful value. In the centre it is mischievous, because cotton-wool (used to represent smoke) obscures the depth of the Wavre cross-road.

An observatory is represented in this model ; and there was an observatory in 1815 erected close to the spot where it is shown on the model. It was erected, however, six weeks before the battle by order of the King of the Netherlands for use in a survey of the country. For this reason it was perched on the highest spot in the neighbourhood. Napoleon is generally credited with taking post here during the battle. Actually he never went there after the conflict had begun. Before 8 a.m., however, he did spend an hour reconnoitring the ground from the observatory, but the convex slopes of the battle-field rendered a nearer position more suitable and he did not again return. (By 1817 this observatory had fallen down.) From about noon, and until after La Haye Sainte fell, Napoleon took up his position on a low knoll near De Coster's house, just behind La

Belle Alliance.   From this spot he could see Hougoumont and La Haye Sainte, and the ground between the farms, his eye could range over the position to the east of the Charleroi road, and Ohain, Fichermont, and the Paris Wood were all in sight. To the north-eastward the heights of Chapelle St. Lambert bounded his horizon.   Centrally placed and close to his Reserves, the Emperor's situation was excellent.   With him was a local guide, De Coster, who did not cut a very heroic figure.

Wellington, although moving about wherever his presence was required, spent much of his time under an elm tree at the cross-roads above La Haye Sainte.   From this position the French line of battle, as well as Hougoumont, La Haye Sainte, and the red-tiled, white farmhouse of La Belle Alliance were all in sight. Far away to his left, eastward of Plancenoit, he could discern, the smoke of Blücher's fight and by its position he could gauge the progress his Ally was making.   The Duke was well placed.

Actually the name of Waterloo was not marked on some of the maps used by Wellington's officers, and Lieut.-Colonel Sir A. Frazer, commanding R.H.A., writing from Brussels at 6 a.m. on the 16th June, stated,

' . . . *I have just learned that the Duke moves in half an hour. Wood* [Colonel Sir George Wood, commanding Royal Artillery] *thinks to Waterloo, which we cannot find on the map.   This is the old story over again.   I have sent Bell* [Lieut. W. Bell, Staff Officer, R.A.] *to Delancey's office, where we shall learn the real name . . .*'   (It is said that Tilly was not shown on the Prussian maps, and Gneisenau added Wavre to his orders on the 17th so as to make the line of the Prussian retreat unambiguous.) In recent times there are many officers who have had a similar experience to that of Sir Augustus Frazer.   Even to-day the maps of theatres of operations are not always complete with all the necessary names.

(B) THE PRUSSIAN PLANS

(Map 5 and Sketch E)

Between 7 and 8 a.m. Major Count von der Gröben (of Röder's Cavalry) came in from the Prussian outposts. He brought a report that a French force, strength about 15,000, had halted overnight at Gembloux, but so far this force showed no signs of moving off. Gröben urged the Field-Marshal, even if the French could dispose of 30,000 men on the right bank, to leave only one Corps to hold the line of the Dyle, and march with every other available man so as to decide the fate of the campaign at Mt. St. Jean. Gneisenau, however, favoured a more cautious plan. He wished to defer stripping the Dyle of troops until noon. Then, if the enemy did not show very large forces in front of Wavre, the Prussian I Corps could follow the IV and II, and possibly also the III Corps might be able to march westward.

Blücher had ordered Bülow to start at daybreak from Dion le Mont and march through Wavre towards Chapelle St. Lambert; and on arrival, if he found Wellington was not engaged in a serious action, Bülow was to conceal his Corps behind Chapelle St. Lambert. But if the French were attacking the Anglo-Dutch Army, Bülow was to engage at once and drive his Corps against Napoleon's right flank.

The II Corps (Pirch I) was to follow immediately behind Bülow, and the I and III Corps were to hold themselves in readiness to march. The four Corps were warned to disengage themselves provisionally of their trains, which were to be sent on to Louvain. Only what was required in action was to be retained with the troops.

So far as Bülow's Corps was concerned the orders were very satisfactory. If Napoleon had not attacked Wellington, it would have been most unwise to show the Emperor that the Prussians were once more ready to co-operate with the Anglo-Dutch Army, as in that case Blücher's plan for the 19th would have come to naught. On the other hand, if Wellington was already being attacked Bülow was rightly ordered to engage directly he reached the field. In this case, so as to ensure against any delay, it was essential to relieve Bülow of all responsibility for deciding whether or not he should engage his Corps.

Unfortunately in other respects the orders were less satisfactory. The choice of Bülow's Corps to lead the advance was sure to result in serious delay, since the IV Corps was farthest from Wellington's battle-field. Further, Bülow's march crossed the advance of Zieten and Pirch I, consequently they had to wait whilst the IV Corps cleared them, and Pirch I had to follow Bülow. Even so, more precious hours were lost because Bülow did not start at daybreak; and, as ill luck had it, whilst the Corps was engaged in traversing Wavre a fire broke out, and blocked the narrow streets of the town. This delayed Bülow for two more hours, and although the van of the Corps did reach Chapelle St. Lambert between 10 a.m. and noon yet the rear of the column did not close up until 3 p.m.

Of the rest, Thielemann's Corps was to remain behind at Wavre and defend the Dyle against Grouchy's 15,000 men. (This underestimate of Grouchy's strength was due to the French infantry columns not being in evidence on the 17th.) Thielemann was also told that, if no serious French advance was made by the time Zieten and the I Corps had started, he was to draw off and move westward with the III Corps. Clausewitz has said, ' Blücher's plan, in its general design, to support the English left with one Corps and throw the remainder against Napoleon's exposed right, could not have been more simple, practical, and effective.'

Blücher further showed that he had risen to the height of the occasion, when, at 9.30 a.m., he dictated his historic letter to Müffling : ' *I have the honour to beg you to say in my name to the Duke of Wellington that, ill as I am, I will march at the head of my Army to attack at once the Right Flank of the enemy, if Napoleon should attempt anything against the Duke. In case the French do not attack to-day, I am of opinion that together we should attack the French Army to-morrow. I desire you to communicate this to the Duke as the result of my firm conviction. In our present situation, I consider this plan the best and the most suitable.*' The invincible Blücher rose superior to his physical ailments, his great age, and the attendant circumstances ; and on the 18th June he obtained from all ranks of the Prussian Army the utmost exertions of which they were capable. Rugged and unpolished Blücher's character probably was, nevertheless he never made difficulties when it was a question of advancing and attacking. From the many plans which his Staff might submit to him, he always preferred and chose the bold and daring course which might lead to a decision. On the other hand, it was only the increasing roar of the opening cannonade which gradually made clear to Gneisenau that Wellington had kept faithful to his promise and stood at Mt. St. Jean.

Whilst Gneisenau remained temporarily at Wavre to decide on the movements of the other Corps, Blücher left Wavre about 11 a.m. and joined Bülow at Chapelle St. Lambert. As he said : ' despite all that he was suffering he would rather have been lashed in the saddle than have missed the battle ', and he infused his spirit and energy into the Prussian advance.

Riding past the marching columns the old Field-Marshal exhorted the infantry to assist in dragging the embogged guns across the muddy valley of the Lasne, galvanizing the men to renewed vigour by an appeal which he knew would make them exert themselves : ' Lads, you will not let me break my word ! ' Even so several hours passed without any direct Prussian intervention ; and only at 4 p.m. did Bülow's Corps begin to exchange shots with the French right. To carry out his orders Bülow had to cross the Lasne and deploy on the left bank. Since Lobau had failed to occupy the Paris Wood this considerably facilitated Bülow's manœuvre. But, even at 1 p.m., when he had three out of his four Brigades in hand, Bülow took no steps to carry out his orders ; and as late as 3 p.m., when his Corps had assembled, Bülow still hesitated about taking the plunge. The Paris Wood had been occupied by a Prussian detachment for some time and an officer of Blücher's Staff had repeatedly requested Bülow to occupy the wood in strength. At last the staff officer rode off to interview Blücher and Gneisenau, but for the moment no decision was reached. Certainly if Wellington was overthrown Blücher's position would have been unenviable. The best means, however, of securing Wellington's position at Waterloo was to attack Napoleon's exposed right immediately and furiously. This is evidently what Grölmann thought, when at this critical juncture he rode up from Wavre. On the staff officer informing him of the state of affairs, Grölmann issued the following order : ' Attack at once ! In the Field-Marshal's name I order you to cross the defile ! ' The order was obeyed immediately, and the energy with which it was executed turned the wavering fortunes of the day and led to overwhelming victory.

The hesitation exhibited up to that time by the Prussian Staff is understandable when it came to giving orders fraught with such possibilities. This made even more admirable the insight and the moral courage exhibited by Grölmann in taking on himself the responsibility for issuing the order for the onslaught.

CHAPTER XVIII

THE BATTLE OF WATERLOO

(Map 4)

THE Battle of Waterloo may be divided into five phases, all of which were distinct, well defined, and separated by perceptible intervals in which merely a hot cannonade was sustained unsupported by any other action of the troops.

1ST PHASE—FROM 11.30 A.M. THE ATTACK ON HOUGOUMONT; AND THE APPEARANCE OF THE PRUSSIANS

Before the battle opened the commander of a cavalry picket near Papelotte, Captain T. W. Taylor (10th Hussars), met a Prussian officer. The latter asked Captain Taylor to inform the Duke that Bülow's Corps, advancing to his assistance, was three-quarters of a league away. Captain Taylor at once sent Lieut. W. H. B. Lindsey to the Duke's head-quarters with this welcome information.

Eleven o'clock sounded from Plancenoit clock-tower before Napoleon took up his position near Rossomme. The day grew brighter, and the array of Napoleon's Army impressed the spectators in Wellington's position. Such masses, such uniformity, such regularity of movement had not been seen in the Peninsula, where the broken and difficult country rarely allowed the French to form up in a recognized order of battle. On this Sunday morning the unaccustomed sight was indescribably grand.

At 11.30 Napoleon began the battle with the assault of Hougoumont. The French advanced, some of their guns opened fire, skirmishers were thrown out, and Bull's Howitzers and Sandham's Field Brigade answered one of Reille's batteries. The first round fired from our position at the attacking infantry, a spherical case, was effective. It occasioned three casualties in the *Ier. Léger* of Bauduin's Brigade in Jérôme's Division. A brisk duel broke out immediately between the British and French guns. But the British gunners, realizing which target was of the greatest importance at the moment, changed on to Jérôme's infantry and broke up a French column with howitzer shells. Our guns were all well served and the officers laid the pieces with unerring aim.

After some fighting around Hougoumont Jérôme carried the copse and field, and his staff then tried to persuade him not to push the attack any farther. He would not listen, however, to this wise advice and sent in his second Brigade, Soye's, against the Château. This attack reached the north front of the courtyard, and an officer of vast strength, Lieutenant Legros, broke open the gate with an axe and burst in followed by a handful of his men. There was a fierce fight before Legros and all his men were killed. Lieut.-Colonel J. Macdonell, Lieut.-Colonel H. Wyndham, Ensigns H. Gooch and J. Hervey, with Sergeants Graham, Brice, Fraser, McGregor, and Alston, Corporal Graham, and Private Lister then slammed to the gates and secured them. Thereafter the defenders held on only to the buildings and gardens.

About 12.30 p.m. four companies of the Coldstreams, and a little later three more companies of the same Regiment, reinforced the post. Before 1 p.m. two more companies arrived to strengthen the garrison, and attack after attack was beaten off. Towards the end of this phase Colonel F. Hepburn reached Hougoumont with the remaining seven companies of the 3rd Guards, and for the rest of the battle Colonel Hepburn was in command at Hougoumont.

Jérôme had entirely misinterpreted Napoleon's project. The Emperor only intended a thrust to be delivered at Hougoumont, so as to draw the Duke's attention to a secondary part of his line and induce him to weaken his centre in order to reinforce his right. Unhappily for the French, Jérôme engaged in a murderous struggle which went in favour of the resolute garrison of Hougoumont, who kept fully employed around the Château a very superior number of assailants, as well as the numerous reinforcements who were drawn into the vortex of strife which raged all day for the possession of the buildings. Finally even one of Foy's Brigades was swallowed up in the profitless fray. There is no doubt that howitzers should have been used against the place from the outset ; but, as it was, the unskilfully conducted attacks merely resulted in heavy losses. All day Prince Jérôme played the maladroit game of staking gold against copper.

On the Emperor's order Kellermann's two horse artillery batteries were pushed up to reinforce the line of guns in action to the south of Hougoumont. The cannonade grew in intensity. More guns opened fire from Wellington's position, and Piré's horse battery, coming into action near the Nivelles road, enfiladed the guns which were engaged in repelling the French attacks.

Meanwhile General Perponcher fortunately noticed the exposed position of Bijlandt's Brigade and ordered the Brigadier to withdraw his regiments behind the Wavre cross-road. As a result of this order, towards noon Bijlandt's Brigade retired and formed up in front of the interval between the Brigades of Kempt and Pack. Bijleveld's Battery followed, and seven of its guns unlimbered on the left of Rogers's Field Brigade. About the same time Captain Mercer, waiting in reserve with G Troop R.H.A. near the farm of Mt. St. Jean, received orders to move to the right of Wellington's second line. Mercer brought his 9-pounders into action, facing south-west, about 1,000 yards to the north of Hougoumont. Here the Troop was in front of the 14th Regiment whose men were lying down in square. In this position Mercer was annoyed by some of Piré's 4-pounders (1,300 yards off and west of Hougoumont) and by occasional howitzer shells, fitted with long fuses, as well as by French round-shot which sailed over the main position and ended among our troops in the second line. The Duke's orders, however, were positive. The Troop was not to fire unless Piré's Cavalry attempted to close. But it was not long before the impatient Mercer opened a slow fire on the French 4-pounders, expecting to gain an easy mastery with his 9-pounders. To his surprise his very first round drew the fire of six heavier pieces (12-pounders), which had been carefully concealed to the east of the 4-pounders. Mercer recognized his blunder. G Troop ceased firing, the French heavy guns did the same, and only the 4-pounders kept up their galling cannonade. This flagrant disobedience of orders had not passed unnoticed. The Duke, seeing a projectile from one of our guns strike a French 4-pounder, sent in haste to have the commander of a neighbouring Field Brigade (Sandham) placed under arrest. Fortunately Captain Sandham was able to offer a satisfactory explanation, and the real offender was not definitely identified until Mercer's *Journal* was published in 1870.[1] After ceasing fire Mercer's Troop remained in its position of observation in front of the 14th Regiment.

The time had nearly come for the main assault of the ridge. To prepare the way for the attack on Wellington's left centre, the Emperor ordered into action a battery of 84 guns. This battery unlimbered along a spur about 250 yards from La Haye Sainte. It included the twenty 12-pounders of the II and VI Corps, forty 8-pounders of the I Corps, and twenty-four 12-pounders from the Guard—the Emperor's ' beautiful daughters '. About midday the French guns opened fire and soon settled down to their task of deluging Wellington's line preparatory to the projected assault. It was this cannonade which attracted the attention of Grouchy and his officers at Walhain, speedily convincing them that a serious action was raging to the south of the Forest of Soignes.

The bombardment had just opened when the Emperor received Grouchy's second letter from Gembloux (written at 6 a.m.), in which the Marshal stated that the Prussians were moving on Brussels. Napoleon evinced no hurry to answer Grouchy's despatch ; and it was 1 p.m. when Soult wrote to inform Grouchy that his advance on Corbais and Wavre was conformable to His Majesty's arrangements. No precise instructions, however, were given to Grouchy to seize any especial points, such as the Dyle passages at Mousty and Ottignies. The Emperor must have realized that this communication would not reach Grouchy before 4 or 5 p.m. and therefore could not influence his operations on the 18th. But, before this letter was despatched, the Emperor had to add a postscript containing some very disquieting information.

The fire of the great French battery was replied to by the Allied guns on Wellington's left wing and a deafening cannonade raged. Although Wellington's infantry were sheltered by the

[1] General A. C. Mercer, Colonel-Commandant R.A., died on the 9th November 1868.

crest of the ridge yet they were necessarily placed fairly close behind their artillery. Consequently their position was a dangerous one, as projectiles, which missed the guns, frequently tore through the infantry in rear. To have drawn back the infantry, to a safe position, would have exposed the guns to the risk of immediate capture by the French cavalry who were close at hand. The discipline and the steadfast nature of Wellington's troops enabled them to hold their ground, despite the fire which was ' so terrible as to strike with awe the oldest veterans on the field '.

At 1 p.m. Ney was waiting for the Emperor's order to lead forward D'Erlon's Corps and storm the advanced posts of La Haye Sainte and the Sand-Pit, and then drive home an assault against Wellington's left centre. Before this great attack was launched and the battle-field became enshrouded in smoke, the Emperor took a last glance round, and away to the north-eastward he saw what appeared to be a dense black cloud emerging from the woods of Chapelle St. Lambert. Officers on the Imperial Staff held different views concerning the composition of this apparition. But it was soon evident that it consisted of troops, although their strength and nationality remained uncertain. A reconnaissance was at once despatched, and all doubts were set at rest when a Prussian orderly officer was brought in. This officer made no attempt to conceal that the troops were the advanced guard of Bülow's Corps, and the Corps was hastening to Wellington's assistance. Napoleon at once realized that it was no longer a simple affair with Wellington. He would now have to reckon with Bülow's Corps of 30,000 fresh troops closing round his right flank. In addition, as the prisoner also disclosed that all Blücher's Army had spent the previous night at Wavre, it was possible the whole Prussian Army might intervene in the battle. Nevertheless Napoleon was undismayed. Turning to Soult the Emperor said : ' This morning we had ninety chances in our favour. Even now we have sixty chances, and only forty against us.'

The Emperor promptly decided to involve Bülow in Wellington's rout, and he never contemplated breaking off the battle. But as Soult's letter to Grouchy had not been despatched the following postscript was added, ' *Une lettre qui vient d'être interceptée porte que le Général Bülow doit attaquer notre flanc droit.*

Nous croyons apercevoir ce corps sur les hauteurs de St. Lambert ; ainsi, ne perdez pas un instant pour vous rapprocher de nous et nous joindre, et pour écraser Bülow, que vous prendrez en flagrant délit.' [1] At last precise orders were sent to Grouchy, but it was twelve hours too late. Unless the Marshal had already crossed the Dyle at Mousty, it would be impossible for him to reach La Belle Alliance before 9 or 10 p.m. By then the Grand Army would have fought its last battle.

Despite the approach of Bülow's Corps, at 1.30 p.m. Napoleon ordered Ney to begin the attack and ruin the Anglo-Dutch Army before the Prussians arrived. To watch the Prussians he ordered Domon and Subervie to move to the right, and shortly after he sent Lobau with his two Divisions to support the Light Cavalry. Lobau was ordered to take up a good intermediate position where his 10,000 men could stop the advance of Bülow's 30,000. Further, Lobau was ordered to attack Bülow vigorously as soon as Grouchy's guns were heard thundering in rear of the IV Corps, announcing that the Marshal had caught Bülow ' *en flagrant délit de concentration* '.

As yet danger from the Prussians was by no means immediate, and it could have been guarded against by smashing in Wellington's line with the least delay. Then the risk of being involved in Wellington's destruction would probably have prevented the circumspect Prussian Generals from engaging. Undoubtedly to drive in Wellington's centre would require the employment of every available man, and to detach Lobau was to weaken the French reserves. On the other hand, as circumstances had changed, it might have been wiser to let Lobau advance in echelon behind the right of the I Corps. Thus placed the VI Corps could strike at Wellington's left, if the Prussians remained onlookers ; or, if they became active, Lobau could wheel up and cover D'Erlon's right. Of course, if the Prussians remained passive spectators, reserve could be piled on reserve to compel the decision : Lobau supporting D'Erlon, and these two Corps being backed up in turn by the Young Guard, Domon, Subervie, Lefebvre-Desnoëttes, and Milhaud's Cuirassiers. In all probability these repeated sledge-hammer blows would have overwhelmed Wellington. At any rate it was no time for half-measures. A crisis had been reached. If he

[1] The letter is given in Appendix II, No. 6.

intended to persevere with his attack on the Anglo-Dutch Army, Napoleon must risk all to gain all, hammer Wellington's line with tremendous energy, and grudge every man not employed in this main battle.

As matters turned out, Lobau drew out at right-angles to the French front between Plancenoit and the Paris Wood. Here for over three hours he was wasted, because the Prussians did not come on seriously until 4 p.m. and were not really danger-ous until 5 p.m. It was not Lobau's Corps which delayed their advance, but their natural hesitation to open an action which might be fraught with such dangerous possibilities for them-selves. One of Jacquinot's Cavalry Regiments would have been sufficient to keep touch with the Prussians. This arrangement would have left at Napoleon's disposal 10,000 more men, horse and foot, to effect Wellington's overthrow in the dwindling time-limit now vouchsafed to the Emperor.

Thus ended the first phase. So far the fighting had gone a little in favour of Wellington, and, to a certain extent, the arrival of the Prussians changed the balance of the strategical situation. Nevertheless Napoleon was not compromised.

CHAPTER XIX

THE BATTLE OF WATERLOO

2ND PHASE: FROM 1.30 P.M. D'ERLON'S ATTACK ON WELLINGTON'S LEFT CENTRE

(Map 4)

AFTER $1\frac{1}{2}$ hours' cannonading the great French battery suspended fire to allow the I Corps to advance. This Corps had to cross the 1,300 yards which separated the two Armies, but the ground, dipping towards the centre, gave it some cover as it marched forward.

The approach formation used by the Corps in this advance was a clumsy one. Three of the four divisions, those of Donzelot, Quiot (Alix), and Marcognet, advanced with their deployed battalions formed one behind the other, each Division (about 5,000 strong) moving forward on a front of one deployed battalion. On his own initiative, however, Durutte formed, not his Division but his two Brigades in a similar fashion; thus he halved the depth of the mass and doubled its fire-power. Durutte's formation was deployable under fire and his Division gained the greatest success of the venture. It seized Papelotte.

Naturally Napoleon was not responsible for the formation which his troops used. The conception was his affair and the details of execution were the business of his subordinates. In the Napoleonic Armies the column was not used as an attack formation although it was used for manœuvre and for advancing to the attack. On reaching decisive range it was always intended to deploy the columns so as to develop fire-power. Hence how did it happen that such an unwieldy, undeployable formation was used by D'Erlon, a formation equal in clumsiness and depth to the Greek phalanx? It is quite possible that the word ' Division ' was the cause of all the trouble and confusion. This word, in the French military phraseology of the period, had a double connotation. Presumably the formation D'Erlon ordered was *Colonne de bataillon par divisions*—in which all the battalions went forward side by side, at deploying interval, each on a double-company (*division*) front. This formation was suitable for crossing any ground, could be deployed under fire, presented a small target, and could swiftly change to square if charged by cavalry. Possibly, however, owing to some mistake in the transmission of the order, it reached divisional commanders thus transposed— *Colonne de Division par bataillon.* This was the formation which was used.

Unfortunately, unwieldy, heavy columns had previously been used for advance, notably at Friedland and at Wagram. Their use had passed unnoticed and the practice crept in. Undoubtedly the formation used by the I Corps was responsible for the loss experienced by the Corps in men and in *moral*, but these losses were aggravated by the tardy support accorded to D'Erlon by the Cavalry. Milhaud was available, although Domon and Subervie were employed in watching the Prussians. Had Milhaud been directed to support the infantry attack, the British Cavalry would not have fallen on D'Erlon's surprised and fully engaged infantry, but would have been met by the Cuirassiers with a furious counter-charge. Whatever the outcome, the French Cavalry would have shielded their infantry from the full force of a storm which, as it was, caught them unprepared. In addition, owing to Wellington's skill in using the brow of the ridge to shield his troops, the Anglo-Dutch line had not been sufficiently shaken by Napoleon's guns, and close-range infantry fire was still required to prepare Wellington's line for the onslaught. To deploy D'Erlon's clumsy columns, however, would be impossible under the deadly, galling fire of the unshaken two-deep British line.

Directly D'Erlon's huge columns gallantly began to climb the slope they were met by heavy fire. The British gunners opened on them with every gun they could bring to bear, and ' the manner their columns were cut up in making the attack was extraordinary, and the excellence of practice in artillery was never exceeded '. The Duke knew that only infantry and cavalry could drive his troops from their position, because in 1815 good, well-posted infantry could not be shot away by artillery. For this reason the Anglo-Dutch guns had reserved their fire for the attacking infantry and cavalry, as D'Erlon's Corps were now to discover.

Confronting the extremities of the I Corps were two advanced posts—Papelotte and La Haye Sainte—which had to be captured before the Duke's line could be overcome. The two flank divisions were entrusted with the task of reducing these places. In accordance with this plan, Durutte headed for Papelotte which he seized, whilst one Brigade of Donzelot's Division diverged to storm La Haye Sainte. The remainder of the I Corps advanced against Wellington's left centre. The left of D'Erlon's Corps was covered by Travers's Cuirassier Brigade, and this Brigade pounced on one of Ompteda's battalions advancing towards La Haye Sainte and cut it to pieces. This was a solitary success. The assault of the farm was met by a hot musketry fire, and Donzelot's Infantry, unaccompanied by guns and not even supported by artillery, failed to storm La Haye Sainte, though they took the orchard and garden.

Napoleon's preliminary bombardment was always intended to crush out the spirit of resistance before he sent in his infantry to win. In many battles the large columns (used for advance and manœuvre) were not even called on to deploy, because the shattered enemy broke at their near approach. Naturally against defended farms and villages the effect of gun-fire was less. Against troops, posted as Wellington could and did post them, the effect of the bombardment was not sufficient to destroy their fighting spirit, or break down their stubbornness and powers of resistance.

During the advance of D'Erlon's Divisions the 95th Rifles, holding the Sand-Pit, caused severe loss to the French and checked the advance of the skirmishers. Then, realizing that both flanks of the Pit were being turned, the three companies fell back and joined the battalion behind the Wavre road.

Immediately after this the French struck into Picton's Division (3,600 muskets) and Bijlandt's Brigade, and just farther to the left were two Hanoverian Brigades, another 5,000 muskets. Mere numbers favoured the French; but the defenders could bring all their muskets into play, whereas the French, unable to deploy from their columns, could not assert their great numerical superiority. Picton's troops were lining a hedge and the fire they poured in, coupled with co-operating gun-fire, caused the French to hesitate whilst they were a hundred yards away. Shouting 'Charge!' gallant old Picton dashed forward and met his death. The engagement became general and a tremendous musketry fight began, in which Donzelot's Brigade opposed Kempt, Pack confronted Marcognet, and Quiot attempted to pass between Pack and Kempt.

Whilst this fight was raging Major Baring's garrison of La Haye Sainte had been reinforced by the 1st Lüneburg Battalion and Donzelot was pressed back. But, as the orchard was then threatened by Cuirassiers and French infantry retook the garden, Baring again retired to the buildings, just as the British Cavalry charged, beat back the Cuirassiers, and broke up the French infantry. Baring asked for a further reinforcement. Two companies of the 1st Light Battalion were thereupon sent up to him, and he rearranged the garrison so as to defend only the garden and buildings and he definitely abandoned the orchard.

By this time D'Erlon's main attack had been very roughly handled. The infantry on both sides had their attention riveted on their immediate foes and clouds of smoke limited the view. The chance to intervene with cavalry had come ; and, fortunately for Wellington, it was Uxbridge at this crisis who seized the chance and engaged his horsemen. Placing himself at the head of Somerset's Brigade, Uxbridge ordered Somerset's and Ponsonby's Brigades to charge the enemy. Passing through the gaps left between the infantry squares, Somerset's Household Regiments crossed the Ohain road and galloped straight at Travers's Cuirassiers. The regiments met in the fairest cavalry fight of this great day. Travers's regiments were overborne and hurled back with considerable loss. Although the ground was slightly in our favour yet Somerset's regiments had just crossed the Ohain road, a minor obstacle but quite sufficient to loosen the formation of any but first-class troops.

About the same time and just to the east, Ponsonby's Union Brigade (Royals, Greys, and Inniskillings) achieved a brilliant success. They swooped down on D'Erlon's infantry and surprised them whilst they were engaged with Picton's Division. The Royals and Inniskillings overthrew Quiot's Division, whilst the Scots Greys charged Marcognet. As the cavalry came galloping through the smoke, Pack shouted to the 92nd Highlanders (220 strong): 'Ninety-second, you must charge!' and then

' The Scots Greys came up, and doubling round our flanks and through our centre, where openings were made for them, both regiments charged together calling out " Scotland for ever ! " and the Scots Greys walked over this column, and in less than three minutes it was totally destroyed . . .' The French, losing heavily in killed, wounded, and prisoners, were chased down the slope and driven back to their first position. In the victors' hands they left 3,000 prisoners and two of their prized Eagles. Captain A. K. Clark of the Royals took the Eagle of the 105th, and Sergeant Charles Ewart of the Greys captured the Eagle of the 45th. Unfortunately the Union Brigade was out of hand. It swept on regardless of consequences—and regardless of Napoleon. The horsemen riding into the great French battery began cutting down the gunners and stabbing the horses. On seeing these reckless British horsemen career amid his guns, Napoleon took prompt action and hurled on them cavalry from right and left : Jacquinot's Lancers and Farine's Cuirassiers. The Union Brigade was nearly destroyed. Its regiments left behind over one-third of their numbers dead and disabled, as well as the dashing leader. Indeed, after this episode, the effective strength of the Brigade was ˅ not above a squadron '.

Somerset's Brigade followed up Travers in rather an imprudent manner, and this Brigade also suffered although not nearly so severely as Ponsonby's. An officer in Vandeleur's Brigade, who witnessed the return of the cavalry, has described the scene, ' On our moving out in front of the left of the position our cavalry were seen riding back to our line in parties of twenty and thirty, followed by the enemy, whose horses were not blown. Our cavalry suffering greatly from our horses being scarcely able to move. On moving to support them we had to cross a deep lane, which broke us, and occasioned some confusion ; however, we got forward as quickly as possible, charged, and repulsed a body of lancers in pursuit of a party of the Scots Greys.' Had Ponsonby been content with his first great success his loss would have been trifling, and the Brigade would have been available to strike a great blow later in the day. Even as it was, Uxbridge's timely charge, by taking the pressure off Picton's highly tried infantry, assisted Wellington to maintain his hold on his position and keep his promise to Blücher.

All through this phase the Anglo-Dutch troops, holding the

main position, west of the Charleroi road, were only subjected to a cannonade. They were able to lie down in shelter on the reverse slope.

Observing the little progress Reille was making on the left, Napoleon ordered some howitzers to open fire on Hougoumont. About 2.30 p.m., after some shelling, the Château burst into flames, forming ' a striking feature in this murderous scene '. Nevertheless the garrison held on grimly to the blazing buildings and could not be dislodged, though so heavy was the firing ' the trees in advance of the Château were cut to pieces by musketry '. Gradually more and more of Reille's Corps became involved and neutralized in this bitter strife for a mere advanced post. The smoke from the conflagration drifted back over the Allied troops preventing a clear view of what was going on. Strengthened by the smoke from the guns and muskets it slowly settled like a pall over Wellington's position.

It may be considered that Picton's Division should have immediately followed up the advantage it had gained over D'Erlon's Corps, and completed its success with the bayonet. Such action, however, would have been most unwise since Napoleon still had ample reserves in hand, and he would have made the Division pay for such temerity. The French then following up the repulsed Division, would have forced the unguarded breach in the left centre of Wellington's line, and the grim struggle would have been over before a Prussian had engaged. The Duke had foreseen this temptation to dash forward in the hour of a temporary triumph ; and, before the action, he issued stringent orders forbidding the troops to leave their allotted positions so as to follow up a local advantage. Consequently D'Erlon's Corps was allowed to fall back, unimpeded by pursuit ; and, by 3.15 p.m., Picton's Division had resumed its original position and three companies of the 95th had reoccupied the Sand-Pit. Then for nearly twenty minutes there was a lull in the battle and each side prepared to make fresh efforts.

Wellington used the pause to carry out the following rearrangements : Lambert's Brigade was moved up into line with Picton's Division, Sir J. Kempt replaced Picton as divisional commander, and La Haye Sainte was reinforced by two companies. At the same time Prince Bernard retook Papelotte from Durutte. Practically all D'Erlon had achieved was obtaining definite knowledge that Wellington was occupying the Mt. St. Jean position in force. This rather obvious information had been dearly bought.

Wellington had expected Prussian intervention by noon, but even at 2.30 p.m. there was no sign of the Prussians entering the battle. The Duke grew anxious. The resisting power of his Army had been highly tried and he must have dreaded having to withstand another attack unaided.

On the stability of his left depended Wellington's connection with the Prussian Army ; and as the Prussians were unacquainted with the topography of the field, the Duke recognized that General von Müffling could be most effectively employed on this flank so as to direct the Prussian troops to their stations on the battle-field. Müffling would also be able to co-ordinate the action of the Anglo-Dutch left and the Prussians, and ensure co-operation and combination between them. Seeing that Müffling had sufficient rank, was well known to both Armies, and was accustomed to take upon himself considerable responsibility, the Duke's selection was a wise one, and the Duke referred the Generals of the Anglo-Dutch left to Müffling, who took over almost at the same moment as General Picton was killed. From his new station Müffling sent officers continuously to Field-Marshal Blücher, so as to keep the latter duly informed of the state of affairs.

Just before the end of this phase Napoleon received another letter from Grouchy, written about 11 a.m. from Walhain (between Gembloux and Wavre). Although this letter showed that Grouchy was heading for Wavre, yet he was 7 miles away from this town, and still on the right bank of the Dyle. If he persisted in this course, no help need be expected from the Marshal at Mt. St. Jean on the 18th. Possibly the Emperor had already given up all hope of seeing Grouchy arrive. If so, after the failure which had attended D'Erlon's attack, Napoleon would have been well advised to draw off his Army, effect a concentration with Grouchy, and wait for a more favourable opportunity of dealing with the Allies. Still determined, however, to complete Wellington's destruction before Blücher could engage, the Emperor resolved to make a fresh attack on the Anglo-Dutch line. This became the third phase of the battle.

CHAPTER XX

THE BATTLE OF WATERLOO

3RD PHASE : FROM 3.30 P.M. ATTACK OF WELLINGTON'S
POSITION CULMINATING IN THE FRENCH CAVALRY
CHARGES ; AND THE OPENING OF BLÜCHER'S ATTACK
AGAINST NAPOLEON'S RIGHT

NOTE.—*Legend of the Hollow Way*

(Map 4)

At 3.30 p.m., as soon as D'Erlon's Corps had partly rallied,
Napoleon ordered Ney to storm La Haye Sainte. Ney led
D'Erlon's least-injured regiments forward in two columns of
attack, but the assault failed and the key of the position remained
in Wellington's possession.

The roar of the cannonade became deafening. Gun after gun
fired in quick succession and gradually a cloak of smoke settled
over the centre. Soon a rearward tendency was discernible on
the plateau, as battalions drew back to screen themselves from the
tempest of iron. Stragglers were dribbling back, and parties
bearing and escorting wounded men were seen leaving the front
line.

Marshal Ney knew that the Emperor intended to support the
infantry attacks with his splendid veteran cavalry. Imagining
the movements on the plateau heralded the opening of a general
retreat, the Marshal decided to compel an immediate decision
with the Cuirassiers. His lack of daring when he was in command
at Quatre Bras on the 16th and on the 17th, rankling in Ney's
mind, may have determined him not to be backward on the
battle-field at Mt. St. Jean. This may explain his desire to
launch the cavalry before receiving Napoleon's orders. Be that
as it may, Ney ordered a brigade of Milhaud's Cuirassiers to
attack. Farine sent two of his regiments ; but his divisional
commander, Delort, refused his permission, and only consented

when he learned that Ney had the Emperor's authority to make the attempt. Ney promptly repeated the order and included the whole Corps of Cuirassiers, whom he then led forward to carry out his premature and reckless enterprise. Unfortunately, Lefebvre-Desnoëttes (who was formed behind Milhaud) saw the Cruirassiers move off, and on his own initiative he determined to support Milhaud. Ney, riding at the head of the Cuirassiers, could not see the strength of the cavalry following him ; and, until the attack was fairly launched, the convexity of the ground prevented Napoleon from noticing what was going on. Even if Ney had noticed Lefebvre-Desnoëttes following Milhaud, the Marshal might have concluded that the Emperor had ordered the Light Horse of the Guard to support Milhaud, and Ney would only have been confirmed in his rash resolve. The glittering mass, launched against Wellington's centre, numbered 5,000 veteran horsemen in forty-three squadrons, the finest body of horse seen on a battle-field since the time of Seydlitz.

In the advance the horsemen inclined considerably to the left, and crossing to the west of the Charleroi road they formed up unseen by Napoleon. The two Allied advanced posts— Hougoumont and La Haye Sainte—limited the frontage available for the charge, as the cavalry had to keep a respectful distance from these two farms to avoid the enfilade fire of their garrisons. Not only, however, had Ney misappreciated the situation, since Wellington was not contemplating retreat, but the part of the Duke's line which the Marshal selected for his onslaught was the strongest and the least shaken. All the senior officers in Wellington's centre who saw the French cavalry form up for attack considered, that so far as the result of any military operation could be foreseen, the defenders were perfectly prepared and secure.

To receive the French Cavalry, the Allied Infantry formed into twenty squares which covered the plateau like a chessboard. The gunners had been ordered by the Duke not to stand to their pieces as the cavalry closed. After firing their last rounds, they were to seek temporary refuge in the nearest squares leaving the guns abandoned in front of the infantry ; then directly the cavalry drew off the gunners were to emerge and serve their guns. The wisdom of this order is questionable. Even in 1815 guns with their flanks even partially protected (as these were by the squares) could be trusted to keep their front clear, so long as they did not run out of ammunition and reserved their fire until the enemy was on top of them. On the other hand, the sudden withdrawal of the gunners might upset the *moral* of any but the most determined infantry ; and, unless the gunners were of the highest class, they might prefer to remain in the squares once they had gained that refuge. The latter never happened on the 18th June, and this proved the quality and disciplined courage of the personnel of our Artillery at Waterloo.

Although, before the French Cavalry advanced, the Infantry had drawn back to their second position, yet the guns were still in action at the edge of the plateau with gaps of a hundred yards between the guns and the squares. To-day such a distance is trivial. In 1815, however, the infantry weapon was the flint-lock muzzle-loading musket ' Brown Bess ', and even a short distance made an appreciable difference in the percentage of the hits. It is true that cavalry, outflanking the guns and wheeling inwards to cut down the gunners, must pass very close to the squares and present a target into which a deadly and telling fire could be poured. The gaps, however, did exist and probably they were the reason for the Duke's order to the gunners. In the existing circumstances the guns could not be drawn back and wedged between the squares. The guns were stuck fast in the mud and could not be run back by hand. Moreover, running back would have restricted the field of fire. Probably the order to retreat into the squares was given by the Duke because he was not so acquainted with the power of artillery as his opponent. Wellington undoubtedly relied chiefly on his infantry ; but he must have trusted the personnel of the artillery very highly to have dared to issue such an order.

It was 4 p.m. when Ney led the Cavalry forward, keeping well to the west of La Haye Sainte. When the intrepid horsemen closed they were received by a hurricane of fire, and the leading squadrons were blown to pieces before the guns were captured. Not only did the restricted space stop the Cavalry deploying, but the sodden ground and deep cornfields prevented rapidity of movement, and the most rapid pace used was a trot or at most a slow canter, robbing the charge of its fury. Over such ground no attempt could be made to break up the squares by the irresistible impulse of a charge delivered at full speed, which might have overwhelmed the living citadels in a torrent which nothing human could withstand.

Our Infantry reserved their fire until the Cavalry were within about 30 yards. Then volley after volley pealed along the front, the horsemen swerved to right and left, and an epic struggle of endurance began. Around each little fortress the horsemen surged and crowded. All their attempts to gain an entrance failed, their numbers dwindled fast. Gradually the splendid body of Cavalry became a wreck surrounded by the impenetrable and immovable masses of infantry, within whose rock-like formation the Cuirassiers became wedged and entangled. There were intervals in this prolonged *mêlée* when the assailants, clearing the front of a square, allowed the French guns to co-operate, and make havoc of our Infantry. Probably most of the losses suffered were occasioned by the French artillery rather than by the horsemen. Whole files were torn away by the round-shot. But, despite the strain, the Infantry stood firm and stopped up the gaps by closing in. According to an eye-witness : ' The French Cavalry made some of the boldest charges I ever saw. They sounded the whole extent of our line which was thrown into squares. Never did Cavalry behave so nobly, or was received by Infantry so firmly. Our guns were taken and retaken repeatedly.'

It became of vital importance to gain a breathing space ; so Lord Uxbridge flung his fresh squadrons, nearly 5,000 strong, against the exhausted Cuirassiers, and the French were forced back from the plateau. As they retired, the gunners ran out from the squares, manned their pieces, and pursued the Cavalry with fire. Strange to say, the guns and their stores had been left intact. No attempt was made to bring away the guns with spare teams, nor were the guns spiked or the sponge-staves broken or carried off. In the turmoil and confusion these things were overlooked.

The French Cavalry rallied, reformed, and advanced once more against the squares. The same scenes were re-enacted, until the horsemen, worn out in the fierce struggle, were charged by Allied Cavalry and again driven off and pushed down the forward slope. The situation, however, was on the mend. Bülow had opened his attack and the sound of the Prussian guns filled Wellington's troops with renewed hope.

Napoleon moved his head-quarters close to the farm of La

Belle Alliance and watched Ney's gallant but premature effort as well as the advance of the Prussians against his right. Thenceforward he had a double rôle to play. Frontally he assailed Wellington ; on his right he fought a defensive battle against Blücher. Since the Emperor had decided to continue the battle with Wellington, despite Bülow's appearance, there was no time to be lost, because at Prussian Head-Quarters, action had obviously taken the place of vacillation. Delay was all in favour of the Allies. The moment had come when Wellington's Army must be closed with, assailed hand-to-hand all along the line, and forced to retreat. As some of the Cavalry were heavily engaged it became imperative to support them with the remainder of the French horse and back the stroke with the Artillery and Infantry of the Guard. The indomitable defence of the Duke's tenacious Infantry must be broken down by the sheer fury and weight of repeated sledge-hammer blows.

At 4.30 p.m. Bülow's attack was only in its initial stages, and there was at least an hour in which to force a decision on the slopes of Mt. St. Jean. Even if Friant's Division of the Old Guard was kept back as a last reserve, yet Morand's Middle Guard and Duhesme's Young Guard were ready to co-operate in this great assault together with every available man of Reille's and D'Erlon's Corps not already engaged.

At this moment a victory over Wellington was by no means impossible ; but it was the last chance offered by Fortune, and Napoleon neglected it. Before launching his Guard against Wellington Napoleon decided to beat back Bülow, although the battle was already raging with Wellington and had hardly begun with Bülow. Since the Emperor decided not to launch his Guard, surely he should have refrained from engaging Kellermann or allowing Ney to employ the remainder of the Cavalry in an unsupported attack which was unlikely to lead to any great result. At this supreme moment he was not true to himself. He did not throw for complete success ; though had he done so he might have seen the battle turn in his favour. He was undone by adopting a half-measure.

Once more the Emperor's glance swept over his battle-field. Then he said : ' Ney's cavalry attack has taken place an hour too soon, but we must stand by what is done.' In furtherance of this decision General de Flahault took an order to Kellermann to charge with his four Brigades of Cuirassiers and Carabiniers. Kellermann's Cavalry were to be supported by Guyot's Heavy Horse of the Guard (Grenadiers and Dragoons)—thirty-seven squadrons in all.

At 5.30 p.m. this fresh tempest struck Wellington's centre. Even now the cavalry was not backed by infantry, nor was it closely supported by horse artillery. Had guns been galloped up in the wake of the cavalry, and, directly our gunners left their guns, opened a case-shot attack of the squares, then nothing could have saved the centre of Wellington's line from being torn to pieces and breached. At this crisis a Senarmont was required by the *Armée du Nord* and the bold independent manœuvre of Friedland would have been attempted. Early in the battle, however, General Desvaux, commanding the Guard Artillery, had been killed close to the Emperor. This proved an irreparable misfortune as Drouot could not be spared.

When Kellermann's and Guyot's squadrons advanced, Milhaud had just been repulsed from the plateau for the second time. The forty-three mangled squadrons rallied as a support to this new attack, and the eighty squadrons (9,000 sabres) fell upon the crippled squares. An hour of confused, chaotic strife followed. The horsemen rode all over the plateau, even to the very rear of the position, and repeatedly charged the blocks of infantry which refused to be broken. During the hottest time of this period Wellington was inside the square of the 73rd Regiment (Alten's Division). The stress became extreme. During the prolonged struggle Wellington used up nearly all his reserves of infantry as well as all his horsemen, except the Brigades of Vivian and Vandeleur. Once again the French did nothing with our abandoned guns. This is the more surprising as they had the previous experience to guide them, and Kellermann could be trusted in a crisis.

The squares shrank visibly. Most of the casualties, however, were occasioned by the French guns and by skirmishers, who crept up close and would not be driven off. To have deployed the Infantry, so as to sweep away the skirmishers, would have meant certain and speedy annihilation by the Cuirassiers. The destruction of the squares would have been inevitable if only the Cavalry had been supported closely by French Infantry and by horse artillery. The French guns would have run no risk, because (by the Duke's orders) our gunners were sheltering in the squares, and to unlimber at the crest of the plateau would have been quite feasible.   Volleys of grape-shot, poured into the squares at point-blank range, would have blown them away.   Guns would have completed in fifteen minutes what Corps of Cavalry failed to accomplish in two hours.   The damage done by casual round-shot is proof of what case-shot must have achieved.   The close co-operation of artillery and infantry was required, since cavalry by itself was incapable of gaining a definite and permanent success over such stubborn opponents.   Had this attack gone right over Wellington's Army nothing could have saved Blücher from extermination, fully committed as he was to his hazardous flank march and with part of his force already engaged.

In this second cavalry episode, Captain Mercer, Commanding G Troop, Royal Horse Artillery, was the one officer to disobey the Duke's order, as Mercer and his gunners remained with their guns when the French cavalry closed.   After the first cavalry charges, Lieut.-Colonel Sir A. Frazer brought up Mercer's Troop at a gallop from its old position on the right near the Nivelles road to a new one in the centre.   Placing the Troop between two squares of Brunswickers, who were suffering heavy casualties, Sir A. Frazer warned Mercer that the Troop would probably be charged by French Cavalry.   Sir A. Frazer then gave Mercer the following order : ' The Duke's orders are positive.   In the event of the French persevering and charging home, you will not expose your men, but retire with them into the adjacent squares of Infantry.'   Sir Augustus left, after advising Mercer to husband his ammunition and to remember the Duke's order.   Captain Mercer took stock of the Brunswickers, to whom he was ordered to entrust the safety of his gunners.   The outlook was not promising.   One square had gaps in every face.   The infantry, mere boys, seemed almost bereft of their senses, stood like wooden figures, and at any moment might break up in panic, throw down their arms, and seek safety in flight.   Indeed the two squares were only kept intact by the personal efforts of the officers and sergeants.   Mercer at once decided that the squares were too unreliable to seek refuge in when the Cavalry closed.   The gunners, running from their guns, would give the signal for the dissolution of the squares and all would be at the mercy of the French.   Worse still, the centre would be pierced, and no one could say how far an incipient panic might spread along the line. Rather than run such a risk it would be far better for the gunners to fall at their posts. Captain Mercer promptly decided to say nothing to his men about the Duke's order, and to let his Troop take its chance, fighting the guns. This attitude Mercer maintained for the remainder of that long June afternoon ; and undoubtedly his wise and courageous decision saved this part of Wellington's centre from annihilation.

Scarcely had Mercer's first gun come up between the squares, when, less than a hundred yards away, the enemy's leading squadrons were seen advancing at a sharp trot. Captain Mercer ordered line to be formed for action, and to load the 9-pounders with grape. As each gun came up it unlimbered and opened fire independently, and the ground in front of the Troop was strewn with men and horses. Still the cavalry came on, though very slowly ; until, at the last, when only 10 yards away, they flinched and, falling into disorder, bolted down the hill, whilst the 6 guns kept up a steady fire of grape. The carnage was frightful.

Three times this grim scene was re-enacted. But in each case, ready for their foes, G Troop received them with a salvo from guns loaded with a round-shot and a grape over it. Fire was invariably withheld until the enmy was within 50 yards and then the effect was terrible. Nearly the whole of the leading rank would be blown away by the grape whilst the round-shot tore through the depth of the column. In addition, the rolling fire delivered, with ever-increasing spirit, by the two Brunswicker squares seconded the efforts of Mercer's boldly handled Troop. The fine discipline and devotion to duty of G Troop had a great effect on the Brunswickers, and gradually the two squares became steady and compact bodies of infantry.

The task of the French horsemen grew hopeless. After a while a rampart of men and mangled horses slowly rose in front of Mercer's gun muzzles. The 9-pounders were admirably placed. Wedged between the two squares, with flanks perfectly protected, the guns easily kept their own front clear. In Mercer's case, therefore, the reason for seeking refuge in the squares was far less cogent than it was for the gunners of more exposed batteries ; and, to some extent, G Troop was protected from French gun-fire by a 2-foot bank which acted as a natural epaulement. Nevertheless the Troop suffered casualties from a cloud of sharpshooters. These snipers crept up within 40 yards and maintained a galling fire, though their loose formation made it merely a waste of gun ammunition to fire at them.

Meanwhile the great cavalry attack had run its course. Most of the Generals were wounded and the squadrons were utterly disorganized. Notwithstanding the horsemen were indefatigable. No sooner were they swept off the plateau than they proceeded to reform at the foot of the slope, where they were sheltered from the fire of the British guns. By gradual recoiling, the guns had lost the advantage derived from their original commanding position, and the deep, greasy ground rendered it impossible for the weary detachments to run them up to the crest, without the aid of horses whom it was unsafe to employ.

Ney, with untiring energy, launched yet another attack to carry the plateau. Riding over to the Brigade of Mounted Carabiniers, whom Kellermann had left behind as a reserve, the Marshal led this body, the last cavalry reserve of the Army, against the stout-hearted Infantry whose diminished squares still covered Wellington's position. The Infantry held firm. At last, despairing of success, the horsemen drew off and descended into the valley, decimated and worn out.

Even then Ney did not despair. Mounting the trumpeter's horse of the 1st Cuirassiers, his fourth horse, the Marshal proceeded to rally around him everyone he could collect, so as to make one last splendid effort. Having gathered together about a thousand carabiniers, horse grenadiers, cuirassiers, dragoons, chasseurs, and red lancers, and accompanied by Lefebvre-Desnoëttes and the wounded Guyot, the lion-hearted Ney placed himself at the head of this mass of desperate men. Then for the tenth time the Marshal climbed the death-strewn slope. With one great resounding shout ' *Vive l'Empereur !* ' this death-ride of heroes burst against the resolute Infantry, standing so confidently in their unbreakable squares. With merciful swiftness came the end. Beaten back, the survivors of this devoted band were driven from the fatal, blood-drenched plateau.

For two long hours the impregnable squares stood between Ney and Victory ; and this wild act was played out by the dauntless Cavalry to a glorious but resultless end—' *ils sont vaincus avec honneur.*'

Only now did Marshal Ney remember that a part of Reille's

Corps (Bachelu's Division and one Brigade of Foy's Division, in all 6,000 bayonets) was available to support and assist the cavalry. Up to this moment Ney had overlooked this body of infantry, although previously its co-operation with the cavalry attacks might have had a far-reaching result. Too late the Marshal noticed these troops and decided to hurl them against the Anglo-Dutch line ; but the unsupported infantry was beaten off and forced back, without shaking Wellington's hold on his position.

About 4.30 p.m. Bülow's two leading Brigades (15th and 16th) debouched from the Paris Wood and drove away the squadrons covering Lobau, who was in position on some heights close to Fichermont. The 7,000 infantry of the VI Corps could not expect to hold back for long a determined attack by Bülow's fresh Corps, 30,000 strong. Nevertheless Lobau showed unconquerable spirit. Presenting a bold front to Bülow, Lobau and the VI Corps fought stubbornly and well. But Lobau, despite the admirable obstinacy which he displayed, had not shown much skill in his selection of a position where ' with 10,000 he could hold off 30,000 Prussians '. Even if he had not dared to dispute the passages of the swollen Lasne, at any rate he should have occupied the Paris Wood. Bülow would then have had to deploy his Corps to master the Wood. The close nature of wood-fighting would have so disordered the Prussians that they must have rallied and reformed before advancing any farther against the French right. Valuable time would have been gained. The Wood, however, was surrendered to Bülow without a blow. Thereafter he used it to screen the Prussian movements and he collected his troops in it before advancing against the French right. Lobau made a serious tactical mistake when he neglected to hold the Paris Wood.

For a time, Lobau held off Bülow's two leading Brigades. Then at 5.30 p.m. the whole of Bülow's Corps came up and pressed back Lobau and Domon to the heights in front of Plancenoit, drove them from there through the village, and at once Prussian round-shot ploughed up the Charleroi road behind Napoleon. With the Prussians in possession of Plancenoit, Napoleon's line of retreat was threatened. The Emperor promptly ordered

Duhesme to reinforce Lobau with the Young Guard and recapture Plancenoit at all hazards. Duhesme attacked at once, dislodged the Prussians, and completely cleared the village. In this way Napoleon freed his right flank and temporarily restored the wavering balance of the battle. It was 6 p.m. So far Bülow's action had not turned the fate of the day, and, if no other Prussian troops had arrived, Napoleon would have beaten Wellington and Bülow.

When troops were first seen issuing from the Paris Wood their nationality was uncertain to the Anglo-Dutch Army. The relief and delight can be imagined when the new-comers' guns opened fire on the French right. The long-expected Prussians had arrived. ' Such a reinforcement during an action was an occurrence so different from former days in the Peninsula, where everything centred in the British Army, that it appeared decisive of the fate of the day.'

Beyond giving a great increase of *moral* to Wellington's battered Army, Bülow's attack compelled Napoleon before 6 p.m. to divert against the Prussians 14,000 men from his general reserve. These numbers would otherwise have been available to drive home the final attack against Wellington's shaken line. It is true that the French had beaten back Bülow, but Pirch's Corps was now drawing near Napoleon's right and Zieten's Corps was approaching Wellington's left. Immediately on Zieten's arrival Vandeleur's and Vivian's fresh Cavalry Brigades (2,600 strong) and Gardiner's Troop R.H.A. would be able to move from the extreme left and reinforce the centre of the Anglo-Dutch line.

It was during this phase Wellington became convinced that no serious attack would be delivered beyond the Nivelles road, and he ordered General Chassé to bring in his Division from Braine l'Alleud. Chassé moved through Merbe Braine and formed up behind the right centre. At the same time, Adam's Brigade (of Clinton's Division), which had been in reserve on the right of the line, was also moved towards the right centre and it formed up behind the ridge to the north of Hougoumont. No orders, however, were sent to the Hal detachment.

For an hour and a half repeated efforts were made to storm La Haye Sainte and gradually the garrison's ammunition ran low, but no further supply was forthcoming. On the other hand, the skirmishers of the 5th Line Battalion, K.G.L., were thrown into this advanced post, and later on 200 Nassauers reached the farm. The French, however, managed to set the place on fire. This created some consternation among the defenders, because, although water was available the means to draw and carry it were wanting, as all the utensils had been broken. Luckily Baring noticed that the Nassauers had large field cooking-kettles. He seized one, filled it with water, and advanced to put out the fire. Others then used the kettles, the fire was got under, and the French were beaten off. Fortunately Major Baring had realized the importance of holding La Haye Sainte to the last, and he was equal to the occasion.

Towards the end of this phase one of Thielemann's aides-de-camp rode up to the Prussian Head-Quarters Staff, and reported that Thielemann, hard pressed at Wavre, was uncertain as to the result of the action. Gneisenau replied : ' Let Thielemann defend himself as best he can. It matters little if he is crushed at Wavre, so long as we gain the victory here.' At last Gneisenau showed that he appreciated the strategical situation. Economy of force meant economy on the whole transaction. The fate of the Wavre detachment was of no importance provided the decision was obtained at La Belle Alliance. ' *Qu'importe l'humanité, il faut suivre un plan !* '

If Grouchy, on the 18th June, had possessed the same clear perception of the relative importance of current events, then, at starting, he would have placed himself between Blücher and Napoleon. At the first sounds of the opening cannonade he would have despatched the greater part of his detachment to the roar of the guns, so as to ensure giving Napoleon as much assistance as possible. Had Davout or Soult been in Grouchy's place, far more effective support would have been rendered to Napoleon.

So far the Emperor had gained no tangible result at La Belle Alliance, despite the desperate nature of the fight. Not only was his Cavalry ruined, but on the eastern horizon lowered ever-increasing masses of Prussian troops. At the end of this Third Phase the growing seriousness of the situation was only too apparent.

NOTE.—*The Legend of the Hollow Way*

Whereas Austerlitz has one myth attached to it, Waterloo has attracted at least two. One of these myths is defamatory ; but this myth has been dissipated for ever by two artillery officers (Major F. Duncan, R.A., and Lieut.-Colonel H. W. L. Hime, R.A.). The second myth is a piece of sheer imagination. It should never have received credence for a moment, but unfortunately it has been repeated by many authors and artists.

This second myth, ' The legend of the hollow way ' (or Ohain road), recounts and describes a fantastical disaster to the French Cavalry in the passage of that exaggerated obstacle. The hollow way was no ravine ; it was just an ordinary country lane, slightly sunk below the level of the ground. At its deepest part, along Wellington's line, it was merely an easy in-and-out jump, complicated by neither hedge nor ditch, either on the taking-off or on the landing side. Crossed under fire this obstacle might have overturned a few French Cuirassiers, or have slightly loosened or disordered the formation of the advancing squadrons. It could never have led to a disaster of any importance or magnitude.

A Brigade of our heavy cavalry (Somerset's) crossed it when they charged Travers's Cuirassiers, and our horsemen triumphed despite the sunken road. Captain J. Shaw, whose Division (Alten's) was posted behind the road, stated, ' the ground between them and us (Alten's Division) presented no natural obstacles whatever ' ; and Picton's A.-Q.-M.-G., Lieut.-Colonel Sir W. Gomm, wrote, ' As for Victor Hugo's monstrous *chemin creux d'Ohain* and its train of catastrophes, there was no *creux* in the whole extent of it, save the Sand-Pit.'

Milhaud, Wathier de St. Alphonse, Dubois, and Ney himself, led the numerous cavalry charges ; consequently they must have been the first to be precipitated to the bottom of the abyss and then crushed under the horsemen who followed them. Strangely enough, out of the four, only Dubois was wounded. Dubois' wound was a sabre cut.

To conclude, neither Milhaud in his report (to Soult), nor his Divisional General, Delort, nor Captain Shaw (Staff Officer to Alten) made any mention at all of this catastrophe. Hence it can be consigned to its fitting resting-place—the limbo of exploded fictions.

CHAPTER XXI

THE BATTLE OF WATERLOO

4TH PHASE : FROM 6 P.M. CAPTURE OF LA HAYE SAINTE

(Map 4)

To ascertain the situation the Emperor passed along his whole line of battle. Although the fire was as hot as ever and several of the generals with him were hit, Napoleon exposed himself freely to give encouragement to his men. Having completed his reconnaissance, Napoleon ordered Marshal Ney to take La Haye Sainte, cost what it might. But the Heavy Cavalry was almost incapable of further effort, and, even if the farm was taken, nothing else would be achieved, unless the Artillery Reserve and the Guard followed up and drove home the success directly the key of Wellington's line was in Napoleon's possession. Even supposing Wellington was then overthrown, only infantry was now available to reap the harvest of victory and no shattering result could be obtained, particularly as Blücher's masses were in such close proximity.

In the last attack on Wellington's right centre, three Brigades of Reille's Corps had been brought to a standstill and forced back after losing a quarter of their strength ; and Ney had to undertake this assault of La Haye Sainte with the wrecks of D'Erlon's Corps. At the same time Durutte advanced on Papelotte and recaptured it.

Just before Ney's assault, the nine companies holding La Haye Sainte took stock of the available ammunition and found that the men had only three or four rounds apiece. At first there was some talk of withdrawing to the main position ; however, at the near approach of the French, the men unanimously informed Major Baring : ' No one will desert you. We will fight and die with you.'

This dearth of ammunition did not arise from the intercep-

tion of communication between La Haye Sainte and Wellington's main line, as the distance was short and the farm was
reinforced several times. It was due, however, to the difficulty
of obtaining rifle ammunition. There was only one cart with
reserve rifle ammunition for the two Light Battalions of the
King's German Legion, and this cart, involved in the premature
retreat of the baggage, had been thrown into a ditch and overturned. Thus it was not possible to replenish the sixty rounds
which was all that each man had when the action opened.

With the buildings almost in ruins and the garrison running
short of ammunition, the assailants soon broke in. Even then
the gallant defenders fought stubbornly, quarter being neither
asked nor given, until at length Major Baring and the survivors
had to retire from the house into the garden and then fall back
singly to the main position. Only forty-two remained of the
original garrison of 376. Baring attached himself and the weak
remnant of his own battalion to the two companies of the 1st
Light Battalion, K.G.L., which occupied the hollow road behind
the farm.

The advanced post of La Haye Sainte fell owing to its importance not having been sufficiently recognized. The original garrison and the defensive arrangements were alike inadequate,
because the place was considered strong enough for all that
was required of it. Its capture gave the French a considerable
advantage. 'The possession of La Haye Sainte, and of the
knoll above it on each side of the great road, enabled the enemy
to keep up a destructive fire of musketry upon the troops posted
for the defence of this important part of the line.'

Ney made immediate use of his success. He brought a battery
into action on a hillock near La Haye Sainte, within 300 yards
of Wellington's position, and pushed a regiment into the Sand-
Pit only 80 yards away. The action broke out furiously along
the Allied front and D'Erlon's shattered Divisions pushed on
up to the Ohain road. Luckily the Prussians applied counter-
pressure. Bülow's Corps attacked, drove the Young Guard out
of Plancenoit, and threatened the right flank of the *Armée du
Nord*.

Marshal Ney noticed a backward tendency here and there
among Wellington's troops, but the French were too exhausted
to press home the advantage which they had gained. Ney,

therefore, asked to be reinforced by a few infantry. The Marshal considered Wellington's troops must be nearly at the end of their powers. But Blücher's round-shot were ranging across the Charleroi road, and with the French cavalry destroyed Napoleon could not, or dared not, comply. Turning to Ney's messenger (Colonel Heymès) he answered roughly: '*Des troupes! Où voulez-vous que j'en prenne? Voulez-vous que j'en fasse?*'

Nevertheless Ney was right. Matters had become exceedingly critical with Wellington directly La Haye Sainte fell. To his eternal credit, however, the Duke himself remained calm, undaunted, resourceful, and fearless, quite confident that he could control and guide the storm raging around him. Officers came up to ask what should be done because the situation was desperate, and they were told there was no other order but to stand fast to the last man. Wellington was carrying out nobly his part of the pact with Blücher. It was Wellington's steadfastness and Blücher's loyalty which triumphed at long last, struck down Napoleon on this field of ' La Belle Alliance ', and consummated the glory of Trafalgar.

If Napoleon meant to use his Guard to force Wellington's position the very last moment had come when such an attack could possibly succeed. Although the Prussian strength was developing visibly yet the key of Wellington's position had been gained, and the Anglo-Dutch troops were showing all the outward signs of having reached their limits of endurance, albeit they had far exceeded the limits which Napoleon had expected. Had the Guard been launched *en masse* at Wellington's centre directly La Haye Sainte fell, the crippled line might have yielded under this terrific impact.

An officer in Vandeleur's Cavalry Brigade, formed up on the reverse slope of the position, gave the following description of the situation, ' There was a regiment of the Pays Bas in square. They were not engaged, nor suffering much from fire, I may say not in the least cut up whilst I saw them. They were immediately in our front, and fancying the affair rather serious, and that if the enemy advanced any farther (as their fears apprehended) they would have to oppose them, they began firing their muskets in the air, and their rear moved a little, intending, under the confusion of their fire and smoke, to move off.

Major Childers, 11th Light Dragoons, and I rode up to them, encouraged them, stopped those who had moved the farthest (10 yards perhaps) out of their ranks, and whilst they were hesitating whether to retreat or to continue with their columns, the Duke rode up and encouraged them. He said to us, " That is right, that is right. Keep them up." Childers then brought up his squadron, and by placing it in their rear they continued steady. The Duke rode away again immediately. Had this one battalion run away at this moment, the consequence might have been fatal.'

The foregoing describes the effect of the prolonged strain on some of the troops. It shows, too, the grip which Wellington kept on his battle, and his coolness when confronted with an incident which might have developed into a general rearward movement.

After La Haye Sainte was captured, a body of Cuirassiers gradually collected in the valley between La Haye Sainte and Hougoumont. Here, sheltered from the fire of the Allied guns, they were well placed to advance and take advantage of any disorder which might be noticed amongst Wellington's troops. Marshal Ney's numerous thrusts, launched against Wellington's centre, had tried the King's German Legion and Hanoverian Battalions of Alten's Division very highly. The 5th Line Battalion, K.G.L., were in square behind the Wavre road, when a French infantry column debouched from La Haye Sainte and advanced towards them. Alten at once sent orders to Ompteda to deploy and attack the advancing infantry. Ompteda demurred. Such a manœuvre must place the battalion at the mercy of the Cuirassiers, lying in wait on the other side of the road. At this moment the Prince of Orange rode up and ordered Ompteda to deploy. The same representation was made to the Prince who impatiently repeated his order. Ompteda then mounted, issued the order to deploy, led the battalion against the French infantry column, and overbore it. Immediately afterwards the French horsemen pounced on their defenceless foes. Taking them in front and flank they rode over them, inflicting tremendous slaughter. Colonel Ompteda was killed and less than twenty survived this fatal charge. This incident shows the result which could have been obtained earlier in the day, if the French infantry had co-operated closely with their cavalry.

At this moment La Haye Sainte and the ground on both sides of the Charleroi road in the immediate vicinity of the farm, were in the possession of the French. Ompteda's Brigade was nearly annihilated, and Kielmansegge's Brigade was so thin that the two together could scarcely hold this position. Hence that part of the battle-line between Halkett's left and Kempt's right was unprotected. This was the centre of the Duke's line, the very part above all which Napoleon desired to gain. The danger was imminent. The result of the great battle wavered in the balance. Wellington's finest tactical qualities had to be displayed now if the battle was to be saved, and nobly the Iron Duke rose to the full height of the perilous situation.

At this juncture Captain J. Shaw (A.-Q.-M.-G. of Alten's Division) found that he was probably the senior Staff Officer present with his Division, the others having been killed or badly wounded. Captain Shaw recognized the very precarious state of affairs, and galloping to the Duke he reported the peril in which the centre stood. The Duke was standing on the right of the Nivelles road, behind the British Guards, when Captain Shaw informed him that his line was open for the whole space between Halkett's and Kempt's Brigades. The Duke received this startling information very coolly, and although ' generally quiet and even apparently indifferent, yet the moment of danger always aroused him and showed the great man '. Wellington's answer promptly rang out :

' I shall order the Brunswick troops to the spot, and other troops besides. Go you, and get all the German troops of the Division to the spot that you can, and all the guns that you can find.'

Carried out as expeditiously as possible, these dispositions closed the dangerous gap with the best available means. Even if the peril arose from the original failure to appreciate the importance of La Haye Sainte, which resulted in its capture, yet the error was nobly amended.

Gaps, too, began to show in other places in Wellington's hard-pressed line. The 30th and 2/73rd had formed a square together nearly all day. About 6.30 p.m., Major Dawson Kelly, sent by the Duke to find out the cause of some confusion which was noticed in Halkett's Brigade, learned that all the officers of the 73rd had been killed or wounded and there was no officer to command the regiment. Major Kelly decided to remain with the 73rd, and assumed temporary command of the battalion. He ordered the colours of the 2/73rd, which were riddled with holes, to be removed from the pole, rolled round the body of a trusty sergeant, and taken to Brussels, as there was no longer an officer to carry them.

At the same time, just to the right of Captain S. Bolton's Field Brigade the Duke noticed six foreign guns, which had been abandoned by their gunners, and he ordered Colonel Sir G. Wood (commanding R.A.) to have them withdrawn to the rear. This duty was entrusted to Lieut. W. C. Anderson and a party from Bolton's Field Brigade, and they successfully withdrew the guns, except a very exposed one which could not be moved. The Duke also ordered D'Aubrêmé's and Detmer's Brigades (of Chassé's Division) to be brought forward to fill the position vacated by the Brunswick troops, who had been pushed into the front line between Halkett and Kruse.

It is time to return to the French right. Bülow had retaken Plancenoit and Napoleon decided he must free his threatened right before reinforcing Ney. To drive back Bülow, the Emperor selected two Battalions of his Old Guard (1/2nd Grenadiers and 1/2nd Chasseurs) and ordered them to storm Plancenoit. The Emperor gave personal instructions to the 1/2nd Grenadiers (Lieut.-Colonel Baron Golzio), ' de ne pas tirer un coup de fusil, mais d'arriver sur l'ennemi à la baïonnette '.

The two Battalions closed on Plancenoit on two points, advancing with drums beating, colours spread, and bayonets fixed. In accordance with the Emperor's orders, they disdained to fire. With the naked steel they forced their way in, overthrew all resistance, and drove out the Prussians. In twenty minutes they swept the village streets and churchyard clear, and hurled back their foe 600 yards beyond.

Many acts of great personal gallantry occurred in this Homeric strife. Not the least picturesque was the feat of the Drum-Major of the Grenadiers, who with his drum-major's staff beat down all who confronted him. The fourteen Prussian battalions in Plancenoit were utterly unable to withstand the avalanche of 1,100 Grenadiers and Chasseurs. All resistance was swept away.

After this devastating hurricane had raged through Plancenoit there lay in its track more than 3,000 Prussians, the price our Allies had to pay for the honour of crossing bayonets with the Old Guard.

The Guard pressed on victoriously up the farther slope, reached the muzzles of the Prussian guns, and even succeeded in capturing some. Bülow then turned round. Realizing he was not confronted by a grand attack of the Old Guard, he concentrated every man he could lay hands on and threw them against the veterans. Slowly the latter gave ground, and withdrawing in good order to Plancenoit they organized a stubborn defence of the village.

The two Battalions had achieved all that was required of them, since, at the end of this terrific twenty minutes, the Young Guard had rallied and Lobau and the VI Corps were able to show front once more. By this sledge-hammer blow the Emperor cleared his right, stopped the advance of the Prussians, and was free to act against Wellington. But Napoleon had depleted still further the Reserve with which he wished to ensure Wellington's defeat. For his last throw he had only 6,000 bayonets of the Old and Middle Guard. The capture, however, of La Haye Sainte had placed Napoleon in a position to drive home his supreme onslaught against the Allied centre and to assist it by a general attack all along the line. The final crisis was at hand.

CHAPTER XXII

THE BATTLE OF WATERLOO

5TH PHASE : FROM 7 P.M. 'THE LAST MADNESS OF DESPAIR ' : THE ATTACK OF THE IMPERIAL GUARD. FAILURE ; AND THE ROUT OF THE *ARMÉE DU NORD*

(Map 4 ; Sketch F)

THE Emperor, relieved temporarily of the threat to his right flank, could concentrate on the task of destroying the Anglo-Dutch Army. But Wellington had profited from the respite accorded to him after the fall of La Haye Sainte, and he had called in his reserves from right and left to reinforce and strengthen his depleted centre. The Duke realized that Napoleon was about to launch his Guard, nevertheless he awaited the supreme moment unflinchingly because he knew the head of Zieten's column had reached Smohain and was about to debouch on the battlefield.

Napoleon also knew that the Prussian I Corps was approaching. In spite of that, instead of drawing off covered by the twelve battalions of Grenadiers and Chasseurs of the Old and Middle Guard, 6,000 strong, he determined to have one last bid for victory. He considered that the Anglo-Dutch troops were exhausted and had no reserves available ; and he sent General de la Bédoyère and other Staff Officers along the ranks of the *Armée du Nord*, to spread the news that Marshal Grouchy was coming up on the French right and would engage the Allied left. Everywhere *moral* was re-established, and the highly tried French Army braced itself for its culminating effort. It was nearly 7.30 p.m. The distant rumble of Grouchy's cannonade became more distinct and the French were convinced that the Marshal was on the point of engaging and neutralizing the Prussians, thus leaving Wellington unsupported to meet the assault of the Guard.

The smoke-wreaths and puffs indicated the situation very

clearly to the Emperor, as he made a scrutiny of Wellington's position. On the right at Papelotte, Durutte was working his way forward up the slope and threatened to outflank the Anglo-Dutch left. In the centre D'Erlon's gallant Corps crowned the ridge which was theirs at last. But the intrepid infantry was worn out, it was powerless by itself to force Wellington's line. Indeed Ney had just remarked to D'Erlon : ' We must die here, because if we are spared by the English grape-shot we shall both be hanged.' Away to Napoleon's left the remnants of the Cavalry and part of Reille's Corps were rallying. Still more to westward the strife around the blazing ruins of Hougoumont raged as furiously as ever. Nevertheless Napoleon deemed that the moment had come to wrest victory from a doubtful battle, and he relied, as he had always done, on ' *l'audace et encore de l'audace, et toujours de l'audace !* '

A grand attack by ' the Invincibles ' might have gone over Wellington's line had it been driven home directly La Haye Sainte fell. Now, so far as Wellington was concerned, the crisis was past, since Zieten was close up and, after some vacillation, had borne down to support the Anglo-Dutch left. A young officer sent on by Zieten to reconnoitre had returned and reported that Wellington's left was retiring. The officer had mistaken the wounded, who were being taken back in large numbers to the dressing stations, for fugitives. In consequence of this report the Advanced Guard of Zieten's Corps was drawn back. As it disappeared, Müffling galloped after the I Corps and sought out Zieten whom he reassured, and then Müffling explained to Zieten the need for immediate action. At the moment Zieten was undecided whether he should engage to support the Duke's left, or manœuvre to rally Bülow. At once Müffling clinched the matter by saying : ' The battle is lost if the I Corps does not go to the Duke's rescue.' Zieten promptly turned his troops about and allowed Müffling to direct his advance. Had Zieten vacillated much longer his Corps would never have engaged on the 18th ; and the effectiveness of the Prussian co-operation at Waterloo was due in no slight degree to Müffling's loyalty to Wellington, as well as to his unhesitating efforts and skilful arrangements.

For the supreme onslaught the Emperor handed over to Marshal Ney only five battalions of the Middle Guard (one each of the 3rd and 4th Grenadiers and 4th Chasseurs, and two of the 3rd Chasseurs). Small this force undoubtedly was, but it was formidable because of the trained valour and splendid reputation of the Regiments. To assist this attack by the Guard, D'Erlon and Reille were ordered to co-operate ; and the Emperor now took up his position near La Haye Sainte.

A French deserter (a cavalry officer) warned Sir Augustus Frazer where the attack would be made in a quarter of an hour. Frazer, involved with artillery details, sent General Adam with the deserter to the Duke, and Wellington received the information in time to make the necessary dispositions. It is going too far to say that this piece of treasonable information saved the Anglo-Dutch Army ; but this incident and de Bourmont's desertion on the 15th showed a distinct trend of popular feeling. If all ranks of the *Armée du Nord* were not loyal to Napoleon, so much less was the nation, and this might prove a grave weakness if disaster overtook Napoleon in Belgium. Even despite this timely warning, Frazer wrote, ' the last struggle was nearly fatal to us '.

This final assault, however, was not a single concentrated effort. Not only did the Guard advance in three echelons and deliver three attacks, but these attacks were delivered on two different parts of Wellington's line. The attack of the first echelon, two Battalions of Grenadiers, was delivered midway between La Haye Sainte and Hougoumont. So as to be in hand to meet any eventuality, the two Battalions crossed the field and climbed the face of Wellington's position in columns, and these two Battalions were accompanied by guns loaded with grape. At the head of the first echelon rode Marshal Ney, with Generals Friant, Roguet, Michel, and other general officers. In the advance General Friant was wounded, and the Marshal's fifth horse was shot and he fell under it. Ney sprang up at once and thenceforward led the attack on foot. At 600 yards from Wellington's position the first echelon of the Guard passed the Emperor, standing in the middle of the road between two batteries, and the Grenadiers gave Napoleon a tremendous salute before throwing themselves against Wellington's line.

The sun was sinking, and the darkened smoke-laden air obscured any clear view of the pandemonium which broke out when the Grenadiers closed.

Sketch F.—At this supreme moment the British Horse Artillery Troops and Field Brigades stood in action on a curve along the ridge above La Haye Sainte and Hougoumont, awaiting the final onslaught. From more than 30 guns a double salvo of grape-shot saluted the advancing columns and took them in flank. The grape tore holes in the ranks of the assailants, but the veterans neither flinched nor faltered. Steadily they pressed on. Closing their shot-scarred ranks, their war-cry pealed high above the din of battle.

The 1/3rd Grenadiers overcame some Brunswickers and seized the temporarily abandoned guns of Major W. Lloyd's Field Brigade, R.A., and Captain A. Cleeves's Battery (K.G.L.). Then, inclining slightly, the Grenadiers bore down on Halkett's Brigade and pressed back the 30th and 73rd Regiments who, forming a square together, stood slightly in advance of the 33rd and 69th. At this ominous moment General Chassé brought up the Horse Battery from Major van der Smissen's Group and placed the 6-pounders on the right of the two British regiments. The grape-shot volleys from van der Smissen's 6-pounders smote the Guard in flank with deadly effect. Chassé then swung up Detmers' Brigade (3,000 strong) and drove it with the bayonet against the left of the shattered French column. The 1/3rd Grenadiers were broken, crushed, and hurled to the bottom of the slope.

Meanwhile the Battalion of the 4th Grenadiers engaged the right of Halkett's Brigade, and the musketry of the Grenadiers was augmented by two of Duchand's guns (of the Guard Horse Artillery Reserve). Under this pressure the highly tried 33rd and 69th wavered. In this crisis, Sir Colin Halkett rose to the occasion, and seizing the flag of the 33rd he stood firm waving it above his head. This example steadied the men and they beat off the 4th Grenadiers. The attack of the first echelon had failed.

The other thrusts at Wellington's line were made just to the east of Hougoumont. After the cavalry charges, Captain S. Bolton's Field Brigade moved forward and unlimbered between Maitland's Brigade of Guards (who were lying down covered by a small bank) and the 52nd Light Infantry. Whilst his guns were in this position, Captain Bolton was killed by a cannon shot and the command devolved on 2nd-Captain C. Napier.

Soon afterwards the Duke rode up to one of Napier's subalterns, Lieut. W. Sharpin, and this conversation took place :

' What are your guns firing at ? '

' On the infantry, my Lord.'

' Can you see them well ? '

' Perfectly well, my Lord.'

On hearing that Captain Napier was in command, the Duke said : ' Tell him to keep a sharp look out on his left, for the French will be with him immediately.'

The attack of the three remaining Battalions of the Middle Guard was delivered in two echelons, the first by two Battalions of the 3rd Chasseurs and the second by one Battalion of the 4th Chasseurs. The Battalions used for the approach march a formation of the period, *colonne contre la cavalerie*. Formed in this way the Battalions advanced in succession in double-company columns at half-company distance, with one-and-a-half-company distance between battalions. This kept the men well in hand and ready to meet any emergency.

Advancing with perfect steadiness, undeterred by the appalling sight of the ground around Hougoumont and of the slopes covered with the remains of the shattered cavalry, the 3rd Chasseurs pressed on undismayed almost to the very crest of the ridge. The gun-fire had slackened, owing to the scarcity of ammunition. For all that, the Chasseurs were pounded with round-shot by Major W. N. Ramsay's Troop (under Lieut. P. Sandilands). Suddenly, in Bolton's Brigade, shouts of ' *Vive l'Empereur ! en avant ! en avant !* ' were heard above the tumult of the battle. At the same moment the head-dresses of the Chasseurs showed over the corn only 50 yards away, their officers in front, waving their swords and cheering on their men. As a result of the Duke's warning to Lieut. Sharpin, Captain Napier had just loaded his guns with grape. As each succeeding body of troops topped the rise, Napier opened point-blank fire and almost to a man they were swept away. Even so Napier's guns had to fire several rounds of grape before these magnificent veterans slowed their advance. Invariably the cheers of the gunners acted as a spur, and once more on they came. At last they were so close that it was difficult to depress the guns so as to fire into them. Now as they received each discharge the Chasseurs swayed like standing corn blown by the wind.

So it went on, till the guns had expended all their ammunition. Then, just before the 3rd Chasseurs reached the Ohain road, they were confronted by a thin red line. It was the British Guards who barred a further advance. On Wellington's command, ' Up Guards, ready ! ' they rose from their lair in the standing corn. Bringing their muskets to the present they fired a smashing volley at 20 yards' range, and the head of the 3rd Chasseurs went down in one weltering mass. The Chasseurs had just reached the very summit of our position. Their bodies lay there to prove it.

An attempt made to deploy the Chasseurs was ineffectual. It merely served to increase the disorder and confusion spreading through their ranks. But for ten long minutes the Chasseurs refused to acknowledge defeat. Then, detecting their condition, Wellington ordered his troops to charge. In a moment the British Guards leaped on their foe with the bayonet, swept them back, and flung them down the slope as far as the enclosures around Hougoumont.

Still another foe came looming through the smoke. It was the 4th Chasseurs, advancing to extricate their comrades. The British Guards halted, and then fell back to their original position, followed closely by the French who were received with volleys of grape-shot. The British Guards and W. Halkett's Brigade stood astride the advance of the 4th Chasseurs, and the 3rd Hanoverian Brigade, emerging from Hougoumont, began to fire into their rear. But the end of this last desperate throw for victory came with a catastrophic suddenness, foretelling the final overthrow of Napoleon and the First Empire.

Until this moment the 52nd Light Infantry (of Adam's Brigade) had remained concealed on the reverse slope, to the right front of Maitland's Guards. Not a bayonet showed. Only the head of the commanding officer, Sir John Colborne, was visible above the crest. He watched and calculated his chance as the 4th Chasseurs passed within a hundred yards. At last the head of the Battalion drew level with the 52nd's left. The moment had come, and Colborne ordered his regiment to advance. Clearing the crest, under heavy fire from the Chasseurs, the 52nd threw its right shoulders forward and brought the point-blank fire of its deployed line to bear on the heavy mass before it. The 71st nobly supported the 52nd. Withered by the deadly

fire the leading Chasseurs gave ground, and soon a thick pall
of smoke settled over the combatants. Cheers and shouts were
heard. The 52nd pressed forward. A more rapid roll of musketry broke out. Then—the end came with startling abrupt-
ness. The Chasseurs broke and fled in mingled confusion.
Driven obliquely by the charge towards the Charleroi road, they
carried with them in disorder all the troops on their right.

It was 8 p.m. when the dread cry rang out : ' *La Garde
recule !* ' Along the battle-line it pealed. It paralysed the
French and prevented their further efforts. On the other hand
it stimulated the Allies into immediate and decisive action, and
Wellington determined to finish off the last of the Grand Armies
then and there. The Duke rode to the crest of the position,
took off his hat, and waved it in the air. 40,000 men came
pouring down the slopes in the twilight, the drums beat, and
the trumpets sounded the charge.

Catching up the 52nd, the Duke called out : ' Go on, Colborne, go on ! Give them no time to rally ! ' Hastily correct-
ing the alignment, the regiment (with the 71st covering its right)
hastened forward as fast as the heavy state of the ground would
permit. So soft were the fields that the men occasionally sank
in up to their knees. Across this quagmire Wellington had
compelled Napoleon to attack all day.

In this great hour Wellington loosed on the wavering foe his
last cavalry reserve, the Brigades of Vivian and Vandeleur, and
the French at once abandoned La Haye Sainte and the enclosures
around Hougoumont. Panic spread like wildfire and transformed
the French left and centre into a rudderless horde. A British
officer wrote, ' I have seen nothing like that moment, the sky
literally darkened with smoke, the sun just going down, and,
until then it had not for some hours broken through the gloom
of a dull day, the indescribable shouts of thousands, where it
was impossible to distinguish between friend and foe. Every
man's arm seemed to be raised against that of every other.
Suddenly, after the mingled mass had ebbed and flowed, the
enemy began to yield, and cheerings and English huzzas announced
that the day must be ours.'

The rapidity with which the end had come is testified by
another eye-witness, ' On our Brigade (Vandeleur) getting to
the point where we overlooked them (the French), they were

seen running away on every side in the greatest haste and confusion. Not knowing when we moved to the front which had succeeded, it was a sight I shall never forget.'

At the same moment as the Guard failed, another great success was obtained by the Prussians against the French right. Zieten's Corps had at last linked Wellington's left with Pirch I and Bülow. Zieten then confronted the right-angle at the north-east corner of the French front. Under the extreme pressure exerted by the Prussian masses at the apex of the angle, the front of the French troops, holding this part of the line, was driven inwards, leaving open a way straight to the heart of the *Armée du Nord*. Durutte, however, with his troops formed in Napoleon's ' mixed order ', still fought on grimly. Not for long could the Prussians be kept back. Through the widening gap their horsemen poured, to meet, at La Belle Alliance, the British Cavalry who had crashed across the débris of the fight to the east of Hougoumont.

The one great risk, against which Napoleon had to guard during this campaign, was the unlikely one of being caught on a battle-field between the two closing jaws of the Allied vice. The unlikely had happened and further resistance was of little avail.

Lobau and the troops under his command held firm to cover the retreat of the Grand Army along the Charleroi road. But the retreat quickened into flight as the ever-increasing roar of Blücher's guns drew in nearer and nearer to Plancenoit. All honour to Lobau. Here, as at Essling on the Danube's bank, he held the blazing ruins of a village to save his Emperor's Army from annihilation. Lobau's courage afforded Napoleon a chance to rally the Army he had used so hardly. Then, when hope was gone, the heroic defence of Plancenoit kept open for the Emperor and the débris of the *Armée du Nord* an avenue of escape from the accursed field. General Duhesme was killed in this desperate fight for Plancenoit. ' *C'était un soldat intrépide, un général consommé.*'

When his attacks collapsed, Napoleon still had in hand, near La Haye Sainte, the 2nd battalions of the 1st Chasseurs, 2nd Grenadiers, and 2nd Chasseurs, under Generals Cambronne, Roguet, and Christiani. The Emperor was just forming up these troops, whom he intended to lead across the plateau to give the *coup de grâce* to Wellington. Suddenly he saw ruin everywhere and realized that the best use which he could make of the three battalions was to form with them a human dike, and behind this cover rally the *Armée du Nord* and march off. For this purpose he formed the three battalions into three squares, with their right resting on the Charleroi road about a hundred yards distant from La Haye Sainte. These squares withstood Vivian's charges. Thereupon (unchecked by the four head-quarters squadrons, which the Emperor launched against them) the Allied horsemen turned on the flying masses and cut down all whom they could reach.

Meanwhile Wellington's Infantry and two British Horse Artillery Troops (Major Whinyates's and Lieut.-Colonel Sir R. Gardiner's) and a British Field Brigade (Major Rogers's) closed with the squares. The guns opened with grape at 60 yards and the infantry swarmed round the Guard, who were un-favourably placed to reply to the fire poured into them. See-ing this, the Emperor ordered the squares to withdraw, and with a few mounted Chasseurs, he galloped off to La Belle Alliance to select a position for reforming the *Armée du Nord*. Napoleon also sent an order to General Piré to move his Light Cavalry to the entrance of the village of Genappe, to stem the tide of flight and rally and reform the fugitives.

Enemies surrounded the three battalions of the Guard as they withdrew; but their retreat, although slow, was carried out with precision and order. It was amidst this tumult that, on being asked if he would surrender, General Cambronne made the curt answer which a few days later was improved into the immortal phrase: '*La Garde meurt, elle ne se rend pas!*' At last, on reaching La Belle Alliance, the dwindling squares were submerged by the crowd of assailants; and, as they dissolved, the survivors mingled with the remnants of the *Armée du Nord*.

It was at this time that disaster overtook Captain Mercer's Troop of Royal Horse Artillery; and the incident serves to demonstrate the disorder which existed even among the victors in the hour of their triumph. A disorder which partly resulted from the Allied Armies effecting their concentration on the battle-field.

See Inset Sketch F.—Just when the day had been won, a battery, which seemed to have dropped from the clouds about 400 yards away, opened a heavy enfilade fire on the left of Mercer's Troop. The Troop was raked from end to end. Every shot took effect. Slowly and laboriously, owing to the heavy ground, the tired gunners swung round the two left flank guns and brought them to bear on their new foe. Soon afterwards, a Black Brunswicker Officer galloped up in a great state of excitement and asserted that the Troop was firing on its own good friends—the Prussians ! Mercer patiently explained that in a *mêlée* one could only tell the tree by the fruit. This fruit was deadly as it threatened to annihilate his Troop ; and if the offenders were Prussians, they were behaving very uncivilly. As a result of the Black Brunswicker's protest, Mercer ceased fire against the enfilading battery, but the raking round-shot only came in thicker than ever. The Black Brunswicker himself had a narrow escape, and disappeared. Gradually Mercer's Troop was reduced to a confused wreck. It was only saved from complete extinction by the advent of a Belgian Horse Artillery Battery which un-limbered close on Mercer's left, where it could enfilade indiffer-ently either the Troop or the Prussian Battery. Mercer induced the Belgians to open fire on the Prussians. Taken in flank, our Prussian allies soon retired. Shortly after this an aide-de-camp galloped up to Mercer, shouting out : ' Forward, Sir, Forward ! It is of the utmost importance that this movement is supported by artillery.' In answer Mercer merely pointed to the remains of his famous Troop, and the over-zealous aide-de-camp galloped off. The Troop was a jumbled mass of guns with the trails interlocked. 140 (out of 200) of its horses had fallen, and the personnel had suffered severely. In consequence the Troop had to spend the night in its battle-position, covered by the huge rampart of slaughtered cavalry which, even from La Belle Alliance, showed up as an immense heap of dark objects, which ' formed a remarkable feature on the field '.

With the battle lost, Marshal Ney, standing close to the road, determined to die a soldier's death. The Marshal was almost unrecognizable. He was splashed with mud, bare-headed, his face blackened by powder-smoke, with an epaulette shot away, and his sword-blade broken to the hilt. Just then a mass of fugitives was swirling past in confusion. Suddenly Ney caught sight of Brue's Brigade (Durutte's Division), the only troops of the line which still maintained any formation, though the Brigade by this time was reduced to two battalions. Ney's chance had come. The Marshal stopped the Brigade. Placing himself at its head he flung it upon the foe, electrifying the men by shouting : ' *Venez voir mourir un maréchal de France !* ' But nothing could stop the victorious Allies in the hour of their triumph. Brue's Brigade was swiftly broken and scattered ; and the commanding officer of the 95th of the Line had to seize the Eagle of his Regiment and run with it towards a square of the Guard. At first he was refused shelter ; but the Eagle, the treasured emblem of the Regiment's honour, gained him the necessary permission to enter.

Still Ney was undaunted. But to save himself from immediate capture he had to enter the same square of the Guard. When the square finally broke up he left the field on foot, supported by a corporal of the Guard until he had passed through Genappe. Major Schmidt, of the Red Lancers, then recognized the Marshal and gave his horse to *le brave des braves*.[1]

Previously the Emperor had formed the 2/3rd Grenadiers (Lieut.-Colonel Belcourt) in square and placed it on the left flank near Hougoumont. Here, when the *Armée du Nord* gave way, the square was in the position of an isolated redoubt. The square held its ground although subjected to a heavy gun-fire which tore bloody breaches in its flanks ; and, after a charge, the Allied Cavalry left 200 of their number as a glacis to this impenetrable work. Another charge was delivered with the same lack of success. A third time the cavalry charged. Fifteen or twenty horsemen did win an entrance, but they were bayoneted instantly in the square. The time had come, however, for the square to retire, and, reduced from 500 to 300, the Grenadiers moved off to Rossomme. On the way the square became an asylum for many wounded men, who begged to be escorted from the field. This proved its undoing. No longer could the Grenadiers form a large and roomy square three deep, they had to form a triangle, two deep only, with the apex directed at Rossomme. The Allies prepared to deliver a fourth assault on the living fortress which had defied them for so long. Close

---

[1] Marshal Ney was tried by the Chamber of Peers after the Restoration. Found guilty and condemned to death on the 5th December, 1815, Marshal Ney was shot at 9.15 a.m. on the 7th December, 1815, in the Avenue de l'Observatoire.

to La Belle Alliance the end came.   A last furious charge broke in.   After a desperate fight between bayonet and sabre, the Grenadiers outnumbered and crushed—disappeared.   The 2/3rd Grenadiers had done their duty nobly.

The last scene of the battle, fought out near de Coster's house, redounded to the glory of the French Army.   With ruin all around them, calmly waiting in squares stood the two Battalions of the 1st Grenadiers of the Guard, under General Petit, with the Emperor himself in the centre of the 1st Battalion.   With these living bastions Napoleon meant to cover the disorganized flight of the Grand Army and save it from the horrors of a close pursuit.   A 12-pounder battery of the Guard Artillery was in action on the prolongation of the squares, though it had but one round a gun.   The pursuing cavalry closed.   A last salvo of grape-shot was belched from the mouths of the guns.   Then the gunners, standing beside their empty pieces, were cut down where they stood.   Notwithstanding, the two squares stood firm and beat off the assailants.   The attacks had merely the same effect as have handfuls of sand blown against the granite pyramids of Egypt.   Petit's Grenadiers defied all efforts to break them as they stood there alone.   Two Battalions confronting two Armies.

By this time Lobau's defences were down.   The Prussians driving the defenders from the blazing ruins of Plancenoit, both pursued and pursuers debouched pell-mell on to the Charleroi highway.   Despite the awful *débâcle* the Grenadiers remained undaunted.   In self-defence they had to clear the faces of the squares with fire, lest foes should enter the two citadels along with the friends who sought refuge therein.   At length the Emperor ordered the Grenadiers to fall back.   They drew off in perfect order, halting continually to rectify their line and arrest the pursuit by effective enfilading fire.   In this supreme hour the Old Guard was worthy of itself and of France.   If on the Champ de Mars the bearing of the Grenadiers was magnificent, here in the hour of defeat at La Belle Alliance it was majestic and superb.   The 1st Grenadiers of the Old Guard knew how to die, they did not know how to surrender.   Fame's unfading splendour is their reward.

Meanwhile the Emperor had been induced to leave the square. Accompanied by a small staff and a tiny escort, he pushed on to Le Caillou. Here he found his personal escort, the 1/1st Chasseurs, and with this Battalion Napoleon slowly took the road to Charleroi.

It was after 9 p.m. when Field-Marshal the Duke of Wellington and Field-Marshal Prince Blücher met near the farm of 'La Belle Alliance' and greeted each other as victors. It was almost dark, but the battle-field was still feebly lit by a red and sinister glow from blazing Plancenoit. Wellington's troops were too weary and Blücher undertook to carry on an immediate pursuit. The Prussian Field-Marshal ordered Gneisenau to lead the pursuit in person, and the Prussian Corps Commanders were directed to press on so long as they possessed a man and a horse able to stand.

It has been estimated that the Prussian troops, engaged in the great Battle, numbered approximately :
At 4.30 p.m., 16,000 (including 2,700 sabres) and 64 guns ; at 6.30 p.m., 30,000 (including 2,700 sabres) and 64 guns ; and at 7.30 p.m., 52,000 (including 8,800 sabres) and 104 guns.
The Prussian formations actively engaged in the fighting were :
Bülow's IV Corps ;
5th Brigade (Tippelskirch) of Pirch I's II Corps ;
1st Brigade (Steinmetz) of Zieten's I Corps ; and
Röder's Cavalry.
On the 18th June, the Allied losses were apportioned as follows :

	Killed, wounded, and missing
Anglo-Hanoverian	7,400
Dutch-Belgian	3,200
Nassauers and Brunswickers	1,300
Total loss suffered by Wellington's Army .	11,900

The Prussian casualties numbered about 7,000.
Truly might Wellington say at the close of this day : ' I have never fought such a battle, and I trust I shall never fight such another.'
The heavy sustained fire which they had kept up rendered many of our guns unserviceable. On the 18th June, the eight

Troops, R.H.A., and five Field Brigades, R.A., fired 9,476 rounds. Of this total, Captain Sandham's Field Brigade, R.A., expended 1,100 rounds ; and Major Whinyates's Troop, R.H.A., 309 round-shot, 236 spherical case (shrapnel), 15 case, and 52 rockets. The Prussian Artillery loosed off 4,800 rounds.

The losses on the French side can only be given approximately :

$$
\begin{array}{l}
\text{25,000 killed and wounded ;} \\
\text{8,000 captured ;} \\
\text{8,000 deserted or straggling ;}
\end{array}
$$

Total   41,000 men.

The *Armée du Nord* lost two Eagles, and abandoned on the battle-field over 120 guns and more than 210 artillery vehicles.

The fierce fighting on Sunday the 18th June was so concentrated that the 43,000 killed and wounded lay on an area of only three square miles. ' The face of the hill near La Haye Sainte, and from thence to Hougoumont, had more the appearance of a breach carried by assault than an extended field of battle ', with ' rider and horse in one red burial blent ' ; and ' the 27th Regiment (Inniskillings) was lying dead in square '. At the end of the Battle the position, which our Infantry had held so gallantly and so stubbornly throughout the long, trying hours of that Sunday in mid-June, was marked by the red line of our dead and wounded, lying along it shoulder to shoulder. Six days after the Battle an officer in E Troop, R.H.A., wrote : ' Everyone felt a difference between this battle and all others we ever fought [in the Peninsular War]. Here was suspense ; heretofore we carried all our own way.'

The Duke wrote afterwards to Marshal Beresford : ' Never did I see such a pounding match. Both were what the boxers called gluttons. Napoleon did not manœuvre at all. He just moved forward in the " old style " in columns, and was driven off in the " old style ". The only difference was that he mixed cavalry with his infantry, and supported both with an enormous quantity of artillery. I had the infantry (Anglo-Dutch) for some time in squares, and we had the French Cavalry walking about as if they had been our own. I never saw the British Infantry behave so well.' The day after the Battle the Duke owned ' it had been a damned nice thing—the nearest run thing you ever saw in your life '.

The foregoing remarks show the severe strain placed on Wellington and on his troops. Although a large proportion of the British Infantry were young soldiers, yet that made their performance the finer. It is true that the British Infantry may have manœuvred indifferently ; but the essential was to fight and no one can gainsay that they fought splendidly. The position so skilfully chosen for occupation by Wellington only taxed their fighting qualities ; and all day the crest of the ridge sheltered the young troops from the searching bombardment and annihilating case-shot attack.

Wellington's skill and leadership combined with the admirable tenacity and fighting spirit displayed by his troops enabled the Anglo-Dutch Army to hold its position and wear down the *Armée du Nord*. Blücher's arrival and whole-hearted co-operation then enabled the Allies to overwhelm the last of the Grand Armies. Nevertheless throughout this hazardous day surely the Duke of Wellington's motto was : ' *Speravi, oravi, vici !* '

CHAPTER XXIII

THE PURSUIT—AFTER 9.15 P.M.

(Map 1)

THE pursuit need only be considered briefly. It is unnecessary to prolong the last agonies of the *Armée du Nord.*

The Emperor had to contend with the darkness of the night, which prevented his soldiers from recognizing him, increased the growing confusion, and made it impossible to restore order. Napoleon had just entered his campaign carriage when he heard the shouts of Röder's pursuing horsemen ; jumping out, he leaped on his horse and rode off. Immediately afterwards the Prussians seized the carriage and looted it.

Marshal Soult, the Grand Marshal (Bertrand), and General Drouot of the Guard, accompanied the Emperor on the dreary night ride to Charleroi, and the party was escorted by a detachment of the Red Lancers of the Guard. At Genappe the narrow street was so choked that the Emperor took an hour to traverse it, and it was 1 a.m. before he reached Quatre Bras. Here the Emperor hoped to find Girard's Division (Reille's Corps), which had remained at Sombreffe on the 17th, and this weak but rested Division could have taken up a rallying position and checked the pursuit. Unfortunately, Colonel Matis (who replaced Girard) had withdrawn to Charleroi.

From Quatre Bras Napoleon sent Captain Dumonceau to Grouchy to inform the Marshal of the desperate turn which affairs had taken and the perilous position in which the Right Wing had been placed. Hardly had Dumonceau started when the Prussians seized the houses at the cross-roads and opened fire. Napoleon, thinking Girard's Division might still be at Sombreffe, at once sent Major Baudus to Fleurus to warn this Division of its danger ; and, if he found the Division on the Ligny battlefield, Baudus was told to conduct it across the Sambre. After the departure of Baudus, the Emperor and his party remounted and

236

rode for Charleroi past Gosselies. At Charleroi, reached about 5 a.m., the disorder and congestion was as great as at Genappe, and the Emperor halted for an hour before he set out for Philippeville, where he arrived at 9 a.m. on the 19*th June.*

Meanwhile Blücher's Army was putting into practice two of the Marshal's precepts : ' For pursuit, brigades are not necessary, battalions will suffice ' ; and ' It is not enough to be victorious, we must know how to turn the victory to account. If we do not press the enemy at close quarters he will rally, and we shall have to attain by a fresh battle what we can gain now, if we act with energy.' At the end of the Battle of Waterloo, the Prussians were well placed to open and carry out an immediate and close pursuit ; seeing that Bülow's Corps had advanced straight against the French right near Plancenoit, there was no doubt which road the French were using, and the choked way through Genappe, on the main line of the French retreat, gave the Prussians time to come up, re-establish contact, and improve the Allied victory in every way. In this era, before the advent of aircraft, the red harvest of victory had to be cut with the cavalry scythe, so Röder's horsemen were ordered to lead the hunt.

Gneisenau and the troops he led met with no organized resistance. The *Armée du Nord* was a beaten host, and its rout was accentuated by the hunger and the weariness of the men. After Genappe was passed, 4,000 Prussians sufficed to keep 40,000 Frenchmen on the run. All honour, therefore, to those small bands of determined men who marched grouped around the valued Eagle of each regiment, and brought it safely away, in this hour of ruin and black despair. Not a single Eagle was lost during the retreat, although the bulk of the French Army soon became a defenceless mob, which, driven out of seven successive bivouacs, drifted next morning across the Sambre.

Gneisenau's boldly handled force placed the crown on the victors' strategy. Even when the troops led by the Prussian Chief of Staff dwindled to a few squadrons and a detachment of infantry, yet, mounted on one of Napoleon's carriage horses, a drummer continued to beat the charge.

Having passed Frasnes, Gneisenau considered he was not justified in carrying on this man-hunt by moonlight,[1] partly

[1] On the day of the Battle of Waterloo the moon was three days before full and had risen well before sunset.

because of the small numbers of the pursuing troops and partly on account of the fatigue experienced by his men and horses. He called a halt. The chase stopped at a little inn which bore the prophetic inscription—*À l'Empereur*.

*   *   *   *   *   *   *

Surely the ruin which overtook the *Armée du Nord* was due primarily to Napoleon's obstinacy, and to the inexorable pride which possessed him on this fatal day. Obstinacy and pride which bade him persevere with a battle from which no satisfactory result could be obtained, and which threatened dire disaster in the case of failure. His reckless confidence, coupled with his waning powers, induced him to make a fatal miscalculation. He showed no hesitation in asking the utmost from his soldiers, though he failed to give them the assistance they required in their desperate fight ; assistance, which his former glorious campaigns had taught them to expect from him. This help alone could have prevented their overthrow by ensuring their success. Maintaining the bitter struggle with all his old stubbornness and ruthlessness, Napoleon dared no longer compel Fortune to crown his eagles by staking all so that he might gain all.

As the battle ran its course, the chances of Napoleon achieving success waned visibly hour by hour. At last, in a moment of despair, the Emperor made a final, but half-hearted bid for victory, which was then beyond his grasp. Swift on the heels of his failure, the Allies sprang forward to plough red furrows through the crippled mass which had been the proud *Armée du Nord*. From Napoleon's weakening grasp the sword was struck for ever. The Sun of Austerlitz sank to rise no more.

CHAPTER XXIV
SOME COMMENTS ON WATERLOO

DURING the description of the Battle many comments have been made, but the following four subjects require rather more detailed consideration.

THE FIGHTING QUALITIES OF THE BRITISH AND KING'S GERMAN LEGION TROOPS IN 1815

Tribute has already been paid to the gallant and meritorious performances of our Allies and the share they all had in this great victorious campaign. The casualty lists of the 15th, 16th, and 18th June show that all the nations suffered heavily for the cause which they had espoused ; and it was essential for them to do so if Napoleon was to be defeated. But, in a critical study, it is necessary for an Englishman to consider the fighting qualities of our own troops.

In 1815, not only did Napoleon neglect to take sufficient account of Blücher's steadfast loyalty and Wellington's tactical skill and unshaken firmness, but he underestimated the dogged British and K.G.L. troops. These misjudgments eventually turned the scale in favour of the Allies. The dangers confronting Napoleon in 1815 were twofold : defeat in detail, or failure to overcome the immediate foe within the time available for the decisive stroke. The *Armée du Nord* ran very little risk of failure from the first cause. Blücher's Prussians were not veteran troops, and Wellington's Army was not homogeneous enough to beat 40,000 men in forty minutes. Napoleon did not have to fear a lightning overthrow, like Salamanca, which would upset his calculations by annihilating one of his covering forces before the Reserve could be swung in to obtain the decision.

On the other hand, the grim determination, the power of

endurance, the unyielding discipline of the British and K.G.L. troops, and the skill and undaunted courage of their Chief, threatened serious danger to the Emperor in 1815. So that the fighting quality of our troops may be appreciated, we will quote some opinions of them which were expressed by eye-witnesses of their performances in the long wars of this period. Müffling has written :

' For a battle there is not perhaps in Europe an Army equal to the British ; that is to say none whose discipline and whole military tendency is so purely and exclusively calculated for giving battle. The British soldier is vigorous, well-fed, by nature both brave and intrepid, trained to the most rigorous discipline, and admirably well-armed. The infantry resist the attacks of cavalry with great confidence ; and when taken in flank, or rear, British troops are less disconcerted than any other European Army. These circumstances in their favour will explain how this Army, since the Duke of Wellington com- manded it, has never yet been defeated in the open field.'

Marshal (then Lieut.-Colonel) Bugeaud, one of our gallant foes in the Peninsula, has testified to the effect produced on their enemies' minds by the disciplined silence which enshrouded our troops whilst awaiting attack, and the impression made on their assailants by the unequalled unconcern and phlegm exhibited by the British Infantry in battle, as well as the imposing spectacle of that long red wall which so often lay athwart a French attack, barring a farther advance. The French were disconcerted by the outward impassiveness of the British and the lack of notice which they took of their foes, as the latter drew near with noisy shouts. The attacking French infantry realized that the fire, so long withheld, would be murderous when it was delivered, and the storm, so long preparing, would be overwhelming when it burst. The moral effect of studied calm over wild disorder sank deep into the minds of the assailants. Bugeaud considered that the fire delivered by the British was more effective than any which the French troops at that era were called on to face.

Marshal Bugeaud wrote, ' the British Infantry are the best in the world '. He was careful, however, to add, ' fortunately there are not many of them '. Ninety-nine years later the same remarks would have been equally true. Indeed they are to-day.

General Foy, an artillery officer who fought against us in the Peninsula and in Belgium, thought there were no more redoubtable foes than the British, for holding a defensive position. He eulogized their firmness under fire as well as their fine fire-action, and stated that their officers were the bravest and most patriotic in Europe. Of our artillery he wrote, ' the British artillerymen are especially noticeable for the fine spirit which animates them. In action their energy is adequate, their observation of events is perfect, and the courage they exhibit is stoical.'

The French officers, with the ex-Emperor on H.M.S. *Bellerophon*, said to Captain Maitland : ' There is no such infantry in the world, there is no making any impression on them. You may as well attempt to charge through a wall, and their fire is tremendous.'

Particular attention has been bestowed on our infantry, because in 1815 infantry was the ' Queen of the battle-field '. It was the unyielding discipline possessed by our men, which enabled them to stand up to the heavy punishment which was in accordance with accepted tradition. Blücher's soldiers had failed to do this at Ligny. Thus, on the 16th, Napoleon's time-limit was not upset.

On the 18th, however, the skill with which the Duke chose and occupied the position in which he was prepared to give battle and the undaunted front shown all day by his troops, enabled Wellington to defy Napoleon long enough to allow Blücher to arrive and combine in dealing a fatal stroke. It was this unlikely combination which Napoleon slighted.

Our troops stood for hours on the 18th and never flinched from the ordeal. The surging flood of French horse, the ceaseless hail of death sweeping over from the French guns, the point-blank discharges of the Guard, failed to break the steadfast British and King's German Legion Infantry who had taken root on the reverse slope. They proved that the Duke's trust in them was not misplaced, and it was their inflexible spirit which secured the time necessary for Blücher to intervene.

But this wonderful Infantry lacked manœuvring power. Müffling wrote on the 24th June, ' the British have little manœuvring power and are extremely slow '. Here Wellington showed his skill. He accepted battle in such a position and fought it in such a way that his Infantry were hardly called on to manœuvre. The Duke showed that the art of leadership consists in the practical adaptation of the means at hand to the attainment of the object in view.

The Battle of Waterloo proved clearly enough that mere defence, even coupled with indomitable tenacity, could achieve nothing by itself. In the end everything depended on the Allies assuming the offensive. This most difficult task was rendered comparatively easy for Wellington at Waterloo, by the co-operation of Blücher and his Prussian Army. The blow they struck was deadly, because the Allied concentration was made on the battle-field.

The remaining three points to be considered concern the French Army.

The Hour at which the Battle began

Some authors suggest that Napoleon should have begun the battle at 6 a.m. But he could not have attacked at 6 a.m., or even at 7 a.m., because it was necessary for his troops to have a meal, and, in addition, the depth covered by the overnight bivouacs of the French Army prevented him from opening a general action before 9 a.m. at earliest. The unfortunate dispersion resulted from the straggling which Napoleon's rapid pursuit of the Anglo-Dutch Army had induced, the confusion into which the columns were thrown, and the fatigue of the troops. All, however, that Napoleon had to ensure was Wellington's defeat before Blücher engaged in force. So it was only necessary for the action to have been as fully developed at 10 a.m. as it actually was at 1 p.m. At 10 a.m. Napoleon might have combined a frontal attack against Wellington's centre and left centre with an envelopment of the Anglo-Dutch left and employed all his available troops to compel a decision. He would have kept in hand only the Young Guard and the Light Cavalry of the Guard, whom he might have pushed out towards Fichermont to strengthen and cover his exposed right flank. As a result of this onslaught, the Anglo-Dutch Army would have been overpowered and hurled back on Brussels by 3 p.m. at latest. The delay in opening the action saved Wellington's Army.

Bülow only debouched from the Paris Wood after 4 p.m. and did not become dangerous until about 5 p.m., more than four hours after the action had entered on a serious phase. There is no reason to suppose that Bülow would have marched any quicker, even if the guns had been heard thundering away two hours earlier. Nor could he have intervened so effectually, because at the opening stage of the action he would have been farther from the battle-field. He could hardly have engaged before 3 p.m. ; but by then, exposed to Napoleon's merciless blows, Wellington would have suffered defeat. Neither Pirch I nor Zieten could have engaged any earlier than Bülow. Pirch followed Bülow on the same road, consequently Pirch could not have out-distanced the IV Corps. Zieten did not reach Ohain until seven hours after the cannonade had reached its maximum intensity ; and he would not have marched any quicker, even supposing he had started two hours earlier. Consequently Zieten would have reached Ohain at 5 p.m. at earliest. Finding Wellington in full retreat, he would not have compromised his command but would have taken up a position to rally Bülow, just as he actually attempted to do.

Napoleon had a distinct chance of winning a decisive victory at Mt. St. Jean and he could have done so, even without Grouchy's direct intervention. But he could only effect this by advancing the time of attack by at least two hours. This over-delay must rest on the Emperor's shoulders. General Drouot's advice, to delay the opening of the action so as to allow the ground to dry and permit the artillery to manœuvre, possibly induced the Emperor to put back the opening of the battle. Nevertheless the responsibility for his decision was Napoleon's alone. The Emperor knew the strategic outlook at the moment. He alone could decide whether events did, or did not, permit of this delay. In reality the same reason accounted both for the delay in attacking Wellington and the neglect to order up Grouchy to Plancenoit. This reason was Napoleon's failure to solve the Prussian plans.

Thinking the Prussians could not take a hand in the game for several days, Napoleon decided he could take his time in destroying Wellington and need not hurry on matters at Mt. St. Jean. This misappreciation of the strategic situation cost him the battle and his throne.

THE ATTACK OF THE MIDDLE GUARD

Napoleon's determination to launch his Middle Guard led directly (once the attack failed) to the ruin of the *Armée du Nord*. Napoleon had no chance of achieving a decisive success after the destruction of his Cavalry ; and on the conclusion of these magnificent but murderous episodes he should have considered how he could draw off.

Critics have urged that, at this supreme moment, retreat was no longer possible or practicable, and the only hope of safety lay in this last desperate assault. This was not the case. At 7 p.m. the two intrepid battalions of the Old Guard had cleared Plancenoit for the second time, and Napoleon still had a reserve left of twelve battalions of the Old and Middle Guard. He could have formed up these veterans checker-wise, in two lines, with the battalions placed so that the squares in the second line covered the intervals in the first line. Even at the eleventh hour these incomparable troops could have acted as a mighty rampart, behind which the Emperor could have rallied the *Armée du Nord* and drawn it off. As a matter of fact, after the battle had been hopelessly lost, no impression whatever was made on General Petit's Grenadiers of the Old Guard by the hosts of pursuers, flushed with an unprecedented success. If two battalions could withstand two Armies, what might not have been expected from twelve battalions of these heroes, joined, somewhat later, by the troops engaged at Plancenoit, and supported by all the rest of the Army who were still in fighting trim ? Further, the Reserve Artillery of the Guard, unlimbered in the intervals between these living bastions, would have pounded an enemy who sought to approach too close. As necessity arose, the guns could have retired by alternate groups, covering one another's withdrawal by fire.

Even at 7 p.m., it was not too late for Napoleon to open a retreat and carry it out in good order. By nightfall the French Army would have crossed the Dyle and have reformed behind it ; and, on the 19th, Napoleon would have been able to face Wellington and Blücher with over 50,000 men. Tried far above its breaking strain, the *Armée du Nord* dissolved in the hour of defeat.

SHOULD NAPOLEON HAVE BROKEN OFF THE FIGHT WHEN BÜLOW'S APPROACH WAS SIGNALLED? AND THE COURSE HE MIGHT HAVE ADOPTED

At 1.30 p.m. Napoleon must have recognized that Grouchy's arrival at La Belle Alliance was problematical. Was he wise, therefore, to risk a pitched battle with such odds against him? He could only effect a timely concentration with the French Right Wing by calling in Grouchy's detachment, and moving himself in the Marshal's direction. To carry out this manœuvre Napoleon had to retreat from in front of Wellington. Of course this move would not prevent Wellington and Blücher from joining hands, and the Emperor would only be able to oppose a total force of 100,000 to their 135,000. But surely it was better to postpone a general action than to continue it with the almost certain result that it must prove disastrous? Further, as he slipped away from Wellington and marched to concentrate with Grouchy, Napoleon might score some success against the Prussians. The Prussian plans were based on the hypothesis of a battle being waged at Mt. St. Jean between Napoleon and Wellington; or, in the event of Napoleon remaining quiescent in his position, the Allies would deliver a joint attack on the French. Napoleon must have disarranged the Allied plans by declining wager of battle and slipping away on the 18th, and he might have made it difficult for the Allies to avoid taking some serious risk or even making a mistake.

The Anglo-Dutch Army, standing on the defensive, had taken up its position to await the French onslaught. Wellington's Army was singularly ill-adapted to change rapidly from the defensive to the offensive. The manœuvring power of the Anglo-Dutch Army, particularly in attack, was not to be compared with its splendid defensive qualities. Consequently Marshal Ney, with the I and II Corps, together with Kellermann's Cuirassiers, could have held back the Anglo-Dutch Army, and delayed and regulated its advance in pursuit of the retiring French Army. The Marshal would have had 45,000 men, a force which was ample to control Wellington's 67,000; particularly as Ney shone in rear-guard fighting, and was a real master of the art of compelling an enemy to consume an hour in advancing over every mile of ground.

Meanwhile Napoleon would have moved off the remainder of the *Armée du Nord* through Plancenoit. On the Dyle, at Mousty, he would have met Grouchy's detachment whom he would have summoned thither. By 6 p.m. the French concentration on the Dyle would have been effected; and Napoleon, at the head of 50,000 men, would have been in a position to attack any Prussian troops between Lasne and Dyle. If the Emperor advanced on Wavre he could have been opposed only by Pirch I and Thielemann, with 40,000 men. These two Prussian Corps would have been annihilated. The case would not have been altered had Bülow attempted to support them. During this time, Ney would have continued his retreat towards Genappe. Doubtless at 1.30 p.m. Napoleon could not be expected to know all the Prussian movements accurately. But it was logical to think that Bülow would not have marched to support the Anglo-Dutch Army alone and at least one other Corps would have moved to strengthen Wellington's left. Merely by upsetting this combination the chance for delivering a telling blow might arise.

At the worst the French Army could retire across the Dyle at Mousty and effect concentration with Ney on the 19th, and then the whole *Armée du Nord* would be reunited once more. A retrograde manœuvre of this description might give Napoleon the opportunity to deal powerful blows, such as no ordinary retreat could have afforded. No chance of disaster was involved, and Napoleon would have avoided the risk of a mortal wound, which the two Allies must deal him directly they succeeded in effecting a battle-field concentration.

Ney's mistake on Saturday the 17th, was certainly a vital one, since it ruined the campaign strategically. It cannot, however, be regarded as the cause of the overwhelming disaster which on Sunday, the 18th, overtook the French Army at Mt. St. Jean. That disaster was brought about primarily by the Emperor. He it was who opened the battle late. When it became imperative to break off the action, he persisted with it until his troops were worn out. These were the direct causes of the defeat and ruin of the *Armée du Nord* at Mt. St. Jean.

CHAPTER XXV

MARSHAL GROUCHY ON THE 18TH JUNE

(Map 5 ; Sketch E)

Sketch E.—The information which came in during the night of the 17th–18th showed Grouchy that three of the four Prussian Corps were moving on Wavre. The Marshal failed to appreciate the meaning of this manœuvre. He considered Wavre was merely a convenient halting-place for Blücher's Army on its march to Brussels. He did not establish any connection between the battle which was impending with the Anglo-Dutch Army and Blücher's presence at Wavre. Nor did he realize how well placed Blücher was to support Wellington on the 18th, if the Prussians were not prevented from carrying out a comparatively short flank march. At any rate, so far as Grouchy was concerned, the Marshal's duty was to prevent the combination of Blücher's and Wellington's forces against Napoleon. To be in a position to prevent this concentration, Grouchy must cross the Dyle at Mousty, in order to ensure communication with Napoleon and to take the Prussians in flank, if they attempted to cross the belt of country between Dyle and Lasne. Grouchy could achieve nothing by an advance along the right bank of the Dyle. The Marshal was already outside the Prussians ; and he would merely succeed in driving the Allies together by any advance *via* Walhain and subsequent attack on Wavre from the south-east. If the Prussians left a force to hold the river line at Wavre, it might take the French Right Wing many hours of fighting to overpower this detached force if it was resolutely handled. By advancing along the left bank of the Dyle the bridges could be gained with no delay.

If Blücher retreated to Brussels on the 18th, that city was easily reached from Wavre, and once at Wavre the Marshal could follow the Prussians. But if Blücher headed westward so as to support Wellington, the apparition of 33,000 men on the left bank of the Dyle, threatening the Prussian flank, must delay the manœuvre. Even if the Allied concentration was effected on the 18th, yet, directly he was on the left bank of the Dyle, the Marshal could move to the Emperor's assistance, and either fight alongside the *Armée du Nord* or manœuvre in such a way as the Emperor might order.

The Marshal, however, modified in no particular his orders of the 17th. He determined to make for Wavre, but he did not counter-order Pajol's wide eastward sweep *via* Grand Leez. At 6 a.m. Grouchy wrote (from Gembloux) to the Emperor, stating that Blücher was moving on Brussels, *via* Wavre, so as to concentrate with Wellington, and he (Grouchy) was moving to Wavre with the Right Wing.

By 4 a.m. on a morning in mid-June it is quite light enough to march, but the Marshal was content to order Vandamme to start at 6 a.m. and Gérard to follow at 8 a.m. When every moment was vital Grouchy alone was responsible for this delay. Even so, punctuality was not observed in keeping these late starting hours. Exelmans' Dragoons at Sauvenière were to lead the advance ; and this body of horse did not parade until 6 a.m., although at this hour it should have been in position to take over the tactical protection of Grouchy's force. As a result Vandamme only cleared Gembloux between 7 a.m. and 8 a.m., and Gérard started at the same hour. All these troops were to use the same road, apparently for no more cogent reason than to preserve the correct precedence of the Corps on the road. Had the Right Wing advanced in two columns—one *via* Sauvenière and Walhain and the other *via* Ernage and Nil Pierreux—both could have concentrated at the same time at Corbais.

Grouchy waited at Gembloux till the troops had started, and after riding along the marching column he overtook the van at Walhain. Then the Marshal let the troops file on, whilst he dismounted to send a report to the Emperor that the Prussians had passed Wavre heading north-eastward. Probably Grouchy was only too eager to believe this comfortable news which he desired so ardently to hear. The Marshal also informed the Emperor that he would concentrate the Right Wing at Wavre by nightfall and asked for orders for the next day. When this letter was completed he despatched it to the Emperor by Major de Fresnaye. It reached Napoleon about 4 p.m.

This duty completed, Grouchy sat down serenely to his breakfast in the house of Notary Hollaërt at Walhain. The Marshal had just reached the strawberries when Gérard entered the room, having ridden on ahead of the IV Corps. Shortly afterwards there was a more serious interruption. About noon, Colonel Simon Lorière (Gérard's Assistant Chief of Staff) came in and reported that he and some other officers had heard the opening roar of a cannonade. Grouchy at once accompanied Gérard and Lorière into the garden. The guns were distinctly audible. Gérard at once advocated marching to the sound of the cannon. Grouchy demurred, saying it was nothing more than a rear-guard affair. Opinion as to the serious nature of the engagement was quickly dispelled, the gun-thunder grew louder, the reports of the discharges increased in rapidity, and away to the northwestward vast smoke-clouds gathered and grew. It was evident that a general action was in progress. Its location was soon discovered. A peasant informed the Marshal that the firing was 4 or 5 hours' march away at Mt. St. Jean ; or 8 or 9 miles distant, according to Notary Hollaërt. Gérard and some of the other officers reiterated the opinion that the Right Wing must march to the sound of the guns. Grouchy became annoyed at his officers offering a Marshal of France gratuitous advice and in so open a manner ; and he possessed an understandable distaste for counsel which was thrust upon him. Marshal Grouchy desired to adhere to the letter of the Emperor's instructions, which he considered would cover him whatever happened, rather than hearken to Gérard's hazardous advice, which apparently ran counter to the Emperor's commands.

As might have been expected, Grouchy summed up against Gérard's outspoken proposal. The Marshal informed the officers gathered around him that the Emperor had apprised him of the action which was impending with Wellington ; further, had the Emperor desired his help he would not have detached him just as the *Armée du Nord* was moving against the Anglo-Dutch Army. Grouchy went on to say that the cross-country roads, between the Dyle and Lasne, were in so boggy a condition that they would prevent the arrival of the Right Wing before nightfall. Even if the Right Wing started immediately, it would not be able to render any useful aid in the battle which had just begun. The Chief Engineer of the IV Corps, General Valazé, offered with his three companies of Sappers to settle all difficulties arising from the bad roads. This promise must not be taken too literally. A rapid march could not be undertaken if the road had to be put in good order with pick and shovel as the troops advanced. On the other hand there was no reason to suppose that such a task was necessary. Indeed the Prussians showed that the roads were traversable by all three arms and at a sufficiently rapid rate.

The discussion went on until Gérard, who was working himself up, made a bad blunder. ' Marshal,' he ejaculated, ' it is your duty to march to the cannon.' This settled matters. Grouchy was really offended that his duty should have been pointed out in such uncompromising tones by a subordinate, particularly in the presence of several other subordinates. The Marshal replied sternly :

' My duty is to execute the Emperor's orders, which direct me to follow the Prussians. It would be infringing his commands to pursue the course of action which you recommend.'

Immediately after this a diversion was caused by the arrival of an aide-de-camp from Exelmans. This officer reported that the Dragoons were in touch with a strong Prussian rear-guard which was in position covering Wavre. As everything showed that the Prussian Army had passed through Wavre, the General wished to cross the Dyle at Ottignies. This report strengthened Gérard's proposal. For all that, still obsessed with his preconceived idea of the course taken by Blücher, Grouchy considered that Exelmans' report was confirmation of his previous deductions. He looked on the Prussian rear-guard as a cloak to such action. Calling for his horse, he decided to proceed to the front and give orders personally to Exelmans. Just before Grouchy left, Gérard made one final attempt to alter the Marshal's decision. The General asked for leave to take his own (the IV) Corps, with Vallin's Hussars to cover his march, and move with these troops as rapidly as possible to Mt. St. Jean. He pledged his word that he would arrive in time to be useful. Grouchy, however, would not split his force, because he feared he would be courting disaster if the enemy got touch with either part.

It is at least doubtful if the Marshal's conclusion was a wise one. Grouchy's duty was not to fight a pitched battle on the 18th but to assist Napoleon in the struggle at Mt. St. Jean. That was the essential. With it was coupled the task of neutralizing Blücher for at least the next twenty-four hours. Consequently, by detaching Gérard, Grouchy would have ensured that a valuable reinforcement reached the *Armée du Nord* at a critical time ; and, if energetically pushed, the advance of the remainder on Wavre might have held up a considerable portion of Blücher's force.

Such action, too, was in accord with the underlying idea of Napoleon's plan for manœuvring in Belgium with the *Armée du Nord* organized in two Wings and a Reserve. The Emperor had contemplated adding his Reserve to one Wing, so as to win a decisive victory. He had also planned to augment his Reserve from the other, or containing, Wing.[1] Grouchy should have realized that the time had come when he should deplete his command of the largest possible force and send it at once to join the Emperor, so as to ensure a decisive result on the 18th. Then with the remainder of the Right Wing the Marshal would have manœuvred, as skilfully and energetically as he was able, so as to locate and hold up the largest possible proportion of Blücher's troops.

Had Gérard intervened at Plancenoit by 7 p.m., victory might have declared for Napoleon. The certainty of the proximity of this powerful support must have determined the Emperor to launch his final attack directly La Haye Sainte fell, and to have used the whole of the Guard for the decisive stroke. This might have ensured Wellington's overthrow before Zieten engaged.

Meanwhile, to hold the Prussians at Wavre, Marshal Grouchy should have pushed on immediately one of the Dragoon Divisions of Exelmans' Cavalry Corps and the leading Infantry Division of Vandamme's Corps, with orders to threaten an attack on Wavre so as to deceive the Prussians. This detachment would also have served as a stationary flank guard to cover the right flank of the other columns, as they wheeled westward heading for the Dyle passages abreast of Walhain. The bulk of Vandamme's Corps and Exelmans' remaining Dragoon Division might have passed the Dyle at Ottignies (the lower passage), whilst Gérard's Corps, in rear, would have used the upper passage at Mousty. At the

[1] See Appendix II, No. 2.

same time Pajol would have been brought in from Tourinnes and ordered to follow Vandamme. Teste's Division (VI Corps) would have followed Pajol. Had this been done, Gérard, leaving Walhain about noon, would have reached Mousty by 4 p.m. His cavalry would have seized the crossing by 2 p.m. Protected in his further advance by Vandamme, Gérard would have reached Plancenoit by 7 p.m., in time to render inestimable service to Napoleon at the crisis of the great battle.

These dispositions would have kept in view the necessity of rendering timely support to the *Armée du Nord*. They would also have provided security for the flank march, which would have been too risky had no precautions been employed such as the direct threat at Wavre.

Gérard's suggestion was sound, because, when the distant cannon-thunder was first heard, no other course could obtain any important, let alone decisive, result. Gérard's proposal provided the only way for the Right Wing to perform any useful service on the 18th, instead of being wasted. Certainly Grouchy should not have set aside his subordinate's suggestions. But even so at daybreak on the 18th, Napoleon had failed to call in the Marshal when he saw the battle was impending with Wellington. Had Grouchy received such orders and headed for the Dyle at 7 a.m. he would have reached Plancenoit by 2 p.m. Then the result would not have been in doubt. Before 5 p.m., Napoleon, with the whole of the *Armée du Nord* massed under his hand, would have hurled back northward and westward the shattered Anglo-Dutch Army. As the Emperor failed to call in Grouchy to his aid at daybreak, he (Napoleon) must be regarded as chiefly, although not altogether, responsible for the non-intervention of his lieutenant at Waterloo.

Naturally it was immeasurably unfortunate for the Emperor that Marshal Grouchy did not handle the Right Wing with foresight, intelligence, and resolution. Granted that at noon on the 18th there was no possibility of mistake with reference to the instructions which the Marshal had received, yet the peculiar circumstances of the moment, the reports to hand, the increasing cannon-thunder, made it every moment more palpable that those instructions had been issued on a false hypothesis. Grouchy knew the bulk of Blücher's Army was at Wavre. His ears told him that Wellington had accepted battle to the southward of the Forest of Soignes.   All the Marshal had to do was to consider the possibility of Blücher manœuvring so as to co-operate with Wellington.   The chances were strongly in favour of this. Otherwise, why had Blücher abandoned his line with Liége ? What had induced Wellington to accept battle single-handed with Napoleon, after declining it on the 17th ?   By advancing direct on Wavre, along the Dyle's right bank, the Marshal would be acting contrary to the spirit of his instructions.   Grouchy's failure to appreciate the strategical situation showed that he did not possess the qualifications necessary in an independent commander.

Directly Grouchy had negatived Gérard's proposal, the Marshal mounted and galloped off to join Exelmans, who, at 10 a.m., had been informed by his patrols that a large Prussian force of all arms was on the heights above Wavre.   The General considered his Dragoons were insufficient to engage the enemy in such difficult country ; but he did recognize that Blücher was manœuvring to join Wellington.   Deciding that a direct advance on Wavre was useless, he spread out his cavalry to secure the Dyle passage at Ottignies as well as to cover the present advance. Meanwhile Vandamme had halted at Nil St. Vincent, in accordance with Grouchy's orders issued on the 17th.   It was 1 p.m. before Grouchy reached Nil St. Vincent and ordered the III Corps to resume its march.

Just before 2 p.m. Exelmans' two advanced squadrons were attacked at Mt. St. Guibert by a Prussian detachment (one cavalry regiment, two infantry battalions, and 2 guns), under Colonel Ledebur.   At first Ledebur did not realize he was in the midst of enemies, though Vincent's Brigade (Strolz's Division) was just to the east of Ottignies.   As the French advanced, Ledebur saw that his retreat to Wavre was threatened and, using his cavalry to hold back Exelmans, he occupied some woods with his infantry.   The Prussian Hussars forced back the leading French squadrons.   Then Exelmans and the main body came up and the Hussars retired through their infantry whom Exelmans could not dislodge.   In the end Vandamme's leading troops had to attack, as, reinforced by two more battalions, Ledebur was making an obstinate defence.   Grouchy decided to outflank Ledebur, and he ordered Exelmans to take his 3,000 Dragoons and turn the Prussian position.   Ledebur, however, drew back to Wavre before Exelmans could cut his line of retreat. Vandamme advanced as Ledebur drew off, and Grouchy ordered Vandamme to pursue the Prussians as far as Wavre and then take up a position pending further orders.

Meanwhile the guns, booming away to the left with increasing violence, aroused in Grouchy's mind doubt and uncertainty. The Marshal, therefore, galloped off to Limelette so as to come to a definite opinion about the cause of the cannonade. After being convinced that a general action was in progress on the southern border of the Forest of Soignes, Grouchy returned to the Wavre road just before 4 p.m. Here he received Soult's letter despatched at 10 a.m. from Le Caillou. The bearer had taken nearly six hours to cover at most 25 miles. The delay, however, was not vital. In this despatch the Marshal was merely directed to march on Wavre, thus it only served to confirm him in the decision which he had taken. The despatch was not happily phrased, it was rather ambiguous, and Grouchy misread it. Soult should have given the Marshal a definite order to cross the Dyle before he closed on Wavre, and to send an officer's patrol to La Belle Alliance, so as to learn the latest news of the situation ; and Soult should have despatched the order at 4 a.m. instead of at 10 a.m.

Map 5.—At this same time (4 p.m.) the Marshal received a report from Pajol stating that he had discovered no traces of the enemy. Orders were immediately sent to Pajol to move to the left flank and force the bridge at Limal, and he would be supported by Teste's Division. Pajol, however, was 9 miles from Limal, whilst Vallin's Hussars were within 3 miles ; and Hulot's Division (Gérard's Corps) was nearer to the bridge than Teste's Division. The Marshal never waited to consider such matters, and after issuing the order he galloped off to Wavre. There he found that Vandamme had already opened the action, despite the orders which had been given to him.

*   *   *   *   *   *   *

In considering the lack of resolution shown by Marshal Grouchy on the 17th and 18th June, it must not be forgotten that Napoleon had always discouraged initiative in subordinates who were under his control. In 1799 General Bonaparte wrote, ' commandants are to take no independent action, but they will await

the issue of orders from head-quarters '.   In 1806 the Emperor
wrote to Berthier, ' keep strictly to the orders I give you. . . .
I alone know what I have to do ' ; and in 1807 Berthier, writing
to Ney, said, ' None realize his (the Emperor's) designs.'

Not having been trained to think for himself, Grouchy was
unwilling to accept any responsibility whilst he was acting in
fairly close contact with Imperial Head-Quarters.   In moments
of crisis men like Grouchy looked to Napoleon for orders, and
they followed blindly such orders as the Emperor issued to them.
This deplorable lack of initiative was partly the result of the
military atmosphere in which Grouchy and his contemporaries
had been raised.   It was also partly due to the dominating personality of Napoleon.

CHAPTER XXVI

THE ACTION OF WAVRE, 18TH JUNE

(Map 5)

THE Dyle from Limal to Basse Wavre was unfordable below Limelette. The river was about 30 feet wide and its low parallel banks made it look like a ' muddy canal '. The low-lying ground intersected by deep ditches, full to the brim with storm-water, had become a serious obstacle to the free movement of assaulting troops, and the whole valley bottom was soft and treacherous. Consequently the wooden bridges at Limal, Bierges, and Basse Wavre, and the two stone bridges at Wavre, and the approaches to these bridges, were of paramount value to an assailant.

Map 5.—Thielemann, with 16,000 men and 36 guns, held the river-line from Limal to Basse Wavre. The General had disposed his troops as follows : one Brigade (Stülpnagel's) and one Battery of Horse Artillery were on the high ground behind Bierges, with one company placed to cover the bridge. Another Brigade (Kemphen's) was on the heights behind Wavre, to the left of Stülpnagel's. In rear of Wavre, a third Brigade (Luck's) was halted astride the Brussels road. The cavalry (Hobe) were in reserve, formed in column on the southern side of the Brussels road, and the guns were on the heights above Wavre. Leaving a detachment to hold Basse Wavre, Borcke dropped three battalions and two squadrons in Wavre, and with the rest of his Brigade he followed the II Corps to Waterloo. Similarly Zieten left three battalions and three squadrons (under Stengel) to cover Limal bridge. In addition, from Bierges to Basse Wavre, the river bank was lined with Prussian skirmishers. Thielemann's whole front covered about 3 miles and he could only deploy about 5,000 to the mile to oppose Grouchy's very superior force. The General, perforce, had to rely on rear-guard tactics in order to neutralize Grouchy all day and gain the time for Blücher to intervene at Waterloo.

At first Thielemann mistook Exelmans' Dragoons for a mere screen. Impressed by the heavy cannonade, the General had decided to follow Zieten westward, leaving a rear-guard of two battalions to hold Wavre to cover this movement. Just as he reached this decision, Vandamme launched his attack. Thielemann promptly counter-marched the troops who had started and they took up their recently vacated positions, except the officer in command in Wavre (Zepelin) who had not time to complete his arrangements before the French attacked.

Vandamme was as impetuous as ever. He disregarded the orders which he had received from Grouchy, undertook no preliminary reconnaissance, and dispensed with even a semblance of any preparatory bombardment. Only at 4 p.m., when Habert's infantry attacked Wavre, did three French batteries open fire on the town from the high ground some 600 yards from the river. The attack was delivered with great dash. The French at once drove the Prussians out of the suburb on the right bank but then came to a standstill in front of the Dyle. The barricaded bridges were swept with grape from guns placed in the steep streets overlooking them, and the houses on the left bank were crammed with Prussian sharpshooters. The affair was short and deadly. In a few minutes Habert's Division lost 600 men, including the General. Retirement was impracticable. The streets behind the French were swept by fire from end to end, and Grouchy arrived to find Habert's luckless Division ' wedged in a real *cul-de-sac* '. Luckily Hulot's Division (Gérard) was near at hand.

Grouchy surveyed the scene. After some deliberation he decided to assist Vandamme's effort by two other attacks, one above and one below Wavre. Habert's Division was reinforced, and Lefol (Vandamme) was ordered to take one of his battalions and storm the bridge at Bierges whilst Exelmans' Dragoons threatened Basse Wavre. Hardly had Grouchy made these arrangements when he received Soult's despatch timed 1.30 p.m. This informed him that battle had been joined with Wellington at Waterloo. In the postscript of this letter Grouchy was told the alarming news that Bülow's Corps was in sight near Chapelle St. Lambert ; and the Marshal was ordered to turn westward at once and crush Bülow before the Prussian Corps effected its concentration with Wellington.

This 1.30 p.m. despatch was imperative and precise enough. At last, when it was too late, Grouchy realized the situation. Just as Ney at Quatre Bras was powerless to comply with the Emperor's demands on the 16th, after he appreciated the full significance of Major Baudus' message, so, on the 18th, Grouchy was impotent when at last he perceived his duty. It was 5 p.m. already. The Marshal had no troops on the Dyle's left bank. Not a single river-passage was in his hands, and to force the river at once a heavy blow was requisite. Even so, Grouchy's efforts at this moment were not very brilliant.

The Prussians in Wavre and at Bierges might have been neutralized by Habert and the three batteries, supported by Lefol's Division. Basse Wavre could have been neglected; and Berthézène and Exelmans should have been ordered to storm the bridge at Limal. The Limal bridge was the all-important one to gain, so as to allow the Right Wing to march to Waterloo without delay or counter-marching. Directly it was captured Grouchy could threaten the flank of the Prussian columns as they marched to the Lasne. Habert and Lefol could have covered the rest of the Right Wing as it passed across the Dyle at Limal.

It was, however, not on the 18th that the Marshal was to retrieve his reputation as, unfortunately, he only adopted half-measures. Grouchy was still determined to carry Wavre and he decided to allow half his force to continue the attack, whilst the other half was to move on St. Lambert after crossing the Dyle at Limal. To effect this, Grouchy left Exelmans and Vandamme to attack Basse Wavre and Wavre and he despatched an order to Pajol to hasten his advance on Limal. The Marshal then rode over to La Baraque to order Gérard to take the IV Corps and storm the Limal bridge. Possibly the head of Gérard's column had gone astray and made for Wavre so as to avoid undue loss of time, since Gérard brought Vichéry's and Pécheux's Divisions to Wavre instead of to Limal. As matters were, this mistake was of no importance. Previously Gérard's other Division (Hulot) had reached the heights above Wavre about 5 p.m.

Meanwhile the fight raged along the Dyle. Lefol failed to

carry Bierges bridge, but this failure only stimulated Grouchy to fresh exertions. Determined to master this bridge, which was only suitable for infantry, the Marshal ordered Gérard to renew the attack with one of Hulot's battalions. Gérard pointed out that it would be a better arrangement to support Lefol with troops drawn from the same Corps (the III) as the assailants. Grouchy rejected this advice, and Gérard then ordered Hulot to co-operate with Lefol. Hulot led the attack in person. The assailants had to cross broad, deep ditches (over 4 feet deep) running perpendicular to the line of advance, and the attack was so delayed and broken up that the battalion fell back. Grouchy, and Gérard who was leading up a supporting battalion, appeared at this juncture. Gérard himself led the next attack, in which he was severely wounded by a musket ball which struck him in the chest. Grouchy then ordered General Baron Baltus (commanding the Artillery of the IV Corps) to take Gérard's place and lead the assault. Baltus declined. Marshal Grouchy never lacked personal courage. Without a moment's hesitation, he sprang from his charger and headed the assault himself. Nevertheless this attack failed. Grouchy then left Hulot's Division at Bierges and rode off to lead Gérard's two other Divisions towards Limal.

Although one may admire the courage of Marshal Grouchy, who in his long and honourable career was wounded twenty-three times, yet the same admiration can hardly be accorded to the Marshal's handling of the Action of Wavre. In this fight Grouchy degenerated into a mere troop leader. He was everywhere at once and ready to head any attack. For too long he had been a subordinate. When he was perplexed and anxious he did what was second nature to him, and his efforts at Wavre were the mechanical and methodical ones of a subordinate.

Whilst skirmishing continued at Basse Wavre a desperate fight was being waged for the possession of Wavre. Vandamme's thirty-one battalions delivered thirteen assaults on the town, yet they failed to wrest the place from its defenders who fought fiercely and stubbornly to hold the French at bay. More than once Vandamme's men stormed the bridges and entered the near-by houses. But, even when they were driven from the bottom floors, the Prussians retreated to the upper storeys and fought on with great determination. The French could neither penetrate into the town nor make good their foothold on the left bank. Each time this obstinate defence allowed the Prussian reserves to arrive and drive back the assailants over the bridges. Actually not more than four Prussian battalions were engaged in holding up Vandamme's Corps for seven hours, so the fight raged on for the remainder of the day and at 11 p.m. was still raging.

But the Dyle was forced elsewhere. When the Marshal reached Limal with Gérard's two Divisions he found the bridge had been captured by Pajol's horsemen. Pajol decided to attempt at Limal the daring expedient which had been employed at Montereau in 1814, showing once again that in war the happiest inspiration is often only a recollection. Pajol charged the bridge with Vallin's Hussars (Gérard's Corps Cavalry), although it was only wide enough to allow four horses abreast and was defended by a Prussian battalion. The audacious adventure succeeded. The Prussians were ridden into, broken through, and dispersed. Teste's Division then crossed to the left bank in the wake of the Hussars and made permanent the temporary success achieved by Vallin's gallant horsemen.

Had the Limal bridge been barricaded this bold manœuvre would never have been attempted. This oversight lost the river-crossing to the Prussians, and probably the failing light may also help to explain the success which was gained.

The rest of Pajol's Cavalry Corps followed Teste to the left bank ; but Stengel, realizing the importance of time, fought truculently to retain the village of Limal and stem a French advance. At last, under the pressure of superior numbers, Stengel relinquished Limal, but, rallying his men, he took up another position on the high ground to the north of the village. Despite the poor light Teste attacked at once ; and Grouchy came up with Gérard's two Divisions in the nick of time, just as Thielemann moved Stülpnagel's Brigade and Hobe's Cavalry to support Stengel. In the growing darkness the Prussian rein-forcements encountered a ravine, their advance was stopped by the fire of infantry, and French cavalry threatening to outflank their right, the Prussians drew back into the large woods.

The fight went on until 11 p.m. when the French succeeded in obtaining possession of the plateau. At last the road to Mt. St. Jean lay open and Grouchy could move to his Master's assistance when he pleased. But the cannonade had died away and a death-like silence reigned to the westward. No one could tell what this silence presaged.

The critical hours of Waterloo had passed before Grouchy succeeded in wresting one of the Dyle passages from its defenders. This reflects the greatest credit on Thielemann's excellent dispositions and the desperate fight which his troops made to hold back Grouchy's very superior forces at this vital time.

When the French debouched on the left bank of the Dyle it was too late to affect the main issue, because at 8 p.m. the great struggle was over and the fate of the day had been decided. Even if Grouchy had been able to march westward at 5 p.m., when he received Soult's 1.30 p.m. despatch, yet he could have effected nothing of importance. Bülow was already attacking Plancenoit and it was too late to detain Pirch I or Zieten. Grouchy would have reached the fatal field only to find his Master defeated and the *Armée du Nord* spread-eagled over southern Brabant. Grouchy must then have shared in their disaster, and by no means could he have altered the fortunes of the day. But the precise order given in the postscript of Soult's 1.30 p.m. despatch made clear to the Marshal that a crisis had been reached. This did galvanize Grouchy into action and awoke his cavalry spirit. Immediately he was up and doing. He struck hard at last, albeit he struck unskilfully. It is fair to ask what might have happened, had as definite orders been issued at daybreak on the 18th, and received by Marshal Grouchy before he left Gembloux ?

*   *   *   *   *   *   *

As darkness had fallen, Thielemann's and Grouchy's troops bivouacked in front of one another. The French left rested in squares on the plateau which they had won, whilst the Prussians occupied the woods to the north of them. The opposing outposts bickered all night and the repose of the troops was constantly disturbed by outbursts of musketry.

About 11.30 p.m. Grouchy sent orders to Vandamme to bring the III Corps to Limal. The Marshal's idea was to finish off the action by rolling up the river line from the south. Then he would move on Brussels so as to join the *Armée du Nord*, as a rumour spread that Napoleon had beaten Wellington.

Marshal Grouchy must have forgotten Blücher, or where did he expect the Prussian Field-Marshal was ? Thielemann, however, knew the true state of affairs. He had received the reassuring news that the Allies had gained a crushing victory and the French Army was in full retreat. Thielemann could take a justifiable pride in his share of the great day's work. With only 16,000 Prussians he had kept at bay the French Right Wing of 33,000 men commanded by a Marshal of France.

CHAPTER XXVII

19TH JUNE: THE CONCLUSION OF THE ACTION OF WAVRE

MARSHAL GROUCHY HEARS THE RESULT OF THE BATTLE OF WATERLOO AND OPENS AN IMMEDIATE RETREAT

(Map 5 ; Sketch E)

Map 5.—Intending to attack at daybreak, Thielemann concentrated during the night in the vicinity of the plateau. He disposed his force as follows :

Garrisons still held Wavre, Basse Wavre, and Bierges ;
Eight companies held the edge of the woods ;
Three battalions were at the eastern salient of the big wood ;
Seven battalions and two squadrons were between the big wood and Bierges ;
Four battalions were behind Wavre ;
Two battalions were behind the bridge at Bierges ; and
Hobe's Cavalry were to the north of the wood.

Marshal Grouchy massed four Divisions on the Limal plateau : Pécheux, Vichéry, Teste (Lobau) were in the first line, and Hulot (Gérard) was in reserve. The French left was covered by Pajol.

At dawn Hobe advanced and his two horse batteries opened on the French bivouacs. Grouchy's guns answered, and the French infantry moved forward in three columns. Teste advanced on Bierges, Vichéry against the centre, and Pécheux against the Prussian right. A swarm of skirmishers, with a battery in action at the head of each Division, covered and prepared these attacks ; and Pajol prepared to manœuvre against Thielemann's right.

Thielemann's troops fought stubbornly, but gradually they were forced back by superior numbers ; and at 8 a.m. they were in the following position :

Four battalions held the small wood north-west of Bierges with the remainder of Stülpnagel's Brigade farther to the rear ;

Three battalions of Luck's Brigade and 15 guns were behind the large wood ; and

The right flank, as far as the Lasne, was covered by Hobe's two Cavalry Brigades.

Between 8 and 9 a.m. Pirch I sent Thielemann definite news of the result achieved at Waterloo, and Pirch informed Thielemann that the II Corps had pushed on so as to cut off Marshal Grouchy's force when it withdrew. The news inspired Thielemann's hard-pressed troops with fresh ardour and the fighting broke out again as fiercely as ever. The Prussians drove the French out of the large wood, but they could not maintain their hold on it, and once more they were forced back. The French pushed home their success and Teste carried Bierges. Thielemann's left was turned ; and, as Pajol was threatening the Prussian right, Thielemann about 10 a.m. ordered a general retreat along the Brussels road. Even so Thielemann had succeeded not only in retaining Grouchy at Wavre, but in drawing the French well over the Dyle. Thus he had gained extra time for Pirch I to place the II Corps well astride the French line of retreat.

Necessarily the tactical reverse sustained by Thielemann at Wavre was absorbed in the great triumph gained by the Allies at Waterloo. Just as on the 16th it was the victor in the secondary action who was placed in a perilous position.

Wavre, not attacked on the 19th, was abandoned by Colonel Zepelin, and the garrison drew off in several columns followed by Vandamme. Zepelin formed up at La Bavette, but Vandamme at once attacked the Prussians and dislodged them. Hobe's Cavalry and four batteries then took over the duties of rear-guard. The French cavalry, supported by its infantry, advanced to attack Hobe, whereupon the Prussian horse fell back and took up another position to the north of La Bavette. The French cavalry followed and the French infantry occupied La Bavette. With this resolute advance the action came to an end. It was 10.30 a.m.

On each side the losses were about 2,400 men. The Prussians abandoned 5 guns. Thielemann's casualties, about 15 per cent of his effective strength, bore testimony to the stubborn resistance of the III Corps on the 18th June. Nevertheless Thiele-mann's force had not suffered in vain.

Borcke and the 9th Prussian Brigade had reached St. Lambert on the 18th. Then, in the morning, hearing that a French force had crossed the Dyle near Limal, Borcke counter-marched and took up a position at the edge of the St. Lambert woods. Despite the long range his guns opened on the French cavalry as they swept past the big wood. The French horsemen, how-ever, were not to be denied in the hour of victory and Pajol, detaching three regiments to observe the Prussians, continued the advance with the remainder of his force.

For the moment Grouchy was unsuspicious of danger, though the presence of the Prussians near St. Lambert might have caused him to wonder whether all was well at Mt. St. Jean. Naturally he could not yet know that, on the previous night, the Prussians had almost reached the Sambre at Charleroi, and Pirch I was advancing to cut off his retreat. Unconscious of all this, Grouchy prepared to march on Brussels.

Just as he came to this decision an officer of the Imperial Staff rode up. The new-comer (Captain Dumonceau) was the pictured embodiment of disaster and despair. It was some time before he could tell a coherent story. Gradually, by piec-ing together such details as were understandable from his broken and confused ramblings, Grouchy learned the calamitous and alarming news which Dumonceau sought to deliver. The full significance of the ruin which had overtaken the *Armée du Nord* at Waterloo then burst upon the Marshal. From this moment energy and skill replaced vacillation and blundering. In the dark closing hours of this great campaign the rapidity and reso-lution of the Marshal's manœuvres must enhance his reputation.

The destruction of Napoleon's Army dissipated the military atmosphere which had enveloped Grouchy for so many years. No longer was Napoleon available to lean on in this crisis, and the Marshal recognized that he must think and act for himself. This was no time for grief or vain regrets. If the Marshal wished to save the Right Wing of the *Armée du Nord* he must manœuvre at once and with vigour. He perceived that Blücher would spare no effort to cut his line of retreat to France, so as to ensure that a catastrophe befell the French Right Wing. This the Marshal was determined to prevent.

Before he acted, however, he could not resist one last explanation. Drawing his Generals around him, he said : ' My honour makes it a matter of duty to explain myself, with regard to the dispositions which I took yesterday. The instructions which I had received from the Emperor left me free to manœuvre in no other direction than Wavre. Therefore I was obliged to refuse the advice which General Gérard thought he had a right to offer me. I freely admit General Gérard's talents and brilliant valour ; but doubtless you were as surprised as I was, that a General Officer, ignorant of the Emperor's commands and all the information which influenced the Marshal of France under whose orders he was placed, should have presumed to dictate to the latter his line of action. The advanced hour of the day, the distance from the point where the cannonading was heard, the condition of the roads, made it impossible to arrive in time to combine in the battle which was taking place. At any rate, whatever the subsequent events may have been, the Emperor's orders, whose tenour I have disclosed to you, did not permit of my acting otherwise than I have done.'

Even admitting that the Emperor did direct the Marshal to move on Wavre, yet his earliest order in which Wavre was mentioned was the despatch written at 10 a.m. on the 18th. This despatch did not come into Grouchy's hands until the Marshal had reached Wavre with the head of his column. Nor was Grouchy ever ordered to keep to the right bank of the Dyle. This latter was the fatal mistake which Grouchy committed after Gérard's intervention, but it is not necessary to labour that point any further. Grouchy in his explanation did not furnish one single logical reason for his failure on the 18th June to help his Emperor and the *Armée du Nord* in their hour of dire need at Mt. St. Jean.

CHAPTER XXVIII

MARSHAL GROUCHY'S RETREAT TO FRANCE *VIA* NAMUR

(Map 1 ; Sketch E)

DURING the retreat from La Belle Alliance the Emperor despatched several officers to Grouchy. These officers carried orders for the Right Wing to recross the Sambre at Namur and move by Laon to effect its junction with the *Armée du Nord*. It is uncertain whether Grouchy ever received these instructions. At any rate the Marshal appreciated that the bridge at Namur was the only one over the Sambre which he had a chance of using. He decided to retreat on Namur, gain the Meuse Valley, and win a way back to France. Realizing that he must secure Namur without delay and hold the bridge for the passage of the French Right Wing, Grouchy despatched Exelmans to seize the place. Pushing through at speed Exelmans reached Namur at 4 p.m., an admirable performance.

Meanwhile Grouchy had decided to retreat to Gembloux in two columns, and he ordered Vandamme and the III Corps to recross the Dyle at Wavre and march to Gembloux, *via* Tourinnes. The 20th Regiment of Dragoons (Exelmans) were attached to Vandamme to act as Corps Cavalry and replace Domon's Cavalry Division which had accompanied the Emperor. Gérard's Corps and Vallin's Hussars were ordered to cross the Dyle at Limal and march direct to Gembloux. They were to be followed by Teste and Pajol, who took over the duty of rearguard and marched *via* Sauvenière.

Even before Grouchy's retirement began, Pirch I and his Corps (II) were at Mellery, within striking distance of the line of withdrawal ; but Pirch's men were weary and he halted. Had Pirch pressed on he must have intercepted the French Right Wing and either captured it or destroyed it. It was later in the day that Thielemann learned of Grouchy's retreat, but he did not feel justified in pressing the Marshal on the 19th. In this way the chance of capturing Grouchy disappeared. Once he opened his retrograde movement the Marshal slipped through on the 19th without becoming engaged. At night, when the French had concentrated around Gembloux, the most anxious time was over.

The Prussians would have been more likely to intercept the French Right Wing if the leading Corps, Bülow's, had been turned off the Charleroi road at Quatre Bras as early as possible on the 19th. This Corps, reaching Sombreffe at 7 a.m., could have pushed on 2,000 horsemen, each mounted man carrying an infantryman behind him, or the infantry could have ridden in captured wagons. This mobile force would have occupied Namur as rapidly as possible. Bülow, marching the rest of the IV Corps to Gembloux, would have prepared to bar Grouchy's retreat southward, and Thielemann would have been ordered to hang on to Grouchy's rear and retard his withdrawal.

Be all that as it may, Pirch I and Thielemann exhibited little dash or initiative in the pursuit of Grouchy. Possibly this may be explained by the Prussian Corps Commanders (except Bülow) having been chosen because they were junior to Gneisenau. This emphasizes the need for choosing Bülow, the victor of Dennewitz, for the task in question. Bülow's selection would have facilitated Thielemann's co-operation, since Thielemann was very junior to Bülow.

20TH JUNE

Even after Grouchy's force had safely concentrated at Gembloux, Vandamme caused it to run a needless risk. The General went off to pass the night in a house and missed the orders which Grouchy issued for the 20th. As a result of this, the III Corps did not remain until noon in position astride the Gembloux road, so as to cover the withdrawal of the rest of the force to Namur. The III Corps (on the initiative of the Divisional Commanders) began to move towards Namur at 7 a.m. ; and, as Gérard's (IV) Corps did not start until 9 a.m., the flank of the IV Corps was uncovered. Whilst still some distance from

Namur the IV Corps were attacked by Hobe and a horse battery whom Thielemann had pushed ahead at 5 a.m. This collision synchronized with an advance of the II Corps down the Nivelles–Namur main road. Marshal Grouchy's instincts as a leader of horse stood him in good stead in this emergency, and his demeanour was cool and confident. At this critical moment in his withdrawal personal leadership was required, and fortunately the Marshal rose to the occasion. Placing himself at the head of Vallin's Hussars he fell on Hobe's horsemen, who were then threatening the Namur road, and he beat them back. This success kept the road open for the IV Corps to retire to Namur.

Having freed the IV Corps, Grouchy promptly led Vallin's Hussars to assist Vandamme who had just been attacked. The Prussians had had some success in this quarter, so Grouchy's intervention was most welcome. Vallin's Hussars and Briqueville's Dragoons (Exelmans) charged Hobe's cavalry and readjusted matters by driving off the Prussians. Thereupon Grouchy ordered Vandamme to take up a position covering Namur, whilst the rest of the French Right Wing passed through the place. In his turn Vandamme drew off and followed the IV Corps. Teste alone remained to hold the antiquated fortress until nightfall, so as to cover the movement of the rest of the force up the Meuse valley.

For the defence of the time-worn and broken-down fortifications of Namur, Teste could muster only 2,000 men and 8 field guns. Quite undismayed, this small force boldly manned the old ramparts and held the gates. Hardly had the positions been occupied when Pirch I delivered an assault, to prevent the French escaping. The Prussians were met by a salvo of grapeshot and heavy musketry fire. This reception caused the assailants to wheel sharp round on the glacis and draw back, leaving the slope littered with their dead and wounded. Without delay Pirch I ordered a second assault. Teste's ammunition was now running low ; but his men, reserving their fire until the attackers could not be missed, once more mowed down the Prussians on the glacis. These two assaults cost the II Corps 1,500 men, and Pirch I decided to break off the fight.

Teste considered that he had performed the duty which Grouchy had allotted to him. The light was failing, his available ammunition hardly warranted his risking another attack, so he began to retire. This withdrawal was noticed by the Prussians. Dashing forward, they burst into Namur and pressed on to seize the Sambre bridge. General Teste, however, had provided for this danger by placing a party of engineers in loop-holed houses covering the river-crossing. The fire of this detachment checked the Prussians whilst the rear-guard passed through the ' Gate of France ', already prepared for demolition. When all were clear, the sappers set light to the bundles. The roaring flames spreading from the gate to the houses in the vicinity prevented any further pursuit. In the meantime, as a result of Teste's spirited resistance, the main body had reached Dinant unmolested. The period of suspense was over.

On the 21*st* the French Right Wing retired across the frontier ; and, beneath the walls of Givet, the Marshal concentrated all the men, horses, and guns which had been placed under his command. It was entirely due to Marshal Grouchy's resolute and skilful handling that the Right Wing escaped out of the very dangerous situation in which it was placed after the destruction of the *Armée du Nord*. The Marshal rose superior to all the difficulties which had confronted him in his retreat. When it was too late to save France, he put on record a performance which at any other time must have gained him great honour.

Nevertheless the Marshal's rapid and vigorous manœuvres on the 19th and 20th June altered nothing. The decisive battle on the 18th June at *La Belle Alliance* had irrevocably settled the fate of the campaign and of France. Although he did extricate his force from the dangerous situation in which it had been placed, Grouchy was unable to nullify the result which Wellington and Blücher had gained on the red slopes of Mt. St. Jean ; nor could the Marshal and his detachment wring better terms for France from the all-conquering hosts of the Seventh Coalition.

CHAPTER XXIX

THE ADVANCE OF THE ALLIES ON PARIS AND THE END OF THE HUNDRED DAYS

(Map 1)

THIELEMANN and Pirch I gave up the chase of the French Right Wing after Grouchy had escaped through Namur. Pirch I moved from Namur to Thuin (*21st*). Thereafter the II Corps was employed in the reduction of the French frontier fortresses ; whilst Thielemann, moving through Charleroi (*21st*) and Beaumont (*22nd*), reached St. Germain on the *1st July*.

Meanwhile on the *19th* the Emperor had halted at Philippeville to write the bulletin of Ligny and Waterloo for the *Moniteur*, and to write to Joseph. Even in this dark hour, the letter to Joseph reveals in every line the inflexible personality of its author. Beginning with the words ' *Tout n'est point perdu* ', it ends on the high note ' *Surtout du courage et de la fermeté !* '

Before leaving Philippeville the Emperor issued orders for Grouchy to retire to Laon, where Soult was to collect the débris of the *Armée du Nord*. Rapp's Corps, with the French troops around Belfort and in La Vendée, were to move to Paris. The time for this concentration would be gained by the stubborn defence of the frontier fortresses. The rallying of the *Armée du Nord* was left to Marshal Soult. Events imperiously demanded the Emperor's immediate presence in Paris, in order to organize the last means of resistance ; for as yet the Emperor did not acknowledge defeat. Other armies could be raised, other material could be provided. In the circumstances this might require heroic efforts, and only Napoleon could rouse the Nation to make a last supreme stand for the Empire.

In the meantime, Marshal Soult was to collect the *Armée du Nord* as follows :

271

I, II, and VI Corps at Laon ; the Cavalry at Marle, St. Quentin, Réthel, Vervins, and Reims ; the Artillery at La Fère ; and the Imperial Guard at Soissons.

Reille reported, whilst Napoleon was still at Philippeville, and he was ordered to organize all the troops as they arrived. At the moment, the force at Napoleon's disposal at Philippeville and Avesnes was only about 10,000 men. Having issued his orders Napoleon set off for Paris *via* Marienbourg, Rocroi, Mézières, and Laon, so as to ensure that his journey should not be interfered with ; and completely worn out in mind and body, he reached his capital on the 21*st*. He had been absent just ten days.

It was soon made clear to the Emperor that he had to face hostility far nearer home than the enemy in the field. The Chambers were openly opposed to him ; and, to prevent their dissolution by the Emperor, they declared themselves in permanent session. On the 22*nd* Napoleon heard that he had been granted a choice between deposition or resignation. He yielded and signed his abdication, resigning in favour of his son (the King of Rome), who was to reign as Napoleon II. On the 25*th* the ex-Emperor moved to Malmaison.

Whilst the Chambers turned against Napoleon, the foe was closing in. Heading for Paris, the Allies were determined to press the beaten foe relentlessly. Blücher's Army advanced past Charleroi (19*th*), Avesnes (22*nd*), Guise (24*th*), St. Quentin (25*th*), Compiègne (27*th*), St. Denis (29*th*), and St. Germain (1*st July*). Blücher reached Versailles on the 3*rd July*. Wellington's advance was not so rapid. The Duke's Army had spent the 19*th* at Nivelles, refitting after the battle. Then it marched to Paris through Maubeuge (20*th*), Le Câteau Cambrésis (22*nd*), Cambrai (25*th*), Péronne (26*th*), and Louvres (30*th*). It reached St. Denis on the 1*st July*. During the advance Wellington was somewhat in rear of Blücher, yet the Duke was always within supporting distance of the Prussians.

After he had rallied the wrecks of the *Armée du Nord* at Laon, Soult marched to Soissons on the 25*th* so as to effect a junction with Grouchy ; and the Right Wing, moving through Givet (21*st*) and Réthel (24*th*), reached Soissons on the 26*th*.

At Laon the Provisional Government's instructions were received. Marshal Grouchy was ordered to take command of the whole Army, and Marshal Soult left and returned to Paris.[1] Grouchy withdrew his force (some 60,000) through Villers Cottérêts (*27th*), and Nanteuil (*28th*). This force reached Paris on the *29th*, the day on which the heads of Blücher's columns were sighted to the northward of the city. It is true that Wellington's Army was not yet in sight, but Blücher's isolation exposed the Prussians to no serious danger. The remaining Armies of the Seventh Coalition were fast closing in. At this stage a local reverse to the Allies could not prevent final disaster from overwhelming France.

Early on the *29th* Blücher detached a flying column to capture Napoleon dead or alive. On the previous day (*28th*) the Emperor had sent General de Flahault to the French Government to ask that two frigates should be placed at the ex-Emperor's disposal, or he would not leave Paris. Flahault interviewed Fouché and Davout. Davout informed Flahault that the ex-Emperor must leave or he (Davout) would arrest him himself. Flahault at once told Davout that the Marshal must be his own messenger, and he (Flahault) refused to carry such a message. If this refusal entailed resigning his commission, Flahault placed it unreservedly in Davout's hands. On returning to Malmaison Flahault told the ex-Emperor what had transpired, but Napoleon only said : ' *Eh bien, qu'il y vienne.*'

Before this Napoleon, through General Becker, had offered his services to the Provisional Government. Serving merely as General Bonaparte, he wished to place himself at the head of the available French forces and surprise and beat Blücher and Wellington in detail, as the Armies were two days' march apart. To Napoleon's disappointment his offer was negatived. Thereupon, not wishing to be captured by the Prussians, at 5 p.m. on the *29th June* Napoleon (accompanied by Bertrand, Savary, Gourgaud, and Becker) left Malmaison and set out for Rochefort—and exile.

Already Schweidnitz, Schwarzenberg, and Bianchi were submerging France and fastening securely on the country. Schweid-

---

[1] On the 26th September, 1847, Marshal Soult was elevated to the dignity of *Maréchal Général* ; a dignity which he shares with de Turenne, de Villars, and de Saxe. When Soult died in 1851 (aged 82) he had been a Marshal of France for forty-seven years.

nitz reached Laon and Reims on the 7th July. Schwarzenberg's Austrians entered Melun (13th), and Tonnerre and Montbard on the 21st. Bianchi, having crossed the Simplon, reached Geneva and Mâcon by the 11th July and spread northwards to Besançon. A column under Frimont crossed the Simplon on the 1st July and another under Bubna crossed the Mt. Cenis ; both reached Lyon by the end of July. At the same time Barclay de Tolly and his Russians arrived on the Rhine. Despite the wide area covered by the advancing Armies of the Seventh Coalition the risk they ran was infinitesimal. In France all hope was gone.

During this invasion, Colonel Bugeaud [1] and the 14th Regiment of the Line fought a gallant and successful action, on the 28th June, at Conflans and l'Hôpital on the Arly River, to oppose the advance of General Trenck and 10,000 Austrians over the Little St. Bernard. Colonel Bugeaud had just heard the news of the disaster at Waterloo and of Napoleon's abdication ; so he fought for France. Bugeaud's 1,800 men beat off the Austrian attacks, killed or wounded 1,500 and made 500 prisoners. With this parting gleam of splendour the Napoleonic Wars ended.

Within a week, Paris, menaced by Blücher and Wellington, had to choose between standing a siege or capitulating to the Allies. On the 3rd July it was decided to make terms, and the capitulation was arranged. On the 4th, Wellington and Blücher approved the Convention, and Marshal Davout led the French Army out of Paris towards the Loire. The Allies occupied the suburbs on the same day, and on the 7th they made their triumphal entry into Paris. On the 8th, Louis XVIII returned to the Tuileries.

As this history began with Napoleon, it must allude to his surrender ; as ever since his return from Elba Napoleon had been the central figure of the drama, around him it had revolved, for him his men had fought, for him they had laid down their lives.

After reaching Rochefort, Napoleon, on the 8th July, embarked on the frigate La Saale, and, accompanied by another frigate (La Méduse), proceeded to the roads of Aix. The ex-Emperor wished to escape to the United States. On the 10th a favourable

---

[1] Bugeaud de la Piconnerie, Duc d'Isly, was made a Marshal of France on the 18th September, 1844. Bugeaud died on the 10th June, 1849.

wind sprang up, but a British Fleet of eleven ships hove in sight. The vigilance of the British could not be eluded ; and, after waiting three days, the ex-Emperor opened up communication with Captain Maitland, commanding H.M.S. *Bellerophon* of the blockading squadron. Maitland thereupon informed Napoleon that he would not be permitted to sail to America.

By the 13*th* Napoleon realized that it was hopeless to think of flight by sea, and he arranged to surrender to Captain Maitland. Before doing so, however, Napoleon on the 14th July wrote from Aix a personal letter to the Prince Regent of England, claiming protection and hospitality. The letter ended with this noble sentence : ' *Je me mets sous la protection de ses lois, que je réclame de Votre Altesse Royale, comme du plus puissant, du plus constant, et du plus généreux de mes ennemis. Napoléon.*' [1]

On the following day, the 15*th July*, Napoleon went on board the *Bellerophon* and formally entrusted his person to the British Nation. The Hundred Days had come to an end—St. Helena lay beyond the horizon.

[1] *Correspondance*, 22066.

CHAPTER XXX—AND LAST

NAPOLEON IN 1815

SUCH varying opinions have been given about Napoleon's state of health and capability in 1815 that the subject requires consideration. Some critics have professed the belief that Napoleon was broken down, physically and mentally. Some indeed appear to think that he might have been suffering from a disease akin to ' sleeping sickness '. M. Henri Houssaye, however, held the opposite opinion, so far as Napoleon's physical faculties were concerned. He wrote : ' For practically four days, between 3 a.m. 15th June and about 2 a.m. 19th June, this man whom writers are so eager to represent as broken down, depressed by disease, lacking in energy, unable to overcome sleep, and incapable of keeping in the saddle, scarcely took 20 hours' rest. Even although he was probably on foot for three-quarters of the time which the two great battles lasted, yet he remained in the saddle for 37 hours.

' In 1815 Napoleon was in sufficiently good health to enable him to bear the great fatigues of war, and his brain had lost none of its power. But with him his moral power no longer upheld his genius. . . . He no longer believed in success, his boldness gave way with his confidence. . . . He dared not seize and force circumstances. . . . With his faith in his destiny he had always been a daring and audacious gambler. Now that Fortune showed itself contrary he became a timid player. He hesitated, no longer followed his inspiration, temporized, weighed the chances, saw the pros and cons, and would risk nothing save on a certainty.'

Thiers also thought, ' Whatever may have been Napoleon's state of health in 1815, it did not in any way affect his activity.'

Another writer, Colonel Chesney, put it more strongly : ' Certain French writers are disposed to impute a large share of their country's disaster to some supposed falling off in the physical energy and mental powers of the Emperor. The simple reply

to this is, that his warlike capacity had never been more splendidly
displayed than during that part of the struggle with the Allies
in the spring of 1814, known as the Week of Victories. The
General of Arcola and Rivoli was not more full of resource, nor
more sudden and deadly in his strokes, than he of Montmirail
and Champaubert!' In 1814, however, Napoleon staked all
that he held dear. This acted like a stimulant, whilst there
remained a hope of success. Under this influence Napoleon
became once more the personal embodiment of energy, audacity,
and resolution ; but, like all prolonged mental strains, there was
the after-effect to reckon with.

A great French critic, Colonel Grouard, considered that in
1813 and 1814 Napoleon made the fatal mistake of underrating
his adversaries, conceiving that they would shake in terror at the
very sound of his name and tremble when opposed to him. On
the morrow of the great Victories of Austerlitz, Jena, and Friedland, such a state of affairs may have existed, possibly even after
Wagram. But in 1813 there was not the same reason to hold such
feelings about the Emperor. He had laid the foundations of his
own ruin in the calamitous and never-ending war in the Spanish
Peninsula, which, perpetually breaking out afresh, continued to
eat away his means of resistance. His downfall was brought
nearer by the disastrous Russian Campaign. In 1813, in 1814,
and especially in 1815, his adversaries had a great advantage in the
task to which they had set their hands. At last Napoleon had
taught them something of the art of war, and they were able
to profit from the knowledge they had acquired slowly and
painfully in the years of their defeats. In 1815 Napoleon no
longer possessed the same prestige. He had shown that he was
conquerable, and the Allies were more formidable foes than they
had been of yore.

Undoubtedly too, in 1815, the physical and mental state of the
Emperor partly account for his brilliant conception being marred
and then ruined in execution. The Emperor's conduct of the
campaign is inexplicable, if it is assumed that Napoleon still
retained all his powers of mind and body. Until his last campaign the Emperor's bodily health had not penalized him. But on
his return from Elba it was noticed that he had grown stouter.
The enforced comparative inaction at Elba may have had a
prejudicial effect on his health.

In 1815 was Napoleon suffering from some definite illness which seriously affected his activity ? It is well established that the ex-Emperor died at St. Helena of cancer of the stomach in May 1821. Even so, cancer was not the disease from which Napoleon suffered in June 1815. The ex-Emperor remarked to Antommarchi at St. Helena that he had always had a stomach of iron and he had felt no inconveniences until the onset of what proved to be his fatal illness. It was not until September 1820 that the growth became acutely malignant, and the disease then slew the sufferer before there was time to produce much wasting.

Modern medical opinion, however, leans to the belief that in 1815 Napoleon was suffering from the comparatively rare disease of Acromegaly.[1] Whatever may have been the injury which was responsible for the perverted function of the pituitary gland, this disease probably started early in Napoleon's adult life, since he seems to have possessed some of its unmistakable signs : separation of the teeth, spade-like hands, curvature of the upper portion of the back, etc.

The emotional shocks caused by such terrific hammer-blows as those dealt him by Fate—the awful failure of his Russian campaign in 1812, the appalling disaster at Leipzig in 1813, his enforced abdication in 1814—may have assisted in accentuating the already-present disease.

Napoleon's recurring fits of lethargy during the campaign of 1815, his extreme depression at the conclusion of the struggle, his occasional irritability, his false estimate of what Blücher would do after Ligny (amounting to a delusion), are explained by his suffering from acromegaly. All are well-known symptoms of that malady.

Unfortunately the undermined physical condition of the Emperor in 1815 assisted materially in bringing about his final overthrow by a united Europe in arms. This being so, Napoleon's conduct of his Campaign in Belgium must now be considered in order to determine the extent that his enfeebled activity, or positive lethargy, curtailed his personal supervision of events or caused dangerous delays at critical times.

[1] I am indebted to my friend, Dr. R. H. Leaver, for explaining to me the nature of the disease from which Napoleon was suffering in 1815, and enlightening me about it. Acromegaly was first described by Marie in 1880.

By following Napoleon during the progress of the Campaign it is possible to notice certain facts, which taken by themselves might mean nothing, though in the aggregate they afford proof that he no longer retained his earlier mental and bodily powers.

At the outset of the Campaign in Belgium, Napoleon's appreciation of the true measure of his offensive means and his distribution of his soldiers on the theatre of war were unworthy of the victor of Ulm and Austerlitz. Penalized as he was in this fashion before hostilities began, it was scarcely possible that he could succeed. Nevertheless his concentration was so brilliant that it gave him an undeniable chance of victory. Gradually this chance passed away.

On the 15th the Emperor was early in the saddle, yet on the far side of Charleroi he succumbed to drowsiness from which even the cheers of his soldiers failed to wake him. This lethargy might have been caused by the heat. If it had been unrepeated, it would only have shown that his powers of endurance were no longer limitless. Unfortunately it was not a solitary instance. On the evening of the 15th Napoleon was so thoroughly overcome by fatigue that his orders for the 16th were not sent out until 9 a.m. on that day, and probably he did not begin to work at them before 6 a.m. at the earliest.

In the Battle of Ligny Napoleon was stationary for most of the time, and the strain on his physical powers was slight. Yet at nightfall the Emperor was unwell. He went to bed without issuing orders to Grouchy to open an immediate pursuit of the Prussians. Then on the 17th when Grouchy, on his own initiative having pushed out Pajol and Exelmans, came to Imperial Head-Quarters for instructions, the Emperor was sleeping and only awoke at 7.30 a.m.

This day was the vital one of the whole campaign. Either Blücher's ruin was to be brought about, or Wellington must be held fast at Quatre Bras, until the Emperor could swing in the French Reserve and effect the destruction of the Anglo-Dutch Army. Unless he was prepared to leave too much to chance, the Emperor, at an early hour, was required to make certain of Blücher's line of retreat by his own personal reconnaissance, and at daybreak to send Ney precise orders to attack and hold Wellington at Quatre Bras. Disastrously for France, Napoleon's lethargy allowed these critical hours to pass by unused. Had

Ney behaved correctly the lethargy would not have mattered ; but it was Napoleon's business to ensure that Ney did behave correctly. This the Emperor failed to do, consequently he did not repair the errors of the previous day.

Had Napoleon been himself, he would have been afoot at 4 a.m. on the 17th, as he was in his earlier campaigns. Had he pushed the bulk of his horsemen northward towards Wavre, in the only dangerous direction, then before they reached Mt. St. Guibert the French Cavalry must have established contact with the retiring Corps of Zieten and Pirch I. Napoleon would have appreciated the meaning of this retreat and realized that, if the decision was to be obtained, it must be gained on the 17th at Quatre Bras. Had he moved to the assault of the open left of the Anglo-Dutch Army with those troops who were ready to advance at short notice—Lobau's (VI) Corps, Milhaud's Cuirassiers, and the Guard—and called up Lefebvre-Desnoëttes and Kellermann to co-operate, there can be no doubt that the Anglo-Dutch Army would have been smashed long before the great storm broke. The remnants would have been driven off to the westward before 3 p.m. Junction with Blücher would have been out of the question.

So early as 4 a.m. on the 17th, it was impossible in the complicated situation for Grouchy to distinguish the essential. It is true the Prussians had been beaten. But the Battle of Ligny finished in the darkness, touch was lost, and no one knew for certain whither Blücher's Army had gone. Nor was it known at Imperial Head-Quarters what had happened at Quatre Bras, where Wellington was known to be concentrated and almost within gun-shot of the *Armée du Nord*. D'Erlon's recall indicated that Ney was hard pressed. Consequently, at 4 a.m. on the 17th, the situation was beyond the range of the subordinates at Ligny.

Ney's duty alone was clear : to grip Wellington and await further instructions. Although Ney was ignorant of the result of Ligny, yet he could have deduced that Napoleon had the battle with Blücher in hand, since D'Erlon had been allowed to march back to Quatre Bras without any attempt to recall the I Corps to Ligny. If Ney was still in doubt, then an officer's patrol, sent to Ligny at daybreak, would have found the French in possession of the field with the Prussians nowhere visible.

Indeed the patrol could have got all the necessary information from Durutte who had seen the end of the battle. Ney's failure to hold Wellington fast at Quatre Bras on the 17th was an almost irreparable error.

Naturally the orders for the *Armée du Nord* at Ligny could only be issued by Napoleon. Marshal Grouchy was now the commander of the Right Wing, and no longer merely commander of the Cavalry, so the order to reconnoitre northward at 4 a.m. should have come from the Emperor. By failing to be available at 4 a.m. the Emperor showed that the old energy was dimmed. By failing to recognize at dawn that reconnaissance to the northward was essential, Napoleon showed that he seriously underestimated Blücher and the *moral* of the gallant Prussian Army. The Emperor easily convinced himself that Blücher and his Prussians must seek safety behind the Meuse. Even so, he did not ensure Wellington's immediate annihilation. His mental powers as well as his physical powers had deteriorated. He was no longer the Napoleon of 1805.

After Grouchy had been despatched to find and neutralize Blücher, the responsibility for scouting northward shifted to the Marshal. The blunders which Grouchy made need not be gone into again, though it is obvious the Emperor did not recognize that intelligence of the Prussians should be sought first of all in the direction of Mt. St. Guibert. This is astonishing when Napoleon's almost superhuman strategical faculty is recalled. But, in 1815, his mind had lost its flexibility and not for a moment did he suspect the significance of the Allied plan. On this particular morning there was no adequate reason to cause Napoleon to change his strategical plan ; but a crisis had been reached, and it was essential not to lose even minutes by over-confidence. On the morning of the 17th Napoleon's impaired health caused him to lose valuable hours which he was never able to make up. The hours thus lost proved to be vital, owing to Ney's failure to retain the Anglo-Dutch Army at Quatre Bras, and to Grouchy's feeble and false manœuvres, which, by nightfall, placed the French Right Wing outside the Prussian Army. These fatal errors, together with the initial faults of distribution and Napoleon's own mental and physical decadence (due to acromegaly), were opposed to the strongest of combinations : Marshal Blücher's remarkable loyalty, the Duke of Wellington's iron fortitude and singleness of purpose, coupled with the stubborn tenacity and intrepidity of the British troops and the King's German Legion ; and this combination brought about Napoleon's ruin at Waterloo.

It is true that the Emperor in his chase after Wellington's rear-guard on the 17th showed a blaze of the old energy, since even in a thunderstorm he rode at the head of the pursuit for 7 miles, and immediately afterwards dictated orders, dealt with correspondence, and later on made a round of his outposts.   But it is only by comparison with the Napoleon of earlier years that the Emperor's performance in the Waterloo Campaign can be judged.   In 1815 there is no doubt that Napoleon's powers of mind and body were seriously impaired, although that is very far from saying that he was worn out.   After a good night's rest he was still capable of vigorous action, if he desired to take it. In 1815, however, it was unlikely that such action would outlast the circumstances which had demanded this particular outburst of activity.

In the Battle of Waterloo Napoleon was full of energy.   If he slept during the battle, he took his rest during some non-critical period.   During all the critical phases he was wakeful and active, because the stimulus of battle galvanized him into at least a resemblance of his old self.

In 1815 Napoleon's powers resembled a dying fire.   Occasionally there were brilliant flashes, but they came at ever-lengthening intervals.   At the opening of the campaign there was the concentration around Beaumont.   This was swiftly followed by the forcing of the Sambre at Charleroi, when the necessary incentive was provided by the news of the delay of Vandamme's Corps. This spur to action caused the Emperor to hurry to the front with the Guard and storm the bridge.   Directly the reason for immediate action was removed, the exertion took its full toll of his powers and his lethargy at Charleroi was the result.   The flame had died down.

The next flash came at Gilly, where with a thunderclap Napoleon drove Pirch II's Prussians in headlong flight on Fleurus. But at night the Emperor was not himself and he was late in issuing his orders on the 16th.   Then came the great Battle of Ligny.   The exertion and particularly the mental strain proved too much for Napoleon.   On that night he was unwell.   After this the embers smouldered.   Such flashes as shot up were short and spasmodic. Finally on the fatal field of La Belle Alliance the fire was quenched for ever.

In all the earlier and glorious campaigns Napoleon's capacity for hard mental work had only been equalled by his great physical powers. His iron frame never wearied. At the close of the longest and most tiring day his mind was clear and ready to grasp the most complex problem. However unexpected or however disheartening were the reports which came to hand, Napoleon was always calm, dispassionate, capable of weighing events, seeing things as they were, and appreciating everything at its correct value. Then, without hesitation, he reached a rapid, definite, and appropriate decision, and carried through his plans without loss of time or irresolution.

A great commander must have both character and genius. Generals with much genius and little character are top-heavy. They are the least suited for command in the field. In Napoleon genius and character were equally blended. His genius and character were even more admirable than his magnificent physical powers. His genius enabled him to foresee what the enemy would do. His imagination allowed him to create the decisive manœuvre. His resolution enabled him to carry through his plan, despite the dangers and accidents which always occur in execution. Thus he accomplished great ends with means which would have been utterly inadequate for any of his contemporaries. No other leader of any era compares with Napoleon for grandeur of intellect and military genius. No one among his contemporaries could have led the French hosts through Berlin and Vienna, or carried the Grand Army through Russia to Moscow. His genius and strength of character have made Napoleon immortal. He ' was not of the stuff of which kings are made—he was of the marble from which gods are hewn '.

In 1815, even if his mental powers and his health and activity were no longer all they had been, yet Napoleon was still a power to reckon with. He was still incomparably the greatest General in the world. His organizing and administrative ability had deteriorated little, as the Army which he raised and equipped, in the three short months vouchsafed to him, bore testimony. His strategical concentration, his surprise of his enemies, the subtle restraint which left to his foes the apparent chance of co-operation, luring them to attempt that hazardous forward concentration, together with his determination to take and maintain the initiative, and the magnificently simple formation of the *Armée du Nord* for the advance in Belgium, all proclaim that Napoleon was still *un grand homme de guerre.*

Napoleon attracts the chief interest and attention in this tragedy. He stands out distinct from all the other leaders, and his generalship is still the absorbing study in this Campaign. He failed ; but what he dared and what he achieved against over-whelming odds, vouch that Napoleon, the Emperor of Battles, was in truth *le génie incarné de la guerre.*

Vive L'Empereur !

APPENDICES

APPENDIX I   COMPOSITION AND ORGANIZATION OF THE OPPOSING FORCES

(A) L'ARMÉE DU NORD—(JUNE 1815)

Commander-in-Chief, Napoléon Bonaparte, Emperor of the French.
Major-Général (Chief of the Head-quarters Staff), Marshal Soult, Duke of Dalmatia.
Commanding Artillery, Lieut.-General Ruty.
Commanding Engineer, Lieut.-General Baron Rogniat.

CORPS.	DIVISIONS.	BRIGADES.	REGIMENTS.
I. Lieut.-General Drouet, Count d'Erlon. Chief of the Staff, Maj.-Gen. Baron Delcambre. Assistant Chief of the Staff, Viala.	1st. Lieut.-General Alix (in Alix's absence, Baron Quiot commanded the division).	Quiot.	54, 55.
		Bourgeois.	28, 105.
	2nd. Lieut.-General Baron Donzelot.	Schmitz.	13th Light, and 17.
		Aulard.	19, 51.
	3rd. Lieut.-General Baron Marcognet.	Nogués.	21, 46.
		Grenier.	25, 45.
	4th. Lieut.-General Count Durutte.	Pégot.	8, 29.
		Brue.	85, 95.
	Cavalry Division. Lieut.-General Jacquinot.	Bruno	7 Hsrs. and 3 Chassrs.
		Gobrecht.	3 and 4 Lancers.
	Artillery. Baron Desales. (6 Batteries.)		

NOTE.—The Emperor was attended by 8 general aides-de-camp and orderly officers; and the Imperial and Head-quarters Staff comprised 79 officers.

Each Corps had a staff of 6 officers, including officers to command the Artillery and Engineers; and each Divisional Commander had a Chief of the Staff.

The Staff of the Imperial Guard consisted of 8 officers.

The command of the Left Wing was given (on the 15th June) to Marshal Ney, Prince of the Moskowa and Duke of Elchingen.

L'ARMÉE DU NORD—*continued*

CORPS.	DIVISIONS.	BRIGADES.	REGIMENTS.
II. Lieut.-General Count Reille. Chief of the Staff, Lieut.-General Baron Pamphile Lacroix. Assistant Chief of the Staff, Lecouturier.	5th. Lieut.-General Baron Bachelu.	Husson. Campy.	2nd Light, and 61. 72, 108.
	6th. Lieut.-General Prince Jérôme Bonaparte.	Bauduin. Soye.	1st Light, and 3. 1 and 2.
	7th. Lieut.-General Count Girard.	Devilliers. Piat.	11th Light, and 82. 12th Light, and 4.
	9th. Lieut.-General Count Foy.	Gauthier. Jamin.	92, 93. 4th Light, and 100.
	2nd Cavalry Division. Lieut.-General Baron Piré.	Huber. Wathiez.	1 and 6 Chasseurs. 5 and 6 Lancers.
	Artillery. Baron Pelletier. (6 Batteries.)		
III. Lieut.-General Count Vandamme. Chief of the Staff, Lieut.-General Count Guilleminot. Assistant Chief of the Staff, Trezel.	8th. Lieut.-General Baron Lefol.	Billard. Corsin.	15th Light, and 23. 37, 64.
	10th. Lieut.-General Baron Habert.	Gengoult. Dupeyroux.	34, 88. 22, 70.
	11th. Lieut.-General Baron Berthézène.	Dufour. Lagarde.	12, 56. 33, 86.
	3rd Cavalry Division Lieut.-General Baron Domon.	Dommanget. Vinot.	4 and 9 Chasseurs. 12 Chasseurs.
	Artillery. Maj.-General Doguereau. (5 Batteries.)		

CORPS.	DIVISIONS.	BRIGADES.	REGIMENTS.
IV.			
Lieut.-General Count Gérard.	12th. Lieut.-General Baron Pécheux.	Rome.	30, 96.
		Schoeffer.	6th Light, and 63.
Chief of the Staff, Maj.-General St. Remy.	13th. Lieut.-General Baron Vichéry.	Le Capitaine.	59, 76.
		Desprez.	48, 69.
Assistant Chief of the Staff, Simon Lorière.	14th. Lieut.-General de Bourmont (afterwards Major-General Hulot).	Hulot.	9th Light, and 111.
		Toussaint.	44, 50.
	7th Cavalry Division. Lieut.-General Maurin.	Vallin.	6 Hussars.
		Berruyer.	8 Chasseurs.
	Artillery. Maj.-General Baron Baltus. (5 Batteries.)		
VI.			
Lieut.-General Mouton, Count of Lobau.	19th. Lieut.-General Baron Simmer.	Bellair.	5, 11.
		M. Jamin.	27, 84.
Chief of the Staff, Maj.-General Durrieu.	20th. Lieut.-General Baron Jannin.	Bony.	5th Light, and 10.
		Tromelin.	47,[1] 107.
Assistant Chief of the Staff, E. Janin.	21st. Lieut.-General Baron Teste.	Lafitte.	8th Light, and 40.[2]
		Penne.	65, 75.
	Artillery. Lieut.-General Baron Noury. (4 Batteries.)		

[1] This regiment had been detailed to join the force operating in La Vendée.
[2] This regiment was mobilizing at its depôt at Senlis, and probably did not take part in the campaign.

L'ARMÉE DU NORD—*continued*
Cavalry Reserve, Marshal Count de Grouchy.

CORPS.	DIVISIONS.	BRIGADES.	REGIMENTS.
I. Lieut.-General Count Pajol. Chief of the Staff, Picard.	4th. Lieut.-General Baron Soult.	St. Laurent.	1 and 4 Hussars.
		Ameil.	5 Hussars.
	5th. Lieut.-General Baron Subervie.	A. de Colbert.	1 and 2 Lancers.
		Merlin.	11 Chasseurs.
	2 Horse Artillery Batteries.		
II. Lieut.-General Count Exelmans.	9th. Lieut.-General Strolz.	Burthe.	5 and 13 Dragoons.
		Vincent.	15 and 20 Dragoons.
	10th. Lieut.-General Baron Chastel.	Bonnemains.	4 and 12 Dragoons.
		Berton.	14 and 17 Dragoons.
Chief of the Staff, Feroussat.	2 Horse Artillery Batteries.		
III. Lieut.-General Kellermann, Count of Valmy. Chief of the Staff, Tancarville.	11th. Lieut.-General Baron Lhéritier.	Picquet.	2 and 7 Dragoons.
		Guiton.	8 and 11 Cuirassiers.
	12th. Lieut.-General Roussel d'Hurbal.	Blancard.	1 and 2 Carabiniers.
		Donop.	2 and 3 Cuirassiers.
	2 Horse Artillery Batteries.		
IV. Lieut.-General Count Milhaud. Chief of the Staff, Baron Chasseriau.	13th. Lieut.-General Wathier St. Alphonse.	Dubois.	1 and 4 Cuirassiers.
		Travers.	7 and 12 Cuirassiers
	14th. Lieut.-General Baron Delort.	Farine.	5 and 10 Cuirassiers.
		Vial.	6 and 9 Cuirassiers.
	2 Horse Artillery Batteries.		

L'ARMÉE DU NORD—*continued*

The IMPERIAL GUARD. Marshal Mortier, Duke of Treviso.[1]
Aide-Major-Général de la Garde, Lieut.-General Count Drouot.

OLD GUARD (on foot). Lieut.-General Count Friant.
  1st and 2nd Grenadiers.
      (1st Grenadiers, General Petit.)
      (2nd Grenadiers, General Christiani.)
  1st and 2nd Chasseurs.
      (1st Chasseurs, General Cambronne.)
      (2nd Chasseurs, General Pelet.)

MIDDLE GUARD (on foot). Lieut.-General Count Morand.
  3rd and 4th Grenadiers (Generals de Morvan and Harlet).
  3rd and 4th Chasseurs (Colonel Mallet and General Henrion).

YOUNG GUARD (on foot). Lieut.-General Count Duhesme.
  1st and 3rd Voltigeurs (Colonel Hurel).
  1st and 3rd Tirailleurs (Colonels de Malcolm and Pailhès).

LIGHT CAVALRY. Lieut.-General Lefebvre-Desnoëttes (Lancers and Chasseurs).

RESERVE CAVALRY (Heavy). Lieut.-General Count Guyot.
(Mounted Grenadiers, Dragoons, and *Gendarmes d'élite.*)

ARTILLERY. Lieut.-General Desvaux de St. Maurice.
(3 Horse Artillery, and 13 Field Artillery Batteries.) [2]

---

[1] Marshal Mortier was left behind, on the 15th June, at Beaumont, on the sick list. He was not replaced at the head of the Guard, the orders thereafter passing through the deputy head of the General Staff of the Guard, Lieut.-General Count Antoine Drouot. The Staff of the Guard consisted of 8 officers.

[2] In the Decree of 8th April, 1815, the organization of the Guard was to be as follows :—
Infantry. Each regiment composed of 2 battalions, each battalion of 4 companies, each company of 200 men.
Cavalry. Each regiment composed of 4 squadrons, each squadron of 2 companies, each company of 150 men.
Artillery. 8 horse artillery (6-gun) batteries (4 with the cavalry and 4 with the reserve) ; 2 field artillery (8-gun) batteries, attached to the infantry of the Old Guard ; 4 field artillery (6-gun) batteries, attached to the 2 divisions of the Young Guard ; 8 12-pounder (8-gun) batteries (4 being manned by the artillery of the Old Guard) to be attached to the Guard Artillery Reserve.
General Gourgaud stated that the Artillery was organized as follows : Each division had a (field) battery of 8 guns, and with each infantry corps there was a reserve (field) battery of 8 12-pounders. Each cavalry division also possessed a (horse artillery) battery of 6 guns.
The artillery of the Guard numbered 96 guns ; comprising 24 horse, and 72 field artillery guns.
The strength of the Guard varied in the different campaigns of the First

The total strength of the *Armée du Nord* was about 125,000 men (including 20,000 to 22,000 Cavalry), and 370 guns ; or 180 squadrons, 50 batteries, and 175 battalions.

Empire : it was 12,000 in 1805, in 1806 it was 15,000 ; it remained about this strength until 1809, when it rose to 24,000 ; it was 32,000 in 1810 ; 52,000 in 1811 ; 56,000 in 1812 ; 81,000 in 1813 ; and it attained its maximum strength, 102,000, in 1814 ; dropping to a little over 20,000 in 1815.

(B) THE PRUSSIAN ARMY

Commander-in-Chief : Field-Marshal Prince Blücher von Wahlstatt.
Quartermaster-General and Chief of the Staff : Lieut.-General Count von Gneisenau.
Chief of the General Staff : Major-General von Grölmann.[1]

CORPS.		BRIGADES.[2]
I		Von Steinmetz.
		Von Pirch II.
		Von Jägow.
Lieut.-General von Zieten II.		Henckel von Donnersmarck.
	Cavalry :	Von Röder.
		Von Treskow II.
		Von Lützow.
	Artillery :	Lehmann.

Corps Artillery : One horse artillery, two 12-pounder, seven 6-pounder field batteries ; one howitzer battery. 31,000 and 80 guns (including 20 howitzers).

II.		Von Tippelskirch.
		Von Krafft.
		Von Brause.
		Von Langen.
Major-General von Pirch I.	*Cavalry :*	Von Jürgass.
		Von Thümen.
		Von Sohr.
		Von der Schulenburg.
	Artillery :	Von Röhl.

Corps Artillery : One horse artillery, two 12-pounder, seven 6-pounder field batteries, and one battery of howitzers. 31,500 and 80 guns (including 20 howitzers).

[1] The Head-Quarters Staff under General von Grölmann numbered 6 officers. The remainder of the Staff numbered 49, including the officer commanding the artillery, head-quarters commandant, surveyors, surgeons, auditor, provost-marshal, etc. The whole of the Prussian Head-Quarters Staff totalled 58 officers.

Each Corps had a staff of about 20 officers ; and the Brigades each had a staff of about 5 officers. A Prussian battery normally consisted of 6 guns and 2 howitzers.

[2] There was no divisional organization in the Prussian Army of 1815 ; the Brigades were each about the strength of a French division.

THE PRUSSIAN ARMY—*continued*

CORPS.	BRIGADES.
III.	Von Borcke.
	Von Kemphen.
	Von Luck.
Lieut.-General	Von Stülpnagel.
von Thiele-	*Cavalry :* Von Hobe.
mann.	Von der Marwitz.
	Von Lottum.
	Artillery : Monhaupt.

Corps Artillery : One horse artillery, one 12-pounder, four 6-pounder field batteries, and one battery of howitzers. 24,000 and 48 guns (including 12 howitzers).

CORPS.	BRIGADES.
IV.	Von Hake.
	Von Rijssel.
	Von Losthin.
General Count	Von Hiller.
Bülow von	*Cavalry :* Prince William of Prussia.
Dennewitz.	Von Schwerin.
	Von Watzdorf.
	Von Sydow.
	Artillery : Von Braun.

Corps Artillery : Two horse artillery, three 12-pounder, and six 6-pounder field batteries, and one howitzer battery. 30,800 and 88 guns (including 22 howitzers).

Total strength, about 117,000 men (including 12,000 sabres) with 296 guns (or 136 battalions, 137 squadrons, and 41 batteries).

(C) ANGLO-DUTCH ARMY

Commander-in-Chief, Field-Marshal the Duke of Wellington.
Chief of the Staff, Colonel Sir William Howe de Lancey.
Adjutant-General, Major-General Sir E. Barnes.
Commanding Royal Artillery, Colonel Sir G. A. Wood.
Commanding Royal Engineers, Lieut.-Colonel J. C. Smyth.
Prussian *Attaché* at the British Head-Quarters, Major-General Baron von Müffling.

CORPS.	DIVISIONS.	BRIGADES.
I. H.R.H. the Prince of Orange. Q.M.G. Major-General Baron de Constant Rebecque.	Major-General G. Cooke. 1st Division (B.).	Maitland (B.), (Guards, 2/1st and 3/1st). Sir J. Byng (B.), (Guards, 2/2nd and 2/3rd). *Artillery:* Lieut.-Colonel S. G. Adye. Captain Sandham's Field Brigade, R.A. Major Kühlmann's Horse Artillery Troop, K.G.L.
	Lieut.-General Count Sir C. Alten. 3rd Division (B.).	Sir C. Halkett (B.), (30, 33, 69, and 73). Baron von Ompteda (K.G.L.), (5 and 8; 1 Light and 2 Light). Count Kielmansegge (H.). *Artillery:* Lieut.-Colonel J. S. Williamson. Major Lloyd's Field Brigade, R.A. Captain Cleeves's 4th Foot Battery, K.G.L.
	Lieut.-General Baron de Perponcher. 2nd Dutch-Belgian Division.	Van Bijlandt. Prince Bernard of Saxe-Weimar. *Artillery:* Van Opstall. 1 Horse (Bijleveld) and 1 Field (Stevenart) Battery.
	Lieut.-General Baron Chassé. 3rd Dutch-Belgian Division.	Detmers. D'Aubrémé. *Artillery:* Van der Smissen. 1 Horse (Krahmer de Bichin) and 1 Field (Lux) Battery.

ANGLO-DUTCH ARMY—*continued*

CORPS.	DIVISIONS.	BRIGADES.
II.	Lieut.-General Sir H. Clinton. 2nd Division (B.).	Adam (B.), (52, 71, 2/95, 3/95). Du Plat (K.G.L.), (1, 2, 3, 4). W. Halkett (H.). *Artillery:* Lieut.-Colonel C. Gold. *Captain Bolton's Field Brigade, R.A.* Major Sympher's Horse Artillery Troop, K.G.L.
Lieut.-General Lord Hill.	Lieut.-General Sir C. Colville. 4th Division (B.).	Mitchell (B.), (14, 23, 51). Johnstone (B.), (35, 54, 59, 91). Sir J. Lyon (H.). *Artillery:* Lieut.-Colonel J. Hawker. *Major Brome's Field Brigade, R.A.* Captain v. Rettberg's Hanoverian Field Battery.
	Troops of the Netherlands under Prince Frederick. 1st Dutch-Belgian Division. Lieut.-General Stedman.	D'Hauw. De Eerens. *Artillery:* 1 Field Battery (Wynands). Indian Brigade: Anthing. *Artillery:* 1 Field Battery (Riesz).

NOTE.—British Brigades are denoted by the letter 'B.' in brackets (the numbers show the regiments); King's German Legion Brigades, by 'K.G.L.'; and Hanoverian Brigades, by 'H.'

The British Field Brigades R.A., which are shown in italics were not engaged at Waterloo.

ANGLO-DUTCH ARMY—*continued*

BRIGADES.

DIVISIONS.

Lieut.-General Sir T.
Picton, 5th Division
(B.).

Sir J. Kempt (B.), (28, 32, 79, 1/95).
Sir D. Pack (B.), (1, 42, 44, 92).
Vincke (H.).

Artillery: Major Heise.
Major Rogers's Field Brigade, R.A.
Captain Braun's Hanoverian Field Battery.

Lieut.-General Sir L. Cole
(absent), 6th Division
(B.).

Sir J. Lambert (B.), (4, 27, 40, 81).
Best (H.).

Artillery: Lieut.-Colonel H. Brückmann.
Major Unett's Field Brigade, R.A.
Captain Sinclair's Field Brigade, R.A.

British Reserve Artillery.
Major P. Drummond.

Lieut.-Colonel Sir H. Ross's Troop (A, R.H.A.).
Major Bean's Troop (D, R.H.A.).
Major Morisson's Company, R.A.
Captain Hutchesson's Company, R.A.
Captain Ilbert's Company, R.A.

7th Division.

7th British Brigade (25, 37, 78).
British Garrison Troops.

Brunswick Corps.
H.S.H. the Duke of
Brunswick.

Von Buttler.
Olfermanns.

Artillery: Von Lubecq.
1 Horse (von Heinemann) and 1 Field (von Moll) Battery.

Hanoverian Reserve Corps.
Van der Decken.

Von Bennigsen.
Von Beaulieu.
Von Bodecken.
Von Wissel.
Von Kruse.

Nassau Contingent.

Reserve : Field-Marshal the Duke of Wellington.

ANGLO-DUTCH ARMY—*continued.*

Cavalry : Lieut.-General the Earl of Uxbridge.

BRIGADES.

British and King's German Legion Cavalry.
{
Lord E. Somerset (B.), (1 and 2 L.G., R.H.G., and 1 K.D.G.).

Sir W. Ponsonby (B.), (1, 2, and 6 Dragoons).

Sir W. von Dörnberg (B. and K.G.L.), (1 and 2 Light Dragoons, K.G.L., and 23 Light Dragoons).

Sir J. Vandeleur (B.), (11, 12, 16 Light Dragoons).

Sir C. Grant (B. and K.G.L.), (7 and 15 Hussars ; and 2 Hussars, K.G.L.).

Sir H. Vivian (B. and K.G.L.), (10 and 18 Hussars ; and 1st Hussars, K.G.L.).

Baron F. Arenschildt (B. and K.G.L.), (13 Light Dragoons ; and 3 Hussars, K.G.L.).
}

R.H.A. Troops attached to the Cavalry.
Commanding : Lieut.-Colonel Sir A. Frazer.
  E Troop (Lieut.-Colonel Sir R. Gardiner) ;
  F Troop (Lieut.-Colonel J. Webber Smith) ;
  G Troop (2nd Captain A. C. Mercer) ;
  H Troop (Major W. N. Ramsay) ;
  I Troop (Major R. Bull) ;
  2nd Rocket Troop (Captain E. C. Whinyates).
Hanoverian Cavalry Brigade : Baron von Estorff.
  Brunswick Cavalry.

Dutch-Belgian Cavalry Division.
Lieut.-General Baron de Collaert.
{
Trip.

Baron de Ghigny.

Baron van Merlen.

Artillery : 2 ½-Horse Batteries (Petter and van Pittius).
}

Total strength, about 110,000 men (including 14,000 cavalry) ; or 133 battalions, 109 squadrons, and 34 batteries, with 222 guns.[1]

¹ This total includes all the garrison troops. The available Field Army was about 93,000 men and 196 guns.

The Duke of Wellington had 9 Aides-de-camp, and the Head-Quarters Staff numbered 60 other officers.

The Prince of Orange had 7 A.D.C.s and 1 Brigade-Major ; the Earl of Uxbridge, 5 A.D.C.s ; Lord Hill, 5 A.D.C.s ; General Picton, 4 A.D.C.s ; the other Divisional Commanders had 1 or 2 A.D.C.s, and in some cases Brigade-Majors ; Brigadiers had an A.D.C. and a Brigade-Major each.

An interesting comparison may be made with the B.E.F. on the Western Front (France and Belgium) in the Great War. In August, 1914 (after the arrival of the 4th Division) the B.E.F. had 410 guns (30 13-pounders ; 270 18-pounders ; 90 4·5-in. howitzers ; and 20 60-pounders). On the 11th November, 1918 (Armistice Day) the strength of the B.E.F. was 1,385,247 men and 7,601 guns and howitzers, together with 102 squadrons, R.A.F., with 1,576 (serviceable) aeroplanes. The staff at G.H.Q., B.E.F., numbered : 1st Echelon, 308 officers ; Administrative Services and Departments, 203 officers. In addition four missions were attached to G.H.Q., viz. French (4), Belgian (8), Italian (1), and American (3).

The General Officers of the Allied Powers officially present in 1815, on the Duke of Wellington's staff, were :—

Russia—General Pozzo de Borgo ;
Prussia—Major-General Baron v. Müffling ;
Austria—General Baron Vincent ;
Spain—General Miguel Alava.

The British officer attached to the Prussian Staff was Lieut.-Colonel Sir H. Hardinge.

In 1815 the British Artillery was the only one which possessed in its equipment spherical case (or shrapnel as they are now termed). The advantage of possessing the only serious man-killing projectile, capable of being used at longer ranges than 500 yards, was very considerable. Under 500 yards case-shot (or grape) could be used by the guns of all nations, and with deadly effect, but case-shot (and grape) were almost innocuous beyond 500 yards.

NOTES

NOTE (i)

THE PRESENT-DAY (1935) DESIGNATIONS OF THE WATERLOO R.H.A. TROOPS AND FIELD BRIGADES, R.A.

Waterloo Designation	[Armament]	Present-Day Designation (1935)
A Troop, R.H.A. (Capt. (Bt. Lt.-Col.) Sir H. D. Ross).	[9-pdrs.]	A Battery, R.H.A.
D Troop, R.H.A. (Capt. (Bt. Major) G. Bean).	[6-pdrs.]	V Field Battery, R.A.
E Troop, R.H.A. (Capt. (Bt. Lt.-Col.) Sir R. W. Gardiner).	[6-pdrs.]	E Battery, R.H.A.
F Troop, R.H.A. (Capt. (Bt. Lt.-Col.) J. Webber Smith).	[6-pdrs.]	D Battery, R.H.A.
G Troop, R.H.A. (2nd Capt. A. C. Mercer).	[9-pdrs.]	G Battery, R.H.A.
H Troop, R.H.A. (Capt. (Bt. Major) W. N. Ramsay).	[9-pdrs.]	H Field Battery, R.A.
I Troop, R.H.A. (Capt. (Bt. Major) R. Bull).	[Heavy $5\frac{1}{2}$-in. Hows.]	I Battery, R.H.A.
2nd Rocket Troop, R.H.A. (Capt. E. C. Whinyates).	[5 6-pdrs. and Rockets.]	O Battery, R.H.A.
Capt. C. F. Sandham's Field Brigade, R.A.	[9-pdrs.]	7th Field Battery, R.A.
Capt. (Bt. Major) T. Rogers's Field Brigade, R.A.[1]	[9-pdrs.]	R.A. Fixed Defences, Southern Ports.
a 2nd Capt. J. Sinclair's Field Brigade, R.A.	[5 9-pdrs. and 1 $5\frac{1}{2}$-in. How.]	9th Heavy Battery, R.A.
b Capt. S. Bolton's Field Brigade, R.A.	[4 9-pdrs. and 2 $5\frac{1}{2}$-in. Hows.]	82nd Field Battery, R.A.
Capt. (Bt. Major) W. J. Lloyd's Field Brigade, R.A.[1]	[9-pdrs.]	27th Heavy Battery, R.A.
Capt. (Bt. Major) J. Brome's Field Brigade, R.A.[2]	[9-pdrs.]	12th Heavy Battery, R.A.
Capt. (Bt. Major) G. W. Unett's Field Brigade, R.A.[2]	[9-pdrs.]	10th Heavy Battery, R.A.

[1] These 2 Field Brigades were present at Quatre Bras on the 16th June.
[2] On the 18th June these 2 Field Brigades were at Hal.
a Capt. F. Gordon's Company, but he was in Canada.   b Capt. C. G. Alms's Company, but he was in Ceylon.

NOTE (ii)

' BROWN BESS ' AND THE BAKER RIFLE

In 1815 the firearms used by the British Infantry were either the flint-lock musket ' Brown Bess ', or the Baker rifle.

Brown Bess and its 17-inch bayonet weighed over 12 lb. The calibre of this musket was ·753 in. and the diameter of the bullet was ·68 in. The bullets weighed 14½ to the lb., and the infantry soldier carried 60 rounds of ball ammunition in his pouches. Three flints were allowed for each 60 rounds. The powder charge was 6 drs. F.G. ; and though (since 1775) the powder had doubled in power yet the charge remained unaltered.

The Baker rifle, the only rifle used (between 1800 and 1838) by rifle units in the British Service, was 3 ft. 9½ in. long and weighed 10 lb. 5 oz. The calibre of this rifle was ·615 in. and its leaden spherical bullets had a diameter of ·6 in. The rifle was a muzzle-loading flint-lock, rifled with 7 grooves. The bullets weighed 20 to the lb., the charge was 4 drs. F.G., the muzzle velocity was 1200 f.s., and the rifle was sighted to 200 yards.

In 1815, the British Infantry soldier, with his ammunition, carried about 4 stone (including 3 days' biscuit ration in the haversack). The weight was made up by the accoutrements, knapsack, canteen, camp-kettle, blankets, great coat, and clothing.

NOTE (iii)

LOSSES IN THE WATERLOO CAMPAIGN

The losses suffered by the *British* units were :

16th June.	157 officers,	2,292 men ;
17th June.	3 officers,	64 men ;
18th June.	380 officers,	6,002 men ;
Total . .	540 officers,	8,358 men.

In the same period the *K.G.L.* lost 129 officers, 1,343 men, and 215 missing ; practically 25 per cent. of the K.G.L. effective fighting strength.

The total losses suffered between the 15th and 18th June, by the *Dutch-Belgians and Nassauers* were 158 officers and 4,114 men.

APPENDIX II

DOCUMENTS

No. 1

Report rendered in the evening of the 15th June by Lieut.-General Lefebvre-Desnoëttes, commanding the Light Cavalry of the Imperial Guard, to Marshal Ney, commanding the Left Wing of the *Armée du Nord*.

To the Marshal Prince of the Moskowa.

FRASNES,

9 p.m., 15 June, 1815.

MY LORD (MONSEIGNEUR),

When we reached Frasnes, in accordance with your orders, we found it occupied by a regiment of Nassau Infantry (some 1,500 men), and 8 guns. As they observed that we were manœuvring to turn them, they retired from the village where we had practically enveloped them with our squadrons. General Colbert [commanding the Lancers of the Guard] reached within musket shot of Quatre Bras on the high road, but as the ground was difficult and the enemy fell back for support to the Bossu Wood, keeping up a vigorous fire from their 8 guns, it was impossible for us to carry it.

The troops which were found at Frasnes had not advanced this morning and were not engaged at Gosselies. They are under the orders of Lord Wellington, and appear to be retiring towards Nivelles. They set light to a beacon at Quatre Bras, and fired their guns a great deal. None of the troops who fought this morning at Gosselies have passed this way, they marched towards Fleurus.

The peasants can give no information about a large assembly of troops in this neighbourhood, only that there is a Park of Artillery at Tubize, composed of 100 ammunition wagons and 12 guns ; they say that the Belgian Army is in the neighbourhood of Mons, and that the head-quarters of the Prince of Orange is at Braine-le-Comte. We took about 15 prisoners, and we have had 10 men killed and wounded.

To-morrow at daybreak, if it is possible, I shall send a reconnoitring party to Quatre Bras so as to occupy that place, for I think that the Nassau troops have left it.

A battalion of Infantry has just arrived [from Bachelu's Division], and I have placed it in front of the village. My Artillery not having rejoined me, I have sent orders for it to bivouac with Bachelu's Division, it will rejoin me to-morrow morning.

I have not written to the Emperor, as I have nothing more important to report to him than what I am telling your Excellency.

I have the honour, etc.,

LEFEBVRE-DESNOËTTES.

No. 2

To Marshal Ney, Prince of the Moskowa, Commanding the Left Wing of the *Armée du Nord*.

CHARLEROI, 16 June, 1815.

MY COUSIN,

My Aide-de-Camp, General de Flahault, is directed to deliver this letter to you. The *Major-Général* [Soult] should have given you orders, but you will receive mine first because my officers travel faster than his. You will receive the operation orders for the day, but I wish to write to you in detail because it is of the highest importance.

I am sending Marshal Grouchy with the III and IV Infantry Corps to Sombreffe. I am taking my Guard to Fleurus, and I shall be there myself before midday. I shall attack the enemy if I find him there, and I shall clear the roads as far as Gembloux.

At that place, according to the circumstances, I shall come to a decision—perhaps at 3 p.m., and perhaps this evening.

My intention is that, immediately after I have made up my mind, you will be ready to march on Brussels. I shall support you with my Guard, who will be at Fleurus, or at Sombreffe, and I shall wish to reach Brussels to-morrow morning. You will set off with your troops this evening, if I make up my mind early enough for you to be informed of my intention by day, and then this evening you will cover three or four leagues [8 to 10 miles] and reach Brussels by 7 a.m. to-morrow morning.

Therefore you will dispose your troops as follows :—

1 Division 2 leagues [5 miles] in front of Quatre Bras, if it is not inconvenient ; 6 Infantry Divisions around Quatre Bras ; and a

Division at Marbais, in order that I can move it myself to Sombreffe, should I need its assistance, besides it will not delay your march.

The Corps of the Count of Valmy, who has 3,000 Cuirassiers, picked troops, will be placed where the Roman road cuts and crosses the Brussels road, in order that I can call him in to me if necessary. As soon as my course of action has been taken you will order him to move and rejoin you. I should desire to have with me the Division of the Guard [Cavalry] commanded by General Lefebvre-Desnoëttes, and I send you two divisions of the Count of Valmy's Corps to replace it. But in my actual scheme I prefer placing the Count of Valmy so that I can recall him if I wish to, and I do not wish to cause General Lefebvre-Desnoëttes to make unnecessary marches, since it is probable that I shall decide to march on Brussels this evening with the Guard. You will cover the Lefebvre Division by the Cavalry Divisions belonging to D'Erlon's and Reille's Corps, in order to spare the Guard. If any fighting occurs with the English, it is preferable that this should fall on the Cavalry of the Line rather than on the Guard.

I have adopted for this campaign the following general principle, to divide my Army into two wings and a reserve. Your Wing will be composed of four divisions of the I Corps, four divisions of the II Corps, two divisions of Light Cavalry, and two divisions of the Corps of the Count of Valmy. This ought not to fall short of 45,000 to 50,000 men.

Marshal Grouchy will have almost the same force, and will command the Right Wing.

The Guard will form the Reserve, and I shall bring it into action on either wing just as the actual circumstances may dictate.

The *Major-Général* issues the most precise orders, so that when you are detached you should not find any difficulty in obeying such orders as you receive. General officers commanding Corps will take orders directly from me when I am present in person.

According to circumstances I shall draw troops from one wing to strengthen my Reserve.

You understand how much importance is attached to the taking of Brussels. From its capture certain things would happen, because such a quick and sudden movement would cut the English Army from Mons, Ostend, etc. I desire that your dispositions may be well conceived, so that at the first order your eight divisions will take the road at once and march rapidly and unhindered to Brussels.

NAPOLÉON.

No. 3.

Wellington to Blücher.

On the heights behind FRASNES,
10.30 a.m., 16 June, 1815.

MY DEAR PRINCE,

My army is disposed as follows :

The Prince of Orange's Corps has a division here at Quatre Bras, the remainder are at Nivelles.

The Reserve is now marching from Waterloo to Genappe, where it will arrive at midday.

At the same hour the English Cavalry will have reached Nivelles. Lord Hill's Corps is at Braine-le-Comte.

I do not see many of the enemy in front of us, and I await the receipt of news from Your Highness, and the arrival of my troops, to decide on my operations for this day.

Nothing has been seen in the direction of Binche, nor on our right.

Your very Obedient Servant,

WELLINGTON.

No. 4

To His Excellency the Duke of Dalmatia.

FRASNES,
16 June, 1815, 10 p.m.

MARSHAL,

I have attacked the English position at Quatre Bras with the greatest vigour ; but an error of Count D'Erlon's deprived me of a fine victory, for at the very moment when the 5th and 9th Divisions of General Reille's Corps had overthrown everything in front of them, the I Corps marched off to St. Amand to support His Majesty's left ; but the fatal thing was that this Corps, having then counter-marched to rejoin my wing, gave no useful assistance on either field.

Prince Jérôme's Division fought with great valour ; His Royal Highness has been slightly wounded.

Actually there have been engaged here [on our side] only 3 Infantry Divisions, a Brigade of Cuirassiers, and General Piré's Cavalry. The Count of Valmy delivered a fine charge. All have done their duty, except the I Corps.

The enemy has lost heavily ; we have captured some guns and a flag.

We have lost about 2,000 killed and 4,000 wounded. I have called for reports from Generals Reille and D'Erlon, and will forward them to Your Excellency.

Accept, Marshal, the assurance of my deep respect,

The Marshal Prince of the Moskowa,

NEY.

No. 5

Napoleon's attack orders.
To each Corps Commander.

11 a.m., 18 June, 1815.

Directly the Army has formed up, and soon after 1 p.m., the Emperor will give the order to Marshal Ney and the attack will be delivered on Mt. St. Jean village in order to seize the crossroads at that place. To this end the 12-pounder batteries of the II and VI Corps will mass with that of the I Corps. These 24 guns will bombard the troops holding Mont St. Jean, and Count D'Erlon will begin the attack by first launching the left division, and, when necessary, supporting it by the other divisions of the I Corps.

The II Corps also will advance, keeping abreast of the I Corps.

The company of Engineers belonging to the I Corps will hold themselves in readiness to barricade and fortify Mt. St. Jean directly it is taken.

[In pencil in Marshal Ney's writing, and added by Marshal Ney :—
' Count D'Erlon will note that the attack will be delivered first by the left instead of beginning from the right. Inform General Reille of this change.']

(On the back :
' Order dictated by the Emperor on the field of battle of Mt. St. Jean, on the 18th June, at 11 a.m., and written by the Marshal Duke of Dalmatia, *Major-Général*.')

No. 6

Soult to Grouchy.

[From the battle-field of Mt. St. Jean.]

1 p.m., 18 June, 1815.

MARSHAL,

You wrote to the Emperor at 6 a.m. this morning that you would march on Sart à Walhain ; your further plan was to proceed to Corbais, or to Wavre. This movement is conformable to His Majesty's arrangements, which have been communicated to you. Nevertheless His Majesty directs me to tell you that you ought always to manœuvre in our direction. It is for you to ascertain our exact whereabouts, to regulate your movements accordingly, and to keep up your communication with us, so as to be prepared at any moment to fall upon and to crush any of the enemy's troops which may endeavour to annoy our right flank. At this moment the battle is raging [*engagée*] near Waterloo, in front of the Forest of Soignes, the enemy's centre is at Mt. St. Jean ; manœuvre, therefore, to join our right.

THE MARSHAL DUKE OF DALMATIA.

P.S.—A letter, which has just been intercepted, states that General Bülow is about to attack our right flank. We believe that we can see this corps on the heights of St. Lambert. So do not lose a moment in drawing near to us, and effecting a junction with us, in order to crush Bülow whom you will catch in the very act of concentrating [with Wellington].

BOOKS CONSULTED AND USED

NAPOLÉON IER—
  *Correspondance de Napoléon I*er* (particularly Vol. XXVIII ; Paris, 1869).
  *Commentaires de Napoléon I*er* (particularly Vol. V ; Paris, 1867).

GENERAL GOURGAUD—
  The Campaign of 1815 (English trans., 1818).

CAPITAINE HIPPOLYTE DE MAUDUIT—
  Les Derniers Jours de la Grande Armée (Paris, 1847).

HENRI HOUSSAYE—
  1815, *Les Cent Jours* (29th ed.).
  1815, *Waterloo* (59th ed.).

COLONEL ALPHONSE GROUARD—
  Critique de la Campaigne de 1815 (1904).
  Réponse à M. Houssaye (1907).

E. LENIENT—
  La Solution des énigmes de Waterloo (1915).

LE MARÉCHAL DROUET, COMTE D'ERLON—
  Ma Vie Militaire (Paris, 1844).

COLONEL F. FOCH—
  Des Principes de la Guerre (2nd ed.).

L. NAVEZ—
  Les Champs de Bataille de la Belgique, II.
  Le Champ de Bataille de Waterloo, 1815, et actuellement.

THE EARL OF KERRY—
  The First Napoleon (unpublished documents from the Bowood Papers), (1925).

GENERAL C. VON CLAUSEWITZ—
  La Campagne de 1815 (*en France*) (French trans., 1900).

BARON VON MÜFFLING—
  Passages from My Life (English trans., 2nd ed., 1853).

FR. VON KAUSLER—
  Atlas des plus memorables Batailles, Combats, et Sièges (Merseburg, 1839).

GENERAL ALBERT POLLIO—
  Waterloo, 1815 (French trans., 1908).

BIBLIOGRAPHY

CAPTAIN W. SIBORNE, 9TH FOOT—
History of the Campaign of 1815 (3rd ed., 1848) and Atlas.

MAJOR-GENERAL H. T. SIBORNE, R.E.—
Waterloo Letters (1891).

GEORGE JONES—
The Battle of Waterloo (11th ed., 1852).

GENERAL SIR J. SHAW KENNEDY, K.C.B.—
Notes on the Battle of Waterloo (London, 1865).
(In 1815 the author was Captain J. Shaw, A.-Q.-M.-G. of Alten's Division.)

COLONEL C. C. CHESNEY, R.E.—
Waterloo Lectures (3rd ed.).

COLONEL SIR AUGUSTUS FRAZER, K.C.B., R.H.A.—
Letters Written in the Peninsular and Waterloo Campaigns (London, 1859).

GENERAL CAVALIÉ MERCER, R.A.—
Journal of the Waterloo Campaign (London, 1870).

LIEUT.-COL. TOMKINSON, 16TH LIGHT DRAGOONS—
The Diary of a Cavalry Officer (2nd ed., 1895).

CAPTAIN SIR J. KINCAID—
Adventures in the Rifle Brigade (1909 ed.).

CAPTAIN BATTY, 1ST GUARDS—
Historical Sketch of the Campaign of 1815 (2nd ed., 1820).

AN EYE-WITNESS—
The Crisis and close of the action at Waterloo (1833).
(The author was Major G. Gawler—in 1815 he was a lieutenant in the 52nd Light Infantry.)

A BRITISH OFFICER—
Letters from Portugal, Spain, and France during 1811–1813, *and from Belgium and France in* 1815 (Edinburgh, 1819). (The writer was Lieut. James Hope, 92nd Highlanders.)

THE EARL STANHOPE—
Conversations with the Duke of Wellington.

THE EARL OF ELLESMERE—
Personal Reminiscences of the Duke of Wellington.

LIEUT.-COLONEL GURWOOD—
Despatches, etc., of Field-Marshal the Duke of Wellington, Vol. XII and Vol. VIII (editions, 1838 and 1852), also Vol. X, *Supplementary Despatches,* 1863 ; and Vol. XIV, *Appendix to the Supplementary Despatches* (1872).

DUKE OF WELLINGTON—
Memo. on Battle of Waterloo (given in the *Supplementary Despatches,* Vol. X, pp. 513–31).

MAJOR N. L. BEAMISH, K.G.L.—
History of the King's German Legion (London, 1832 and 1837).

LIEUT.-COLONEL W. H. JAMES, R.E.—
The Campaign of 1815, chiefly in Flanders.

F. DE BAS ET LE COMTE DE T'SERCLÆS DE WOMMERSON—
La Campagne de 1815 aux Pays Bays, d'après les rapports officiels néerlandais.

NOTE.—I do not profess to have read the whole of each book which I have included in the above list, nor by including a book do I mean that I agree with all the author has to say about 1815.

MAPS

The modern Belgian Official Maps which have been found most useful are :—

General—
' Carte de la Belgique,' $\frac{1}{160000}$ (1898 ed.),
' Carte de la Belgique,' $\frac{1}{40000}$.

Waterloo—
' Champ de Bataille de Waterloo,' $\frac{1}{20000}$ (Belgian Survey), and ' Plan du Champ de Bataille de Waterloo, $\frac{1}{12500}$, dressé par W. B. Craan, Ingénieur (1816).'

INDEX